W9-CBI-113

ORACLE®   *Oracle Press*™

OCP Oracle9*i* Database: Fundamentals I Exam Guide

Oracle Press™

OCP Oracle9i Database: Fundamentals I Exam Guide

Jason S. Couchman

Sudheer N. Marisetti

Osborne/**McGraw-Hill**

New York   Chicago   San Francisco
Lisbon   London   Madrid   Mexico City   Milan
New Delhi   San Juan   Seoul   Singapore   Sydney   Toronto

McGraw-Hill/Osborne
2600 Tenth Street
Berkeley, California 94710
U.S.A.

For information on translations or book distributors outside the U.S.A., or to arrange bulk purchase discounts for sales promotions, premiums, or fund-raisers, please contact **McGraw-Hill**/Osborne at the above address.

OCP Oracle9*i* Database: Fundamentals I Exam Guide

Copyright ©2002 by The McGraw-Hill Companies. All rights reserved. Printed in the United States of America. Except as permitted under the Copyright Act of 1976, no part of this publication may be reproduced or distributed in any form or by any means, or stored in a database or retrieval system, without the prior written permission of the publisher, with the exception that the program listings may be entered, stored, and executed in a computer system, but they may not be reproduced for publication.

Oracle is a registered trademark and Oracle 9*i* is a trademark or registered trademark of Orale Corporation.

1234567890 FGR FGR 0198765432
Book p/n 0-07-219541-X and CD p/n 0-07-219542-8
parts of
ISBN 0-07-219540-1

Publisher
    Brandon A. Nordin

Vice-President & Associate Publisher
    Scott Rogers

Acquisitions Editor
    Jeremy Judson

Project Manager
    Jenn Tust

Acquisitions Coordinator
    Athena Honore

Technical Editor
    Trevor Davies

Cover Series Design
    Damore Johann Design, Inc.

Composition and Indexing
    MacAllister Publishing Services, LLC

This book was composed with QuarkXPress™.

Information has been obtained by **McGraw-Hill**/Osborne from sources believed to be reliable. However, because of the possibility of human or mechanical error by our sources, **McGraw-Hill**/Osborne, or others, **McGraw-Hill**/Osborne does not guarantee the accuracy, adequacy, or completeness of any information and is not responsible for any errors or omissions or the results obtained from use of such information.

    Oracle Corporation does not make any representations or warranties as to the accuracy, adequacy or completeness of any information contained in this Work, and is not responsible for any errors or omissions.

To my wife Stacy
—*Jason Couchman*

To my wife Sujani and my sons, Rahath and Rishabh
—*Sudheer Marisetti*

About the Authors

Jason S. Couchman
Jason S. Couchman is a database consultant and the author of
Oracle8i Certified Professional DBA Certification Exam Guide, also
from Oracle Press. He is a regular presenter on Oracle and OCP at
international Oracle user conferences and meetings. His work has
been published by *Oracle Magazine*, Harvard Business School
Publishing, and Gannett Newspapers, among others.

Sudheer N. Marisetti
Sudheer N. Marisetti is a database, Unix, and Web administrator and
president of Abacus Concepts Inc., a New Jersey-based consulting
firm specializing in designing, building, and maintaining database
systems. He is an adjunct faculty member at Columbia University
teaching advanced Oracle administration classes. He holds a master's
degree in electrical engineering.

OracleCertified Professional

About the Oracle Certification Exams

The expertise of Oracle database administrators (DBAs) is integral to the success of today's increasingly complex system environments. The best DBAs operate primarily behind the scenes, looking for ways to fine-tune day-to-day performance to prevent unscheduled crises and hours of expensive downtime. They know they stand between optimal performance and a crisis that could bring a company to a standstill. The Oracle Certified Database Administrator Track provides DBAs with tangible evidence of their skills with the Oracle database.

The Oracle Certified Professional (OCP) Program was developed by Oracle to recognize technical professionals who can demonstrate the depth of knowledge and hands-on skills required to maximize Oracle's core products according to a rigorous standard established by Oracle. By earning professional certification, you can translate the impressive knowledge and skill you have worked so hard to accumulate into a tangible credential that can lead to greater job security or more challenging, better-paying opportunities.

Oracle Certified Professionals are eligible to receive use of the Oracle Certified Professional logo and a certificate for framing.

Requirements for Certification

To become an Oracle Certified Database Administrator for the Oracle9*i* track, you must pass four tests. These exams cover knowledge of the essential aspects of the SQL language, Oracle administration, backup and recovery, and performance tuning of systems. The certification process requires that you pass the following four exams:

- Exam 1: Introduction to Oracle9*i*: SQL (1Z0-007)
- Exam 2: Oracle9*i* Database: Fundamentals I (1Z0-031)
- Exam 3: Oracle9*i* Database: Fundamentals II (1Z0-032)
- Exam 4: Oracle9*i* Database: Performance Tuning (1Z0-033)

If you fail a test, you must wait at least 30 days before you retake that exam. You may attempt a particular test up to three times in a twelve-month period.

Recertification

Oracle announces the requirements for upgrading your certification based on the release of new products and upgrades. Oracle will give six months' notice announcing when an exam version is expiring.

Exam Format

The computer-based exams are multiple-choice tests, consisting of 50–65 questions that must be completed in 90–120 minutes.

Contents at a Glance

Contents

PART I
Preparing for OCP Database Administration
Fundamentals I Exam

PART 2
OCP Oracle9*i* DBA Fundamentals I Practice Exams

Preface

ason's interest in Oracle certification began in 1996 when he read about the Oracle DBA certificate offered by the Chauncey Group. He found it difficult to prepare for that certification exam for two reasons. First, there was an absence of practice questions readily available. Second, preparation for the exam involved reviewing six or seven different manuals and Oracle Press books, none of which were particularly suited to the task. Judging from the response to the proliferation of titles now available in the Oracle Certified Professional (OCP) Exam Guide Series from Oracle Press, it would seem others have had similar experiences.

This book is divided into two units, the first containing preparatory material for the Oracle9*i* DBA Fundamentals I exam, part of the Oracle's Oracle9*i* DBA certification track. The first unit has six chapters, each containing several discussions that focus on a particular topic or subtopic objective listed by the Oracle Certified Professional Oracle9*i* DBA Track Candidate Guide for the DBA Fundamentals I exam. (For a complete listing of all the topics tested for this exam, see Chapter 1.) These discussions are followed by a For Review section, each listing the three or four most important concepts for you to retain from the discussion. After the review, you'll see two to six exercise questions in exam-based multiple choice or short answer format. Following the questions you will find an answer key for those questions, which should help you master the material even more quickly. Thus, with this book you're never more than a few pages away from demonstrating what you've learned about Oracle9*i* DBA topics for the OCP exam.

At the end of each chapter, you will find a short summary of what was covered in the chapter, followed by a Two-Minute Drill. The Two-Minute Drill contains another bulleted list of fast facts to review, or crib notes for the days leading up to your OCP exam. The chapters conclude with 5 to 20 short answer and exam-based multiple choice questions designed to help you further test your understanding of the materials you learned in the chapter.

The second unit consists of one chapter containing three full-length practice exams. Each test contains exam-based multiple choice and scenario-based questions that are designed to help you strengthen your test-taking skills for the OCP exams. You will also find answers and in-depth explanations for every question in the practice exams in the back of that chapter, along with a reference back to the exam topic and subtopic objectives from the OCP Candidate Guide. This feature should help you determine your areas requiring further improvement with pinpoint accuracy.

Finally, a note about updates and errata. Because OCP covers such vast ground in a short time, this has become a living text. If you feel you have encountered difficulties due to errors, you can check out **www.OraclePressBooks.com** to find the latest errata.

Good luck!

Acknowledgments

here are many people I would like to thank for their help with writing this book. My first and most heartfelt thanks goes to the dedicated readers of other books who took time out of their busy schedules to send feedback on the book. I have listened to your praise and constructive criticism, and made every effort to correct and amplify my work based on the points you made. Next, a note of gratitude to the folks at Oracle who made the book possible. Ulrike Schwinn and Jim DiIanni have both been loyal associates, colleagues, and friends during my ongoing effort to help 110,000-plus readers get Oracle certified. Thanks also to Oracle University for its feedback and assistance with the overall direction for the OCP DBA track. As always, thanks to the fine folks at Osborne and MacAllister Publishing Services for their hard work in assembling the manuscript into a finished product.

This book is dedicated to my wife, Stacy, who makes every part of my life better. Stacy, I strive to be a better husband to you, and to help you grow as a person. As you take this next step in your life from student to professional, I want you to know that I support you wholeheartedly and will do everything in my power to keep our marriage strong and solid—especially when you have to work late! I love you.

—Jason Couchman

I wish to thank Jason for giving me an opportunity to coauthor this book with him. Working with him on this book and the guidance he provided me were invaluable. I thank all the folks at Osborne/McGraw-Hill in helping us complete this book. I also thank Oracle Corporation for reviewing each chapter and providing valuable feedback. I thank all my previous, current, and future students, whose interaction was invaluable in building my technical expertise.

I thank my good friend Ravi Kadeermangalan, whose support and advice helped me in my life and in writing this book. I am fortunate to have such a friend. Most of all I am indebted to my beloved wife, Sujani "Puppala" Marisetti, who held the fort and kept our two active kids preoccupied while I toiled on this book during the weekends and nights. Without her patience, support, and affection I would not have traveled so far in my life.

For your comments, I can be reached at smarisetti@yahoo.com.

—*Sudheer Marisetti, Piscataway, New Jersey*

Introduction

he Oracle Certified Professional DBA certification exam series from Oracle Corporation is a great opportunity for you to demonstrate your expertise on the use of Oracle database software. Called OCP, it represents the culmination of many people's requests for objective standards in Oracle database administration, one of the hottest markets in the software field. The presence of OCP on the market indicates an important reality about Oracle as a career path. Oracle is mature, robust, and stable for enterprisewide information management. However, corporations facing a severe shortage of qualified Oracle professionals need a measurement for Oracle expertise.

The OCP certification core track for DBAs consists of four tests in the following areas of Oracle9*i*: SQL, DBA Fundamentals I and II, and Tuning, with the current content of those exams covering Oracle through Oracle9*i*. As of this printing, each test consists of about 60 multiple choice questions pertaining to the recommended usage of Oracle databases. You have about 90 minutes to take each exam. Obtaining certification for Oracle9*i* through the core track is contingent on taking and passing *all* core examinations. This book will help you prepare for the DBA Fundamentals I exam in the DBA track.

Why Get Certified?

If you are already an Oracle professional, you may wonder, "Why should I get certified?" Perhaps you have a successful career as an Oracle DBA or developer, enjoying the instant prestige your résumé gets with that one magic word on it. With market forces currently in your favor, you're right to wonder. But while no one is saying you don't know Oracle when you put the magic word on your résumé, can you prove how well you *do* know Oracle without undergoing a technical interview? We started asking ourselves that question when Oracle certification began to emerge and were surprised to find out that, after years of using Oracle, developing Oracle applications, and administering Oracle databases for Fortune 500 companies, there were a lot of things about Oracle we *didn't* know. And the only reason we know them now is because we took the time and effort to become certified.

If you're looking for another reason to become certified in Oracle, consider the experience of computer professionals with Novell NetWare experience in the late 1980s and early 1990s. Back then, it seemed that anyone with even a little experience in Novell could count on a fantastic job offer. Then Novell introduced its CNE/CNA programs. At first, employers were okay with hiring Novell professionals whether they had a certificate or not. As time went on, however, employers no longer asked for computer professionals with Novell NetWare *experience*; they asked for CNEs and CNAs. A similar phenomenon can be seen in the arena of Microsoft Windows NT, where the MCSE has already become the standard by which those professionals are measuring their skills. Furthermore, with the latest economic downturn in the technology-driven U.S. economy comes the possibility of involuntary information technologies (IT) job changes. If you want to stay competitive in the field of Oracle database administration or development through those changes, your real question shouldn't be *whether* you should become certified, but *when*.

If you are not in the field of Oracle development or database management, or if you want to advance your career using Oracle products, there has never been a better time to do so. OCP is already altering the playing field for DBAs and developers by changing the focus of the Oracle skill set from "How many years have you used it?" to "Do you know *how* to use it?" That shift benefits organizations using Oracle as much as it benefits the professionals who use Oracle because the emphasis is on *skills*, not attrition.

Managers who are faced with the task of hiring Oracle professionals can breathe a sigh of relief with the debut of OCP as well. By seeking professionals who are certified, managers can spend less time trying to determine if the candidate possesses the Oracle skills for the job, and spend more time assessing the candidate's work habits and compatibility with the team.

TIP
*You can find the exam objectives tested on the OCP
exam on DBA Fundamentals I at the beginning of
Chapter 1.*

How Should You Prepare
for the Exam?

If you spend your free time studying things like the feature that permits Oracle to remove database files after you issue the DROP TABLESPACE command, you are probably ready to take the OCP Oracle9*i* DBA Fundamentals I exam now. For the rest of us, Oracle and other companies offer classroom- and computer-based training options to learn Oracle. Now users have another option—this book! By selecting this book, you demonstrate two excellent characteristics—that you are committed to a superior career using Oracle products and that you care about preparing for the exam correctly and thoroughly. And by the way, the feature that permits Oracle to remove database files after you drop a tablespace is the Oracle-Managed Files feature, and it is tested heavily on the OCP Oracle9*i* DBA Fundamentals I exam. That fact, along with thousands of others, is covered extensively in this book to help you prepare for, and pass, the OCP Oracle9*i* DBA Fundamentals I exam.

DBA Certification Past and Present

Oracle certification started in the mid-1990s with the involvement of the Chauncey Group International, a division of the Educational Testing Service. With the help of many Oracle DBAs, Chauncey put together an objective, fact-based, and scenario-based examination on Oracle database administration. This test did an excellent job of measuring knowledge of Oracle7, versions 7.0 to 7.2. Consisting of 60 questions, Chauncey's exam covered several different topic areas, including backup and recovery, security, administration, and performance tuning, all in one test.

Oracle Corporation has taken DBA certification ahead with the advent of OCP. Their core DBA certification consists of four tests, each about 60 questions in length. By quadrupling the number of questions you must answer, Oracle requires that you have an unprecedented depth of knowledge in Oracle database administration. Oracle has also committed to including scenario-based questions on the OCP examinations, and preparation material for these new questions is included in this book as well. Scenario-based questions require you to not only know the facts about Oracle, but also to understand how to apply those facts in real-life situations.

Oracle's final contribution to the area of Oracle certification is a commitment to reviewing and updating the material presented in the certification exams. Oracle-certified DBAs will be required to maintain their certification by retaking the certification exams periodically, meaning that those who certify will stay on the cutting edge of the Oracle database better than those who do not.

The Next Steps

Next, let's examine the test interface you will encounter on exam day. Figure I-1 contains a diagram of the actual test graphical user interface (GUI). The top of the interface tells you how much time has elapsed and the number of questions you have answered. You can use the checkbox in the upper left-hand corner of the interface to mark questions you would like to review later. In the main window of the interface you'll find the actual exam question, along with the choices.

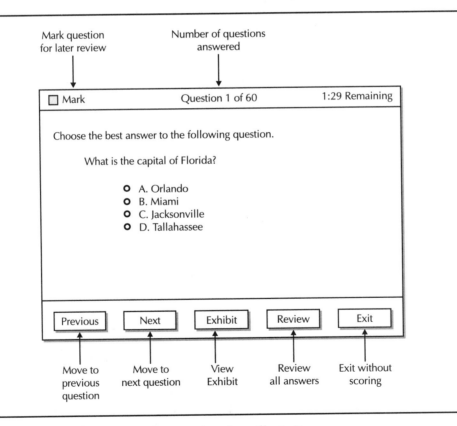

FIGURE I-1   *Sylvan Prometric exam interface illustration*

Generally, the interface enables the user to select only one answer (unless the question specifically directs you to select more answers). In this case, the interface will enable you to select only as many answers as the question requests. After answering a question, or marking the question for later review, the candidate can move onto the next question by clicking the appropriate button in the lower left-hand corner. To return to the previous question on the OCP exam, hit the Next button over to the left. You can score your questions at any time by pressing the Grade Test button on the bottom right-hand side.

The final point feature to cover is the Exhibit button. In some cases, you may require the use of an exhibit consisting of extra information from the database, which is useful in answering a question. If the question does not require the use of an exhibit, the button will be grayed out.

Once you've completed all questions on the exam, the Sylvan Prometric interface will display a listing of all the answers you selected, shown in Figure I-2.

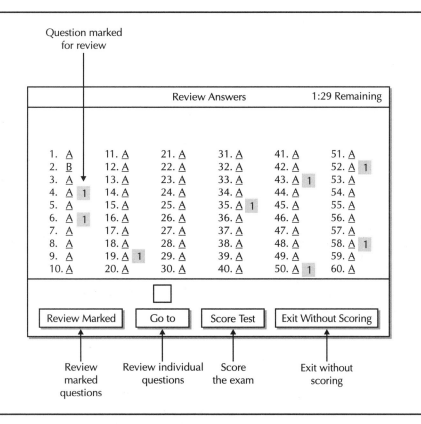

FIGURE I-2 *Sylvan Prometric answer interface illustration*

The questions you marked for later review will be highlighted, and the interface will guide you through a review of all those questions you marked. You can review individual questions or simply have Sylvan Prometric grade your exam.

The assessment test indicates your performance by means of a grade window, such as the one displayed in Figure I-3. It details the number of questions you answered correctly, along with your percentage score based on 100 percent. You will be shown a section-by-section breakdown of how you did according to the topics covered on the exam, as published in the OCP DBA Candidate Guide from Oracle. Finally, a bar graph indicates where your performance falls in comparison to the maximum score possible on the exam. The OCP exam reports your score immediately after you exit the exam, so you will know right then whether you pass or not in a similar fashion as the assessment test. Both interfaces offer you the ability to print a report of your score.

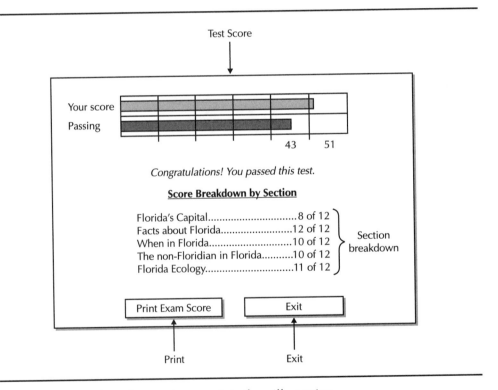

FIGURE I-3   *Sylvan Prometric score interface illustration*

Strategies for Improving Your Score

When OCP exams were first released, the score range for each OCP exam was between 200 and 800. However, Oracle has moved away from scaling the OCP exam score and has experimented lately with reporting only a raw score of the number of questions you answered correctly. However, the bottom line is still the same. Since there are typically 60 questions on an OCP exam, you want to make sure you get at least 75 percent, or 45 of the questions right, in order to pass. Given the recent use of questions with two or even three correct answers on OCP exams, you need to be careful to select *all* correct answer choices on a question or else you may not get full credit for a correct answer. *There is no penalty for wrong answers.*

Some preliminary items are now identified for you to take the OCP exams. The first tip is, *don't wait until you're the world's foremost authority on Oracle to take the OCP Exam.* If your OCP exam is scaled as it was when the exams were first released, the passing score for most exams is approximately 650. You have to get 45 to 50 questions right, or about 75 to 80 percent of the exam. So, if you are getting about four questions right out of five on the assessment test or in the chapters (more on chapter format in a minute), you should consider taking the OCP exam. Remember, you're certified if you pass with 77 or 96 percent of the correct answers.

If you can't answer the question within 30 seconds, mark it with the check box in the upper left-hand corner of the OCP interface for review later. The most significant difference between the OCP interface and the assessment test interface is a special screen appearing after you answer all the questions. This screen displays all your answers, along with a special indicator next to the questions you marked for review. This screen also offers a button for you to click in order to review the questions you marked. You should use this feature extensively. If you spend only 30 seconds answering each question in your first pass on the exam, you will have at least an hour to review the questions you're unsure of, with the added bonus of knowing you answered all the questions that were easiest to you first.

Third, *there is no penalty for guessing.* If you answer the question correctly, your score goes up; if not, your score does not change. If you can eliminate any choices on a question, you should take the chance in the interest of improving your score. In some questions, the OCP exam requires you to specify two or even three choices; this can work in your favor, meaning you need to eliminate fewer choices to get the question right.

A Note about Updates and Errata

You can typically find related information such as posted updates, corrections, and amplifications for all Oracle Press books on **www.OraclePressBooks.com**. Check back on this site often, as new issues arise all the time in the pursuit of OCP. Good luck with OCP and best wishes for your Oracle career!

PART
I

Preparing for OCP
Database Administration
Fundamentals I Exam

The following list shows the topic and subtopic objectives covered on the OCP Oracle9i Database Fundamentals I exam:

1. Oracle Architectural Components
   1.1. Describe Oracle architecture and its main components
   1.2. List the structures involved in connecting a user to an Oracle instance
2. Getting Started with Oracle Server
   2.1. Identify the common database administrative tools available to a DBA
   2.2. Identify the features of Oracle Universal Installer
   2.3. Explain the benefits of Optimal Flexible Architecture
   2.4. Set up password file authentication
   2.5. List the main components of OEM and their uses
3. Managing an Oracle Instance
   3.1. Create and manage initialization parameter files
   3.2. Configure OMF
   3.3. Start up and shut down an instance
   3.4. Monitor the use of diagnostic files
4. Creating a Database
   4.1. Describe the prerequisites necessary for database creation
   4.2. Create a database using Oracle Database Configuration Assistant
   4.3. Create a database manually
5. Data Dictionary Content and Usage
   5.1. Identify key data dictionary components
   5.2. Identify the contents and uses of the data dictionary
   5.3. Query the data dictionary
6. Maintaining the Control File
   6.1. Explain the uses of the control file
   6.2. List the contents of the control file
   6.3. Multiplex and manage the control file
   6.4. Manage the control file with OMF
   6.5. Obtain control file information
7. Maintaining Redo Log Files
   7.1. Explain the purpose of online redo log files
   7.2. Describe the structure of online redo log files
   7.3. Control log switches and checkpoints
   7.4. Multiplex and maintain online redo log files
   7.5. Manage online redo log files with OMF
8. Managing Tablespaces and Datafiles
   8.1. Describe the logical structure of the database
   8.2. Create tablespaces
   8.3. Change the size of tablespaces
   8.4. Allocate space for temporary segments

CHAPTER
1

Basics of the Oracle Database Architecture

n this chapter, you will learn about and demonstrate knowledge in the following areas:

- Oracle architectural components
- Getting started with the Oracle server
- Managing an Oracle instance
- Creating an Oracle database

To be a successful Oracle DBA and to pass OCP DBA Fundamental I, you must understand the Oracle database architecture. An Oracle database in action consists of several elements, including memory structures, special processes that make things run faster, and recovery mechanisms that enable the DBA to restore systems after seemingly unrecoverable problems. Whatever the Oracle feature, it's all here. Review this chapter carefully, as these concepts form the foundation for material covered in the rest of unit and book, the OCP exam, and your work as a DBA. This is an important chapter covering approximately 20 percent of the material tested on the OCP DBA Fundamentals I exam.

Oracle Architectural Components

In this section, you will cover the following topics related to the Oracle architecture:

- Oracle server architecture
- Structures that connect users to Oracle servers
- Stages in processing queries, changes, and `commits`

The Oracle database server consists of many different components. Some of these components are memory structures, whereas others are background processes that execute certain tasks behind the scenes. There are also disk resources that store the data that applications use to track data for an entire organization, and special resources designed to allow for recovering data from problems ranging from incorrect entry to disk failure. The memory structures and the background processes constitute an Oracle *instance*, whereas the Oracle instance with the remaining structures constitutes an Oracle *database*. This section explains each component of the Oracle database, as well as what Oracle is doing when users issue queries, data-change or data manipulation language (DML) statements, and save their work to Oracle by issuing `commit` commands.

Oracle Server Architecture

Figure 1-1 demonstrates the various disk, memory, and process components of the Oracle instance. Every Oracle database, from the smallest Oracle application running on a hand-held device to terabyte data warehouses that run on mainframes and supercomputers, has these features working together to manage data. They allow for applications, ranging from online transaction processing (OLTP) apps to N-tier apps to data marts to data warehouses, to process their data efficiently and effectively.

The SGA: Oracle's Primary Memory Component

Focus first on the memory components of the Oracle instance. There are two basic memory structures in Oracle. The first and most important is the System Global Area (SGA). When DBAs talk about most things related to memory, they usually mean the SGA. The SGA consists of several different items: the buffer cache, shared pool, and redo log buffer, as well as a few other items that will be discussed later in the unit. The following subtopics explain the primary components of the Oracle SGA.

 TIP
Although they are not emphasized to a great extent on the OCP exam, you should also be aware that the Java pool and large pool are also part of the Oracle SGA.

Buffer Cache   This memory structure consists of buffers, each the size of a database block, that store data needed by SQL statements issued by user processes. You can imagine buffer cache as a beehive with each unit in it as a buffer and all buffers being of equal size. That is why the size of a buffer cache is indicated in a parameter file as the number of buffers and not in bytes. A database block is the most granular unit of information storage in Oracle, in which Oracle can place several rows of table data. The buffer cache has two purposes: to improve performance for subsequent repeated `select` statements on the same data and to enable Oracle users to make data changes quickly in memory. Oracle writes those data changes to disk later.

Shared Pool   There are two mandatory structures and one optional structure in the Oracle shared pool. The first required component is the *library cache*, which is used for storing parsed SQL statement text and the statement's execution plan for reuse. The second is the *dictionary cache,* sometimes also referred to as the *row cache,* which is used for storing recently accessed information from the Oracle data dictionary, such as table and column definitions, usernames, passwords, and

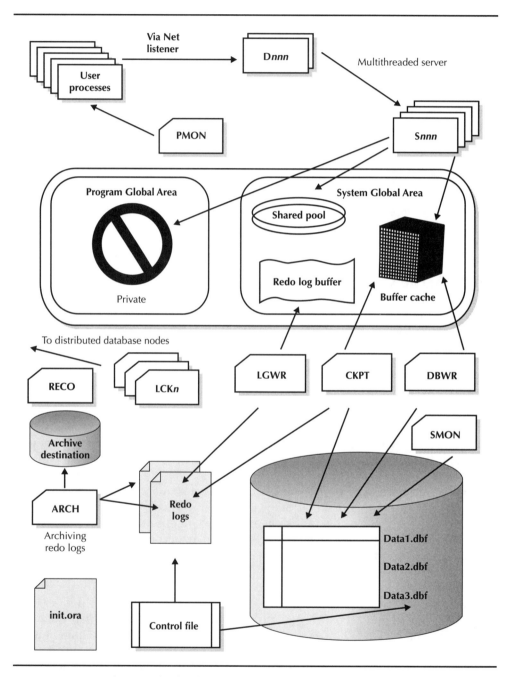

FIGURE 1-1. *The Oracle database architecture*

privileges. (If you don't know what the data dictionary is, you'll find more out about it in the section "More Introductions: SYS, SYSTEM, and the Data Dictionary" later in this chapter.) These two components are designed to improve overall Oracle performance in multiuser environments. The optional shared pool structure contains session information about user processes connected to Oracle. When will Oracle include this optional component in the SGA? You'll find out shortly.

Redo Log Buffer This SGA component temporarily stores in memory the redo entry information generated by DML statements run in user sessions until Oracle writes the information to disk. DML statements include `update`, `delete`, and `insert` statements run by users. What is a redo entry? It is a small amount of information produced and saved by Oracle to reconstruct, or redo, changes made to the database by `insert`, `update`, `delete`, `create`, `alter`, and `drop` statements. If some sort of failure occurred, the DBA can use redo information to recover the Oracle database to the point of database failure.

The PGA: The Oracle User's Memory Area

The other memory structure in the Oracle instance is called the Program Global Area (PGA). The PGA helps user processes execute by storing information like bind variable values, sort areas, and other aspects of cursor handling. Why do users need their own area to execute? Even though the parse information for SQL or PL/SQL may already be available in the library cache of the shared pool, the values upon which the user wants to execute the `select` or `update` statement cannot be shared. The PGA is used to store real values in place of bind variables for executing SQL statements.

Reading Data from Disk for Users: The Server Process

Let's move on to quickly cover Oracle background processes. There are several types of processes running all the time in Oracle. These types are *background, server,* and *network* processes. The most important one from a user perspective is the server process. This process acts on the user's behalf to pull Oracle data from disk into the buffer cache, where the user can manipulate it. There are two ways DBAs can set up Oracle to run server processes: shared servers and dedicated servers. The following subtopics identify the primary differences between these two configurations.

TIP

Think of the Oracle server process as a genie—the magical being from the story of Aladdin—because your want for Oracle data is the server process command!

Dedicated Servers: One Genie, One Master   In this setup, every single user connecting to Oracle will have a personal genie handling data retrieval from disk into the buffer cache. If there are 150 users connected to Oracle, there will also be 150 genies out there grabbing data from disk and putting it in the buffer cache for those users. The architectural setup means that every user gets his or her data retrieval requests acted upon immediately. It also means there will be additional memory and CPU overhead on the machine running the Oracle database, and that each dedicated server process will, depending on the workload and the access method, sit idle most of the time. Still, this is the setup chosen by many DBAs for overall performance reasons when hardware resources are readily available.

Shared Servers: One Genie, Many Masters   In this setup, there is a small pool of server processes running in Oracle that support data retrieval requests for a large number of users. Several users are served by one server process. Oracle manages this utilization by means of a network process called the *dispatcher*. User processes are assigned to a dispatcher, and the dispatcher puts the user requests for data into one queue, and the shared server processes fulfill all the requests, one at a time. This does not mean that there will be only one dispatcher process for the entire database. You will be able to configure the database to have many dispatchers and many server processes. This configuration can reduce memory and CPU burden on the machine that hosts Oracle, as well as limit server process idle time. On the contrary, in dedicated server mode, the user process has to take time to create a dedicated server process for each connection that comes through, whereas in shared server mode, they save time by being served by an existing dispatcher process and server process. That is why MTS is preferred in cases where there are a large number of users in the database as well as when a large number of users connect and disconnect from the database (Internet databases).

TIP
In addition to server processes, Oracle uses background processes for a multitude of operations. These processes include DBW0 (or database writer), LGWR (or log writer), CKPT (or checkpoint), SMON (or system monitor), PMON (or process monitor), and a host of others. We will discuss the functionality of these background processes as they relate to other components of the database and as they are tested on the OCP exam.

Locating User Session Info: Shared Pool or PGA?

Let's return to the point raised earlier about the optional component of the shared pool, where user session information is stored in Oracle. Oracle will store session information in the shared pool only if the DBA configures Oracle to use shared servers to handle user data retrieval requests. This option is known as the *multithreaded server* (MTS) architecture. Otherwise, if dedicated servers are used, user session information is housed in the PGA.

For Review

1. Be sure you understand the difference between an Oracle instance and the Oracle database.

2. Know the main memory structure in Oracle. Be sure you can list its components for OCP. Also, understand the components of the PGA.

3. Understand the purpose of background processes in the Oracle database. At this point, you should be able to name at least two and describe their function. LGWR writes redo information to disk in the background, whereas DBW0 writes data blocks from the buffer cache to disk periodically.

Exercises

1. **You are managing an Oracle database. Which of the following choices correctly describes the difference between an Oracle instance and an Oracle database?**

A. An Oracle instance is a saved version of Oracle on disk, whereas a database is a running version of Oracle server.

B. An Oracle instance is the background processes of Oracle server, whereas a database is the memory allocated to the server.

C. An Oracle instance is the memory and background processes of a running Oracle server, whereas a database consists of an instance and files on disk.

D. The term "Oracle instance" is synonymous with the term Oracle database.

2. **You are managing an Oracle database. Which of the following is not a component of Oracle server's shared memory allocation when dedicated servers are being used?**

A. Buffer cache

B. Shared pool

C. Redo buffer

D. Program Global Area

3. **You are managing an Oracle database. Which of the following choices identifies the background process that handles writing data blocks to disk on a periodic basis?**

   A. LGWR

   B. CKPT

   C. DBW0

   D. S000

4. **You are configuring the Oracle database for user activity. Which of the following choices identifies where user session information will be stored when multithreaded servers are being used?**

   A. Shared pool

   B. Large pool

   C. Buffer cache

   D. Log buffer

Answer Key
1. C. 2. D. 3. C. 4. A.

Structures That Connect Users to Oracle Servers

Let's spend another quick moment covering a few other important Oracle network processes. The first is called the *listener process*. The Oracle listener process does just that—it listens for users trying to connect to the Oracle database via the network. When a user connects to the machine hosting the Oracle database, the listener process does one of two things. If dedicated server processes are being used, the listener tells Oracle to generate a new dedicated server and then assigns the user process to that dedicated server. If MTS is being used, the listener sends the user process to another process called the *dispatcher process*, which has already been mentioned. Once the listener hands over the user connection to either a dedicated server or a dispatcher, it is no longer involved in that connection. It will return to servicing new incoming connections.

The term "request from a user" is actually more precise than it sounds. It is a single program-interface call that is part of the user's SQL statement. When the database is operating in MTS mode, when a user makes a call, the dispatcher servicing the user process places the request in the *request queue*, where it is picked up by the next available shared server process. The request queue is in the SGA and is shared by all dispatcher processes of an instance. The shared server processes check the common request queue for new requests, picking up new requests on a first-in-first-out basis. One shared server process picks up one request in the queue and makes all the necessary calls to the database to complete that request. When the server completes the request, it places the response on the calling dispatcher's response queue. Each dispatcher has its own response queue in the SGA. The dispatcher then returns the completed request to the appropriate user process. That is the magic of how users are connected to an Oracle server.

TIP

Here's a quick summary of server, background, and network processes. The server process handles user requests for data. Background processes are Oracle processes that handle certain aspects of database operation behind the scenes. Network processes are used for network connectivity between user processes running on other machines to server processes running on the machine hosting the Oracle database.

For Review

1. Be sure you can distinguish between background, server, and network processes that operate in conjunction with the Oracle database.

2. Be sure you understand the different procedures Oracle undertakes to connect users to servers when the dedicated server or MTS architecture is being used.

3. Know the performance implications for using shared versus dedicated servers. Understand the circumstances where it is appropriate to use MTS versus dedicated servers as well.

4. Understand that the loss of a listener process will not affect existing connections to the database, but that it will prevent new users from connecting until the listener gets restarted.

Exercises

1. You are configuring the use of servers in your Oracle database. Which of the following statements describes what happens after the listener process detects a user attempting to connect to Oracle when dedicated servers are being used?

   A. The listener spawns a new server process.

   B. The listener passes the request to a dispatcher.

   C. The listener passes the request to LGWR.

   D. The listener passes the request to DBW0.

2. You are configuring the use of MTS on your Oracle database. Which of the following statements describes what happens after the listener process detects a user attempting to connect to Oracle when MTS is being used?

   A. The listener spawns a new server process.

   B. The listener passes the request to a dispatcher.

   C. The listener passes the request to LGWR.

   D. The listener passes the request to DBW0.

3. Finish the following sentence: When a listener process fails, _____(A) _____ users will not be able to _____(B)_____ to the Oracle database, whereas _____(C)_____ users remain unaffected by the listener process failure.

4. You are configuring the server architecture of your Oracle database. Which of the following choices identifies a situation the MTS architecture is designed to handle more effectively than the dedicated server architecture?

   A. Small workgroup database configurations

   B. Internet database configurations

   C. Single-user configurations

   D. Configurations on systems with plenty of available memory

---

Answer Key

1. A. 2. B. 3. (A) new; (B) connect; (C) existing (connected is also okay). 4. B.

Stages in Processing Queries, Changes, and `commits`

Now that you know how Oracle connects a user process with a server process, it's time for you to learn how Oracle behaves when the user wants to do something with the server, such as selecting Oracle data. You already know most of the main players, including the server process, user process, buffer cache, and library cache of the shared pool. You know all players, that is, except one—the Oracle relational database management system (RDBMS). SQL is a functional programming language, as opposed to a procedural language like COBOL or C. You write your code in terms of your desired outcome, not the process by which Oracle should get there. The RDBMS translates the outcome defined in your SQL statement into a process by which Oracle will obtain it.

Stages in Processing Queries

With all components established in the world of processing Oracle queries, let's look now at how Oracle processes queries. There are several for processing an Oracle `select` statement. The operations involved in executing both `select` statements and DML statements fall into a general pattern, which is shown in Figure 1-2. The specific flow of operation in processing a `select` statement is as follows:

1. *Search shared pool.* The RDBMS will first attempt to determine if a copy of this parsed SQL statement exists in the library cache.

2. *Validate statement.* The RDBMS accomplishes this step by checking SQL statement syntax.

3. *Validate data sources.* The RDBMS ensures that all columns and tables referenced in this statement exist.

4. *Acquire locks.* The RDBMS acquires parse locks on objects referenced in this statement so that their definitions don't change while the statement is parsed.

5. *Check privileges.* The RDBMS ensures that the user attempting to execute this SQL statement has enough privileges in the database to do so.

6. *Parse statement.* The RDBMS creates a *parse tree*, or *execution plan*, for the statement and places it in the library cache, based on what Oracle believes is the optimal method for executing the SQL statement. This is a list of operations the RDBMS uses to obtain data. If a parse tree already exists for this statement, the RDBMS can omit this step.

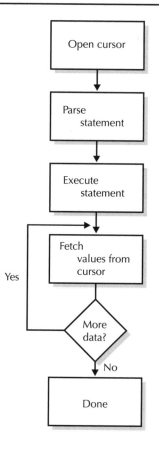

FIGURE 1-2. *Steps in Oracle SQL statement processing*

7. *Execute statement.* The RDBMS performs all processing to execute the `select` statement. At this point, the server process will retrieve data from disk into the buffer cache.

8. *Fetch values from cursor.* Once the `select` statement has been executed, all data returned from Oracle is stored in the cursor. That data is then placed into bind variables, row by row, and returned to the user process.

When complete, both the statement execution plan and the data in blocks retrieved from the disk stick around in the library cache and buffer cache, respectively, for a variable length of time, just in case that user or another user wants to execute the same `select` statement. In multiuser application environments, a performance gain is achieved every time user processes execute the same `select` statement because the RDBMS spends less time parsing the statement, and the server process spends less time retrieving data.

Stages in Processing DML Statements

At this point, meet yet another behind-the-scenes player in Oracle transaction processing—the *undo segment*. The undo segment is a database object in Oracle that stores old versions of data being changed by DML statements issued by the user process. Undo segments only store the old values, not the new values—the new values are stored in the object itself.

With this in mind, return to the processing of DML statements. There are several differences between how Oracle processes `select` statements and how it processes DML statements such as `update`, `insert`, and `delete`. Although the operations involved in executing DML statements fall into the same general pattern as those for `select` statements, shown in Figure 1-2, the specific flow of operation in processing DML statements is as follows:

1. *Parse statement.* The RDBMS creates a parse tree, or execution plan, for the statement and places it in the library cache. This is a list of operations the RDBMS uses to process the data change. If a parse tree already exists for this statement, the RDBMS can omit this step.

2. *Execute statement.* The RDBMS performs all processing to execute the DML statement. For `update` or `delete` statements, the server process will retrieve the data from disk into the buffer cache, implicitly acquire a lock on the data to be changed, and then make the specified data change in the buffer cache. A *lock* is an Oracle internal resource that one user process acquires before updating or deleting existing data to prevent other users from doing the same thing. For `insert` statements, the server process retrieves a block from a disk that has enough space available to house the new row of data, and places that new row into the block. Also, part of executing the DML statement is writing the old and new versions of the data to the undo segment acquired for that transaction. A lock must be acquired on the undo segment to write changes to an undo segment as well.

3. *Generate redo information.* Recall from the prior lesson that the redo log buffer stores redo or data-change information produced as the result of DML operations running in user sessions. After issuing DML statements, the user process must write a redo entry to the redo log buffer. In this way, Oracle can recover a data change if damage is later done to the disk files containing Oracle data.

TIP
Acquiring a lock is how one Oracle user says to the other users, "Hey! Hands off this data! I'm changing it now, so that means you can't have it until I let go of my lock!" Locks can be acquired at the row level implicitly as part of update *or* delete *statements, or at the table level through explicit methods described later in the book.*

Moving Data Changes from Memory to Disk

Once the DML statement has been executed, there is no further need to fetch values, as there was for select statements. However, as with select statements, the execution plan for the DML statement sticks around in the library cache for a variable period of time in case another user tries to execute the same statement. The changed blocks in the buffer cache are now considered "dirty" because the versions in the buffer cache and on disk are no longer identical. Those dirty buffers stick around in the buffer cache as well, but they will need to be copied to disk eventually in order for Oracle not to lose the data changes made. Also, new information appears in the redo log buffer as a result of the data changes made by the DML statement. By making all the data changes in memory, Oracle is able to achieve superior response to DML statements. This is achieved because it is faster to change and manipulate data in memory rather than on the disk. Secondly, the user does not have to wait for the changed data to be written back to the disk. Oracle does this by running two background processes called DBW0 and LGWR that write the data changes from buffer cache and redo log buffer to disk; these processes are asynchronous, meaning that they occur sometime after the user actually made the change. The following subtopics explain the role of each background process.

Role of DBW0   Called the *database writer* process, the DBW0 background process writes dirty data blocks from buffer cache to disk. Historically, this process is also called DBWR, but in more recent versions of Oracle, this term has become somewhat obsolete because Oracle now supports use of more than one database writer process. The writes are done for any of the following reasons:

- When the server process needs to make room in the buffer cache to read more data in for user processes.

- When DBW0 is told to write data to disk by the LGWR process.

- Every three seconds due to a timeout.

- The number of dirty buffers reaches a threshold value.

The event that causes LGWR to tell DBW0 to write to disk is called a *checkpoint*. You will learn more about checkpoints in Chapter 2. Because Oracle enables multiple database writers to run on the host machine, the DBW0 process is referred to as *DBW0*, where 0 can be any digit between zero and nine, because there can be one of several database writer processes running in Oracle. Oracle accepts a maximum of ten database writer processes for a single instance.

Role of LGWR   Called the *log writer* process, the LGWR background process writes redo log entries from the redo log buffer in memory to online redo log files on disk. LGWR has some other specialized functions related to the management of redo information that you will learn about in Chapter 2. LGWR also tells DBW0 to write dirty buffers to disk at checkpoints, as mentioned earlier. The redo log buffer writes to the redo log file under the following situations:

- When a transaction commits

- When the redo log buffer is one-third full

- When there is more than a megabyte of changes recorded in the redo log buffer

- Before DBW0 writes modified blocks in the database buffer cache to the datafiles

Stages in Processing `commits`

Issuing a `commit` statement ends the current transaction by making permanent any data change the user process may have issued to the Oracle database. A `rollback` statement discards the data change in favor of how the data appeared before the change was made. The undo segment is how Oracle manages to offer this functionality. By keeping a copy of the old data in the undo segment for the duration of the transaction, Oracle is able to discard any change made by the transaction until the `commit` statement is issued.

Before proceeding any further, make sure you understand the following important point—issuing `commit` does not imply that the data modified by the user process is safely written into the disk by the DBW0 process. Only a checkpoint, a timeout, or a need for room in the buffer cache for blocks requested by users will make DBW0 write dirty blocks to disk. With that fact in mind, what exactly does processing a `commit` statement consist of? The following list tells all:

- *Release table/row locks acquired by transaction.* The `commit` statement releases all row locks (or even table locks, if any were acquired) held by the user transaction issuing the `commit` statement. Other users can then modify the rows (or tables) previously locked by this user.

■ *Release undo segment locks acquired by transaction.* Changes to undo segments are subject to the same locking mechanisms as other objects. Once the change is committed, the space to hold both old and new versions of data for that transaction in the undo segment is available for another user's transaction. However, Oracle is lazy in that it does not actually discard or remove any information from the undo segment. Instead, Oracle merely overwrites the undo segment contents when the space is needed by another transaction.

■ *Generate redo for committed transaction.* Once the commit takes place, a redo entry is generated by the user process stating that all the changes associated with that transaction have now been committed by the user. A commit also results in flushing the content of the redo log buffer into redo log files—committed as well as uncommitted statements.

An interesting question remains: how does Oracle know which DML statement redo entries to associate with each transaction? The answer is the system change numbers (SCNs). An SCN is an ID that Oracle generates for each and every transaction that a user process engages. Every redo entry for every data change lists the change made and the SCN the change is associated with. The redo entry for the commit also identifies the SCN and simply notes that this SCN has been committed. Thus, Oracle can keep easy track of the status of every transaction via the SCN.

For Review

1. Be sure you understand that SQL lets users obtain their data via desired characteristics of that data, rather than via the procedure Oracle should use to obtain the data. Oracle has its own underlying mechanisms for data retrieval—you should be sure you understand these mechanisms for OCP.

2. Know the point at which Oracle server processes actually retrieve data into the buffer cache.

3. Be sure you can describe the function and purpose of undo segments, locks, and system change numbers in Oracle.

4. Be sure you can describe the process that Oracle server executes in order to support DML changes to data, including how changes in actual data and redo entries are moved from memory to disk.

Exercises

1. A user issues a `select` command against the Oracle database. Which of the following choices describes a step that Oracle will execute in support of this statement?

   A. Acquire locks on table queried.

   B. Generate redo for statement.

   C. Fetch data from disk into memory.

   D. Write changes to disk.

2. A user issues an `insert` statement against the Oracle database. Which of the following choices describes a step that Oracle will execute in support of this statement?

   A. Make changes to data block in memory.

   B. Parse statement if parse tree already exists in shared pool.

   C. Write changed records to undo segment.

   D. Write redo for transaction to datafile.

3. A user issues a `commit` statement on the Oracle database. Which of the following choices indicates what Oracle must do next?

   A. Save changes made to data in datafile.

   B. Wait for feedback from user to write redo to disk.

   C. Eliminate data block from buffer cache to make room for new changes.

   D. Write redo indicating transaction has been committed.

Answer Key

1. C. 2. A. 3. D.

Getting Started with the Oracle Server

In this section, you will cover the following topics related to getting started with the Oracle server:

- Common database administrative tools
- The Oracle Universal Installer (OUI)
- Optimal Flexible Architecture (OFA) and its benefits
- Setting up password file authentication
- Using Oracle Enterprise Manager (OEM) components

In the past few years, there has been an explosion in the use of administrative tools for Oracle databases. These tools are designed to simplify many aspects of Oracle database administration, including tablespace, instance, storage, object, and backup and recovery management. However, OCP certification on Oracle7 did not focus on using administrative tools. Instead, it focused on the importance of understanding server internals, such as V$ views and issuing commands from the command line. Although the importance of these Oracle components can hardly be diminished, administrative tools such as Oracle Enterprise Manager matured and expanded their functionality, and these areas have risen to take similar levels of importance in the repertoire of every DBA. Plus, they make your job a heck of a lot easier. Therefore, be prepared to see some questions on administrative tools on the Oracle 9i OCP Database Fundamentals I exam.

Common Database Administrative Tools

The most common database administrative tools that you would use as DBA of an Oracle9i database would be the various configuration assistants. These assistants are used to create databases, configuring Oracle networking and migrating databases from previous versions to Oracle9i. As you will see in subsequent chapters, the Database Configuration Assistant is used to create the databases and/or database templates. Templates are definitions of databases that you could create and store and later use in order to create similar databases. This tool has been enhanced to practically define anything to create a database.

Network Configuration Assistant is another tool that you would use to configure and administer your Oracle networking. This tool helps you to create `listener.ora` or `tnsnames.ora` files. Oracle Migration Assistant can be used to migrate databases from lower releases to Oracle9i. Where appropriate, we'll discuss the use of these tools in addition to covering the command-line options you may need to execute in order to accomplish administrative tasks.

The final tools to be used by DBAs in order to manage the Oracle database include Oracle Enterprise Manager, Oracle DBA Studio, and SQL*Plus. These tools are used for common administrative tasks. In addition, SQL*Plus can be used by end users for accessing and manipulating data in the Oracle database. For the most part, we'll emphasize how to execute common administrative tasks from within SQL*Plus using command-line interface (CLI) statements rather than graphical user interface (GUI) processes.

For Review

1. Be sure you can identify the administrative tools used by Oracle DBAs in order to administer the Oracle database.

2. Understand that the primary administrative tools for handling common DBA tasks are Oracle Enterprise Manager (GUI) and SQL*Plus (CLI).

Exercises

1. **You are administering the Oracle database. Which of the following tools would you use if you wanted to administer the database via statements issued on a command line?**

   A. Database Configuration Assistant

   B. SQL*Plus

   C. Network Configuration Assistant

   D. Enterprise Manager

2. **This is the name of the database management tool that enables you to create a new database via a template: _____.**

3. **This is the name of a file that can be managed via the Oracle Network Configuration Assistant: _____.**

Answer Key

1. B. **2.** Database Configuration Assistant. **3.** `listener.ora` or `tnsnames.ora`.

The Oracle Universal Installer

The Oracle Universal Installer (OUI) is a very versatile tool that Oracle provides in order to make the installation of Oracle software simple, interactive, and wizard-driven. The OUI interface is the same in all operating system platforms because it uses Java run-time environment, enabling it to be used on multiple platforms.

The first thing you will undoubtedly notice when installing your Oracle database is that many versions of Oracle for various host systems now come with the Oracle Universal Installer. Figure 1-3 shows the Oracle Universal Installer running in Windows environments. However, it is important to note that the same version of Oracle Universal Installer and Packager used in Windows environments also works for Sun Solaris.

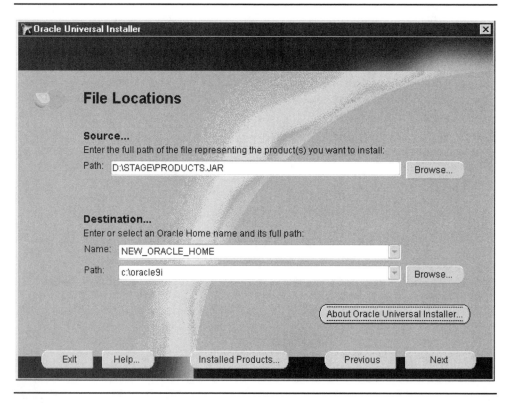

FIGURE 1-3. *Installing Oracle with Oracle Universal Installer and Packager*

TIP
*There won't likely be too many questions about
OUI on the OCP DBA I exam, but you should
understand its capabilities nevertheless.*

Universal Installer Features

The following bullets list some of the features of OUI:

- The look and feel of Oracle Universal Installer and Packager is nice, and at any step of the way, you can obtain help with installing your Oracle software. Some of the new features of this interface include the capability to install Oracle database software, client software, and management and integration software unattended.

- OUI not only installs the database software, but it also provides you with an option to create different types of database using Configuration Assistants. Details follow in later sections.

- It accepts automated software installation if you define a response file for noninteractive installation of Oracle products on a machine. The response file contains information and variable settings that the Universal Installer and Packager needs in order to complete an Oracle software installation.

- It tracks its own activities with a log file, showing the activities of the Universal Installer and Packager.

Installation of Oracle9i Software

You should be aware of a few issues regarding software installation. Oracle9i is a large application that comes on three CDs, and it requires well over 1GB of space on your hard drive just for the application software. In addition, on UNIX systems you will be required to `mount` and `umount` your CD-ROM drive repeatedly as Oracle switches from one CD for installation to another. The booklet that comes with your Oracle9i software distribution CDs has an explanation of how this process is executed. For example, the following code block shows the command used for several operating systems:

```
# HP-UX
nohup /usr/sbin/pfs_mountd &
nohup /usr/sbin/pfsd &
/usr/sbin/pfs_mount -t rrip -x unix /def/dsk/c5t2d0/SD_CDROM
```

```
# IBM AIX
mount -r -v cdrfs /dev/cd0 /cdrom

# SuSE Linux
mount -t iso9660 /dev/cdrom /cdrom

# SPARC/Solaris
mount -r -F hsfs /dev/dsk/c0t6d0s2 /cdrom
```

Additionally, you should be aware of the following steps to unmount the CD-ROM drive in order to eject the current disk and replace it with the next one Oracle requires:

1. In your telnet or xterm window, press the RETURN key to return to the shell prompt.

2. Type cd / to return to the root directory.

3. Type su and press RETURN. This will give you the root privileges you need to unmount the CD-ROM before ejecting. You'll need the password for root in order to become superuser. Involve your system administrator if you don't already have this privilege in your organization.

4. Type unmount/cdrom to unmount the CD-ROM drive. If you try to do this while logged in as oracle, you'll likely get errors indicating the device is busy. If so, return to step 3.

5. Eject the current CD from the CD-ROM drive and replace it with the disk OUI requested.

6. Enter the mount command appropriate for your system from the previous code block.

7. Return to OUI and click OK to continue.

Windows users of Oracle won't need to worry, as changing CDs for installation is more common in those environments. As with all Oracle databases, you should try to have at least three separate disk devices available to dedicate to Oracle resources. For large enterprise installations, you will definitely want at least six or seven, and perhaps as many as 20 to 30, depending on what sort of operation you plan to use your Oracle database for.

For smaller machines, you may find Oracle9*i* Enterprise Edition difficult to install due to memory constraints, even if you follow Oracle's recommendation of having 128MB of RAM at a minimum. In reality, you should have 256 to 512MB of RAM available on the host machine, and even then, the installation process will run slowly because OUI runs completely within a Java Virtual Machine environment. However, you can tailor your Oracle configuration later to minimize the amount of memory the database will require.

We can offer a couple of additional suggestions for installation of Oracle9*i* on smaller machines as well to reduce problems. You can choose the Minimal Installation radio button on the wizard screen for defining the type of Oracle9*i* installation you want to perform, which requires less memory for the installation. This is a good option for installing Oracle9*i* on machines with 256 to 384MB of RAM. Otherwise, if you want to run the typical installation, you should increase the available real memory on the machine hosting the Oracle database to 512MB of RAM or more. On starting the OUI, the following occurs:

- You will be prompted whether you want to install Enterprise or Standard Edition of the software or custom install the software.

- You will then be prompted whether you want to install just the software or you want to have a general installation (install software and preconfigured database) or an installation with a specific type of database. The databases are created during the installation by using the Configuration Assistant tool.

- You will be asked questions related to the software installation location and if you choose to create a database, you will be prompted for the database name and the location for the database files.

- If you have chosen custom installation, you will be prompted to select the components you want to install. Make sure you include OUI in your selection.

- Database Configuration Assistant will be invoked to assist in creating the database. Then the Oracle Net Configuration Assistant will be invoked to create necessary network configuration files and start the listener process. If you are installing in UNIX environment, you will be prompted to run `root.sh` file to handle.

Installation Log

OUI creates the `oraInventory` directory the first time it is run to keep an inventory of products that it installs. OUI creates a file in this directory called `installActions.log` that stores the log of the recent installation. In UNIX, the location of this directory is stored in a file called `oraInst.loc`.

Noninteractive Installation

You may perform a noninteractive installation of the Oracle9*i* software by supplying OUI with a *response file*. OUI uses the information provided in the response file to provide answers to the Installer prompts and completes the installation. For further details, refer to Oracle installation documents provided with your distribution software.

TIP
Operating system-specific information for installing Oracle is not tested on the OCP exam. Nevertheless, you should attempt installation of Oracle9i at least once before taking the OCP DBA Fundamentals I exam to give yourself the hands-on experience necessary for practice of database administration in real life.

For Review

1. Understand the purpose of Oracle Universal Installer and how it differs from versions of Oracle Installer you may have used in Oracle8*i* or earlier editions of the Oracle database.

2. Be sure you understand the host system requirements Oracle9*i* imposes on your organization before upgrading to Oracle9*i* in your company.

3. Understand the basic OUI components required for noninteractive installation and where to look for information Oracle logged during installation.

Exercises

1. **This is the name of the directory OUI uses to store a log of all installation activities: _____.**

2. **Complete the following statement: Oracle Universal Installer runs within the _____ (three words).**

3. **This is the name of the file you would use if you wanted OUI to run in unattended installation mode: _____ (two words).**

Answer Key
1. oraInventory. 2. Java Virtual Machine. 3. Response file.

Benefits of Optimal Flexible Architecture

As we discussed earlier in the chapter, Oracle databases consist of many different files residing within a host system. Some of these files pertain to the application software, whereas others are used for storing actual data in your database. Still others are used for administering your database. As Oracle evolved into a complex and powerful software product, DBAs faced numerous challenges in determining the best way to layout the Oracle software, database, and administrative files on their host systems in order to effectively manage the task of administering Oracle databases. In response to this task, the Oracle Corporation published a specification identifying a standard filesystem configuration that DBAs could use in order to layout the files of a working Oracle database system. The underlying idea was that if DBAs followed this standard for every database used in the organization, it would be much easier for others to find where the filesystem components were located, rather than forcing others to dig around for each component. The result was an Oracle standard called Optimal Flexible Architecture (OFA). Let's now explore OFA in more detail.

What Is OFA?

Optimal Flexible Architecture (OFA) is an industry standard that defines how to set up Oracle software and Oracle databases. OFA provides maximum flexibility in supporting multiple versions of Oracle software and a single listener process to support oracle instances that may be running under different versions of Oracle Software. This brings us to a concept known as ORACLE_HOME. ORACLE_HOME corresponds to the environment in which Oracle products run. The environment could be the location of the installed products files (/u01/app/oracle/product/9.0.1 for UNIX, or C:\oracle\ora90 in Windows) or the PATH variable pointing to the location of the binary files and in the case of Windows NT, the registry entries, service names, and program groups. Figure 1-4 gives you an example of directories on a filesystem laid out in accordance with OFA.

Some Benefits of Using OFA

OFA has been a boon to many DBAs looking to minimize support headaches. Let's now explore why we might want to use OFA rather than just simply come up with our own organizational standards for database layout:

- OFA is designed to organize large amounts of database data files and Oracle software on disks to improve the performance of the database and minimize I/O contention among many disks that house the databases.

- OFA is designed to be flexible enough to facilitate the growth of the databases.

```
                        /u02/
                            oradata/
                                db01/
                                    system01.dbf
                                    control01.ctl
                                    redo0101.rdo
                          .     db02/
                                    system01.dbf
                                    control01.ctl
                                    redo0101.rdo
                        ...


                        /u03/
                            oradata/
                                db01/
                                    users01.dbf
                                    control02.ctl
                                    redo0102.rdo
                                db02/
                                    tools01.dbf
                                    control02.ctl
                                    redo0102.rdo
```

FIGURE 1-4. *Optimal Flexible Architecture*

■ OFA encourages consistent database file-naming conventions. This enables the DBA to clearly distinguish the data files, control files, and other files that belong to one database from the other. OFA also helps in associating data files to their corresponding tablespaces.

■ By keeping the contents of the tablespace separate, OFA minimizes fragmentation and I/O contention. Take for example the separation of tables and indexes in different tablespaces. This gives the flexibility to move the tablespaces to different disk drives in the event the I/O contention goes up.

■ OFA supports multiple ORACLE_HOME locations. This enables you to execute multiple releases of Oracle concurrently. For example, you could have a database instance running on 8.1.7 while at the same time have another database instance running on 9.0.1 without causing any disruption to each other.

■ OFA enables you to have one listener spawning connections to databases of multiple Oracle software home directories.

■ OFA keeps the administration information of the each of the database separate.

For Review

1. Be sure you can define what OFA is and why it is beneficial to you as the DBA and to your organization.

2. Know what ORACLE_HOME means with respect to Oracle database running environments.

Exercises

1. **You are implementing Oracle in your organization. Which of the following identifies a feature of Optimal Flexible Architecture?**

    A. OFA lumps software, database, and administrative files into one area so they are easy for DBAs to locate.

    B. Use of OFA enables DBAs to define their own filesystem layouts using proprietary naming conventions in order to facilitate management of Oracle databases.

    C. Use of OFA reduces support headaches by standardizing filesystem layouts for all Oracle installations.

    D. OFA lumps all database objects like tables and indexes into one tablespace so they are easy for DBAs to manage.

2. **Finish the following sentence: Use of OFA is _____ when creating, configuring, and managing Oracle databases.**

3. **Finish the following sentence: When configuring an Oracle database on your host system, OFA minimizes _____(A)_____ contention because different _____(B)_____ can be placed on different _____(C)_____.**

Answer Key
1. C. 2. Optional. 3. (A) I/O; (B) tablespaces; (C) disks.

Setting Up Password File Authentication

How you plan to support the Oracle database you create determines to a large extent how you will set up Oracle to handle *administrative authentication*. Authentication requires the DBA to provide a password in order to gain entry for administrative tasks onto the machine hosting Oracle, the database itself, or both. There are two methods of providing administrative authentication: operating system and password file authentication. If you plan to connect to the machine hosting the Oracle database via `telnet`, `xterm`, or a Windows client such as Citrix Metaframe in order to administer the database, operating system authentication might be acceptable. But realistically, if you plan to manage the site from software running on your desktop computer, such as Enterprise Manager, then you should set up a password file authentication.

Another nice feature about a password file is that it enables many DBAs to manage databases, each with varying levels of control. For example, the organization might want the junior DBA to handle backups and user creation, but not the startup and shutdown of the instance. Password files work well to support organizations wanting a team of DBAs to have a range of capabilities on the machine.

More Introductions: SYS, SYSTEM, and the Data Dictionary

Another round of introductions is in order. *SYS* and *SYSTEM* are two users Oracle creates when you install your database. Each has its own default password. The default password for SYS is `change_on_install`, and for SYSTEM it is `manager`. Be careful to protect the passwords for both these users by changing them after installing Oracle. These two privileged users have the power to administer most any feature of the Oracle database. SYS is more important than SYSTEM because SYS will wind up owning all Oracle system tables from which the data dictionary is derived.

The Oracle data dictionary is the system resource you will turn to in order to find out just about anything about your database, from which users own what objects to the initialization parameter settings, to performance monitoring, and more. There are two basic categories for Oracle database views: those that show information about database objects and those that show dynamic performance. The views showing information about objects are the data dictionary views. The views showing information about performance are dynamic performance views. You'll learn more about setting up and using the data dictionary in Chapter 2.

Using Operating System Authentication

Operating system authentication offers the comfort of a familiar face to old-school UNIX folks, in the same way as using the vi text editor and Korn shell. Because of this, the discussion of operating system authentication will focus primarily on its implementation in UNIX. However, operating system authentication has few real advantages and many disadvantages compared to the password file method of authentication. The main benefit operating system authentication offers is easy login to Oracle via the slash (/) character, as shown in the following:

```
UNIX(r) SYSTEM V TTYP01 (23.45.67.98)
Login: bobcat
Password:
User connected. Today is 12/17/99 14:15:34
[companyx] /home/bobcat/> sqlplus /
SQL*PLUS Version 8.1.7.0.0
(c) 2001 Oracle Corporation(c) All rights reserved.
Connected to Oracle9i Enterprise Edition 9.0.1 - Production
With the Java option.
SQL>
```

The disadvantages to operating system authentication are many. For one thing, you must have a machine login to use Oracle. When might this pose a problem? For example, you may not want to make the host machine's command prompt accessible to your 10,000+ user base for a production system. For development and test environments, however, operating system authentication may be fine.

To use operating system authentication, a special group must be created on the operating system before you even install your Oracle software called dba. Later, when Oracle is installed and configured, you can log into the operating system via Telnet as a user belonging to the dba group (such as the Oracle software owner). From there, you run SQL*Plus in line mode and perform startup and shutdown operations after issuing the connect *name* as sysdba command and then providing the appropriate password as well. The sysdba keyword denotes a collection of privileges that are used for the administration of Oracle databases, including the capability to start and stop the database. The following block illustrates simple usage:

```
SQL> connect sys as sysdba
Password:
Connected.
```

TIP
Those old-school Oracle DBAs who are familiar with the connect internal *command should know that* connect internal *is gradually being desupported along with Server Manager in Oracle8i and later releases. Use* connect sys as sysdba *instead.*

Oracle creates some other operating system roles as part of its UNIX installation that must be granted to the DBA, such as osoper and osdba. These operating system roles are given to the Oracle software owner and must be granted to other operating system users who would be DBAs via operating system commands. These roles cannot be revoked or granted from within Oracle. However, there are two equivalent Oracle privileges used when you authenticate with a password file— sysoper and sysdba, respectively.

There are some small differences between the osoper and sysoper, and osdba and sysdba, which you may use to your advantage for breaking out DBA roles and responsibilities. The osoper role and sysoper privilege enable you to start and stop the instance, mount or open the database, back up the database, initiate archiving redo logs, initiate database recovery, and change database access to restricted session mode. The sysoper and sysdba roles offer the same privileges as osoper and sysoper, and add the capability to execute and administer all Oracle system privileges, the create database privilege, and all privileges required for time-based incomplete database recovery. Obviously, osoper or sysoper is given to the DBA to ultimately be responsible for the operation of the database.

TIP
The implementation of operating system authentication in Oracle depends heavily on the operating system you use. Because operating system-specific issues are not part of the OCP DBA Fundamentals I exam, they will not be covered here. If you need more information on operating system authentication, consult the appropriate operating system-specific Oracle administrative manual.

Some Initialization Parameters to Remember for Operating System Authentication

You need to set the REMOTE_LOGIN_PASSWORDFILE = NONE when your database is initially created in order to configure operating system authentication. This ensures that you can only start and stop your database from a terminal session on the actual machine hosting the Oracle database or from the console for that machine. In Oracle9*i*, the default value for this parameter is NONE.

Special Notes for Windows Users

When setting up operating system authentication on Windows, you must execute the following additional steps:

I. Create a new local Windows NT users' group called ORA_*SID*_DBA and ORA_*SID*_OPER that is specific to an instance, or ORA_DBA and ORA_OPER that is not specific to an instance.

2. Add a Windows NT operating system user to that group. Once you access this domain, you are automatically validated as an authorized DBA.

3. Ensure that you have the following line in your `sqlnet.ora` file: SQLNET.AUTHENTICATION_SERVICES = (NTS)

4. Set the REMOTE_LOGIN_PASSWORDFILE parameter to NONE in your `init.ora` file.

5. Connect to the database with the privilege SYSDBA or SYSOPER:

```
SQL> CONNECT JASON AS SYSDBA
Password:
Connected.
```

Authentication with the Password File

Oracle's other method of authenticating DBAs is the *password file*. It is far more important that you understand this option than operating system authentication for the OCP DBA Fundamentals I exam. The DBA creates the password file, and passwords for all others permitted to administer Oracle are stored in the file. The password file is created with the ORAPWD utility. The name of this executable varies by operating system. For example, it is `orapwd` on both UNIX and on Windows.

When executing ORAPWD, you will pass three parameters: FILE, PASSWORD, and ENTRIES. To determine what to specify for FILE, you usually place the password file in $ORACLE_HOME/dbs and name it `orapwsid.pwd`, substituting the name of your database for `sid`. For PASSWORD, be aware that as you define the password for your password file, you are also simultaneously assigning the password for logging into Oracle as SYS. Later, if the DBA connects as SYS and issues the `alter user name identified by password` command, the password for SYS, and the password file are all changed. The final parameter is ENTRIES, specifying the number of user entries allowed for the password file. Be careful, because you can't add more later without deleting and re-creating the password file, which is risky. The actual execution of ORAPWD in Windows may look something like this, from the command line:

```
D:\oracle\bin\>orapwd FILE=D:\oracle\dbs\orapworgdb01.pwd
PASSWORD=jason ENTRIES=5
```

In UNIX, it may look something like this:

```
/home/oracle> orapwd \
FILE=/u01/app/oracle/product/9.0.1/dbs/orapwdorgdb01.pwd \
 PASSWORD=jason ENTRIES=5
```

After creating the password file, you must do a few other things to provide administrative access to the database. First, set the value for the REMOTE_LOGIN_PASSWORDFILE parameter in the init*sid*.ora parameter file. This parameter accepts `none`, `shared`, and `exclusive` as its values. The `none` setting means the database won't allow privileged sessions over nonsecure connections. When operating system authentication is used, the REMOTE_LOGIN_PASSWORDFILE is set to `none` to disallow remote database administration. Setting REMOTE_LOGIN_PASSWORDFILE to `shared` means that only SYS can log into Oracle to perform administrative functions remotely. Finally, setting REMOTE_LOGIN_PASSWORDFILE to `exclusive` means that a password file exists and any user/password combination in the password file can log into Oracle remotely and administer that instance. If this setting is used, the DBA may use the `create user` command in Oracle to create the users who are added to the password file, and grant `sysoper` and/or `sysdba` system privileges to those users. After that, users can log into the database as themselves with all administrator privileges. In addition, EXCLUSIVE indicates that only one instance can use the password file and that the password file contains names other than SYS. SHARED indicates that more than one instance can use the password file. The only user recognized by the password file is SYS.

After creating the password file with the ORAPWD utility and setting the REMOTE_LOGIN_PASSWORDFILE parameter to `exclusive` in order to administer a database remotely, the DBA can then connect to the database as a user with `sysdba` privileges as shown in the following:

```
SQL>  CONNECT sys AS SYSDBA;
Password:
Connected.
```

TIP
Remember two important points about password files. First, to find out which users are in the database password file, use the V$PWFILE_USERS dynamic performance view. (More on the data dictionary will be presented in Chapter 2.) Second, any object created by anyone logging in as sysdba *or* sysoper *will be owned by SYS.*

Password File Default Locations
Password file default locations depend on the operating system hosting the Oracle database. On UNIX, the password files are usually located in the $ORACLE_HOME/dbs directory. On Windows, the password file is usually located

in the %ORACLE_HOME%\DATABASE directory. You can specify a nondefault location of the password file in the Windows registry with the key ORA_*SID*_PWFILE. You can set the password during installation by using the Custom Installation option.

For Review

1. Understand that there are two methods for administrative authentication in Oracle: operating system and password file. In general, you should understand how to set up and use password file authentication.

2. Know that the OCP DBA Fundamentals I exam will focus on use of password file authentication.

3. Remember that the REMOTE_LOGIN_PASSWORDFILE init.ora parameter is used for configuring use of password file authentication, whereas the ORAPWD utility is used for actually creating the password file.

4. Understand the SYS and SYSTEM users and their purpose in the Oracle database architecture.

Exercises

1. **You are configuring password file usage for administering the Oracle database. You want to set it such that DBAs listed in the password file will be able to administer a single database. Which of the following choices identifies the appropriate REMOTE_LOGIN_PASSWORDFILE setting in the init.ora file?**

   A. NONE

   B. SHARED

   C. EXCLUSIVE

   D. ORAPWD

2. **You are creating a password file in Oracle. Which of the following choices identifies how you will specify this command if you want your password file named orapwdORCL.pwd, located in /u01/app/oracle/database, to allow up to 100 other DBAs to connect and administer the database?**

   A. orapwd directory=/u01/app/oracle/database
   file=orapwdORCL.pwd

    B. `orapwd file=/u01/app/oracle/database/orapwdORCL.pwd password=oracle entries=100`

    C. `orapwd file=/u01/app/oracle/database/orapwdORCL.pwd entries=100`

    D. `orapwd file=orapwdORCL.pwd password=oracle entries=100`

3. **You execute the ORAPWD utility to generate your password file in Oracle, specifying `password=fritz26`. Which of the following users will have his or her password set to `fritz26`?**

    A. OUTLN

    B. SYS

    C. SYSTEM

    D. None, the PASSWORD parameter is used for authentication of the user running ORAPWD to create the password file.

Answer Key
1. C. 2. B. 3. B.

Using Oracle Enterprise Manager Components

Oracle Enterprise Manager (OEM) is a suite of applications that enable you to manage your Oracle database in a GUI. Almost anything you can do from SQL*Plus, you can do from OEM, provided you have set up a password file for remote database administration. More about how to do this appears in the next section. If you do not have a password file set up for administering your Oracle database remotely, then you cannot start up and shut down the Oracle database using OEM, but you can do most anything else.

    There is no such thing as easy database administration, but using the administrative tools available in OEM can simplify many areas of managing your database. OEM is usually run from your desktop. Assuming you use Windows, the location of OEM components under your Start button can vary. One way you can identify the tools at your disposal as part of OEM is by looking under Start | Programs | Oracle Enterprise Manager, or under the Tools | Applications menu within the Enterprise Manager application itself. Figure 1-5 illustrates Enterprise Manager and both the Tools | Applications menu and the Applications button bar,

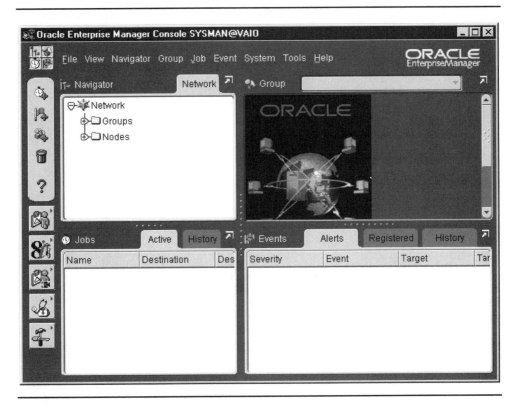

FIGURE 1-5. *Oracle Enterprise Manager administrative applications*

both of which can be used to access any of the administrative applications available in OEM. The following list identifies the applications available for OEM, along with a brief description of their use:

- **Tools and wizards for data management**   Used to load and reorganize data in databases

- **Tools and wizards for backup management**   Used to back up, restore, and recover databases, and to manage redo log files

- **Instance Manager**   Handles management of an Oracle instance, including session, in-doubt transaction, and initialization parameter information

- **Replication Manager**   Manages configuration, scheduling, and administrative functions of replication between nodes on a network running Oracle databases

- **Schema Manager**   Manages table, index, cluster, and other object creation and management in an Oracle database

- **Security Manager**   Handles user access privileges and role administration

- **SQL*Plus Worksheet**   Used to execute SQL statements from scripts in a graphical interface more advanced than SQL*Plus

- **Storage Manager**   Handles configuration and management of logical and physical disk resources for the Oracle database

- **Software Manager**   Used as part of an enterprise-wide management of Oracle software application design, distribution, and asset management

- **Repository Manager**   Used to create, validate, and drop OEM repositories

TIP
In addition to the administrator tools listed previously, other applications are available for different cartridges you may have installed on your Oracle database, such as ConText Cartridge System Administrator. Administrative tools accompany add-ins like the Diagnostic Pack as well, including the Lock Manager, Performance Manager, and others.

Enterprise Manager Architecture

Version 2 and later of OEM extend the client/server architecture introduced with version 1 to a highly scalable three-tier model. The first tier consists of a Java-based console and integrated applications that can be installed or run from a Web browser. The second-tier component of OEM version 2 is the Oracle Management Server (OMS). The main function of the OMS is to provide centralized intelligence and distributed control between clients and managed nodes, which process and administer all system tasks. Sharing of the repository is also possible. The OMS uses the OEM repository as its persistent back-end store. This repository maintains system data, application data, and the state of managed entities distributed throughout the environment. Version 2 enables multiple users to access and share repository data for systems where responsibilities are shared. The third tier is composed of targets, such as databases, nodes, or other managed services. The Intelligent Agent functions as the executor of jobs and events sent by the OMS.

Using the OEM Console

You can choose to run the Enterprise Manager Console first. This program has methods that enable you to start and use the other components mentioned. The first time you run OEM console, it will ask you to set up your management server and repository.

Using SQL*Plus Worksheet

This tool is fairly easy to use, and you can start it either from the Start button in Windows or from within the OEM console. Once you've started the tool and logged into Oracle, you should see two windows. The top window is where you enter your SQL statements as you would in SQL*Plus. The bottom window is where you see the output generated by Oracle in response to your SQL query. On NT, you should experiment to determine whether you can access the SQL*Plus worksheet from the OEM console under Database Applications. The regular SQL*Plus is available on the Start | Programs | Oracle-ora8i | Application Development.

Using Instance Manager

Because so much of your effort in this chapter will focus on managing the Oracle instance and opening and closing the Oracle database, the tool we will focus on is Instance Manager. The basic purpose of Instance Manager is—you guessed it—managing the Oracle instance. You can start and stop the instance with this tool (provided you've set up your password file—more information on how to do this in a moment), view and modify `initsid.ora` parameters, view current sessions and in-doubt transactions, and apply database configuration information you have available on your desktop. Figure 1-6 displays the Instance Manager login prompt. To open this tool, either click on the Tools | Applications | Instance Manager menu item from OEM, or click on Start | Programs | Oracle Enterprise Manager | Instance Manager from the Windows console. In OEM 2.1, Instance Manager is in the DBA Studio; however, this is a minor point because you will only be tested on OEM 2.0 for OCP, and furthermore, OEM is a minor component of the OCP exam. After providing appropriate username, password, and TNS connect information, notice the fourth text box, where the tool prompts you to choose how you want to connect. The options are `normal`, `sysdba`, and `sysoper`. The first option enables you to connect as the username you provided, but gives you no administrative abilities on the database. Thus, you can view database initialization parameters, but cannot start up or shut down the database. Use of the other two options is for administrative authentication, and both will be explained in the next section.

TIP
Instance Manager will not prompt you for login information if you run it from OEM. Instead, it will use the login info you provided when you started OEM.

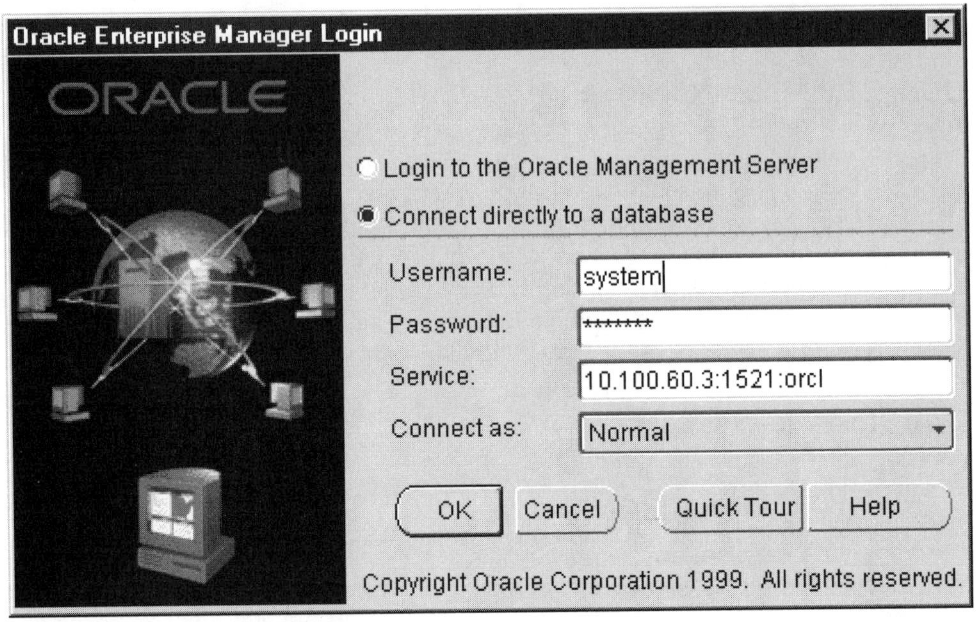

FIGURE 1-6. *Instance Manager tool in OEM*

After login, you will see the Instance Manager interface. The left-hand window is the navigator window. On it, there are several nodes you can drill down into to find information. You drill into each node by clicking on the plus sign (+) to the left of the node. The names of each node are self-explanatory. For example, if you drill into the Sessions node, as shown in Figure 1-7, you will see all the sessions currently happening in Oracle listed below the node. On the right side is the work interface. If you click on the name of the node or the File Folder icon to the left of that name, the relevant information will be displayed in the work window. As another example, if you click on the name of one of the connected sessions in the navigator window, you will see some additional information about that session appearing in the work window.

Along the top of the interface is a set of several menus. From left to right, they are File, View, Database, Sessions, Transactions, Configuration, and Help. The options under the File menu enable you to change database connection, enable roles, or exit the application. The options under the View menu enable you to modify the tools available in Instance Manager and expand or collapse nodes in the left window. The Database menu permits startup and shutdown operations,

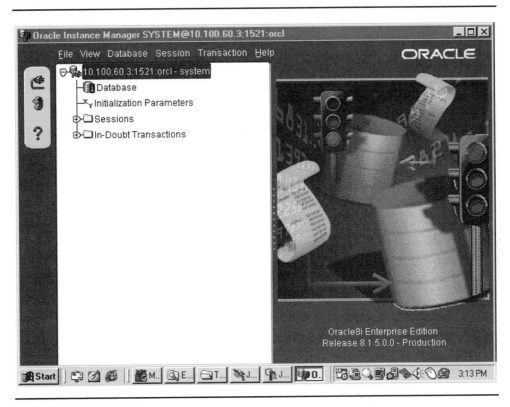

FIGURE 1-7. *Instance Manager interface*

archiving, and other things. The Sessions menu permits management of sessions, including the ability to disconnect a session, restrict access to the database to only those users with `restricted session` privileges, or allow all users to access the database. The Transactions menu enables the DBA to force `commit` and `rollback` operations to happen in the database. The Configuration menu enables you to change or remove database configurations from the database to the desktop. Finally, the Help menu gives you access to online help.

For Review

1. Be sure you understand the basic purpose of Enterprise Manager, namely to assist DBAs in support of Oracle databases by providing a GUI interface for handling most administrative tasks.

2. Know the different categories of tools OEM provides. It is not important to know how to use them for OCP, but you should be able to identify the existence of tools identified in this discussion.

3. Be able to describe the role an Oracle Management Server plays within Enterprise Manager.

Exercises

1. The _____ Manager tool helps you to start and stop a running Oracle server.

2. The _____ Manager tool lets you create database objects like tables and indexes.

3. The _____ (two words) tool is used for obtaining an overall view of all Oracle databases in an organization.

Answer Key
1. Instance. 2. Schema. 3. OEM Console.

Managing an Oracle Instance

In this section, you will cover the following topics related to starting and stopping the instance:

■ Creating and managing your parameter file

■ Configuring Oracle-Managed Files (OMF)

■ Stating and shutting down your database

■ Monitoring the log and diagnostic files of the database

After installing the Oracle software, the DBA should master the management of an Oracle instance. There are several important things that should be done to manage the Oracle instance before even thinking about setting up the Oracle database. Important questions about authentication must be answered, and the parameter file must be developed and managed. This parameter file is generically referred to as *initsid.ora* by many DBAs. Starting up and shutting down the instance, and opening and closing the database are key areas both before and after the database is created. Finally, the management of sessions and places to look for information about the Oracle instance in action are covered in this section.

Creating and Managing Initialization Parameter File

How well or poorly your database performs is determined to a great extent by how you configure your Oracle instance. You configure your instance dynamically when you start it, using a parameter file. This parameter file is commonly referred to by DBAs as the init*sid*.ora file. The real name of the parameter file for your database is arbitrary and completely up to you; however, when you install Oracle and create your first database, Oracle will generate a parameter file for you named after the database if you use the Oracle Database Configuration Assistant to create your Oracle database. Thus, if your database is named ORGDB01, your default name for the init*sid*.ora file will be initORGDB01.ora. Throughout the discussions in this book, this file will be referred to as init.ora or init*sid*.ora file.

You can create your parameter file from scratch, but why bother when Oracle creates one for you? The parameter file Oracle creates for you will contain several different options for the most essential initialization parameters you need to include when creating a new database. However, Oracle has hundreds of initialization parameters, documented and undocumented. The following code block shows a sample parameter file in use on a small Oracle database running under UNIX. It was created automatically when the Oracle Database Configuration Assistant created the database and was then later modified manually. The pound sign (#) is used to denote comments in the parameter file.

```
##########################################################
# Copyright (c) 1991, 2001 by Oracle Corporation
##########################################################
##########################################################

# Cache and I/O
##########################################################
db_block_size = 8192
db_cache_size = 20971520


##########################################################
# Cursors and Library Cache
##########################################################
open_cursors = 300


##########################################################
# Diagnostics and Statistics
##########################################################
```

```
background_dump_dest=/u01/app/oracle/product/9.0.1/admin/oracle/bdump
user_dump_dest=/u01/app/oracle/product/9.0.1/admin/oracle/udump
core_dump_dest=/u01/app/oracle/product/9.0.1/admin/oracle/core
# timed_statistics = TRUE


##########################################################
# Distributed, Replication, and Snapshot
##########################################################
db_domain = ""
remote_login_passwordfile = EXCLUSIVE


##########################################################
# File Configuration
##########################################################
control_files = ("/u01/oradata/oracle/control01.ctl",
                 "/u02/oradata/oracle/control02.ctl",
                 "/u03/oradata/oracle/control03.ctl")


##########################################################
# MTS
##########################################################
dispatchers="(PROTOCOL=TCP)(SER=MODOSE)", "(PROTOCOL=TCP)
(PRE=oracle.aurora.server.GiopServer)", "(PROTOCOL=TCP)
(PRE=oracle.aurora.server.SgiopServer)"


##########################################################
# Miscellaneous
##########################################################
compatible = 9.0.0
db_name = oracle


##########################################################
# Network Registration
##########################################################
instance_name = ORCL


##########################################################
# Pools
##########################################################
java_pool_size = 10485760
large_pool_size = 1048576
shared_pool_size = 31457280


##########################################################
# Processes and Sessions
##########################################################
processes = 15
```

```
#######################################################
# Redo Log and Recovery
#######################################################
fast_start_mttr_target = 300


#######################################################
# Resource Manager
#######################################################
resource_manager_plan = SYSTEM_PLAN


#######################################################
# Sort, Hash Joins, Bitmap Indexes
#######################################################
sort_area_size = 524288


#######################################################
# System Managed Undo and Rollback Segments
#######################################################
undo_management = AUTO
undo_tablespace=UNDOTBS


#######################################################
# Other Database Parameters
#######################################################
utl_file_dir = /u01/oradata/oracle/misc
```

In general, when working with parameter files, it is best not to start from scratch. Use the Oracle default or borrow one from another DBA. However, be sure that you alter the parameters in the file to reflect your own database, including DB_NAME, DB_BLOCK_SIZE, CONTROL_FILES, and others. You should remember where you store your parameter files on the machine hosting the Oracle database. Do not leave multiple copies in different directories; this could lead you to make a change to one but not the other, and then start your instance with the old parameter file later, and have problems. However, it can be useful to have a few different copies of a parameter file for various administrative purposes, such as one for production environments and one for running the database in restricted mode for DBA maintenance operations.

By default, a pointer to the `init.ora` file in your OFA-compliant `admin/SID/pfile` administrative directory (where *SID* is replaced with the name of your Oracle database) is located in the `$ORACLE_HOME/dbs` directory on a UNIX machine. In Windows, the actual `init.ora` file is located in the %ORACLE_HOME%\database directory. If the `init.ora` is not in the default location, it has to be explicitly specified while bringing up the database. If you don't, Oracle will complain.

Once your instance is started, several different ways exist for obtaining the values set for the instance on initialization. The first and least effective way to view parameter values in your database is to look at the init*sid*.ora file. This choice does not give you all parameters, and what's more, the parameters in your parameter file may have changed since the last time you started Oracle. A much better way to obtain parameter values is to select them from a special view in Oracle called V$PARAMETER. Still another effective way for obtaining parameter values in Oracle is to use SQL*Plus. The show parameter command will list all parameters for the instance. Finally, you can use the OEM Instance Manager to display instance parameters, as shown in Figure 1-8. Can you guess where Instance Manager and SQL*Plus draw their initialization parameter information from? If you said V$PARAMETER, you were right!

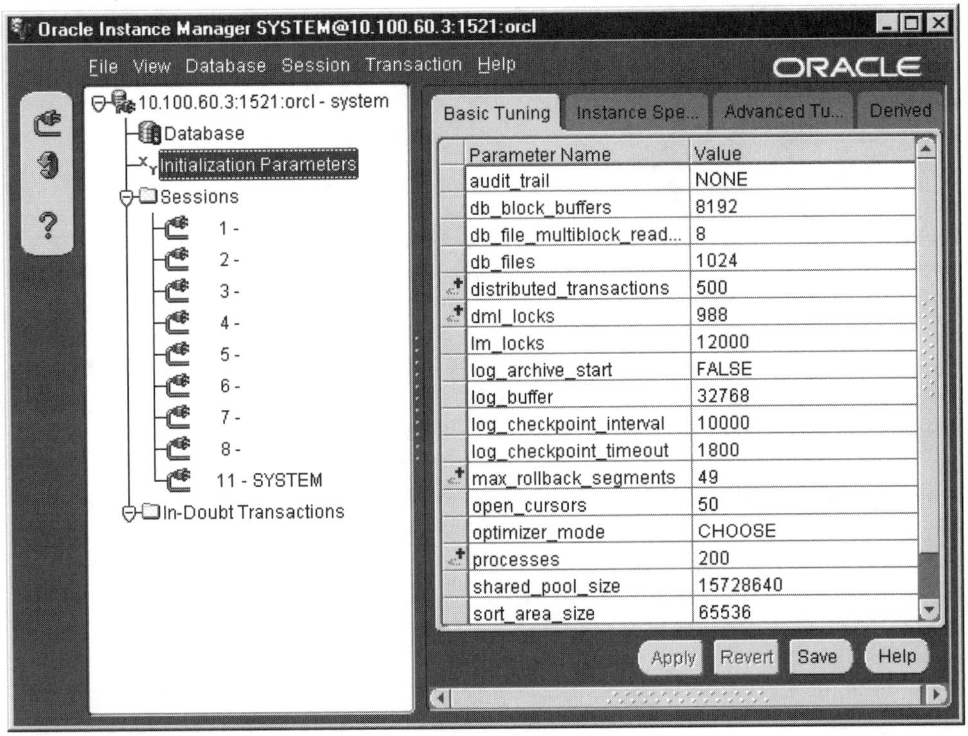

FIGURE 1-8. *Instance parameters in Instance Manager*

TIP

Some other important V$ views available in the Oracle9i database to be aware of include V$FIXED_TABLE, V$SGA, V$PARAMETER, V$OPTION, V$PROCESS, V$SESSION, V$VERSION, V$INSTANCE, V$THREAD, V$CONTROLFILE, V$DATABASE, V$DATAFILE, V$DATAFILE_HEADER, and V$LOGFILE.

Setting parameters is done in one of two ways. By far, the most effective way to set a database parameter is to add the name of the parameter and the value to the init*sid*.ora file for your instance. After that, shut down and start up your instance using the init*sid*.ora file. Unfortunately, in the world of multiuser database environments, DBAs do not always have the luxury of bouncing the database whenever they want. You can always try to schedule this sort of thing, or if the need is not critical, wait until the weekend. Another method for setting parameters is with the alter system, alter session, or alter system deferred commands. This used to not be an effective method for changing parameters, because not all initialization parameters could be changed using this command, but Oracle9*i* has changed this fact along with the introduction of server parameter files, which will be discussed shortly.

TIP

Query the V$PARAMETER or V$SYSTEM_PARAMETER view to list information about the modified parameter. Pay particular attention to the Boolean values in the ISMODIFIED, ISDEFAULT, ISADJUSTED, ISSYS_MODIFIABLE, and ISSES_MODIFIABLE columns. They can be used to identify whether the default value for that parameter is modified or adjusted and whether the value is modifiable with the alter system or alter session commands, respectively.

For Review

1. Be sure you understand the purpose of an init.ora file in Oracle, and that you know some ways for obtaining the values set for parameters on a running database.

2. Understand the use of the `alter system`, `alter session`, and `alter system deferred` commands in order to change values set for parameters once the instance is up and running.

3. Be sure you know where to find actual copies of `init.ora` files and where links to actual copies of `init.ora` files exist in your Oracle database.

Exercises

1. **You are configuring initialization parameters in your Oracle database. Which of the following choices identifies a file where parameter values can be specified?**

   A. `init.ora`

   B. Instance Manager

   C. SQL*Plus

   D. `control01.ctl`

2. **You are managing the Oracle database. Which of the following choices correctly identifies when Oracle reads the contents of the `init.ora` file?**

   A. When the instance is started

   B. When the database is mounted

   C. When the database is opened

   D. When the database is closed

3. **You are managing an Oracle database. Which of the following choices indicates a V$ view where the values set in the `init.ora` file can be viewed for the currently active Oracle instance?**

   A. V$SESSION

   B. V$PARAMETER

   C. V$DATABASE

   D. V$VERSION

Answer Key
1. A. 2. A. 3. B.

Configuring Oracle-Managed Files (OMF)

Oracle**9i**
and higher In the past, Oracle DBAs have always faced a conundrum when working with database administrative tasks. Not only does database administration require a thorough knowledge of how Oracle works, but it also requires that DBAs have a strong understanding of how the underlying operating system works as well. Why would this be the case? Because often DBAs have to perform administrative cleanup tasks following important database management activities.

Nowhere is this more apparent than in the creation and removal of datafiles related to tablespace management. You'll learn more about creating tablespaces in Chapter 2, but for now try to understand that tablespaces are logical areas where Oracle stores the contents of database objects like tables and indexes. Underlying the logical concept of tablespaces is the physical datafile or datafiles where the bits and bytes are actually stored. As the last statement implies, a tablespace can be comprised of one or more datafiles in Oracle. In past versions of Oracle, when a DBA removed a tablespace from Oracle using the appropriate command (which, incidentally, is `drop tablespace`, but we're getting ahead of ourselves here), all the DBA really did was remove reference to the datafiles comprising that tablespace from the Oracle data dictionary. The actual datafiles still existed on the host system, which required that the DBA find the datafiles and remove them manually using whatever operating system-specific command was appropriate for the job. If the DBA forgot to remove those datafiles, it was possible that later the disk might fill up with datafiles Oracle wasn't using, which could cause unexpected administrative problems.

Oracle-Managed Files (OMF) is a new feature introduced in Oracle9*i* to simplify database administration with respect to database files. In previous versions of Oracle, when you created new tablespaces using the appropriate command (`create tablespace`, but again, we're getting ahead of ourselves), Oracle expected you to specify the filesystem location and filename for all datafiles to be used in conjunction with storing information in this tablespace. In Oracle9*i* with OMF enabled, you would instead specify two simple components:

- A location of your OMF file directory in your `init.ora` file using a parameter
- The name of the data file to be created and its size

From there, Oracle takes care of creating the data file in its appropriate location with the name you specify. By using this feature, DBAs relieve themselves of the obligation to delete the datafiles later when the tablespace is dropped. Instead, Oracle9*i* will remove them for you.

Implementing OMF—Initialization Parameters

As we indicated earlier, you implement OMF in two steps. First, you specify the location of OMF directories by setting appropriate parameters in your `init.ora` file. You can specify directory locations using two parameters. The first is DB_CREATE_FILE_DEST, and it is used to identify the filesystem location Oracle will use for automatically creating datafiles. If no filesystem directory is specified in any command that Oracle must create a file to complete, this directory will be used. The directory you specify must exist before you assign it as a value for this parameter. If the directory does not exist, Oracle will not create it for you. An example of how to set DB_CREATE_FILE_DEST is shown in the following code block:

```
DB_CREATE_FILE_DEST = /u01/oradata/oracle
```

The second parameter to set is DB_CREATE_ONLINE_LOG_DEST_*N*, where *N* is set to some numeric value. This parameter is used for setting default online redo log directory locations for all your online redo logs. For greater fault tolerance and improved performance, Oracle recommends that you set at least two locations. An example for doing so in a UNIX environment is shown in the following code block:

```
DB_CREATE_ONLINE_LOG_1 = /u02/oradata/oracle
DB_CREATE_ONLINE_LOG_2 = /u03/oradata/oracle
```

TIP
In both cases, the directory specified for either of these OMF parameters must be set so that the user on your host system who owns all Oracle software has read and write permissions for that directory.

OMF in Action

Now that the appropriate parameters are set you can omit the specification of filesystem locations in commands that would ordinarily require you to specify a filesystem location, such as create tablespace. We will see some examples of how to use OMF in action when we cover the creation and removal of tablespaces and datafiles in Chapter 2.

TIP
When online redo log locations are specified using the appropriate parameter, Oracle automatically handles the setup of online log multiplexing for you. For more information on multiplexing, see Chapter 2.

For Review

1. Understand what is meant by Oracle-Managed Files. Your understanding should include the functionality OMF provides.

2. Be sure you know which `init.ora` parameters to set as part of OMF, including those for datafiles and for online redo logs.

Exercises

1. You issue the following command in Oracle: `create tablespace BOB_TBS datafile "bob01.dbf" size 2M;`. Later queries against the database reveal that the tablespace is located in the /u01/oradata/oracle directory. Which of the following choices identifies how Oracle likely determined what directory to place `bob01.dbf` in?

A. DB_CREATE_FILE_DEST

B. DB_CREATE_ONLINE_LOG_1

C. DB_CREATE_ONLINE_LOG_2

D. The directory is an operating system-specific default value in Oracle that can neither be specified manually nor changed.

2. You have configured OMF on your Oracle database system. After careful analysis, you determine that a tablespace must be removed from the database. Which of the following choices identifies how OMF can assist you in this task?

A. OMF will automatically update the data dictionary to remove reference to the tablespace datafiles.

B. OMF will automatically remove the underlying datafiles from the host environment.

C. OMF will tell Oracle to automatically stop using the datafiles associated with the tablespace.

D. None of the above choices identifies the functionality provided by OMF.

3. Choose the appropriate choice to complete the following statement: **If you want to use OMF to handle specifying the location of your online redo logs, then you must specify at least _____ destinations for Oracle to use through the definition of OMF-related `init.ora` parameters.**

   A. One

   B. Two

   C. Three

   D. Four

Answer Key
1. A. 2. B. 3. B.

Starting an Instance

Recall that we made an important distinction earlier between an Oracle instance and an Oracle database. To refresh your memory, the Oracle database is a set of tables, indexes, procedures, and other objects used for storing data. More precisely, an Oracle database, identified by the database name (DB_NAME), represents the physical structures and is composed of operating system files. Although it is possible to use a database name that is different from the name of the instance, you should use the same name for ease of administration. The Oracle instance, on the other hand, is the memory structures, background processes, and disk resources, all working together to fulfill user data requests and changes.

With that distinction in mind, let's consider starting the Oracle instance. You must do this before creating a new database, or before allowing access to an existing database. To start the instance, follow these steps:

I. From the command line on the host machine, start SQL*Plus and log in as `sysdba`:

```
[ oracle : orgdbux01 ] > sqlplus
Oracle SQL*Plus Release 8.1.7.0.0 - Production
(c)Copyright 2000, Oracle Corporation. All Rights Reserved.
Enter user-name: sys as sysdba
Enter password:
Connected to an idle instance.
SQL>
```

TIP

The password for user sys *when logging in as* sysdba *is usually set to* oracle *by default. Obviously, you'll want to change the password from its default in order to avoid security problems from knowledgeable DBAs!*

2. From within SQL*Plus, use the startup *start_option* [*dbname*] command to start the instance. Several options exist for *start_option*, including nomount, mount, open, and open force. If Oracle cannot find the init.ora file where it expects to find it ($ORACLE_HOME/dbs in UNIX and X:\%ORACLE_HOME%\admin\SID\pfile on Windows), the PFILE parameter should be used to identify the exact init*sid*.ora file you want to use. An example of startup nomount is shown in the following code block:

```
SQL> startup nomount
ORACLE instance started.
Total System Global Area          227174560 bytes
Fixed Size                            42764 bytes
Variable Size                      93999104 bytes
Database Buffers                   81920000 bytes
Redo Buffers                       51208192 bytes
SQL>
```

Options for Starting Oracle

You can also start a database with OEM Instance Manager. All the options discussed for SQL*Plus are available via Instance Manager, except through a GUI. You may also want to note that starting Oracle databases in Windows is not necessarily handled with SQL*Plus or even OEM, but instead may be handled as a *service*. A service in Windows is similar to a *daemon* in UNIX. Both of these operating system functions let Oracle start automatically when the machine boots. (We're getting a little off the topic here, but if you're interested in more information, consult the *Oracle9i Installation Guide for Windows NT*, which comes with that distribution of Oracle.) There are several different options for starting Oracle instances, with or without opening the database.

startup nomount   This option starts the instance without mounting the database. That means all the memory structures and background processes are in place, but no database is attached to the instance. You will use this option later for creating the Oracle database. You can specify this option with or without specifying an init*sid*.ora file for the PFILE parameter. If you do not specify PFILE, Oracle has some default places it will check in order to find the initialization file. For UNIX, Oracle looks in the $ORACLE_HOME/dbs directory. For Windows, Oracle looks in the X:\%ORACLE_HOME%\admin\SID\pfile directory. If Oracle doesn't find an initialization file, and you don't supply an explicit value for PFILE, Oracle will not start your database. In summary, starting an instance without mounting the database includes the following tasks:

■ Reading the parameter file `init.ora`

■ Allocating the SGA

■ Starting the background processes

■ Opening the ALERT file and the trace files

Note that neither control files nor the database data files are opened in this mode.

startup mount   This option starts the instance, reads the control file, and attaches the database, but it does not open it. You can't mount a database you haven't created yet. This option is useful in situations where you have to move physical database files around on the machine hosting Oracle, or when database recovery is required. You can specify this option with or without specifying an `initsid.ora` file for the PFILE parameter. If you do not specify PFILE, Oracle has some default places it will check in order to find the initialization file. For UNIX, Oracle looks in the $ORACLE_HOME/dbs directory. For Windows, Oracle looks in the X:\%ORACLE_HOME%\admin\SID\pfile directory. If Oracle doesn't find an initialization file, and you don't supply an explicit value for PFILE, Oracle will not start your database. If the instance is already started but the database is not mounted, use `alter database mount` instead. In summary, mounting the database includes the following tasks:

■ Associating a database with a previously started instance

■ Locating and opening the control files specified in the parameter file

■ Reading the control files to obtain the names and status of the datafiles and redo log files

startup open   This option starts your instance, attaches the database, and opens it. This is the default option for starting Oracle. It is used when you want to make your database available to users. You can't open a database you haven't created yet. You can specify this option with or without specifying an `initsid.ora` file for the PFILE parameter. If you do not specify PFILE, Oracle has some default places it will check in order to find the initialization file. For UNIX, Oracle looks in the $ORACLE_HOME/dbs directory. For Windows, Oracle looks in the X:\%ORACLE_HOME%\admin\SID\pfile directory. If Oracle doesn't find an initialization file, and you don't supply an explicit value for PFILE, Oracle will not start your database. If the instance is started and the database is mounted, use `alter database open` instead. If you omit the `open` keyword when issuing the `startup` command, `startup open` is assumed. Opening the database includes the following tasks:

- Opening the online datafiles

- Opening the online redo log files

```
SQL> startup open
ORACLE instance started.
Total System Global Area   148808972 bytes
Fixed Size                     70924 bytes
Variable Size               40566784 bytes
Database Buffers           108093440 bytes
Redo Buffers                   77824 bytes
Database mounted.
Database opened.
```

startup force   This option forces the instance to start and the database to open. It is used in situations where other `startup` options are met with errors from Oracle, and no `shutdown` options seem to work either. This is an option of last resort, and there is no reason to use it generally unless you cannot start the database with any other option. You can specify this option with or without specifying an `initsid.ora` file for the PFILE parameter. If you do not specify PFILE, Oracle has some default places it will check in order to find the initialization file. For UNIX, Oracle looks in the $ORACLE_HOME/dbs directory. For Windows, Oracle looks in the X:\%ORACLE_HOME%\admin\SID\pfile directory. If Oracle doesn't find an initialization file, and you don't supply an explicit value for PFILE, Oracle will not start your database.

Two other cases for database startup include `startup recover` for handling database recovery and `startup restrict` for opening the database while simultaneously preventing all users but the DBA from accessing database objects.

TIP

Oracle9i introduces a new mode of operation called quiescing. When a database is placed in quiesced state, only DBA transactions, queries, or PL/SQL statements are allowed to execute. This is achieved by the statement `alter system quiesce restricted.`

The Oracle Enterprise Manager Console or Instance Manager enables the DBA to change and view the initialization parameters. They can be stored either in a local parameter file or in the Oracle Enterprise Manager repository by using stored configurations. If using stored configurations, the DBA must be connected by the way of an Oracle Management Server (OMS) to get access to a repository. In earlier versions of Oracle Enterprise Manager (1.*x*), the initialization parameters were stored locally in the Windows NT registry.

Other Modes of Database Operations

Oracle9*i* has introduced at least two other modes of database operations. The database can be brought in a *quiescing* state where only DBA transactions, queries, or PL/SQL statements are allowed to execute. This is achieved by the statement `alter system quiesced restricted`. This state is best suited for DBAs for their maintenance work. Oracle9*i* also can suspend and resume the databases. Suspending a database will halt all input and output to datafiles and control files, but all preexisting I/O operations are allowed to complete. New database accesses are placed in a queued state. The `alter system suspend` statement suspends the database and the `alter system resume` statement resumes the database operation.

TIP

If you suspend database operation from a SQL*Plus prompt while logged in as `sysdba`, *the only statement you can issue following* `alter system suspend` *is* `alter system resume`. *Issuing any other statement will cause your session to hang.*

Starting the Database Automatically

Most DBAs want their database to start automatically whenever the host machine is rebooted. In Windows environments, the database can be opened by starting the OracleServiceSID service. This service is created for the database instance SID when you install Oracle on Windows environments. To start the database automatically, you will have to make sure that the parameter `ORA_SID_AUTOSTART` is set to TRUE in the Windows registry. For more information, refer to the Oracle software installation guide specific for the Windows operating system. On UNIX, automating database startup and shutdown can be controlled by the entries in the `oratab` file in the /var/opt/oracle directory. For more information, refer to the Oracle software installation guide for a UNIX operating system, such as Solaris.

Read-Only Database Features

Any database can be opened as read-only, as long as it is not already open in read/write mode. The feature is especially useful for a standby database to offload query processing from the production database. If a query needs to use a temporary tablespace—for example, to do disk sorts—the current user must have a locally managed tablespace assigned as the default temporary tablespace; otherwise, the query will fail. For the user SYS, a locally managed tablespace is required.

For Review

1. Be sure you understand the difference between starting an Oracle instance and opening an Oracle database for use. Know the commands for each.

2. Understand why Oracle has so many different modes for starting an instance and opening the database, rather than just simply having one command to do the job.

Exercises

1. You are administering the Oracle instance for startup. Which of the following choices indicates the names of tools that can be used for starting Oracle instances and databases?

   A. Schema Manager

   B. Server Manager

   C. SQL*Plus

   D. Network Configuration Assistant

2. You are administering an instance of your Oracle database. Which of the following choices identifies a command that can be used to tell Oracle to temporarily cease database operations?

   A. `startup nomount`

   B. `alter database open read only`

   C. `alter system suspend`

   D. `alter system resume`

3. Complete the following statement: When you issue the `startup nomount` command, the Oracle instance is _____(A)_____ and the database is _____(B)_____ opened.

Answer Key
1. C. 2. C. 3. (A) started; (B) not.

Shutting Down an Instance

Shutdown of the Oracle instance works in much the same way as starting the instance. You must either be logged onto Oracle as a user with sysdba privileges. The task can be accomplished from SQL*Plus or OEM Instance Manager, or as a Windows service. The steps for shutting down an Oracle database from SQL*Plus are as follows:

1. From the command line on the host machine, start SQL*Plus, and log in as sysdba:

```
[ oracle : orgdbux01 ] > sqlplus
Oracle SQL*Plus Release 8.1.7.0.0 - Production
(c)Copyright 2000, Oracle Corporation. All Rights Reserved.
Enter user-name: sys as sysdba
Password:
Connected to an idle instance.
```

2. From within SQL*Plus, use the shutdown *shutdown_option* command to shut down the instance. Several options exist for *shutdown_option*, including immediate, normal, or abort. An example of shutdown immediate is shown in the following code block:

```
SQL> shutdown immediate
ORA-01507: database not mounted
ORACLE instance shut down.
```

Options for Stopping Oracle

There are four priorities that can be specified by the DBA for shutting down the database. They include shutdown normal, shutdown immediate, shutdown abort, and shutdown transactional. The next four subtopics will explain each of these options and give cases where their use might be appropriate.

shutdown normal   This is the lowest-priority shutdown. When shutdown normal is issued, Oracle will wait for users to log out before actually shutting down the instance and closing the database. There are three rules Oracle follows during shutdown normal. First, Oracle will not let new users access the database. Second, Oracle will not force users already logged onto the system to log off in order to complete the shutdown. Third, this is the most graceful shutdown of all. Therefore, when a database is shut down this way, Oracle will not need to do an instance recovery when the instance is brought up again.

```
SQL> shutdown normal
Database closed.
Database dismounted.
ORACLE instance shut down.
```

`shutdown immediate`   This is a higher-priority shutdown that the DBA can use when `shutdown normal` would take too long. The `shutdown immediate` command shuts down a database as follows. No new users will be able to connect to the database once the `shutdown immediate` command is issued. Oracle will not wait for a user to log off as it does for `shutdown normal`; instead, it terminates user connections immediately and rolls back uncommitted transactions. Immediate database shutdown, although more drastic than `shutdown normal`, does not require any instance recovery. The output of the `shutdown immediate` command is shown in the beginning of this discussion.

`shutdown abort`   This is the highest priority database shutdown command. In all cases where this priority is used, the database will shut down immediately. All users are immediately disconnected, no transactions are rolled back, and media recovery will be required when the database starts up again. You use this option only when media or disk failure has taken place on the machine hosting your Oracle database.

```
SQL> shutdown abort
ORACLE instance shut down.
```

`shutdown transactional`   A transactional shutdown prevents clients from losing work. A transactional database shutdown proceeds with the following conditions: no client can start a new transaction on this particular instance, a client is disconnected when the client ends the transaction that is in progress, and a `shutdown immediate` occurs when all transactions have finished. The next startup will not require an instance recovery.

```
SQL> shutdown transactional
Database closed.
Database dismounted.
ORACLE instance shut down.
```

For Review
Understand the command used for shutting down an Oracle instance and closing the database. Be sure you can name the four different priorities for database shutdown.

Exercises

1. You need to shut down the Oracle database on short notice. Which of the following choices indicates the command you would use if you were prepared to let Oracle execute instance recovery the next time the database was opened?

   A. `shutdown abort`

   B. `shutdown transactional`

   C. `shutdown normal`

   D. `shutdown immediate`

2. You are shutting down the Oracle database. If you use the shutdown command for this purpose with no priority identified, what priority would Oracle shut down your database with?

   A. `abort`

   B. `transactional`

   C. `normal`

   D. `immediate`

Answer Key
1. A. 2. C.

Monitoring Use of Diagnostic Files

There are tons of situations where you as the DBA might want to find out more information about what Oracle is doing behind the scenes in order to address issues related to its operation. Two ways exist for doing so—you can either guess or use diagnostic files. For the record, Oracle recommends that you use diagnostic files. There are two types of diagnostic files in a typical Oracle configuration that Oracle will utilize while your database is up and running. These two types of files are *log files* and *trace files*. Let's look at each in more detail.

Trace Files

Background processes generate trace files whenever something goes wrong with the background process' operation. Network processes generate trace files as well whenever they malfunction. Additionally, network processes enable you to specify that you want trace files generated upon request for troubleshooting purposes.

The name of a background process trace file typically contains the name of the background process concatenated with the value specified by INSTANCE_NAME in the `init.ora` file. Any trace file generated by Oracle will have the filename extension `.trc`. Trace files generated by background processes are stored in the directory specified by the parameter BACKGROUND_DUMP_DEST in the parameter file. If you want, review the discussion on `init.ora` files presented earlier in the chapter to see the example of an `init.ora` file—there you'll find an example of BACKGROUND_DUMP_DEST with a directory value set. The name of the trace file also indicates which background process has generated it. They contain detailed information about what caused the background process to malfunction. It is a good procedure to check these trace files when the database behaves or crashes abnormally. They mostly contain information that only Oracle support could decipher. Many times you will be requested by Oracle support to provide these trace files for them to pinpoint the source of the problems.

Other processes such as the listener process may also generate trace files from time to time. These trace files are stored in locations specified in their corresponding configuration files. For example, the listener process configuration file is `listener.ora`. The detail of the trace information in these trace files can be regulated. They are extremely useful in troubleshooting Oracle networking problems. However, make sure that you turn them off when not in need as they could grow very fast and fill the disk.

TIP

Server processes managing data on behalf of Oracle users may also generate trace files if you request them to. These trace files can be found in the directory specified by USER_DUMP_DEST. Oracle typically names user session trace files after the process ID number generated in the background for the server process acting on behalf of the user. You usually have to dig through user session trace files or else look at the date and time the file was created in order to figure out which is which.

Log Files

The second type of diagnostic files that Oracle generates are the log files. The most important log file that you should be aware of and monitor often is the *alert log file*. The alert log file is created automatically by Oracle as soon as you create an instance. It is also stored in the location specified by the parameter

BACKGROUND_DUMP_DEST in the `init.ora` file. The name of this file is `alert_SID.log` or `SIDALRT.log`, where *SID* is the name specified by the parameter INSTANCE_NAME in `init.ora`.

The alert log file stores information that is extremely useful in order to know the health of the database. It records the starting and stopping of the databases, creation of new redo log file (which happens every time a log switch occurs), creation of tablespaces, addition of new datafiles to the tablespaces, and most importantly the errors that are generated by Oracle. This is the most often requested file by Oracle support. It tends to grow big with passage of time. Parts of the file need to removed or archived on a regular basis.

One of the best practices as a DBA is to scan this file periodically for any error reports (they usually start with ORA-). A much better approach is to have an automated script that scans this file at regular intervals and pages the DBA if it comes across any ORA- occurrences in the file. Other processes such the Oracle network processes also generate log files. These log files give enough information to gauge the health of Oracle and its network processes. The main difference between log files and trace files is that the log files are needed all the time by DBAs, as only important information is reported in them. The trace files are needed for troubleshooting. Oracle reports much more information in trace files than via log files.

TIP
If you start getting really weird errors in your database and your ALERT log contains `ORA-00600` *errors, you should call Oracle Support and start looking in the USER_DUMP_DEST and BACKGROUND_DUMP_DEST directories ASAP!*

For Review

1. Be sure you understand the difference between trace files and log files. Know the types of files as well as the processes that might generate those files that are stored in the directory identified by the BACKGROUND_DUMP_DEST and USER_DUMP_DEST parameters.

2. Understand when background processes generate trace files. Also, know what gets stored in the ALERT log file. Know that this is the first place you look if your database crashes abnormally.

Exercises

1. **The following excerpt of a trace file was taken from an Oracle database:**

```
Tue Jul 18 17:04:33 2000
alter database dismount
Completed: alter database dismount
archiving is disabled
Dump file c:\Oracle\admin\orcl\bdump\orclALRT.LOG
Tue Jul 18 17:05:00 2000
ORACLE V9.0.1.0.0 - Production vsnsta=0
vsnsql=d vsnxtr=3
Windows NT V4.10, OS V192.0, CPU type 586
Starting up ORACLE RDBMS Version: 9.0.1.0.0.
System parameters with non-default values:
  processes              = 59
  shared_pool_size       = 15728640
  java_pool_size         = 20971520
  disk_asynch_io         = FALSE
  control_files          = c:\Oracle\ORADATA\orcl\control01.ctl,
c:\Oracle\ORADATA\orcl\control02.ctl
  db_block_buffers       = 200
  db_block_size          = 2048
  compatible             = 9.0.1.0.0
  log_buffer             = 8192
  log_checkpoint_interval = 10000
  log_checkpoint_timeout  = 0
```

   Which of the following choices identify the most likely name for that trace file?

   A. `orclDBW0.trc`

   B. `orclLGWR.trc`

   C. `orclALRT.trc`

   D. `orcl13095.trc`

2. **You are trying to identify the location of a trace file generated by the listener process. Where would you look for that information?**

   A. `init.ora`

   B. BACKGROUND_DUMP_DEST

   C. `listener.ora`

   D. USER_DUMP_DEST

3. **You are exploring background process trace files for your LGWR process. Under which of the following scenarios would you find a trace file generated for this process?**

   A. When specifically requested by the user

   B. When the database is closed

   C. When the database crashes

   D. When Oracle cannot write to the alert log

Answer Key
1. C. 2. C. 3. C.

Creating an Oracle Database

In this section, you will cover the following topics related to creating an Oracle database:

- Prerequisites necessary for creating a database
- Creating databases using Oracle Database Configuration Assistant
- Creating the database manually

The act of creating a database is nothing but the creation of a *physical* database. Before a physical database is created, the database designers design the *logical* database using an Entity-Relationship diagram (ERD). The ERD shows the relationship between the tables, columns they contain, the constraint, and other information. A DBA translates this logical design into a physical design by mapping where the tables need to be created, what tablespaces they should reside in, how large they have to be, and so on. Just as in installing the Oracle software, there are many tasks a DBA has to do before and after the creation of the database. The focus of the OCP DBA Fundamentals I exam is on the tasks required to create the physical database. In this section, we'll cover how to perform preinstallation tasks, creating a database using Oracle's wizard-driven Database Configuration Assistant and then creating a database manually.

Prerequisites for Database Creation

There are a few things you should do at the operating system level before creating your database. Because every operating system is different, you'll be introduced to the general concepts here for the purpose of preparing for OCP. If you have further questions, refer to the operating system-specific Oracle installation guide that came with your software distribution. Some of these steps are things you should be aware of at the time you install the Oracle software on your host machine, whereas others can wait until the time you are ready to issue the `create database` statement. In general, you should make sure your machine has the capacity to handle Oracle. At a minimum, make sure you have at least three separately controlled disk resources. Configuring certain environment settings is an important task executed at this point as well. If you are installing Oracle on a machine that currently hosts another Oracle database, make sure you shut down and back up the other Oracle databases running on the host. Finally, if it's appropriate, make sure that operating system patches recommended by Oracle are installed on the machine. More details about each of these items follow:

- *Make sure your machine has the capacity to handle Oracle.* Almost any machine made these days has the capacity to install Oracle successfully. However, not every machine has the guts to run a full-scale Oracle enterprise database application. Before creating an Oracle environment, be sure to assess whether your host machine has the CPU power, memory, and disk space it takes to run an Oracle database in a multiuser environment.

- *Ensure that you have at least three separately controlled disk resources.* A running Oracle database has many moving parts. Often, these parts are also moving at the same time. Putting every Oracle resource on the same hard drive is a recipe for slow performance on all but the smallest single-user database setups. Oracle recommends three separately controlled disk resources. An enterprise production installation of Oracle can require 20 or more. Again, think before you create.

- *Configure certain environment settings.* You may need to configure a few environment variables before creating your database, such as ORACLE_BASE, ORACLE_HOME, ORACLE_SID, ORA_NLS33, LD_LIBRARY_PATH, and others. These are items that you will set up in your machine configuration files or user configuration files. Where possible, you should try to follow the OFA. This is Oracle's recommended guideline for file-system directory paths, and following it will help Oracle Support find files for you when you call in the inevitable emergency production-support issue.

- *Shut down and back up other Oracle databases running on the host.* Unless you like long hours spent in a computer room handling recovery, don't care about your data, or both, you should never install an Oracle database on a machine already hosting Oracle without shutting down and backing up that other database first. The `reuse` keyword in the `create database` command as well as the CONTROL_FILES parameter in your init*sid*.ora file make it possible for one Oracle database to overwrite the files of another database on the same machine. Avoid problems by taking the extra time to back up your data, and put different Oracle database files in different directories.

■ *Install Oracle-recommended operating system patches on the machine.* This final point is as much an Oracle software installation issue as it is a database creation issue. Because the exact operating system version and required patches vary from operating system to operating system, you should consult the Oracle installation guide that came with your software for specifics, while being mindful that operating system patches may need to be applied for Oracle to work properly.

■ *Perform UNIX specific tasks.* Specifically for UNIX, edit oratab file to include the name of the database being created, its ORACLE_HOME, and whether it has to automatically shut down in event of system start or shutdown. This task is not mandatory for working of Oracle but essential for many of the administration tasks.

Using Optimal Flexible Architecture

Implementing the OFA standard may be the most important thing you have to do in order keep your administration simple and prevent accidents from happening. We have already discussed the details of OFA in previous sections in this chapter. Make sure to create the administration directory under ORACLE_BASE (you configure a directory for ORACLE_BASE such as the Oracle software owner's home directory as part of configuring environment settings) to store the database administration and diagnostic files. If the datafiles of the database being created are stored in their own directories as recommended in OFA, then make sure to create the directories. In UNIX, these datafiles will not be created unless the directories exist.

Preparing the Parameter File

You've already learned about the parameter file, so now focus on the values that must be set in order to create a new Oracle database. As mentioned, Oracle provides a generic copy of that parameter file, init*sid*.ora, in the software distribution used to install Oracle server on the machine hosting Oracle. Generally, the DBA will take this generic parameter file and alter certain parameters according to his or her needs. Several parameters *must* be changed as part of setting up a new database. The following subtopics identify and describe the parameters you need to change.

DB_NAME This is the local name of the database on the machine hosting Oracle and one component of a database's unique name within the network. If the value for this parameter is the same as another Oracle database running on the host, permanent damage may result in the event that a database is created. Try to limit this name to approximately eight characters. Do not leave the name as DEFAULT. There is a name for the database and a name for the instance, and they should be the same. DB_NAME is required for the creation of the database, and it should be unique among all Oracle databases running in your organization.

DB_DOMAIN This identifies the domain location of the database name within a network. It is the second component of a database's unique name within the network. This is usually set either to WORLD or to the domain name appearing in your e-mail address at your organization, such as EXAMPILOT.COM.

DB_BLOCK_SIZE This is the size in bytes of data blocks within the system. This is also called standard block size in Oracle9*i*. Data blocks are unit components of datafiles into which Oracle places the row data from indexes and tables. This is one parameter that cannot be changed once the database is created. Oracle9*i* supports multiple block sizes. The *standard block size* is defined by the parameter DB_BLOCK_SIZE and it supports additional four nonstandard block sizes. The standard block size is used for system tablespace, whereas nonstandard block size may be specified when creating tablespaces.

CONTROL_FILES This is a name or list of names for the control files of the database. The control files document the location of all disk files used by the Oracle. If the name(s) specified for this parameter does not match filenames that exist currently, then Oracle will create a new control file for the database at startup only when you create a new database. Otherwise, Oracle simply tells you it won't start because it can't find the control files it needs to open your existing database. Only during the creation of a new database will Oracle overwrite the contents of a file of the same name as the control file you specified in `initsid.ora` with the physical layout of the database being created. Beware of this feature, as it can cause a control file on an existing database to be overwritten if you are creating a second database to run on the same machine.

DB_CACHE_SIZE DB_BLOCK_BUFFERS continues to exist in Oracle9*i* but for backward compatibility. Unlike DB_BLOCK_BUFFERS, which specifies the number of data block-sized buffers that can be stored in SGA, Oracle9*i* introduces a new parameter, DB_CACHE_SIZE, which could be used to specify the size of the buffer cache in the Oracle SGA. It specifies the size of the default buffer pool for buffers with the standard block size (as defined in DB_BLOCK_SIZE parameter). Unlike DB_BLOCK_BUFFERS, which is specified in number of buffers, this new parameter is defined in bytes.

LOG_BUFFER   This is the size of the redo log buffer in bytes. As stated earlier, the redo log buffer stores redo log entries in memory until LGWR can write the entries to online redo logs on disk. There will be more about this in Chapter 2.

UNDO_MANAGEMENT   This parameter gets set to AUTO to indicate that Oracle9*i* will handle undo segment management automatically for you. An undo segment is the same thing as a rollback segment. As of Oracle9*i*, you no longer have to create rollback segments manually.

UNDO_TABLESPACE   This parameter is set to the name of the tablespace you want to use to house undo segments generated and managed automatically by Oracle. Make sure you specify and use a tablespace that houses nothing other than undo segments for this purpose.

PROCESSES   This is the number of processes that can connect to Oracle at any given time. This value includes background processes (of which there are at least five) and server processes. This value should be set high in order to avoid errors that prevent users from connecting.

The Server Parameter File Feature in Oracle9*i*

Oracle **9*i***
and higher   The server parameter file is a new feature in Oracle9*i*. It enables you to relieve yourself of the burden of constantly updating your `init.ora` file yourself whenever you decide you need to change an initialization parameter. This is a nice touch, considering that Oracle9*i* also makes it possible to change most every initialization parameter you would ever care to change dynamically while the database is online and available for users. Oracle can also provide a large degree of self-tuning due to its capability to control its initialization parameter settings dynamically as well. Additionally, the server parameter file feature enables Oracle9*i* to remember settings for initialization parameters that were changed dynamically across sessions.

Server parameter files are created from standard `init.ora` files. They are housed inside your Oracle database, so obviously they won't be available until the database is created. You can create a server parameter file in the following way:

1. You define the settings you want in your initial Oracle9*i* database configuration before the database is actually created, using the guidelines we've already discussed so far, by creating an `init.ora` file. You can use one you already have, so long as you make the changes we've already discussed.

2. You then create the database.

3. Once the database exists, you issue the `create spfile` command to create your server parameter file in the following way:

```
SQL> create spfile from
  2  pfile = '/u01/app/oracle/admin/oracle/pfile/init.ora';
```

From there, Oracle9*i* will create a server parameter file on the machine hosting the Oracle database. Oracle9*i* will be able to update that file every time you use the `alter system set` *init_parm* = *value* command to change a parameter's setting dynamically. Oracle9*i* will also read that file every time the instance starts in addition to your `init.ora` file, in order to determine what settings to use initially when the instance starts. A new clause exists on the `alter system` command called `scope` as well, in order to help you specify whether you want Oracle to update its server parameter file with the new setting or not. The `scope` clause has three possible settings: SPFILE, MEMORY, or BOTH. If you define the scope of the dynamic parameter change to be SPFILE or MEMORY, then Oracle9*i* changes the parameter setting in the server parameter file or existing instance memory configuration only, respectively. If you use BOTH, then Oracle9*i* sets the new parameter value in both the server parameter file and makes the change to the current instance. The following code block contains the proper syntax for all three settings:

```
alter system set shared_pool_size = 10485760 scope = spfile;
alter system set shared_pool_size = 10485760 scope = memory;
alter system set shared_pool_size = 10485760 scope = both;
```

TIP
You can also export the contents of your server parameter file to a traditional `init.ora` *file using the* `create pfile from spfile` *command.*

For Review

1. Know that there are certain `init.ora` parameters that must be changed in order to create a new database, such as CONTROL_FILES, DB_NAME, and DB_BLOCK_SIZE, especially if you've copied the `init.ora` file from another database location. If these parameters are not set to a value appropriate for the new database and you have existing databases on the host, you could damage those existing databases.

2. Understand the new SPFILE feature available in Oracle9*i* for dynamic instance parameter configuration, management, and tuning.

Exercises

1. You are preparing to create an Oracle database. Which of the following parameters must be changed in your `init.ora` file in order to create a new database that will not interfere with any existing databases on the machine hosting Oracle when you've copied the `init.ora` file from one of those other databases for use in this one?

   A. CONTROL_FILES

   B. DB_BLOCK_SIZE

   C. DB_DOMAIN

   D. SHARED_POOL_SIZE

2. You are configuring your Oracle `init.ora` file for creating a new database. Which of the following parameters is the newer version of the DB_BLOCK_BUFFERS parameter?

   A. DB_CACHE_SIZE

   B. SHARED_POOL_SIZE

   C. LARGE_POOL_SIZE

   D. JAVA_POOL_SIZE

3. This is the name of the feature that enables Oracle to dynamically manage its own `init.ora` settings (three words):

   _____.

Answer Key

1. A. 2. A. 3. Server parameter files.

Creating Databases Using Database Configuration Assistant

Oracle Database Configuration Assistant (DBCA) is one of the many GUI tools that Oracle provides in support of your Oracle database. DBCA is used to create databases, and it handles a lot of the tricky work behind the scenes so you don't have to. With DBCA, you can perform the following tasks with ease:

- You can create a database from scratch by specifying all the information needed to create one. You can either specify the tool to create the database after you specify information or generate the scripts necessary to create the database manually or store the information in a *template* to be used later to create other databases. It is the last feature that makes this tool very useful to DBAs. You will learn more about it in the following sections.

- You can delete an existing database.

- You can clone an existing database with and without the data. You can reverse-engineer a template of an existing database as well.

TIP
DBCA uses OFA standards, so database files, administrative files, and parameter files follow OFA naming standards and placement practices.

What Are DBCA Templates?

The concept of a template started with Oracle9*i*. A *template* is a definition of a database. Oracle provides a set of predefined templates and DBCA enables you to custom create templates for your own needs. When creating a template, DBCA lets you specify everything possible from the location of control files, redo log file, database datafiles, size of your SGA, location of administrative files, parameters in init.ora file, and many other things. DBCA was made even easier by letting us define variables commonly defined as part of configuring your Oracle operating environment. For example, if you are familiar with UNIX, these environment settings are what you would find in a file such as .profile. These variables, such as ORACLE_BASE, SID, and others can be used in the filenames and such places to replace them with information specific to the instance you are creating.

TIP
Even though Oracle8i version of DBCA provided us with a basic way to create databases, the tool was limited to only creating databases in a few simple ways. DBCA is now a complete product with the capability to define practically any aspect of your databases used for various purposes, including transaction processing databases, decision support systems, data warehouses, and databases for hybrid purposes.

To create a database, you may choose an existing template that Oracle provides or you may create one built to suit your needs. Once you have a database template that looks close to what you are building, you use that template, change few things, and use it to create your database. This is a time-saving tool for the DBAs.

Creating a Database Using DBCA

DBCA can create a database from either predefined templates provided by Oracle or custom-created templates created by you or just create a database without using any of the templates. DBCA wizard goes through the same displays as the one used in template creation and gathers necessary information to create the database. As a final step, you could just create a database, or create a database and save the database creation scripts, or just save the scripts. You may choose the last option to take a look at the scripts and execute them manually to create the database.

For Review

1. Understand the basic use of the Oracle Database Configuration Assistant, and be sure you can describe the advantages of using this tool versus manually creating an Oracle database.

2. Understand the concept of a database template. Be sure you can describe the benefits offered by database templates.

3. Know that any database created by the database configuration assistant will be OFA-compliant in terms of its directory and file layout.

Exercises

1. **You are creating Oracle databases in your host system. Which of the following choices identifies a benefit for using the Database Configuration Assistant for this purpose rather than creating a database manually?**

   A. The Database Configuration Assistant simplifies many of the behind-the-scenes tasks you would otherwise have to handle.

   B. You have more control over the placement of certain datafiles with the Database Configuration Assistant.

   C. The Database Configuration Assistant interface is wizard-driven and therefore complex.

   D. The Database Configuration Assistant simplifies creation of Oracle databases by creating databases suited for only one purpose.

2. **You are using the Database Configuration Assistant to configure your Oracle database. Which of the following terms pertains to the creation of an object from which creation of other databases can be based?**

   A. Clone

   B. Copy

   C. Template

   D. Terminal

Answer Key
1. A. 2. C.

Creating a Database Manually

Of course, you also have the option to create a database yourself manually. Moreover, there are some compelling reasons to do so. First, you retain a great deal of control over the nuances of how your database will be created. Using scripts for database creation also gives you a template of sorts from which you can base the creation of other databases. Scripts may be necessary in situations where you want to create a database on a remote machine as well, and do not have access to the graphical desktop of that remote machine in order to run Database Configuration Assistant on it. Creation of the Oracle database is accomplished with the `create database` statement. The following steps are executed before creating the database:

1. Make sure that `init.ora` file exists and the entries in it refer to the correct database name. You can execute a global search and replace operation to identify and correct discrepancies within any text editor, but be sure you comb through each situation manually so that you don't make a mistake accidentally. Now is also the time to verify one last time that the location of control files in this file is accurate.

2. Make sure the directories specified for BACKGROUND_DUMP_DEST, USER_DUMP_DEST, CORE_DUMP_DEST, UTL_FILE_DIR, and any other administrative directories used by Oracle actually exist on your filesystem. If those directories do not exist, the creation process for your new database may fail when you try to start the instance.

3. Start SQL*Plus and connect to the database as sys as sysdba.

4. Start up the instance in nomount mode so that no existing database is mounted to the instance.

5. Execute the create database statement to create the database by either typing it into SQL*Plus or by running a script with contents similar to the code block containing the create database command shown in the following:

```
CONNECT SYS AS SYSDBA

CREATE DATABASE orgdb01
CONTROLFILE REUSE
LOGFILE
  GROUP 1 ('/u01/oradata/oracle/redo1a.log',
           '/u02/oradata/oracle/redo1b.log') SIZE 5M,
  GROUP 2 ('/u02/oradata/oracle/redo2a.log',
           '/u01/oradata/oracle/redo2b.log') SIZE 5M
MAXLOGFILES 40
DATAFILE '/u03/oradata/oracle/sys01.dbf'
  SIZE 50M AUTOEXTEND ON NEXT 30M MAXSIZE 150M
MAXDATAFILES 240
CHARACTERSET WE8IS08859P1;
EXIT;
```

6. If your database creation process is successful, you can then mount the database you just created using the alter database mount command, and then open it using the alter database open command. Your database now contains one tablespace, called SYSTEM, with one or more datafiles.

7. Then you create the tablespaces for undo segments, users, temp, and other data. We'll see some examples of create tablespace commands in Chapter 2.

8. In versions of Oracle prior to Oracle9i, you would then create the undo segments and bring them online. In Oracle9i, however, all you need to do is create the undo tablespace—Oracle creates its own undo segments.

9. Finally you run the scripts provided by Oracle to create the data dictionary (also called Catalog) and other database objects necessary for database administration.

What Happens When You Execute
the create database Command?

When the database is brought up in nomount mode, Oracle reads the init.ora file, which it uses to figure out where to create the control files. Oracle also uses the settings for parameters in this file to specify the size of the SGA, where to place to log and trace files, and other important information. With this information, it creates the SGA in memory and the background processes.

- When the `create database` command is executed, it creates the control files as specified in `init.ora` file, and the redo log files and the SYSTEM tablespace data file as specified in the command itself.

- SYS and SYSTEM accounts are created. A single undo segment is created in the SYSTEM tablespace.

The Datafiles of the SYSTEM Tablespace

The files created as part of the `datafile` clause of the `create database` command are SYSTEM tablespace datafiles. A *tablespace* is a logical collection of disk files collectively used to store data. The SYSTEM tablespace can be compared to the root directory of a machine's filesystem. The SYSTEM tablespace houses the tables comprising the basis for the Oracle data dictionary, as well as the system undo segments. The tables of the data dictionary and system undo segment will all be owned by user SYS. Oracle creates one system undo segment in the SYSTEM tablespace at database creation for Oracle to acquire at database startup. Without this system undo segment, the database won't start. In the interest of preserving the integrity of the Oracle database, the DBA should ensure that only the data dictionary and system undo segments are placed in the SYSTEM tablespace. No data objects owned by any user other than SYS should be placed in the SYSTEM tablespace. Instead, you will create other tablespaces to store those database objects. You will learn more about tablespaces and datafiles in Chapter 2.

Minimum Two Online Redo Log Groups

Redo logs are created with the `logfile` clause. Redo logs are entries for data changes made to the database. You must create at least two redo log groups for your new database, each with at least one member. In the database created with the preceding code block, redo log group 1 consists of two members, called `log1a.dbf` and `log1b.dbf`, respectively. If any file specified in the `create database` statement currently exists on the system, and the `reuse` keyword is used, Oracle will overwrite the file. Be careful when reusing files to prevent accidentally overwriting the files in your existing database on the host machine. You will learn more about redo logs in Chapter 2.

Other Items in `create database` Statements

Other options set when the database is created include `maxdatafiles` and `maxlogfiles`. The `maxdatafiles` option specifies the initial sizing of the datafiles section of the control file at `create database` or `create` `controlfile` time. An attempt to add a file whose number is greater than `maxdatafiles`, but less than or equal to DB_FILES, causes the control file to expand automatically so that the datafiles section can accommodate more files. You can use the `autoextend` option when defining datafiles. When `autoextend` is used, the datafiles will automatically allocate more space when the datafile fills, up to a total size specified by the `maxsize` keyword. However, you'll want to take care to ensure that Oracle does not try to extend the datafile to more space than the filesystem has available.

The final item in the `create database` statement was `characterset`, which is used to identify the character set used in the Oracle database for information storage. Another option you can use in `create database` commands is `archivelog`. When `archivelog` is used, Oracle archives the redo logs generated. Finally, the `create database` command uses several initialization parameters set in the `initsid.ora` file in database creation. These include DB_BLOCK_SIZE and certain NLS environment settings.

For Review

1. Understand the process for manually creating a database using the `create database` command. Be sure you can identify the various clauses used as part of issuing that command.

2. Be sure you understand that any datafiles created as part of the create database command will belong to the SYSTEM tablespace. Also, know that you must create at least two online redo logs as part of this process.

3. When manually creating an Oracle database, know that your instance must be started but that you cannot have any other database already mounted to that instance.

Exercises

1. **You are about to create a database manually in Oracle. Which of the following `startup` commands would be appropriate for the instance in this context?**

   A. `startup nomount`

   B. `startup mount`

   C. `startup open`

   D. `startup force`

2. You have just created an Oracle database using the `create database` command. To which of the following tablespaces will any datafile identified as part of the `datafile` clause for the `create database` command belong?

    A. DATA

    B. INDEX

    C. UNDO_TBS

    D. SYSTEM

Answer Key
1. A. 2. D.

Chapter Summary

This chapter covered several important topics that got you started in your preparation for the OCP DBA Fundamentals I exam. The first topic we discussed was the theoretical underpinnings of the Oracle database architecture. You learned about the memory structures, disk files, and background processes used in conjunction with Oracle, and explored each of these areas in some detail. We also looked at how Oracle connects users to the database for data access and manipulation. Next, we discussed how to get started as the database administrator of an Oracle system. You learned about installation of Oracle using the Universal Installer and listed the administrative components of Oracle that are shipped with the database. You also covered an overview of Enterprise Manager, Oracle's graphical tool for handling many common administrative tasks. We described how to create password files as well. After that, you focused your attention on how to manage an Oracle instance. A few times in the chapter, we pointed out the difference between an Oracle instance and a database. You learned about how to start up and shut down a running instance, and the various methods for opening and closing a database. We talked a lot about initialization parameters and parameter files as well. You explored the use of log and trace files related to Oracle database administration, an important concept tested on the OCP DBA Fundamentals I exam. The new Oracle9*i* Oracle-Managed Files (OMF) feature was also covered in some depth. Finally, you turned your attention to understanding the process by which databases are created, both with the wizard-driven Database Configuration Assistant and manually using scripts and the `create database` command. This is an important chapter covering approximately 20 percent of the material tested on the OCP DBA Fundamentals I exam.

Two-Minute Drill

- Several structures are used to connect users to an Oracle server. They include memory structures like the System Global Area (SGA) and Program Global Area (PGA), network processes like listeners and dispatchers, shared or dedicated server processes, and background processes like DBW0 and LGWR.

- The SGA consists of the buffer cache for storing recently accessed data blocks, the redo log buffer for storing redo entries until they can be written to disk, and the shared pool for storing parsed information about recently executed SQL for code sharing.

- The fundamental unit of storage in Oracle is the data block.

- SQL select statements are processed in the following way: a cursor or address in memory is opened, the statement is parsed, bind variables are created, the statement is executed, and values are fetched.

- SQL DML statements such as update, delete, and insert are processed in the following way: A cursor or address in memory is opened, the statement is parsed, and the statement is executed.

- Several background processes manage Oracle's capability to write data from the buffer cache and redo log buffer to appropriate areas on disk. They are DBW0 for writing data between disk and buffer cache, and LGWR for writing redo log entries between the redo log buffer and the online redo log on disk.

- DBW0 writes data to disk in three cases. They are every three seconds (when a timeout occurs), when LGWR tells it to (during a checkpoint), or when the buffer cache is full or a server process needs to make room for buffers required by user processes.

- Server processes are like genies from the story of Aladdin because they retrieve data from disk into the buffer cache according to the user's command.

- There are two configurations for server processes: shared servers and dedicated servers. In dedicated servers, a listener process listens for users connecting to Oracle. When a listener hears a user, the listener tells Oracle to spawn a dedicated server. Each user process has its own server process available for retrieving data from disk.

- In shared server configurations (also called multithreaded server [MTS]), a user process attempts to connect to Oracle. The listener hears the connection and passes the user process to a dispatcher process. A limited number of server processes, each handling multiple user requests, are monitored by a dispatcher, which assigns user processes to a shared server based on which has the lightest load at the time of user connection.

■ The `commit` statement may trigger Oracle to write changed data in the buffer cache to disk, but not necessarily. It only makes a redo log buffer entry that says all data changes associated with a particular transaction are now committed.

■ Oracle Universal Installer is the software installer for Oracle products. It is written in Java and runs on multiple platforms.

■ Universal Installer permits automated, noninteractive software installation through the use of a response file.

■ When installing Oracle9*i* on certain platforms, you need to make sure that you install the software to a separate home directory. This is a requirement of the new version of Universal Installer.

■ You can have Universal Installer install a preconfigured database for you with minimal user interaction. In this case, all scripts, such as `catalog.sql` and `catproc.sql`, are run automatically, and a few basic tablespaces, such as DATA, INDEX, and UNDOTBS, are created with the following information:

   ■ SID is `ORC0` or `ORCL`.

   ■ SYS password is `change_on_install`.

   ■ `SYS as SYSDBA` password is `oracle`.

   ■ SYSTEM password is `manager`.

■ Oracle9*i* lets you change most instance parameters dynamically while the database is available for use. For example, SGA parameters can be altered such that Oracle9*i*'s shared memory is changeable while the database is online.

■ The server parameter file feature in Oracle9*i* enables you to create a server parameter file that Oracle9*i* can dynamically modify in support of changes to the configuration of your instance.

■ Server parameter files are created using the `create spfile from 'filename'` command.

■ When you use the `alter system` command in Oracle9*i* to change the settings for instance parameters, you can specify a new clause, `scope`, to determine where Oracle should make the instance parameter change:

- **SPFILE** Oracle9*i* changes the parameter setting in the server parameter file only.

- **MEMORY** Oracle9*i* changes the parameter setting for the current instance only.

- **BOTH** Oracle9*i* changes the parameter setting for both server parameter file and current instance.

- Two user authentication methods exist in Oracle: operating system authentication and Oracle authentication.

- There are two privileges DBAs require to perform their function on the database. In Oracle authentication environments, they are called `sysdba` and `sysoper`.

- To use Oracle authentication, the DBA must create a password file using the ORAPWD utility.

- To start and stop a database, the DBA must connect as `internal` or `sysdba`.

- The tool used to start and stop the database in Oracle9*i* is SQL*Plus.

- Another tool for managing database administration activity is Oracle Enterprise Manager (OEM). OEM has many administrative tools available, including Daemon Manager, Instance Manager, Replication Manager, Schema Manager, Security Manager, SQL Worksheet, Storage Manager, Net8 Assistant, and Software Manager.

- There are several options for starting a database:

  - `startup nomount` Starts the instance and does not mount a database

  - `startup mount` Starts the instance and mounts but does not open the database

  - `startup open` Starts the instance and mounts and opens the database

  - `startup restrict` Starts the instance, mounts and opens the database, but restricts access to those users with `restricted session` privilege granted to them

  - `startup recover` Starts the instance, leaves the database closed, and begins recovery for disk failure scenario

  - `startup force` Makes an instance start that is having problems either starting or stopping

- When a database is open, any user with a username and password and the `create session` privilege can log into the Oracle database.

- Closing or shutting down a database must be done by the DBA while running SQL*Plus and while the DBA is connected to the database as `internal` or `sysdba`.

- There are four options for closing a database:

  - **shutdown normal** No new existing connections are allowed, but existing sessions may take as long as they want to wrap up.

  - **shutdown immediate** No new connections are allowed, existing sessions are terminated, and their transactions are rolled back.

  - **shutdown transactional** No new connections are allowed, existing sessions are allowed to complete current transaction, and then disconnected.

  - **shutdown abort** No new connections are allowed, existing sessions are terminated, and transactions are not rolled back.

- Instance recovery is required after `shutdown abort` is used.

- You can obtain values for initialization parameters from several sources:

  - V$PARAMETER dynamic performance view

  - `show parameter` command in SQL*Plus

  - OEM Instance Manager administrative tool

- Several important run-time logging files exist on the machine hosting Oracle. Each background process, such as LGWR and DBW0, will have a trace file if some error occurs in their execution, and the instance has a special trace file called the ALERT log. Trace files are written whenever the background process has a problem executing. The ALERT log is written whenever the instance is started or stopped, whenever the database structure is altered, or whenever an error occurs in database.

- Trace files and ALERT logs are found in the directory identified by the BACKGROUND_DUMP_DEST parameter in the `initsid.ora` file.

- Before creating the database, assess several things on the operating system level:

  - Are there enough individual disk resources to run Oracle without I/O bottlenecks?

  - Is there enough CPU, memory, and disk space for Oracle processing?

- Are disk resources for different Oracle databases on the same host in separate directories?

- Are environment settings correct for the database creation?

- The first step in creating a database is to back up any existing databases already on the host machine.

- The second step in creating a database is for the DBA to create a parameter file with unique values for several parameters, including the following:

  - **DB_NAME**   The local name for the database

  - **DB_DOMAIN**   The networkwide location for the database

  - **DB_BLOCK_SIZE**   The size of each block in the database

  - **DB_CACHE_SIZE**   The size of DB buffer cache

  - **PROCESSES**   The maximum number of processes available on the database

  - **UNDO_MANAGEMENT and UNDO_TABLESPACE**   Defines how Oracle should handle configuration and management of undo segments

- After creating the parameter file, the DBA executes the `create database` command, which creates the datafiles for the SYSTEM tablespace, an initial undo segment, SYS and SYSTEM users, and redo log files. On conclusion of the `create database` statement, the database is created and open.

- The default password for SYS is `change_on_install`.

- The default password for SYSTEM is `manager`.

- The number of datafiles and redo log files created for the life of the database can be limited with the `maxdatafiles` and `maxlogfiles` options of the `create database` statement.

- The size of a datafile is fixed at its creation, unless the `autoextend` option is used.

- The size of a control file is directly related to the number of datafiles and redo logs for the database.

Fill-in-the-Blank Questions

1. The initialization parameter used for defining the name of your Oracle database is _____.

2. In order to increase the size of a datafile, these keywords can be used so that Oracle can automatically add more space when necessary: _____.

3. Once the database is created, the frequency with which you can alter the database's block size is _____.

4. Of the database shutdown options, this one requires instance recovery the next time the database is started: _____.

5. The utility that supports password file authentication by creating the password file is _____.

Chapter Questions

1. **The user is trying to execute a `select` statement. Which of the following background processes will obtain data from a disk for the user?**

   A. DBW0

   B. LGWR

   C. SERVER

   D. USER

   E. DISPATCHER

2. **In order to perform administrative tasks on the database using Oracle password authentication, the DBA should have the following two privileges granted to them:**

   A. `sysdba` or `sysoper`

   B. CONNECT or RESOURCE

   C. `restricted session` or `create session`

3. **Which component of the SGA stores parsed SQL statements used for process sharing?**

   A. Buffer cache

   B. Private SQL area

C. Redo log buffer

D. Library cache

E. Row cache

4. **Which of the following choices does not identify an aspect of shared server processing architecture?**

   A. Each user gets his or her own server process for data retrieval.

   B. A dispatcher process is involved.

   C. A listener process is involved.

   D. The server process sits idle infrequently.

5. **Which of the following is the init*sid*.ora parameter that indicates the size of each buffer in the buffer cache?**

   A. DB_BLOCK_BUFFERS

   B. BUFFER_SIZE

   C. DB_BLOCK_SIZE

   D. ROLLBACK_SEGMENTS

6. **The datafiles named in a create database statement are used as storage for which of the following database components?**

   A. SYSTEM tablespace

   B. init*sid*.ora file

   C. Redo log member

   D. ALERT log

7. **Changing the password used to manage the password file changes the password for which of the following?**

   A. SYSTEM

   B. RPT_BATCH

   C. CONNECT

   D. internal

8. **Which is the default password for the SYS user?**

   A. change_on_install

   B. NO_PASSWORD

   C. manager

   D. ORACLE

   E. NULL

9. **DBAs who are planning to administer a database remotely should use all of the following choices except which of the following?**

   A. ORAPWD

   B. REMOTE_LOGIN_PASSWORDFILE set to shared

   C. OS_AUTHENT_PREFIX set to OPS$

   D. A password file

10. **Power will disconnect on the machine running Oracle in two minutes, but user JASON has left for the day while still connected to Oracle. His workstation is locked, so he cannot be logged out from his desktop. How should the DBA shut down the instance?**

    A. shutdown normal

    B. shutdown immediate

    C. shutdown abort

    D. shutdown force

    E. shutdown recover

11. **Which of the following administrative tools in OEM can be used to view the initialization parameter settings for Oracle?**

    A. Schema Manager

    B. Instance Manager

    C. Security Manager

    D. Data Manager

    E. Software Manager

12. **Which two of the following items are required for killing a user session?**

    A. Username

    B. SID

    C. Serial number

    D. Password

13. **You are using the Universal Installer and Packager to install Oracle8*i* on a server that already hosts an Oracle7 database. Which of the following should not be performed when installing Oracle8*i* or Oracle9*i* on a machine already hosting earlier editions of the Oracle database?**

    A. Shut down the network listener.

    B. Shut down the database.

    C. Make a backup of existing databases.

    D. Install Oracle8*i* software to the same directory used for Oracle7 software.

Fill-in-the-Blank Answers

1. DB_NAME **2.** AUTOEXTEND ON. **3.** NEVER. **4.** ABORT. **5.** ORAPWD.

Answers to Chapter Questions

1. C.   SERVER

Explanation   The server process handles data access and retrieval from disk for all user processes connected to Oracle. Choice A, DBW0, moves data blocks between disk and the buffer cache, and therefore is not correct. Choice B, LGWR, copies redo entries from the redo log buffer to online redo logs on disk, and therefore is not correct. Choice D, USER, is the process for which the server process acts in support of. Choice E, DISPATCHER, is used in Oracle MTS architecture and routes user processes to a server, but does not handle reading data from disk on behalf of the user process.

2. A.   `sysdba` or `sysoper`

Explanation   Choices B and C are incorrect. Each privilege listed has some bearing on access, but none of them give any administrative capability. Refer to the discussion of choosing an authentication method.

3. D.   Library cache

Explanation   Choice A is incorrect because the buffer cache is where data blocks are stored for recently executed queries. Choice B is incorrect because the private SQL area is in the PGA where the actual values returned from a query are stored, not the parse information for the query. Choice C is incorrect because the redo log buffer stores redo entries temporarily until LGWR can write them to disk. Choice E is incorrect because the row cache stores data dictionary row information for fast access by users and Oracle. Refer to the discussion of Oracle architecture.

4. A.   Each user gets his or her own server process for data retrieval.

Explanation   The shared server or MTS architecture uses several elements that correspond to the choices. A dispatcher process assigns users to a shared server, while the listener process routes user processes either directly to a server in the case of dedicated server processing or to a dispatcher in MTS. The final choice, D, indicates a benefit of the MTS architecture. Because many users utilize the same server process, that server process will sit idle less frequently than in the dedicated server architecture. Choice A indicates the dedicated server architecture only and is the correct answer to the question.

5. C. DB_BLOCK_SIZE

Explanation Because each buffer in the buffer cache is designed to fit one data block, the size of buffers in the database block buffer cache will be the same size as the blocks they store. The size of blocks in the database is determined by DB_BLOCK_BUFFERS. Refer to the discussion of initialization parameters to be changed during database creation.

6. A. SYSTEM tablespace

Explanation Because datafiles can only be a part of tablespaces (more on this in Chapter 2), all other choices must be eliminated immediately. Another reason to eliminate at least choices B and D is that neither the init*sid*.ora file nor the ALERT log are created in the create database statement. So, as long as you know that redo logs are composed of online redo log members, and tablespaces like SYSTEM are composed of datafiles, you should have no problem getting a question like this one right.

7. D. internal

Explanation Choice A is incorrect because the SYSTEM password has no affiliation with the password for the password file. SYS and internal do. Choice B is incorrect because RPT_BATCH is not a password created by Oracle in a create database statement. Choice C is incorrect because CONNECT is a role, not a user. Choice E is incorrect because audit is a command, not a user. Refer to the discussion of creating the password file as part of choosing user authentication.

8. A. change_on_install

Explanation This is a classic piece of Oracle trivia. Memorize it, along with the SYSTEM password, which incidentally is manager. This is all fine for OCP, but beware of others who may also have memorized these facts. Don't let a hacker use this information against you. Make sure you change the default passwords for SYS and SYSTEM after creating your database.

9. C. OS_AUTHENT_PREFIX set to OPS$

Explanation A DBA should use password file authentication when planning to administer a database remotely. This action consists of a password file, the ORAPWD utility, and setting the REMOTE_LOGIN_PASSWORDFILE parameter to shared. The OS_AUTHENT_PREFIX parameter is used to alter the prefix Oracle requires on Oracle users when operating system authentication is being used. This one, obviously, is not required for Oracle password authentication.

10. B. `shutdown immediate`

Explanation   A power outage can cause damage to an Oracle instance if it is running when the power goes out. However, choice C is just too drastic, given that you are basically treating the situation as if it required media recovery. After all, you know that JASON is not executing a transaction, so no additional time to finish the `rollback` will be required before shutdown. Choice A will not do it either, though, because `shutdown normal` will wait all night for JASON to come in and log off. Choice B is the logical choice. Choices D and E are not valid options for shutting down a database instance.

11. B.   Instance Manager

Explanation   The Instance Manager tool handles all instance-related tasks, including display and modification of initialization parameters set in the `initsid.ora` file. Schema Manager handles tasks involving database object creation and modification, eliminating choice A. Security Manager handles user privilege and role management, which eliminates choice C. Data Manager handles the loading and unloading of data from EXPORT binary or flat file format, eliminating choice D. Finally, Software Manager handles enterprise deployment of Oracle software, eliminating choice E.

12. B and C.   SID *and* serial number

Explanation   To disconnect a database user with the `alter system kill session` statement, you must have the SID and serial number. Both these pieces of information for the session you want to kill can be found in the V$SESSION dictionary view. You only need username and password information to establish the connection, not eliminate it, which in turn eliminates choices A and D.

13. D.   Install Oracle8*i* or Oracle9*i* software to the same directory used for Oracle7 software.

Explanation   Using Universal Installer and Packager, you cannot install Oracle8*i* or Oracle9*i* to the same directory that contains a prior release of Oracle installed with an earlier release of Oracle Installer. You should shut down any existing databases and listeners, and make a backup of the existing database before installing a new version of Oracle on a machine already hosting an Oracle database.

CHAPTER
2

Managing the Physical
Database Structure

n this chapter, you will understand and demonstrate knowledge in the following areas:

- Data dictionary views and standard packages
- Managing the control file
- Maintaining redo log files

In this chapter, you will examine Oracle's physical disk resources in detail. Oracle disk resources are broken into two categories: physical and logical. Oracle physical disk resources include control files, datafiles, and redo log files. Logical disk resources, which include tablespaces, segments, extents, and Oracle blocks, will be discussed in the next chapter. After reading this chapter you will get a good understanding of the how the control files, redo log files, and the datafiles work with the background processes to make a working database. With these foundational concepts, you will have a better understanding of the rest of the topics in this book. In addition, you will be introduced to important information that is stored in the SYSTEM tablespace—data dictionary.

Data Dictionary Content and Usage

In this section, you will cover the following points about dictionary views and standard packages:

- Key components of the data dictionary
- Contents of the data dictionary and how they are used
- How to query the data dictionary views

The data dictionary is the first set of database objects the DBA should create after issuing the `create database` command. Every object in the database is tracked in some fashion by the Oracle data dictionary. Oracle generally creates the data dictionary without any intervention from the DBA at database creation time with the use of the `catalog.sql` and `catproc.sql` scripts. If you are using Database Configuration Assistant to create the database, the tool takes care to run these scripts. If you are manually creating the database, make sure to run these scripts soon after the database is created. This section will explain how Oracle creates the data dictionary using these different scripts the components of the data dictionary and how to use the data dictionary.

Constructing the Data Dictionary Views

The first script, `catalog.sql`, is used to create the objects that comprise the data dictionary. The data dictionary supports virtually every aspect of Oracle database operation, from finding information about objects to performance tuning, and everything in between.

To create a data dictionary, you run the `catalog.sql` script from within SQL*Plus while connected as the administrative privilege `sysdba`. This script performs a laundry list of `create view` statements, as well as executing a series of other scripts in order to create other data dictionary views in special areas and special public synonyms for those views. Within the `catalog.sql` script, there are calls to several other scripts, which are listed in the following:

- **`cataudit.sql`** Creates the SYS.AUD$ dictionary table, which tracks all audit trail information generated by Oracle when the auditing feature of the database is used.

- **`catldr.sql`** Creates views that are used for the SQL*Loader tool, which is used to process large-volume data loads from one system to another.

- **`catexp.sql`** Creates views that are used by the IMPORT/EXPORT utilities.

- **`catpart.sql`** Creates views that support Oracle9*i*'s partitioning option.

- **`catadt.sql`** Creates views that support user-defined types and object components of Oracle9*i*'s object features.

- **`standard.sql`** Creates the STANDARD package, which stores all Oracle scalar or simple datatypes like VARCHAR2 and BLOB; STANDARD also contains built-in SQL functions like `decode( )` and others.

It is important to remember that `catalog.sql` calls these other scripts automatically. All the scripts can be found in the `rdbms/admin` directory under the Oracle software home directory. The following code block demonstrates the commands necessary to run the `catalog.sql` file on UNIX:

```
# cd $ORACLE_HOME/rdbms/admin
# sqlplus
Oracle SQL*Plus Release 9.0.1.0.0 - Production
(c)Copyright 2001, Oracle Corporation. All Rights Reserved.
Enter user-name: sys as sysdba
Enter password:
Connected to:
Oracle9i Enterprise Edition Release 9.0.1.0.0 - Production
With the Partitioning and Objects options
SQL> @catalog
```

The second script, `catproc.sql`, creates procedural options and utilities for PL/SQL. There are two different types of scripts that are run by `catproc.sql`. If you look in the script, you will see references to other scripts in the `rdbms/admin` directory, such as `dbmsutil.sql` and `dbmssql.sql`. These scripts ending in `.sql` are package specifications for the various Oracle server packages. Package specification contains the procedure, function, type, and constant definitions that are available in the package, but not actual code. The other type of script is a `.plb` script, such as `prvtutil.plb` and `prvtpipe.plb`. This extension denotes PL/SQL code that has been encrypted using a wrapper program to prevent you from seeing the application code logic.

It is important to remember that `catproc.sql` calls these other scripts automatically. All the scripts can be found in the `rdbms/admin` directory under the Oracle software home directory. The following code block demonstrates the commands necessary to run the `catproc.sql` file on UNIX:

```
/home/oracle/app/oracle/product/9.0.1> cd rdbms/admin
/home/oracle/app/oracle/product/9.0.1/rdbms/admin> sqlplus
Oracle SQL*Plus Release 8.1.7.0.0 - Production
(c)Copyright 2000, Oracle Corporation. All Rights Reserved.
Enter user-name: sys as sysdba
Enter password:
Connected to:
Oracle9i Enterprise Edition Release 9.0.1.0.0 - Production
With the Partitioning and Objects options
SQL> @catproc
```

It is not possible to create the dictionary views unless you have created the database first already. Because you run the scripts while connected as user `sys as sysdba`, the SYS user winds up owning the database objects that comprise the data dictionary, and these objects are stored in the SYSTEM tablespace, neither of which will exist until you issue the `create database` statement. In addition to these two scripts mentioned, there are other scripts that can be executed to create different options. These other scripts will be described as they pertain to matters tested on the OCP exam. You can also refer to Oracle documentation for a complete list of the scripts.

For Review

1. Data dictionary keeps track of every aspect of the database from tables being created to performance information of the database.

2. Executing the `catalog.sql` and `catproc.sql` scripts soon after creation of the database creates the data dictionary.

3. The data dictionary is owned by SYS and created in the SYSTEM tablespace.

Exercises

1. **You are determining when to create your Oracle data dictionary. Which of the following choices indicates the most appropriate time to do so?**

   A. Before the database has been created

   B. Before creating Oracle-supplied packages

   C. Before creating the SYSTEM tablespace

   D. Before giving users access to the database

2. **You are about to create your Oracle-supplied packages for use with the database. Which of the following scripts is most appropriate for doing so?**

   A. `catproc.sql`

   B. `catalog.sql`

   C. `catldr.sql`

   D. `catexp.sql`

3. **You are about to create your Oracle data dictionary for use with the database. Which of the following users would you connect to the database as for this purpose in Oracle9***i*** and later releases?**

   A. SYSTEM

   B. OUTLN

   C. INTERNAL

   D. SYS

Answer Key

1. B. 2. A. 3. D. The INTERNAL user has been made obsolete for Oracle9*i* and later releases.

Key Data Dictionary Components and Contents

Oracle's data dictionary has two components—base tables and user-accessible views. The following discussion covers the differences between the two. You should always remember to use the user-accessible views in the Oracle data dictionary. Never access the base tables directly. Now, let's look at other aspects of the data dictionary components you need to understand for OCP.

Base Tables

Data in the data dictionary is stored in a set of tables that are created during the initial stages of database creation. These tables are called *base tables.* They are the X$ tables created in the SYSTEM tablespace, whose sole purpose is to store these data dictionary base tables. These tables are created during the execution of `catalog.sql` script. Only user SYS as the privileges necessary to access these tables directly. You should avoid logging into Oracle as SYS whenever possible to avoid damaging the dictionary base tables, and you should never grant direct access to base tables to others using the Oracle database.

User-Accessible Views

During the same time the base tables are created and populated, the `catalog.sql` script creates a set of user-friendly views that enables users to view the data dictionary data through these views. Hence, data dictionary that we normally refer to is a set of views and not tables. Oracle creates public synonyms on many data dictionary views so users can access them conveniently. For the rest of the discussion, we'll focus on the views available in the data dictionary rather than on the base tables. The use of the data dictionary is where OCP exams will test your knowledge.

Oracle software uses the data dictionary extensively. It is used from validating the user connections coming into the database to verifying the existence of the tables that are being queried to the looking for indexes of the tables to improve the performance of the transactions. Due to constant access of the data dictionary, it is cached in the *dictionary cache* of the System Global Area (SGA) to improve the access to it.

Available Dictionary Views

A wealth of information about objects and data in your database can be found in a relatively small number of tables owned by a special privileged user in Oracle called SYS. Although Oracle prevents you from looking at these tables directly, several views are available for you to access this information. These views comprise the feature in Oracle known as the *data dictionary*.

Data dictionary views help you avoid referring to the tables of the data dictionary directly. This safeguard is important for two reasons. First, it underscores the sensitivity of the SYS-owned tables that store dictionary data. If something happens to those tables, causing either data to be lost or a table to be removed, the effects could seriously damage your Oracle database—possibly even rendering it completely unusable! Second, the dictionary views distill the information in the data dictionary into highly understandable and useful formats.

What's in a Name?

Let's start by considering an example. Take a look at the following code block. In it, we can see the contents of a dictionary view called USER_TABLES:

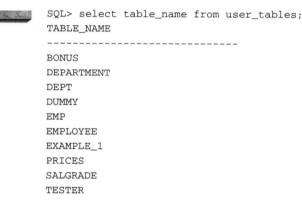

```
SQL> select table_name from user_tables;
TABLE_NAME
------------------------------
BONUS
DEPARTMENT
DEPT
DUMMY
EMP
EMPLOYEE
EXAMPLE_1
PRICES
SALGRADE
TESTER
```

I logged into Oracle as user SCOTT to obtain this output, so you can see that the output of this query displays the name of almost every table we've worked with. Look more carefully for a moment at the name of the view I used: USER_TABLES. Its very name implies two vitally important aspects of this (and indeed every) view in the data dictionary:

- The view's topic (in this case, tables)
- The view's scope (in this case, tables owned by the user SCOTT)

TIP
The scope and topic of the dictionary view are separated by an underscore.

Discerning a Dictionary View's Scope

Let's discuss the view's scope first. Dictionary views are divided into three general categories corresponding to how much of the related topic the database user querying the view is permitted to see. The categories are discussed in the following subsections.

USER   These views enable you to see relevant database objects owned by you. These views have the narrowest scope because they only display the database objects that are in your schema. Therefore, if SCOTT owns a table called EMP and I log into Oracle as user JASON to issue `select * from USER_TABLES`, I'm not going to see EMP listed among the output. Why? Because the table belongs to SCOTT.

ALL   These views enable you to see relevant database objects that you may or may not own but nevertheless are accessible to you. These views have a wider scope than the USER views because they include every relevant object that you can access, regardless of ownership. However, the scope is still limited to you, the user. In order to be able to access a database object, one of three conditions must be true:

- You created the object.

- You were granted access to the object by the object owner.

- The PUBLIC user was granted access privileges on the object by the owner.

TIP
The PUBLIC user in the database is a special user who represents the access privileges every user has. Therefore, when an object owner creates a table and grants access to the table to user PUBLIC, every user in the database has access privileges to the table created.

DBA   These powerful views enable you to see all relevant database objects in the entire database, whether or not they are owned by or accessible to you. These views are incredibly handy for DBAs (and sometimes also for developers) needing information about every database object.

NOTE
You can grant a special role to users called SELECT_CATALOG_ROLE in order to let them look at the DBA views.

Identifying a Dictionary View's Topic

The second part of any dictionary view's name identifies the topic of that view. Based on this fact, we know that the topic of the USER_TABLES view is tables, whereas the topic for the ALL_INDEXES view is all indexes. The views that correspond to areas that have been or will be discussed are listed in the following:

■ **USER_OBJECTS, ALL_OBJECTS, DBA_OBJECTS**   Gives information about various database objects owned by the current user, available to the current user, or all objects in the database, respectively.

■ **USER_TABLES, ALL_TABLES, DBA_TABLES**   Displays information about tables owned by or available to the current user, respectively, or all tables in the Oracle database.

■ **USER_INDEXES, ALL_INDEXES, DBA_INDEXES**   Displays information about indexes owned by or available to the current user, respectively, or all indexes in the Oracle database.

■ **USER_VIEWS, ALL_VIEWS, DBA_VIEWS**   Displays information about views owned by or available to the current user, respectively, or all views in the Oracle database (including dictionary views).

■ **USER_SEQUENCES, ALL_SEQUENCES, DBA_SEQUENCES**   Displays information about sequences owned by or available to the current user, respectively, or all sequences in the Oracle database.

■ **USER_USERS, ALL_USERS, DBA_USERS**   Displays information about the current user or about all users in Oracle, respectively.

■ **USER_CONSTRAINTS, ALL_CONSTRAINTS, DBA_CONSTRAINTS**   Displays information about constraints owned by or available to the current user, respectively, or all constraints in the Oracle database.

■ **USER_CONS_COLUMNS, ALL_CONS_COLUMNS, DBA_CONS_COLUMNS**   Displays information about table columns that have constraints owned by or available to the current user, respectively, or all table columns in Oracle that have constraints on them.

■ **USER_IND_COLUMNS, ALL_IND_COLUMNS, DBA_IND_COLUMNS**   Displays information about table columns that have indexes owned by or available to the current user, respectively, or all columns in Oracle tables that have indexes on them.

■ **USER_TAB_COLUMNS, ALL_TAB_COLUMNS, DBA_TAB_COLUMNS**   Displays information about columns in tables owned by or available to the current user, respectively, or all columns in all tables in Oracle.

■ **USER_ROLES, ALL_ROLES, DBA_ROLES**   Displays information about roles owned by or available to the current user, respectively, or all roles in the Oracle database.

■ **USER_TAB_PRIVS, ALL_TAB_PRIVS, DBA_TAB_PRIVS**   Displays information about object privileges on objects owned by the user or available to the current user, respectively, or all object privileges available to all users in Oracle.

- **USER_SYS_PRIVS, ALL_SYS_PRIVS, DBA_SYS_PRIVS**   Displays information about object privileges on objects owned by the user or available to the current user, respectively, or all system privileges granted to all users in Oracle.

- **USER_SOURCE, ALL_SOURCE, DBA_SOURCE**   Displays the source code for PL/SQL programs owned by the user or available to the current user, respectively, or all PL/SQL source code in the entire Oracle database.

- **USER_TRIGGERS, ALL_TRIGGERS, DBA_TRIGGERS**   Displays information about triggers owned by the user or available to the current user, respectively, or all triggers in the Oracle database.

- **ROLE_TAB_PRIVS, ROLE_SYS_PRIVS, ROLE_ROLE_PRIVS**   Displays information about object privileges, system privileges, or roles granted to roles in the database, respectively.

- **DBA_TABLESPACES, DBA_TS_QUOTAS**   Displays information about all tablespaces in Oracle, as well as space quotas assigned to users in each tablespace.

- **DBA_DATAFILES, DBA_SEGMENTS, DBA_EXTENTS, DBA_FREE_SPACE**   Displays information about datafiles in your Oracle database, as well as segments, extents, and free space in each datafile, respectively.

- **DBA_PROFILES**   Displays information about user profiles in Oracle. Profiles are a way for you as the DBA to restrict the physical resources of the host system (such as process memory allocation, CPU cycles, and so on) that users may utilize in conjunction with Oracle processing.

TIP
These are just some of the views available in the Oracle data dictionary. We'll discuss others as they become relevant to topics tested on the OCP exam.

The Dynamic Performance Views

Another important classification of views in the Oracle database is the dynamic performance views. These are not part of the Oracle dictionary per se, but nevertheless are useful for managing your database. Dynamic performance views are updated constantly by Oracle with important data about database operation. Some examples of dynamic performance views include

- **V$DATABASE**   General information about the database mounted to your instance is kept here.

- **V$SYSSTAT**   Most information about the performance of your database is kept here.

- **V$SESSION, V$SESSTAT**   Most information about performance for individual user sessions is stored here.

- **VLOG, VLOGFILE**   Information about online redo logs can be found here.

- **V$DATAFILE**   Information about Oracle datafiles can be found here.

- **V$CONTROLFILE**   Information about Oracle control files can be found here.

A Look at the Views Themselves

As you know, views do not actually contain any data—they are merely `select` statements stored as objects in Oracle. Every time you refer to a view in your own queries, Oracle dynamically executes the view's underlying `select` statement to obtain the contents of that view. Dictionary view definitions can be quite complex. So that you can appreciate this hidden complexity, the following code block shows you the definition of the ALL_TABLES view in Oracle. Because this view contains a column called TEXT that is defined as the LONG datatype, we have to do a little extra formatting via the `set long 9999` command to ensure that we'll see the output appropriately:

```
SQL> SET LONG 9999;
SQL> SELECT text FROM all_views WHERE view_name = 'ALL_TABLES';
TEXT
--------------------------------------------------
select u.name, o.name, ts.name, co.name,
t.pctfree$, t.pctused$,
t.initrans, t.maxtrans,
s.iniexts * ts.blocksize, s.extsize * ts.blocksize,
s.minexts, s.maxexts, s.extpct,
decode(s.lists, 0, 1, s.lists), decode(s.groups, 0, 1, s.groups),
decode(bitand(t.modified,1), 0, 'Y', 1, 'N', '?'),
t.rowcnt, t.blkcnt, t.empcnt, t.avgspc, t.chncnt, t.avgrln,
lpad(decode(t.spare1, 0, '1', 1, 'DEFAULT', to_char(t.spare1)), 10),
lpad(decode(mod(t.spare2, 65536), 0, '1', 1, 'DEFAULT',
to_char(mod(t.spare2, 65536))), 10),
lpad(decode(floor(t.spare2 / 65536), 0, 'N', 1, 'Y', '?'), 5),
decode(bitand(t.modified, 6), 0, 'ENABLED', 'DISABLED')
from sys.user$ u, sys.ts$ ts, sys.seg$ s,
 sys.obj$ co, sys.tab$ t, sys.obj$ o
where o.owner# = u.user#
and o.obj# = t.obj#
```

```
and t.clu# = co.obj# (+)
and t.ts# = ts.ts#
and t.file# = s.file# (+)
and t.block# = s.block# (+)
and (o.owner# = userenv('SCHEMAID')
or o.obj# in
(select oa.obj#
from sys.objauth$ oa
where grantee# in ( select kzsrorol from x$kzsro))
or /* user has system privileges */
exists (select null from v$enabledprivs
where priv_number in (-45 /* LOCK ANY TABLE */,
-47 /* SELECT ANY TABLE */,
-48 /* INSERT ANY TABLE */,
-49 /* UPDATE ANY TABLE */,
-50 /* DELETE ANY TABLE */)))
```

TIP
*If you want to obtain a full listing of all data
dictionary views available in Oracle, you can
execute* `select * from DICTIONARY`, *and
Oracle will list all the dictionary views for you.
Comments on the use of each dictionary view are
offered in DICTIONARY as well. Some objects in
Oracle that are synonymous with DICTIONARY are
DICT, CATALOG, and CAT.*

For Review

1. Know what the data dictionary is. Be sure you can distinguish between dictionary views and the SYS-owned tables underlying those views.

2. Understand how to identify the topic and scope of a dictionary view based on the name of that view. Also, be sure you can identify all the views defined in this discussion.

3. Be sure you can identify the data dictionary views that will list all the dictionary views available in the Oracle database.

Exercises

1. **You want to list all the indexed columns for objects you own in the Oracle database. Which of the following views would you use?**

    A. USER_TAB_COLUMNS

    B. ALL_TAB_COLUMNS

    C. USER_IND_COLUMNS

    D. ALL_IND_COLUMNS

2. **You are identifying dictionary objects in the Oracle database. Which of the following is a view in the data dictionary?**

    A. V$DATABASE

    B. DBA_TABLES

    C. SYS.AUD$

    D. EMP

3. **This is the user who owns all the data dictionary objects in Oracle:**
    _____.

4. **This is an object you can query to obtain a listing of all data dictionary objects in Oracle:** _____.

5. **Which of the following choices identifies a dynamic performance view in the Oracle database?**

    A. DBA_DATA_FILES

    B. DBA_SEGMENTS

    C. V$DATAFILE

    D. DBA_EXTENTS

Answer Key
1. C. 2. B. 3. SYS. 4. CATALOG, CAT, DICTIONARY, or DICT. 5. C.

Querying the Data Dictionary

We'll now look at some examples of querying the dictionary so you can better understand how useful the data dictionary is in Oracle. (For the purposes of this section, the DBA_ views will be used, except where noted.) Recall that you can use the describe command on data dictionary views, just as if they were tables. The following code block shows what happens when you do so:

```
SQL> describe dba_source
 Name                           Null?    Type
 ------------------------------ -------- ----------------
 OWNER                          NOT NULL VARCHAR2(30)
 NAME                           NOT NULL VARCHAR2(30)
 TYPE                                    VARCHAR2(12)
 LINE                           NOT NULL NUMBER
 TEXT                                    VARCHAR2(4000)
```

The DBA_INDEXES view contains information about the indexes on tables that are available to the user. Some of the information listed in this view details the features of the index, such as whether all values in the indexed column are unique. Other information in the view identifies the storage parameters of the index and where the index is stored. The following shows an example:

```
SQL> column owner format a10
SQL> column index_name format a15
SQL> column table_name format a12
SQL> column uniqueness format a10
SQL> select owner, index_name, table_name, uniqueness
  2  from dba_indexes
  3  where owner = 'SCOTT';
OWNER      INDEX_NAME      TABLE_NAME   UNIQUENESS
---------- --------------- ------------ ----------
SCOTT      PK_01           EXAMPLE_1    UNIQUE
SCOTT      SYS_C00905      DEPARTMENT   UNIQUE
SCOTT      UK_EMPLOYEE_01  EMPLOYEE     UNIQUE
```

TIP
For those of you following along on your own database, I've shown some useful formatting commands for cleaning up the output from these queries.

The next view is the DBA_USERS view. This view is used to give the current user of the database more information about all users known to the Oracle database:

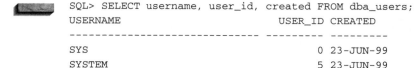

```
SQL> SELECT username, user_id, created FROM dba_users;
USERNAME                              USER_ID CREATED
------------------------------------- --------- ---------
SYS                                         0 23-JUN-99
SYSTEM                                      5 23-JUN-99
```

```
OUTLN                              11  23-JUN-99
DBSNMP                             18  23-JUN-99
AURORA$ORB$UNAUTHENTICATED         23  23-JUN-99
JASON                              27  18-JUL-00
STUDENT2                           46  30-OCT-00
STUDENT1                           45  30-OCT-00
SPANKY                             43  30-OCT-00
JASON2                             48  31-OCT-00
SCOTT                              52  19-MAR-01
JASON3                             49  16-NOV-00
JASON10                            50  18-NOV-00
GIANT                              51  08-DEC-00
```

Querying Dictionary Views for Constraints

Here's a trickier example. In keeping with our work on constraints in this chapter, the next few views are related to constraints. Let's look at combining the contents of two views: DBA_CONSTRAINTS and DBA_CONS_COLUMNS. The DBA_CONSTRAINTS view is used to display information about the constraints that have been defined in the database, while DBA_CONS_COLUMNS displays all columns in integrity constraints in Oracle. Consider the following situation. Say we can't remember whether we have followed the book's advice for naming shared columns in multiple tables the same name. Is this a problem? Not with the Oracle data dictionary on hand! We can still determine the referenced column using DBA_CONSTRAINTS and DBA_CONS_COLUMNS, as shown in the following block:

```
SQL> column table_name format a12
SQL> column column_name format a12
SQL> select a.table_name, b.column_name, c.table_name, c.column_name
  2  from DBA_constraints a, DBA_cons_columns b, DBA_cons_columns c
  3  where a.constraint_name = b.constraint_name
  4  and a.r_constraint_name = c.constraint_name;
TABLE_NAME    COLUMN_NAME          TABLE_NAME    COLUMN_NAME
------------  ------------------   ------------  --------------

EMPLOYEE      DEPARTMENT_NUM       DEPARTMENT    DEPARTMENT_NUM
```

Using Other Dictionary Views

Similar information to the contents of DBA_CONS_COLUMNS can be found in DBA_IND_COLUMNS. However, the dictionary view DBA_IND_COLUMNS will contain columns used in constraint-related indexes as well as columns used in other types of indexes. Check out the following code block:

```
SQL> create index ix_employee_01 on employee (lastname);
Index created.
SQL> select index_name, table_name, column_name, column_position
```

```
  2   from DBA_ind_columns
  3   where table_name = 'EMPLOYEE';
INDEX_NAME       TABLE_NAME    COLUMN_NAME          COLUMN_POSITION
---------------  ------------  -------------------  ---------------
PK_EMPLOYEE_01   EMPLOYEE      EMPID                              1
UK_EMPLOYEE_01   EMPLOYEE      GOVT_ID                            1
IX_EMPLOYEE_01   EMPLOYEE      LASTNAME                           1
```

For Review

Be sure you can develop queries against dictionary views.

Exercises

1. **Use the following code block to answer this question:**

```
TEXT
-----------------------------------------------
declare
  x varchar2(10);
begin
  x := 'hello world';
  dbms_output.put_line(x);
end;
```

   Which of the following queries might have produced this output?

   A. DBA_ERRORS

   B. DBA_SOURCE

   C. DBA_VIEWS

   D. DBA_TRIGGERS

2. **Use the following code block to answer this question:**

```
SQL> select text from DBA_views where view_name =
  2  'DBA_TABLES';
TEXT
-------------------------------------------------------------

select u.name, o.name,
       decode(bitand(t.property, 4194400), 0, ts.name, null),
```

   Which of the following choices identifies a formatting command that can be used for displaying the rest of the output?

   A. `set long 9999`

   B. `column text format a9999`

      C. `set long 50`

      D. `column text format a50`

   3. To identify some aspects about all users in the database, you would use this view: _____.

Answer Key
1. B. 2. A. 3. DBA_USERS.

Maintaining Control Files

In this section, you will cover the following points about managing control files:

- How control files are used

- Examining control file contents

- Managing control files with Oracle-Managed Files

- Obtaining information about control files

- Multiplexing control files

Control files are to the physical structure of the Oracle database what the data dictionary is to the logical structure. The control files keep track of all the files' Oracle needs and where they are on the host machine. The control files also contain information about the redo log member filenames and where they are located in the filesystem. Without control files, the Oracle database server would be unable to find its physical components. The names of the control files are specified in the `init.ora` file for each Oracle instance. In this section, we will talk about how Oracle uses control files, what is stored in the control files, where to obtain information about your control files, and the importance of storing multiple copies of control files on separate disks.

How Control Files Are Used

When you enter SQL*Plus to bring the database online, Oracle looks in the control file to find all the components it needs in order to bring that database online. For example, if the control file on your database has three files associated with it and only two are available, Oracle will complain that the third file was missing, and it won't start your database. After database startup, control files will be modified or used by Oracle in the following situations:

- When new physical disk resources (such as tablespaces) are created

- When an existing disk resource is modified in some way (for example, when a datafile is added to a tablespace)

- When LGWR stops writing one online redo log and starts writing to another (log switch)

Using the CONTROL_FILES Parameter

The CONTROL_FILES parameter in the init.ora file defines the location of your control files on the database server and indicates where Oracle will look on instance startup to find its control files. When you start the instance before creating the database or when you are migrating from one version of Oracle to another, Oracle will create control files based on the filenames and locations you provide in the CONTROL_FILES init.ora parameter. In subsequent instance startups, if Oracle does not find the control files it expects to find based on the content of the CONTROL_FILES parameter, Oracle won't start. You will learn in subsequent sections that if you create Oracle-managed control files then there is no need for the CONTROL_FILES parameter and Oracle will look for default directory or directories for the control files.

By default in both Windows and UNIX environments, the Oracle Database Configuration Assistant (DBCA) will create three control files and put them in the oradata/*database_name* directory under the Oracle software home directory. DBCA gives them the name control*nn*.dbf (although sometimes DBCA may also use the .ctl or .ora extensions), where *n* is a number between 01 and 03 (the number could be operating system specific). You can follow whatever naming convention you like when you define your own control files. You are also not restricted to placing the control files in the directory $ORACLE_HOME/dbs. You can put them wherever you want. For reasons we will explore shortly, Oracle recommends you use multiple control files placed on separate disks. Be sure to include the absolute pathname for the location of your control file when defining values for the CONTROL_FILES parameter.

For Review

1. Control files are used to keep track of all the physical components of the database such as location of the data files, redo logs, name of the database, and so on.

2. Normally, Oracle expects to see the control files at the location indicated by CONTROL_FILES parameter. Starting with Oracle9i, this is not true if

you are using Oracle-Managed Files (OMF). For our purposes, we'll assume you're not using OMF, but be mindful that some OCP questions may take OMFs into account.

Exercises

1. **You are attempting to locate your control files on an Oracle database called ORCL. In which of the following files might you look for this information?**

   A. `control01.ctl`

   B. `pwdORCL.ora`

   C. `catalog.sql`

   D. `init.ora`

2. **Your attempts to start the Oracle database have failed. After looking in the appropriate location, you ascertain the value for the CONTROL_FILES parameter to be set to `/u01/oradata/orcl/control01.ctl`. Which of the following choices identifies the next likely step you would take to troubleshoot the problem?**

   A. Verify the actual directory location of your control file.

   B. Check the hardware to see if the memory card is defective.

   C. Verify the actual directory location of your SYSTEM datafile.

   D. Check to see if you have created two redo logs.

3. **You are configuring your Oracle database. Under which of the following features in Oracle would you not have to configure the CONTROL_FILES parameter for an individual instance?**

   A. When Real Application Clusters are used

   B. When OMF is used

   C. When temporary tablespaces are used

   D. When transportable tablespaces are used

Answer Key

1. D. 2. A. 3. B.

Examining Control File Contents

Control files have several items contained in them. However, you can't just open a control file in your favorite text editor and see what it holds. This is because the control file is written in binary, and only the Oracle database can understand its contents. However, rest assured—we're going to tell you what the control file contains so that you know this information for OCP! The control file contains the following:

- Database name and identifier information that you supplied when you created the database.

- Database creation date and time information that you supplied when you created the database.

- Datafiles and redo log filesystem locations that you supplied when you created the database and when you added datafiles or redo logs.

- Tablespace names and the associations between tablespaces and datafiles that you supplied when you created the database or tablespaces, or when you added more datafiles to existing tablespaces later.

- History of when archive logs were taken. This information is typically generated automatically by Oracle.

- Information about when backups were taken. This information is generated when you take your backups.

- The current online redo log sequence number. This information is typically generated automatically by Oracle.

- Current checkpoint information. Again, this information is typically generated automatically by Oracle.

Re-creating a Control File

Sometimes control files must be re-created for various purposes. For example, you might like to rename the database because you're making a copy of it on the same machine hosting the original database (Oracle doesn't permit two databases to have the same name on the same host system). Or, you might need to change database settings such as maxlogfiles that you set when you created the database. You may have even lost the control file. Whatever the reason, your method is the same. Issue the `alter database backup controlfile to trace` statement. The `trace` keyword in this statement indicates that Oracle will generate a script containing a `create controlfile` command and store it in the trace directory identified in the `init.ora` file by the USER_DUMP_DEST parameter. A sample control file creation script generated by this command is displayed in the following code block:

```
# The following commands will create a new control file and use it
# to open the database.
# Data used by the recovery manager will be lost. Additional
# logs may be required for media recovery of offline data
# files. Use this only if the current version of all online
# logs are available.
STARTUP NOMOUNT
CREATE CONTROLFILE REUSE DATABASE "ORGDB01" NORESETLOGS
NOARCHIVELOG
     MAXLOGFILES 16
     MAXLOGMEMBERS 2
     MAXDATAFILES 240
     MAXINSTANCES 1
     MAXLOGHISTORY 113
LOGFILE
  GROUP 1 ('/oracle/disk_01/log1a.dbf',
'/oracle/disk_02/log1b.dbf') SIZE 30M,
  GROUP 2 ('/oracle/disk_03/log2a.dbf',
'/oracle/disk_04/log2b.dbf') SIZE 30M
DATAFILE
  '/oracle/disk_05/system01.dbf',
  '/oracle/disk_05/system02.dbf'
;
# Recovery is required if any of the datafiles are restored
# backups, or if the last shutdown was not normal or immediate.
RECOVER DATABASE
# Database can now be opened normally.
ALTER DATABASE OPEN;
```

From this script, you can guess what the correct syntax for a `create controlfile` statement would be—you have it right in front of you. For example, if you wanted to clone an existing database, you would follow this procedure:

1. From SQL*Plus, issue the `alter system backup controlfile to trace` command. Oracle generates a script containing the `create controlfile` command similar to the one shown in the previous code block.

2. Shut your existing database down from SQL*Plus using the `shutdown normal` or `shutdown immediate` commands. Do not use `shutdown abort`.

3. Copy all datafiles and redo logs to an alternate filesystem location (preferably using OFA conventions identified in Chapter 1) using operating system commands.

4. Modify the script generated in step 1 using your favorite text editor. You'll need to change the previous reuse database "name" clause to set database "newname". You'll also need to review and modify the filesystem location of every datafile listed in the `datafile` clause of the `create controlfile` command to reflect the new location of the files you copied. You'll need to do the same for online redo logs as well. Also, remove all commented lines beginning with the # character. Later in step 8, you won't necessarily encounter an error if some datafiles weren't copied properly or if Oracle did not find the datafiles where it expected to find them. Thus, it is very important that you verify the filesystem locations for all datafiles and redo logs in your script before proceeding to step 5. Also, remove the `recover database` and `alter database open` commands. You'll perform these steps manually in a later step.

5. Copy the `init.ora` file for the existing database to a new location. In your favorite text editor, change the value set for the CONTROL_FILES parameter in your `init.ora` file to a new filesystem location. In addition, you'll need to modify other `init.ora` settings like DB_NAME and so on, as if you were creating a new database, so refer back to Chapter 1 for further information. If you do not perform this step, then Oracle will not let you rename your new database and may even corrupt your old one!

6. From SQL*Plus, start the Oracle instance with the `startup nomount` command.

7. Run the script you modified in steps 4 and 5 using the `run` or `@` command in SQL*Plus. This step creates you new control file.

8. In SQL*Plus, mount the new database with the `alter table mount` command.

9. In SQL*Plus, open the new database with the `alter table open` command.

10. In SQL*Plus, open the old database with the `startup open` command.

TIP
This is a topic Oracle will most likely cover on the Oracle Database Administration Fundamentals II exam, but explaining it here serves an important purpose—namely, to introduce you to the contents of your control file and how to manipulate it.

For Review

1. Control files are the most important files of a database from a filesystem layout and management perspective. It contains information related to the physical location of every datafile and redo log file in your database.

2. Control files are created the first time you create your Oracle database. If no control file exists already in the location specified by the CONTROL_FILES parameter, then Oracle creates a new control file automatically when the `create database` command is issued. You can re-create a control file for an associated database later using the `create controlfile` command.

3. Control files are opened and read every time the database is opened. The contents of control files are modified every time the structure of the database is changed such as by adding a tablespace, datafile, or online redo log. The control file is also changed when you archive your redo logs, backup the database, and whenever a log switch happens.

Exercises

1. **You are about to create an Oracle database. Which of the following choices identifies a database component not created when the `create database` statement is issued?**

    A. Password files

    B. Control files

    C. Redo log files

    D. Datafiles

2. **You are attempting to rename your Oracle database using the `create controlfile` command. Which of the following choices identifies the step you would most likely take immediately after you shut down your original database to copy the original files to their new locations?**

    A. Issue the `alter database backup controlfile to trace` command.

    B. Modify the script containing your `create controlfile` command to reflect the new filesystem locations for files copied.

    C. Modify appropriate parameters in a copy of the existing database's `init.ora` file.

    D. Remove the control files on your existing database with operating system commands.

3. **BONUS: You are managing control files on an Oracle database. At which of the following points will the contents of your control file not be modified?**

   A. When you open the control file in a text editor

   B. When you issue the `alter tablespace` command

   C. When you issue the `alter database rename file` command

   D. When you issue the `alter database add logfile` command

Answer Key

1. A. **2.** B. Because the question refers to copying files to new locations, the most appropriate next step is to note the new filesystem locations in your script. **3.** A. Although you haven't learned about the commands listed in choices B, C, and D yet, this question should not be too tricky.

Managing Control Files with Oracle-Managed Files

Oracle**9***i*
and higher

In Chapter 1, we introduced the concept of Oracle-Managed Files (OMF). This is a new feature in Oracle9*i* that is designed to minimize the amount of filesystem handling you must execute as an Oracle DBA in support of creating and managing the Oracle database. Let's continue this discussion with respect to the management of your control files. Recall that in order to set up OMF, you must configure appropriate values for the following `init.ora` parameters:

■ **DB_CREATE_FILE_DEST** Defines the location of the default filesystem directory where Oracle will create the datafiles. The following code block shows an OFA-compliant example of how you might set this parameter for a database called DB1:

```
DB_CREATE_FILE_DEST = '/u01/oradata/db1'
```

■ **DB_CREATE_ONLINE_LOG_DEST_*n*** Defines the location of the default filesystem directory for online redo log files and control file creation. The following code block shows an OFA-compliant example of how you might set this parameter for a database called DB1:

```
DB_CREATE_ONLINE_LOG_DEST_1 = '/u01/oradata/db1'
DB_CREATE_ONLINE_LOG_DEST_2 = '/u02/oradata/db1'
```

TIP
When the OMF parameters for defining multiple locations to place online redo logs are specified, then Oracle will place control files in those redo log directories. This multiplexes your control file. You'll learn more about control file multiplexing later in this section.

Changing OMF Settings Later

Values that you set for these two parameters can be dynamically changed using `alter system set parameter = value` command, where *parameter* is the parameter whose settings you want to change, and *value* is the directory you want to change that OMF parameter to. The following code block shows an example:

```
SQL> alter system set DB_CREATE_ONLINE_LOG_DEST_2 = '/u03/oradata/db1';
System altered.
```

Oracle-Managed Control Files During Database Creation

The following are a few facts to keep in mind about OMFs for the OCP Database Administration Fundamentals I exam. If you've specified the CONTROL_FILES parameter in `init.ora` file, but didn't specify values for either OMF parameters, then Oracle will create control files in the locations you defined with the CONTROL_FILES parameter. These files will not be managed by the OMF feature, although Oracle will write any changes in database structure to those control files automatically, as we've already explained. Conversely, if you've chosen not to specify a value for the CONTROL_FILES parameter but instead specified values for OMF parameters, then Oracle creates an OMF-managed control file in the destination you specified for the OMF parameters, subject to the following conditions:

- If you specified a directory for DB_CREATE_FILE_DEST but not for the parameter DB_CREATE_ONLINE_LOG_DEST_*n*, the OMF-managed control file is placed in the directory assigned for DB_CREATE_FILE_DEST.

- If you specified a directory for DB_CREATE_ONLINE_LOG_DEST_*n* but not for DB_CREATE_FILE_DEST, then Oracle places an OMF-managed control file in each directory specified in the DB_CREATE_ONLINE_LOG_DEST_1 and DB_CREATE_ONLINE_LOG_DEST_2 parameters.

- If you specified directories for both parameter types, then Oracle places an OMF-managed control file in each directory specified in the DB_CREATE_ONLINE_LOG_DEST_1 and DB_CREATE_ONLINE_LOG_DEST_2 parameters.

OMF Control File-Naming Conventions

When you use OMF, you relinquish power to Oracle to name the files according to its own conventions. The Oracle-managed control file uses a default naming convention of `ora_%u.ctl`, where `%u` is a unique name generated by Oracle. This name will not necessarily correlate with the name of the database or with parameter settings in `init.ora` such as DB_NAME. The following is an example: `ora_cmr3u45r.ctl`.

TIP
Most DBAs will likely not use OMF for production systems. This is because many files that should be placed on separate disks for performance purposes are all dumped onto the same disk when the OMF feature is used. However, OMFs are great for an organization just getting started with Oracle databases that needs to get up and running very quickly.

For Review

1. Oracle-Managed Files are created by specifying two `init.ora` parameters: DB_CREATE_FILE_DEST and DB_CREATE_ONLINE_LOG_DEST_*n*.

2. When one of these two types of parameters is specified but not the other, then Oracle-managed control files are generated in the filesystem location identified by the parameter that was specified.

3. If both parameters are specified then Oracle-managed control files are created in the locations specified by DB_CREATE_ONLINE_LOG_DEST_*n* parameter.

4. The values set for these parameters can be dynamically changed using `alter system` command.

Exercises

1. **Examine the following excerpt from an `init.ora` file:**

```
DB_CREATE_ONLINE_LOG_DEST_1 = /u01/oradata/db1
DB_CREATE_ONLINE_LOG_DEST_2 = /u02/oradata/db1
DB_CREATE_ONLINE_LOG_DEST_3 = /u03/oradata/db1
DB_CREATE_FILE_DEST = /u04/oradata/db1
```

Which of the following choices does *not* identify the location where Oracle will place your control file when the database gets created?

A. `/u01/oradata/db1`

B. `/u02/oradata/db1`

C. `/u03/oradata/db1`

D. `/u04/oradata/db1`

2. **You are using OMF in conjunction with the management of your Oracle database control file. Which of the following choices identifies an aspect of control file management that Oracle handles regardless of whether OMF is used or not?**

   A. Placement of the control file in the appropriate directory

   B. Multiplexing control files to multiple destinations

   C. Updates to the contents of the control file when new tablespaces are added

   D. Assigning values automatically to the CONTROL_FILES parameter

3. **Complete the following sentence: In order for Oracle to know where to store control files, a value *either* for the _____(A)_____ *or* the _____(B)_____ *and* _____(C)_____ must be specified.**

Answer Key
1. D. 2. C. 3. (A) CONTROL_FILES; (B) DB_CREATE_FILE_DEST; (C) DB_CREATE_ONLINE_LOG_DEST_*n*.

Obtaining Information about Control Files

From time to time, you might need to obtain information about the control files in your Oracle database. You can do so using some important dynamic performance and data dictionary views available to DBAs on an Oracle database. Let's take a look at these views in more detail.

Control Filename and Availability

The main view available in the Oracle data dictionary for control file use and management is the V$CONTROLFILE view. This view has only two columns: STATUS and NAME. Their contents are explained in the following:

- **STATUS** Displays INVALID if the control filename cannot be determined; otherwise, it will be NULL.

■ **NAME** Gives the absolute path location of the file on your host machine as well as the control filename.

The information in the V$CONTROLFILE view corresponds to the values set for the initialization parameter CONTROL_FILES. The following code block shows the SQL statement used to obtain information from the V$CONTROLFILE view about the control files for Oracle on a Windows machine, as well as the output:

```
SQL> select * from v$controlfile;
STATUS    NAME
------    ----------------------------------------
          D:\ORACLE\DATABASE\CTL1D704.ORA
          E:\ORACLE\DATABASE\CTL2D704.ORA
          F:\ORACLE\DATABASE\CTL3D704.ORA
```

Finding Information about Important Control File Contents

You can find other information about your control files from the V$DATABASE view. This dynamic performance view gives information that Oracle normally also stored within the control file. You can see an example of using this view in the following code block, and you should also be aware that several columns in this view give information about your control file:

■ **CONTROLFILE_TYPE** The section type in the control file

■ **CONTROLFILE_CREATED** This indicates when the current control file was created

■ **CONTROLFILE_SEQUENCE#** The current sequence number for the database, which is recorded in the control file

■ **CONTROLFILE_CHANGE#** The current system change number for the database, which is recorded in the control file

■ **CONTROLFILE_TIME** The last time the control file was updated

```
SQL> select * from v$database;

      DBID NAME      CREATED   RESETLOGS_CHANGE# RESETLOGS
---------- --------- --------- ----------------- ---------
PRIOR_RESETLOGS_CHANGE# PRIOR_RES LOG_MODE      CHECKPOINT_CHANGE#
----------------------- --------- ------------- ------------------
ARCHIVE_CHANGE# CONTROL CONTROLFI CONTROLFILE_SEQUENCE#
--------------- ------- --------- ---------------------
CONTROLFILE_CHANGE# CONTROLFI OPEN_RESETL VERSION_T
------------------- --------- ----------- ---------
```

```
1674500680 ORGDB01    21-JAN-00                 33409 21-JAN-00
                    1 06-OCT-98 NOARCHIVELOG                736292
         716268 CURRENT 21-JAN-00                      4412
              736292            NOT ALLOWED 21-JAN-00
```

More Granular Info about Control File Contents

A final view available for displaying control file information is the
V$CONTROLFILE_RECORD_SECTION view. A working control file is divided
into several sections, each storing different information about the database in action.
For example, there is a section in the control file that keeps track of the sequence
number of the current online redo log, a section that contains information about
the physical disk file layout of the Oracle database, and so on. This view displays
information about each of those sections, such as the size of each record in the
control file for that section, the total number of records allocated to each section,
and so on. The following code block shows output from this view:

```
SQL> select * from v$controlfile_record_section where rownum < 6;
TYPE           RECORD_SIZE RECORDS_TOTAL RECORDS_USED FIRST_INDEX LAST_INDEX
-------------- ----------- ------------- ------------ ----------- ----------
LAST_RECID
----------
DATABASE              316             1            1           0          0
        0
CKPT PROGRESS        2036             1            0           0          0
        0
REDO THREAD           228             1            1           0          0
        0
REDO LOG               72            30            5           0          0
        5
DATAFILE              428           400           18           0          0
       20
```

TIP
*You can also find the names of your control files by
issuing* select VALUE from V$PARAMETER
where NAME = 'control_files'. *Be sure that
the parameter name is in lowercase.*

For Review

1. Control file information can be found in several V$ performance views.

2. V$CONTROL_FILE provides the basic information about the status and
   location of the control files.

3. V$DATABASE view provides information such as when the control file is created, and the most recent sequence number and SCN number recorded in the control file.

4. V$CONTROLFILE_RECORD_SECTION shows information stored in different sections of the control file.

Exercises

I. **You want to find out the current sequence number stored in your control file for backup purposes. Which two of the following views would you query?**

    A. V$PARAMETER

    B. V$DATABASE

    C. V$CONTROLFILE

    D. V$CONTROLFILE_RECORD_SECTION

2. **You want to find out the names and locations of all control files in your database. Which two of the following performance views would you query?**

    A. V$PARAMETER

    B. V$DATABASE

    C. V$CONTROLFILE

    D. V$CONTROLFILE_RECORD_SECTION

3. **You want to find out when your control file was created. Which of the following views would you query for this information?**

    A. V$PARAMETER

    B. V$DATABASE

    C. V$CONTROLFILE

    D. V$CONTROLFILE_RECORD_SECTION

Answer Key
1. B and D. 2. A and C. 3. B.

Multiplexing Control Files

If you have multiple disk drives available for Oracle, you should store copies of the control files on different disks to minimize the risk of losing these important physical disk resources. If you stick with the default creation of control files, Oracle recommends that you move these control files to different disk resources and set the CONTROL_FILES parameter to let Oracle know that there are multiple copies of the control file to be maintained. This is called *multiplexing*, or *mirroring*, the control file. Multiplexing control files reduces Oracle's dependence on any one disk available on the host machine. In the event of a failure, the database is more recoverable because multiple copies of the control file have been maintained. In no case should you ever use only one control file for an Oracle database, because of the difficulty in recovering a database when the control file is lost. Having several copies of the control file and parameter file on different disks will minimize the possibility of one disk failure rendering your database inoperable.

Control File Multiplexing: Implementation

The actual process of making additional copies of your control file and moving them to different disk resources is something you handle outside of Oracle. You can create a duplicate copy of the control file by simply using the operating system copy command. In Windows, that command is `copy`, whereas in UNIX it is `cp`. However, that file will be unusable unless you follow these steps:

1. In SQL*Plus, execute the `shutdown normal`, `shutdown immediate`, or `shutdown transactional` command to shut down the instance and close the database.

2. Copy the control file to another disk using your operating system's file copy command.

3. Modify the CONTROL_FILES parameter in `init.ora` to include the additional control file.

4. Restart the instance in SQL*Plus with the `startup open` command. Oracle will now maintain an additional copy of the control file.

TIP
By specifying multiple control files in the `init.ora` *file before database creation, you will start your database administration on that database on the right foot, making the database easy to maintain.*

Backing Up the Control File

You've already seen how to backup your control file using the `alter database backup controlfile to trace` command. As you know, this command generates a script that can be used to re-create the control file later in the event of a problem. You can also use the `alter database backup controlfile` command to make a copy of the actual control file to some alternate location. Once backed up, however, Oracle will not maintain that control file when new datafiles or tablespaces or redo logs are added. Thus, you cannot simply make a backup copy of the control file if you want Oracle to maintain that copy with new information about the database's physical structure. The following code block shows an example of how to use the `alter database backup controlfile` command for making backups of actual control files:

```
SQL> alter database backup controlfile to '/u05/backup/db1/control01.ctl';
Database altered.
```

For Review

1. Oracle can maintain multiple copies of a control file for redundancy purposes. This is called multiplexing.

2. Make sure all your databases have multiplexed control files placed in different physical disks. Their location should be specified in the CONTROL_FILES parameter.

3. You can take regular backups either of the actual control file or of a script to re-create the control file using the `alter database backup controlfile` command.

Exercises

1. **You are implementing control file multiplexing. Which of the following choices identifies the method you can use in order to generate the control file copies that Oracle will maintain?**

   A. Issue `alter database backup controlfile to` *filename*.

   B. Make a copy of the control file with the database shut down.

   C. Issue `alter database backup controlfile to trace`.

   D. Make a copy of the control file with the database still running.

2. **You are implementing control file multiplexing. Which of the following choices identifies how Oracle knows the locations of the control files it is supposed to maintain?**

    A. Values specified for CONTROL_FILES.

    B. Values specified for BACKGROUND_DUMP_DEST.

    C. Values specified in V$DATABASE.

    D. None of the above; Oracle knows automatically where to look.

Answer Key
1. B. **2.** A.

Maintaining Redo Log Files

In this section, you will cover the following points about maintaining redo log files:

- The purpose and structure of online redo logs
- Controlling log switches and checkpoints
- Multiplexing and maintaining redo log files
- Managing online redo log files with OMFs

Redo logs are disk resources that store data changes made by users on Oracle. In this section, we will look at how redo logs are used in Oracle and where you can look to find information about redo log status. The special role of the LGWR background process in maintaining redo logs, and its behavior, will be examined. You will learn more about the importance of maintaining two or more copies of each redo log on your machine, in the same way you do for control files. Finally, we will cover how to manage online redo log files using OMF.

The Purpose and Structure of Online Redo Logs

Oracle uses redo logs to track data changes users make to the database such as changes made to data segment blocks of the tables or indexes. Each user process that makes such a change generates a redo log entry, which identifies the change that was made. This redo log entry is placed in the area of the SGA called the redo log buffer, which you learned about in Chapter 1. The LGWR process writes those changes to files on disk called online redo log files. Oracle expects a minimum of two redo log files. Each of the redo log files is called a *redo log group*. Oracle also enables you to mirror each of the redo log files for sake of redundancy. Those mirrored files are called *members of the group*.

TIP
This discussion covers two official exam objectives listed on the candidate guide for the OCP Database Fundamentals I exam.

The operation of online redo logs occurs in this way. As the redo log buffer fills with redo entries from user processes or if an active transaction gives the `commit` command, then LGWR writes the content of the redo log buffer to each member of the group. This is sometimes referred to as *flushing* the redo buffer. The flushing of the entire redo log buffer happens even if a single active transaction commits. The group being written is considered the current group because LGWR is currently writing into it. LGWR writes redo log entries to the active group until the group is full, at which point LGWR switches to writing redo entries to the next redo log group. This is referred to as *log switch*. When the other group fills, LGWR will then switch to the next available group until it reaches the last redo log file. After filling the last log group, LGWR loops back to the first group and continues writing redo entries.

So, What Happens to the Contents of the First Group?

The answer to that question depends on the archiving mode your Oracle database is running in. A database could be running either in ARCHIVELOG or NOARCHIVELOG mode. When running in the NOARCHIVELOG mode, the LGWR writes into each of the log group and then loops back to the first group and overwrites what it contains. In the event of a failure, this type of mode cannot recover the database to the point of failure. In ARCHIVELOG mode, the redo entries written into the redo groups are copied to a different location by an archiver process (ARC*n*). To speed this archiving process you could activate more than one archiver processes. While running in this mode, the database could recover to the point of failure by applying these archived redo log entries to the restored backup.

Many DBAs with less experience managing Oracle systems at this point wonder the following—if Oracle let's you recover to the point of database failure when the database runs in ARCHIVELOG mode, why would anyone want to run his or her database in NOARCHIVELOG mode? The answer is simple. An Oracle database running in ARCHIVELOG mode runs slower than a database running in NOARCHIVELOG mode, although the performance difference is minimal when the database has been tuned properly. Also, not every Oracle database needs to have all its redo archived. For example, a read-only database used for data warehouse queries wouldn't need to run in ARCHIVELOG mode because once the data has been loaded, users won't be able to make changes anyway.

Another situation where you might not care about archiving user data changes is on development systems. Unlike production systems, wherever user change is important, development systems usually are only utilized by developers coding new programs or enhancing existing systems. The developer may only care that the database structure is the same in development as in production. The developer may populate the development tables with junk data for the purposes of testing. When testing is finished, the developer may want to blow away all the changes and start again from scratch. In this case, archiving all data changes made by the developer would be unnecessary and potentially even counterproductive. Thus, Oracle lets you decide whether or not to archive redo information based on the business needs of the system the database supports.

Switching Archive Modes

In order to switch between these two modes, you must follow these steps:

1. In SQL*Plus, shut down the database you want to change archiving mode on using the `shutdown normal` or `shutdown immediate` command.

2. Start the instance and mount but do not open the database. You can use the `startup mount` command to set up the database in the proper state.

3. Change the archiving status of the database using the `alter database archivelog` or `alter database noarchivelog` command. This command will modify the contents of the control file. If you restart the database using the startup open command, Oracle will bring up the database in the mode you specify here.

4. You should shut down the database at this point and take a complete offline backup. If you don't perform this step and later have to recover the database from datafiles backed up before you changed the archive mode, then the recovered database will not reflect the change in archiving mode. Additionally, if you switched from NOARCHIVELOG mode to ARCHIVELOG mode and didn't backup your database afterward, you will not be able to recover to the point of database failure. This is because the datafiles you use to recover will reflect the fact that Oracle was running in NOARCHIVELOG mode when you took the backup.

5. Reopen the database for normal use with the `alter database open` command.

For Review

1. Online redo log files are the physical files storing the information from the redo log buffers in SGA.

2. Changes made to the data blocks in the database are stored as redo entries in the redo log buffer in SGA.

3. When transactions are committed or this buffer gets full, the redo log entries are flushed into online redo log files.

4. The online redo log files could have mirrored files. Each set of files containing the same data is called a redo log group while the mirrored files in a group are called redo log members.

5. If the database is operating in ARCHIVELOG mode, then the data in online redo log files are archived in the archived redo log files as soon as it gets filled up. This could be done either manually or by using an automatic archiver processes.

6. If the database is operating in NOARCHIVELOG mode, then you do not have to worry about archiving the online redo logs.

Exercises

1. **You are analyzing the redo log structure of your Oracle database. Which of the following choices identifies the name of the background process that writes changes from online redo logs to archived copies in support of a database running in ARCHIVELOG mode?**

   A. LGWR

   B. CKPT

   C. DBW0

   D. ARC0

2. **You are switching your production system from NOARCHIVELOG mode to ARCHIVELOG mode. Which of the following choices identifies the next step to execute after you've issued the appropriate `alter database` statement to change archiving mode?**

   A. Restart the instance.

   B. Mount but do not open the database.

   C. Shut down the database and take a backup.

   D. Open the database and make it available to users.

3. **Finish the following sentence: When transactions get committed, Oracle _____ the contents of the redo buffer to disk.**

Answer Key
1. D. 2. C. 3. Flushes.

Controlling Log Switches and Checkpoints

Redo logs are written sequentially. As Oracle users make changes, the server process generates redo to re-create the changes made within the user's transaction. The redo gets written to the redo buffer. From there, LGWR writes the change to an online redo log. Redo logs are finite in size. When one fills, LGWR has to start writing to the next one in the sequence. A *log switch* occurs at the point at which LGWR completely fills the online redo log group and switches to start writing into the next group.

At every log switch, several events occur. Oracle generates a new sequence number for the online redo log LGWR is about to write. Oracle also performs a checkpoint. A checkpoint occurs every time a log switch occurs. Checkpoints can also occur more often than log switches. During a checkpoint, the checkpoint background process CKPT updates the headers of all datafiles and control files to reflect that it has completed successfully, and signals the DBW*n* to flush the dirty buffers into the data files. The number of buffers being written by DBW*n* is determined by the parameter FAST_START_IO_TARGET (or FAST_START_MTTR_TARGET), if specified. The frequency with which checkpoints occur affects the amount of time Oracle requires for instance recovery. If an instance experiences failure, the dirty blocks that haven't been written to disk must be recovered from redo logs. Even though this instance recovery is handled automatically by SMON, the amount of time it takes to recover depends on the time difference between the checkpoints.

The events that occur at a log switch are as follows. First, LGWR stops writing the redo log it filled. Second, CKPT signals the DBW*n* to flush the dirty buffers into the data files and finally CKPT updates the control files and the data file headers with the checkpoint information. With the checkpointing tasks completed, the LGWR will be allowed to start writing into the next redo log group with a new sequence number.

The DBA has only a small amount of control over log switches. Because users will always change data, there is little the DBA can do to stop redo information from being written. With that said, you can control how often a log switch will occur by changing the size of the online redo log members or manually by forcing a log switch with `alter system switch logfile` command. Larger member files make log switches less frequent, whereas smaller member files make log switches more frequent.

A checkpoint happens not just at the time of log switch, but it can also be configured to happen at the regular intervals by CKPT. You will learn how to do this in the following section. If you configure CKPT to checkpoint at regular intervals, then checkpoints will happen at regular intervals as well as during redo log switch.

Specifying Checkpoint Frequency

If your database redo logs are very large, you should set up the database so that checkpoints happen more often than just at log switches. You can specify more

frequent checkpoints with LOG_CHECKPOINT_INTERVAL or LOG_CHECKPOINT_
TIMEOUT in the `init.ora` file. These two parameters reflect two different
principles on which checkpoint frequency can be based: volume-based intervals
and time-based intervals.

LOG_CHECKPOINT_INTERVAL sets checkpoint intervals to occur on a volume
basis. When LGWR writes as much information to the redo log as is specified by
LOG_CHECKPOINT_INTERVAL, the checkpoint occurs. Periods of high transaction
volume require flushing the dirty buffer write queue more often; conversely, periods
of low transaction volume require fewer redo log entries to be written, and fewer
checkpoints are needed. The effect of using LOG_CHECKPOINT_INTERVAL is much
the same as using smaller redo logs, but it also eliminates the additional overhead of
a log switch, such as the archiving of the redo log.

In versions of Oracle prior to Oracle8*i*, the value you set for
LOG_CHECKPOINT_INTERVAL is the number of operating system blocks
LGWR should write to the redo log (after a log switch) before a checkpoint
should occur. However, this definition changed a little bit with Oracle8*i*. When
LOG_CHECKPOINT_INTERVAL is specified, the target for the checkpoint position
cannot lag the end of the log more than the number of redo log blocks specified by
this parameter. This ensures that no more than a fixed number of redo blocks will
need to be read during instance recovery.

The other way of specifying checkpoint frequency is to use a time-based
interval. This is defined with the LOG_CHECKPOINT_TIMEOUT `init.ora`
parameter. Time-based checkpoint intervals are far simpler to configure than
volume-based ones, although they make checkpoints occur at uniform intervals
regardless of the transaction volume on the system. When
LOG_CHECKPOINT_TIMEOUT is specified, it sets the target for checkpoint
position to a location in the log file where the end of the log was this many seconds
ago. This ensures that no more than the specified number of seconds' worth of
redo blocks needs to be read during recovery. However, there is no difference to
Oracle8*i* except for the formulation. To disable time-based checkpoints, set the
LOG_CHECKPOINT_TIMEOUT to zero. Also, recall the mention of the new
parameter FAST_START_IO_TARGET. This parameter improves the performance of
crash and instance recovery. The smaller the value of this parameter, the better the
recovery performance, because fewer blocks need to be recovered. When the
parameter is set, the DBW*n* writes dirty buffers out more aggressively.

One concern you may have when specifying checkpoints to occur at regular
intervals is that a checkpoint may occur just before a log switch. In order to avoid
log switches causing checkpoints to occur in rapid succession, determine the
average time it takes the redo log to fill and specify a time interval that factors in the
checkpoint that happens at log switches. To do so, review the trace file generated by
LGWR in the directory specified by the BACKGROUND_ DUMP_DEST parameter.

Finally, you can force checkpoints to occur either by forcing a log switch or by
forcing a checkpoint. Both can be done with the `alter system` command. To

force a log switch, issue the `alter system switch logfile` command. To force a checkpoint, issue the `alter system checkpoint` command. Checkpoints that occur without a corresponding log switch are called *fast checkpoints*, whereas checkpoints involving log switches are *full*, or *complete checkpoints*.

For Review

1. A checkpoint is a regular event in the database that signals the database writer to flush the dirty buffers to the data files and to update the control files and the file headers with checkpoint information. This checkpoint frequency is one of the factors that influence the time required for the database to recover from an unexpected failure.

2. Checkpoints occur at least as often as log switches. They can also occur by specifying more frequent intervals using `init.ora` parameters.

3. If the CKPT checkpoint interval exceeds the size of the redo log file, then checkpoints occur only during the redo log switch.

Exercises

1. **You are managing an Oracle database. Which of the following choices describes an event that takes place during a checkpoint?**

    A. DBW0 writes dirty buffers to disk.

    B. LGWR writes new log sequence information to datafile headers.

    C. ARC0 copies archived redo to an alternate location.

    D. CKPT writes redo information to disk.

2. **You would like to reduce the frequency of checkpoints. Which of the following is one way to do so that doesn't impact your `init.ora` file?**

    A. Increase the size of online redo logs.

    B. Adjust LOG_CHECKPOINT_INTERVAL.

    C. Adjust LOG_CHECKPOINT_TIMEOUT.

    D. Disable the ARC0 process.

Answer Key

1. A. 2. A.

Multiplexing and Maintaining Redo Log Files

There are several important details involved in configuring the redo log files of a database. The important detail is the importance of multiplexing your redo logs. In order to improve recoverability in the event of disk failure, the DBA should configure Oracle to multiplex or store each redo log member in a group on different disk resources. This means that Oracle will maintain two or more members for each redo log group. Figure 2-1 illustrates the concept of multiplexing redo log members.

By multiplexing redo log members, you keep multiple copies of the redo log available to LGWR. If LGWR has a problem with a disk that holds the redo log (for example, if the disk controller fails), the entire instance will continue running because another redo log member is available on a different disk. If the redo log group has only one member, or if multiple online redo log members are not multiplexed, and the same failure occurs, LGWR will not be able to write redo log entries and the Oracle instance will fail. This is because LGWR must write redo log entries to disk in order to clear space in the redo log buffer so that user processes can continue making changes to the database. If LGWR cannot clear the space in memory by writing the redo log entries to disk, no further user changes are allowed.

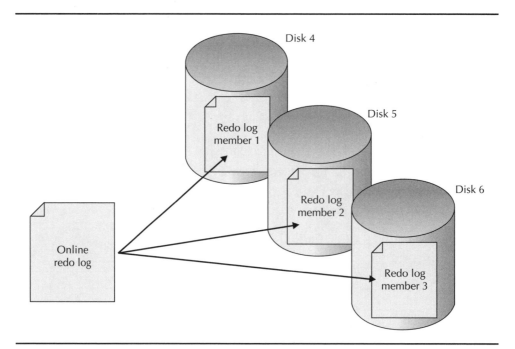

FIGURE 2-1. *Mirroring online redo logs*

Multiplexing redo logs on separate disks benefits the database in other ways, too. The archiver process (ARCn) handles the archiving of redo logs automatically when it is enabled. When the database is run in ARCHIVELOG mode, ARCn can be set up to run. When ARCn is running, it automatically moves archived redo logs to an archive destination specified by the LOG_ARCHIVE_DEST_n parameter in the init.ora file every time a log switch occurs. If redo log groups are on one disk, contention can arise at log switch time when ARCn tries to copy the filled redo log to the archive destination at the same time that LGWR tries to write to the next redo log group. If redo log members and the archive log destination are on different disks, there is little possibility for ARCn and LGWR to contend, because ARCn can work on one disk while LGWR continues on another.

Adding and Removing Redo Logs and Members

A redo log group must have at least one member. To add additional members, use the alter database add logfile member 'filename' to group grpnum, where filename is the name of the file with the absolute path that the group will now have and grpnum is the number of the group to which you are adding the member. You can also add new online redo log groups with the alter database add logfile group grpnum 'filename' statement. Finally, if you have more than two redo log groups, you can remove redo logs, provided at least two logs will remain and the one you want to remove is not currently being written by LGWR. The statement used to remove an online redo log from Oracle is alter database drop logfile group grpnum. Note that dropping the redo log group does not remove the actual file from your host machine. Those files do get automatically removed from the machine when the redo log group or members are dropped.

TIP

Group number and status information for online redo logs can be obtained from V$LOG, as described previously in this chapter.

Renaming Redo Log Files

You can rename redo log member files as well. This functionality can also be used to move an online redo log to another disk location on the machine hosting the Oracle database. In addition, be aware that by moving a redo log, you are also making changes to the control file. If you don't have a backup copy of your control file, it may be difficult to back out of this change to your database later. Thus, you should make a copy of your database (including the control file) before renaming a redo log file. Assuming you've made a backup, the following steps can be used to rename a redo log member file:

1. Issue the `shutdown` command. The database cannot be open while you rename a redo log file.

2. Copy the redo log files from their old location to the new location desired using operating system commands.

3. Start up the instance and mount but do not open the database.

4. Within SQL*Plus, issue the `alter database rename file` command to alert Oracle to the new location of your log file. After issuing this command, you can remove your copy of the redo log from its old (but not its new!) location.

5. Open the database.

6. Make a backup copy of your new control file.

TIP
If the database complains about corrupted redo log file, you can reinitialize the redo log without having to shut down the database. `alter database clear logfile group` *n will do the magic.*

For Review

1. Just like the control file, online redo log files are important for the functioning of database. To prevent accidental loss of them, Oracle enables mirroring of the redo log files. You should definitely mirror members of a redo log group in different disks.

2. If you are archiving the online redo logs, try to alternate the locations of the online redo groups between different disks so that LGWR and ARC*n* do not face disk contention.

3. There will be times when you need to add log groups or log members or drop log groups or log members or even rename log files. Oracle enables you to do all of these using `alter database` commands.

Exercises

1. **Your Oracle database is apparently hung. Users are waiting for their changes to be processed, and no new users can connect to the database. If you wanted to relieve the situation without restarting the Oracle database, which of the following choices identifies a method you might attempt?**

   A. Issue `alter database backup controlfile to trace`.

   B. Issue `alter database archivelog`.

    C. Issue `alter system switch logfile group`.

    D. Issue `alter system set nls_date_format = 'DD-MON-RRRR';`.

2. **You are considering multiplexing your online redo logs in Oracle. Which of the following choices identifies a reason you might consider doing so?**

    A. To reduce contention between the DBW0 and CKPT process

    B. To reduce the risk of database failure due to missing redo logs

    C. To eliminate contention between control file and datafile write activity

    D. To increase DBW0's pace in writing dirty buffers to disk

---

Answer Key
1. C. 2. B.

Managing Online Redo Log Files with OMF

Managing Oracle-managed redo log files is exactly the same as managing Oracle-managed control files. They both use the same `init.ora` parameters and behave in the same way. Refer to the previous section on "Managing Control Files with Oracle-Managed Files" for a full discussion on this topic. We will discuss only the salient points of this feature. Recall that your redo logs are created when you create the database. You can create new redo logs by issuing the `alter database add logfile group` command.

When the database is configured to use OMF by specifying either or both of the `init.ora` parameters for OMF (DB_CREATE_FILE_DEST and DB_CREATE_ONLINE_LOG_DEST_*n*), then there is no need to specify the location or names of the redo log files during the creation of the database. Oracle takes care to create them in a location specified in the OMF parameters and with a standard naming convention. The same is true while creating the redo log groups or members. The value *n* in parameter DB_CREATE_ONLINE_LOG_DEST_*n* specifies the location for a multiplexed copy of the online redo log or control file. You can specify up to five multiplexed copies.

If only DB_CREATE_FILE_DEST parameter is specified, then an Oracle-managed redo log file member is created in the directory specified in the parameter. If both DB_CREATE_FILE_DEST and DB_CREATE_ONLINE_LOG_DEST_*n* parameters are specified, then the later parameter takes the precedence. Whereas the rest of the tablespace Oracle-managed data files are created in the location specified by

DB_CREATE_FILE_DEST, an Oracle-managed log file member is created in each directory specified in the parameters (up to MAXLOGMEMBERS for the database).

The default size of Oracle-managed redo log file is 100MB. This value can be overridden by specifying the size of the redo log files in the `logfile` clause of the `create database` or `alter database` commands. The Oracle-managed redo log file will have the following name format: `ora_%g_%u.log`, where `%g` is the online redo log file group number and `%u` is a unique eight character string. For example, a redo log file could be `/u01/oradata/db1/ora_1_xyz12345.log`. As in the case of any Oracle-Managed Files, when an Oracle-managed online redo log file is dropped its corresponding OMFs on the host are removed automatically.

For Review

1. Online redo logs are created during the database creation and later can be created or dropped using the `alter database` command. In order to create them as Oracle-managed redo log files, two `init.ora` parameters, DB_CREATE_FILE_DEST and DB_CREATE_ONLINE_LOG_DEST_*n*, need to be specified.

2. If only DB_CREATE_FILE_DEST is specified, then all OMFs including redo log files will be created at the location specified by this parameter. Your online redo logs will not be multiplexed in this scenario.

3. When DB_CREATE_ONLINE_LOG_DEST_*n* is specified, regardless of whether DB_CREATE_FILE_DEST is specified or not, the Oracle-managed redo log files will be created in the location specified by the former parameter.

4. If multiple locations are specified by DB_CREATE_ONLINE_LOG_DEST_*n* parameter, then Oracle will create the mirror images of redo logs in each of these locations.

Exercises

1. **You have implemented OMF for redo log management. Which of the following choices reflects a log filename that might be employed when OMF is enabled?**

   A. `log01.log`

   B. `logORCL01.log`

   C. `1_2.log`

   D. `ora_1_asdf1234.log`

2. **Finish the following statement: When values are assigned to initialization parameters DB_CREATE_ONLINE_LOG_1 and DB_CREATE_ONLINE_LOG_2, then Oracle will _____ the redo logs it creates for you.**

Answer Key
1. D. 2. Multiplex.

Chapter Summary

In this chapter, you covered a number of concepts vital in the preparation for the OCP Database Fundamentals I exam. First, you learned about the Oracle data dictionary. You covered how to create the data dictionary using Oracle-supplied scripts. You also covered the difference between dictionary views and base tables, and learned why it is important to use the views and not the base tables. Some of the most important dictionary views in Oracle were also listed in the chapter, along with a description of the data you could find in those views. You learned how to distinguish between dictionary views and dynamic performance views as well. You also learned how to create the Oracle-supplied packages using Oracle-supplied scripts.

After that, we discussed the management of your control files in the Oracle database. You learned about the purpose control files serve in Oracle, as well as how to obtain information from them. You also learned about generating scripts that contain the `create controlfile` command. Last, you learned about managing online redo logs in Oracle. You covered the purpose served by online redo logs and about how to get data about your logs and control files from the data dictionary. Interspersed in these discussions was some coverage of Oracle-Managed Files (OMF), and how to use them pertaining to the creation and maintenance of control files and online redo logs.

Two-Minute Drill

- The Oracle data dictionary contains a host of views to be aware of, which contain information about the contents in and ongoing activities on the Oracle database.

■ Some of the dictionary views to be aware of include those in the following list:

- **USER_OBJECTS, ALL_OBJECTS, DBA_OBJECTS** Gives information about various database objects owned by the current user, available to the current user, or all objects in the database, respectively.

- **USER_TABLES, ALL_TABLES, DBA_TABLES** Displays information about tables owned by or available to the current user, respectively, or all tables in the Oracle database.

- **USER_INDEXES, ALL_INDEXES, DBA_INDEXES** Displays information about indexes owned by or available to the current user, respectively, or all indexes in the Oracle database.

- **USER_VIEWS, ALL_VIEWS, DBA_VIEWS** Displays information about views owned by or available to the current user, respectively, or all views in the Oracle database (including dictionary views).

- **USER_SEQUENCES, ALL_SEQUENCES, DBA_SEQUENCES** Displays information about sequences owned by or available to the current user, respectively, or all sequences in the Oracle database.

- **USER_USERS, ALL_USERS, DBA_USERS** Displays information about the current user or about all users in Oracle, respectively.

- **USER_CONSTRAINTS, ALL_CONSTRAINTS, DBA_CONSTRAINTS** Displays information about constraints owned by or available to the current user, respectively, or all constraints in the Oracle database.

- **USER_CONS_COLUMNS, ALL_CONS_COLUMNS, DBA_CONS_COLUMNS** Displays information about table columns that have constraints owned by or available to the current user, respectively, or all table columns in Oracle that have constraints on them.

- **USER_IND_COLUMNS, ALL_IND_COLUMNS, DBA_IND_COLUMNS** Displays information about table columns that have indexes owned by or available to the current user, respectively, or all columns in Oracle tables that have indexes on them.

- **USER_TAB_COLUMNS, ALL_TAB_COLUMNS, DBA_TAB_COLUMNS** Displays information about columns in tables owned by or available to the current user, respectively, or all columns in all tables in Oracle.

- **USER_ROLES, ALL_ROLES, DBA_ROLES** Displays information about roles owned by or available to the current user, respectively, or all roles in the Oracle database.

- **USER_TAB_PRIVS, ALL_TAB_PRIVS, DBA_TAB_PRIVS** Displays information about object privileges on objects owned by the user or available to the current user, respectively, or all object privileges available to all users in Oracle.

- **USER_SYS_PRIVS, ALL_SYS_PRIVS, DBA_SYS_PRIVS** Displays information about object privileges on objects owned by the user or available to the current user, respectively, or all system privileges granted to all users in Oracle.

- **USER_SOURCE, ALL_SOURCE, DBA_SOURCE** Displays the source code for PL/SQL programs owned by the user or available to the current user, respectively, or all PL/SQL source code in the entire Oracle database.

- **USER_TRIGGERS, ALL_TRIGGERS, DBA_TRIGGERS** Displays information about triggers owned by the user or available to the current user, respectively, or all triggers in the Oracle database.

- **ROLE_TAB_PRIVS, ROLE_SYS_PRIVS, ROLE_ROLE_PRIVS** Displays information about object privileges, system privileges, or roles granted to roles in the database, respectively.

- **DBA_TABLESPACES, DBA_TS_QUOTAS** Displays information about all tablespaces in Oracle, as well as space quotas assigned to users in each tablespace.

- **DBA_DATAFILES, DBA_SEGMENTS, DBA_EXTENTS DBA_FREE_SPACE** Displays information about datafiles in your Oracle database, as well as segments, extents, and free space in each datafile, respectively.

- **DBA_PROFILES** Displays information about user profiles in Oracle. Profiles are a way for you as the DBA to restrict the physical resources of the host system (such as process memory allocation, CPU cycles, and so on) that users may utilize in conjunction with Oracle processing.

- Additionally, there are a host of dynamic performance views that contain information about the ongoing performance of Oracle software. These views include those listed in the following:

  - **V$DATABASE** General information about the database mounted to your instance is kept here.

  - **V$SYSTEM, V$SYSSTAT** Most information about the performance of your database is kept here.

- **V$SESSION, V$SESSTAT**   Most information about performance for individual user sessions is stored here.

- **VLOG, VLOGFILE**   Information about online redo logs can be found here.

- **V$DATAFILE**   Information about Oracle datafiles can be found here.

- **V$CONTROLFILE**   Information about Oracle control files can be found here.

- The `catalog.sql` script creates the data dictionary. Run it after creating a database while connected to Oracle administratively through SQL*Plus.

- The `catproc.sql` script creates the Oracle-supplied packages used often in PL/SQL development. Run it after creating a database while connected to Oracle administratively through SQL*Plus.

- Understand all Oracle physical disk resources—they are control files, redo logs, and datafiles.

- Control files are used to tell the Oracle instance where to find the other files it needs for normal operation.

- The contents of a control file can be found in the script to create it, which Oracle generates with an `alter database backup controlfile to trace`. This file is then found in the directory specified by the USER_DUMP_DEST initialization parameter.

- You will find information about control files, such as where they are located on your host machine, in V$CONTROLFILE, V$CONTROLFILE_RECORD_SECTION, and V$DATABASE.

- It is important to multiplex control files in order to reduce dependency on any single disk resource in the host machine. This is done using the CONTROL_FILES parameter in `init.ora`.

- The Oracle redo log architecture consists of the following components: redo log buffer to store redo entries from user processes, LGWR to move redo entries from memory onto disk, and online redo logs on disk to store redo entries taken out of memory.

- Online redo logs are referred to as groups. The group has one or more files, called members, where LGWR writes the redo log entries from memory. There must be at least two online redo log groups for the Oracle instance to start.

■ Checkpoints are events in which LGWR tells DBWR to write all changed blocks to disk. They occur during log switches, which are when LGWR stops writing the filled log and starts writing a new one. At this point, LGWR will also write the redo log file sequence change to datafile headers and to the control file.

■ Understand the process LGWR uses to write redo data from one log to another and then back again, what happens when archiving is used, what the role of the ARCH process is, and how LGWR can contend with ARCH.

■ Understand how to multiplex redo logs using both the `create database` and `alter database` statements, and why it is important to do so.

■ The OMF feature in Oracle can be used to manage the placement of control files and redo logs on disk. Be sure you understand the use of the appropriate parameters for configuring OMF and the standard filename formats Oracle employs when OMF is used.

Chapter Questions

1. **Flushing dirty buffers out of the buffer cache is influenced to the greatest extent by which of the following processes?**

   A. LGWR

   B. SMON

   C. ARCH

   D. SERVER

2. **How can you decrease the number of checkpoints that occur on the database?**

   A. Set LOG_CHECKPOINT_INTERVAL to half the size of the online redo log.

   B. Set LOG_CHECKPOINT_INTERVAL to twice the size of the online redo log.

   C. Set LOG_CHECKPOINT_TIMEOUT to the number of bytes in the online redo log.

   D. Set LOG_CHECKPOINT_TIMEOUT to half the number of bytes in the online redo log.

3. **Which of the following strategies is recommended when customizing the redo log configuration?**

   A. Store redo log members on the same disk to reduce I/O contention.

   B. Run LGWR only at night.

   C. Store redo log members on different disks to reduce I/O contention.

   D. Run DBW0 only at night.

4. **By allowing user processes to write redo log entries to the redo log buffer, how does Oracle affect I/O contention for disks that contain redo log entries?**

   A. Increases because user processes have to wait for disk writes

   B. Decreases because user processes have to wait for disk writes

   C. Increases because user processes do not have to wait for disk writes

   D. Decreases because user processes do not have to wait for disk writes

5. **Which of the following choices identifies a database component that will be used for multiplexing control files?**

   A. `init.ora`

   B. V$CONTROLFILE

   C. V$DATABASE

   D. DBA_DATAFILES

6. **By default, checkpoints happen at least as often as _____.**

   A. Redo log switches.

   B. `update` statements are issued against the database.

   C. The SYSTEM tablespace is accessed.

   D. SMON coalesces free space in a tablespace.

7. **If all redo log members become unavailable on the database, _____.**

   A. The instance will fail.

   B. The instance will continue to run, but media recovery is needed.

   C. The database will continue to remain open, but instance recovery is needed.

   D. The system will continue to function as normal.

Answers to Chapter Questions

1. A. LGWR

Explanation At a checkpoint, LGWR signals DBW0 to write changed blocks stored in the dirty buffer write queue to their respective datafiles. Choice B is incorrect because SMON handles instance recovery at instance startup and periodically coalesces free space in tablespaces. Choice C is incorrect because ARCH handles automatic archiving at log switches, and even though checkpoints happen at log switches, the overall process is not driven by ARCH. Choice D is incorrect because the server process retrieves data from disk in support of user processes.

2. B. Set LOG_CHECKPOINT_INTERVAL to twice the size of the online redo log.

Explanation The other three choices are incorrect because each of them actually increases the number of checkpoints that will be performed by Oracle. In addition, choices C and D indicate that values set for LOG_CHECKPOINT_TIMEOUT depend on the size of the redo log in bytes, which is not true. LOG_CHECKPOINT_TIMEOUT is a numeric value that determines the timed intervals for checkpoints. Refer to the discussion on checkpoints.

3. C. Store redo log members on different disks to reduce I/O contention.

Explanation Choice A is incorrect because storing all redo log members on the same disk increases I/O contention when log switches occur. Choices B and D are incorrect because DBWR and LGWR should be running at all times on the database. Refer to the discussion on redo logs.

4. D. Decreases because user processes do not have to wait for disk writes

Explanation Allowing users to write redo entries to the redo memory buffer while LGWR handles the transfer of those entries to disk does reduce I/O dependency for user processes. This means that choice D is correct. Choices B and C are paradoxical statements—how can increased wait times lead to better throughput or vice versa? Choice A is the logical opposite of choice D, meaning that choice A is the wrong answer.

5. A. `init.ora`

Explanation Choice A is the `init.ora` file, which contains the CONTROL_FILES parameter. This parameter is where you would define whether you wanted to use multiple copies of the control file and where Oracle should look for them. All other choices are incorrect. They refer to places where you can look for data about your control file, but remember this—the data dictionary can only inform you of the database configuration, never modify it.

6. A.   Redo log switches.

Explanation   Choice A is the only choice given that relates to checkpoints. Refer to the discussion of checkpoints. Working with the SYSTEM tablespace and SMON's coalescing behavior have nothing whatsoever with the behavior of checkpoints. You might be able to make a small case for `update` statements, but even then you have little indication of whether the data change is frequent, infrequent, heavy, or light, and these are the things you'd need to know in order to determine checkpoint intervals. In addition, `update` activity still won't determine checkpoints if you are using LOG_CHECKPOINT_TIMEOUT. Oracle also ensures that the number of redo blocks between the checkpoint and the most recent redo record is less than 90 percent of the size of the smaller redo log. Oracle does this to ensure that the position of the checkpoint has advanced to the current log before that log completely fills.

7. A.   The instance will fail.

Explanation   If a disk becomes unavailable that contains all redo log members for the redo log currently being written, the instance will fail. All other choices are incorrect because they depend on the instance being fully available, which is not the case in this situation. Refer to the discussion of redo log components.

CHAPTER
3

Managing Tablespaces and Datafiles

n this chapter, you will understand and demonstrate knowledge in the following areas:

- Describing the logical structure of the database
- Creating tablespaces
- Changing tablespace size using various methods
- Allocating space for temporary segments
- Changing tablespace status
- Changing tablespace storage settings
- Implementing OMF for tablespaces

Oracle tablespace management is a fascinating concept because it involves mapping plain old files on a disk in your host system to a more abstract concept of space that your Oracle database can store information in. The physical and logical component being mapped together is the basis for understanding what we'll present in this chapter. In it, you will learn about what a tablespace is, how it is managed, and what you must do as an Oracle DBA to keep things flowing smoothly from a storage management perspective. Be sure to pay close attention, because the concepts presented in this chapter will constitute a full 9 percent of material tested on the OCP DBA Fundamentals I exam.

Describing the Logical Structure of the Database

Meet three players in the world of logical Oracle disk resources: tablespaces, segments, and extents. A *tablespace* is a logical database structure that is designed to store other logical database structures. Oracle sees a tablespace as a large area of space into which Oracle can place new objects. Space in tablespaces is allocated in segments. A *segment* is an allocation of space used to store the data of a table, index, undo segment, or temporary object. When the database object runs out of space in its segment and needs to add more data, Oracle lets it allocate more space in the form of an extent. An *extent* is similar to a segment in that the extent stores information corresponding to a table, index, undo segment, or temporary object. You will learn more about segments and extents in the next chapter on storage structures and relationships, so for now, we will focus on tablespaces. When you are logged into Oracle and manipulate storage factors, you are doing so with the logical perspective of tablespaces.

The other perspective you will have on your Oracle database is that provided by the operating system of the host machine. Underlying the logical storage in Oracle is the physical method your host system uses to store data, the cornerstone of which is the *block*. Segments and extents are composed of data blocks, and in turn, the blocks are taken together to comprise a *datafile*. Recall that you specified a value in bytes for an initialization parameter called DB_BLOCK_SIZE. This parameter determined the standard size of each Oracle block. Block size is typically specified as a multiple of operating system block size. Oracle blocks are usually 2KB, 4KB, 8KB, and sometimes 16KB.

Prior versions of Oracle released before Oracle9*i* required that the entire database use only one block size and that once the block size for the database was defined, you couldn't change it later. In Oracle9*i*, Oracle enables you to specify up to five nonstandard block sizes for your database, providing a great deal more flexibility in terms of using one database to fill multiple data management roles in your organization. More information about standard and nonstandard block sizes is discussed in the next chapter.

A tablespace may consist of one or many datafiles, and the objects in a tablespace can be stored by Oracle anywhere within the one or multiple datafiles comprising the tablespace. Although a tablespace may have many datafiles, each datafile can belong to only one tablespace. Figure 3-1 shows you the glasses through which you can view logical and physical disk storage in your Oracle database.

How Oracle Handles Space Management in Tablespaces

Free space management is an important task for Oracle because without it, Oracle would not know where to put things like tables or indexes when you wanted to create and modify them. Prior to Oracle8*i*, all tablespaces were created as *dictionary-managed* tablespaces. Dictionary-managed tablespaces rely on Oracle populating data dictionary tables housed in the SYSTEM tablespace to track free space utilization. With Oracle8*i* and later, there is a new type of tablespace called the *locally managed* tablespace. Locally managed tablespaces use bitmaps stored within the header of the datafiles comprising a tablespace to track the space utilization of the tablespaces. This bitmap represents every block in the datafile, and each bit in the map represents whether that block is free or not.

Within tablespaces, Oracle manages free space by coalescing it into contiguous segments. The system monitor, or SMON background process, in Oracle handles this coalescing activity automatically. When new database objects are created, Oracle will acquire the requested amount of contiguous storage space in the form of a segment for the new object. The amount of space SMON will use is based either on the object's own `storage` clause, the `default storage` clause for that tablespace, or on the uniform extent allocation configured for the tablespace. For OCP, remember that SMON is the process that handles this coalescing of free space

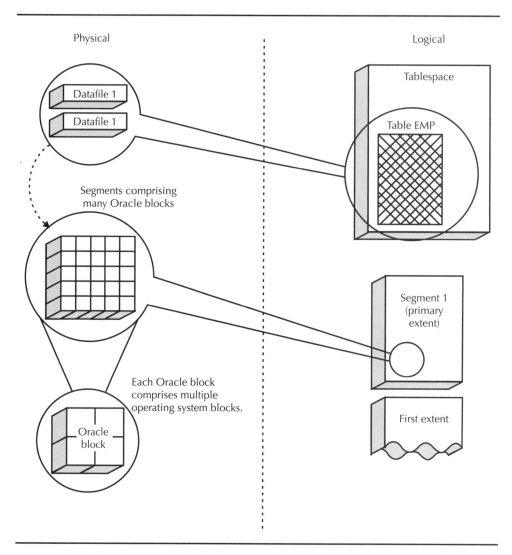

FIGURE 3-1. *The logical and physical views of a database*

into contiguous chunks on an ongoing basis while Oracle is running. As SMON coalesces free space, it either updates the dictionary tables in the SYSTEM tablespace to notify Oracle where the free space is in dictionary-managed tablespaces, or it maintains the bitmap in the datafiles of the tablespace when locally managed tablespaces are used.

TIP
The SYSTEM tablespace is always a dictionary-managed tablespace. Why? Because the dictionary files are in the SYSTEM tablespace anyway, so you don't really get much performance gain with locally managed SYSTEM tablespaces if the data dictionary is already local to the tablespace!

Why might we want to use locally managed tablespaces rather than dictionary-managed tablespaces? Locally managed tablespaces offer better performance because Oracle stores the storage information in file headers and bitmap blocks, eliminating the recursive operations that are required with dictionary-managed space allocation. Beginning in Oracle9*i*, the default space management for tablespaces other than the SYSTEM tablespace is locally managed. However, you can explicitly specify that you want to create a dictionary-managed tablespace.

TIP
We'll discuss the syntax of creating locally managed and dictionary-managed tablespaces in a later section.

Permanent Tablespaces versus Temporary Tablespaces

Regardless of how you configure Oracle to handle space management in your tablespace, the tablespace itself will generally be configured to store two types of segments: permanent and temporary. A permanent segment is one designed to store data for a table or other object that's going to house data for a long time in your database. For example, if you're using Oracle to manage employee information for a large corporation, chances are the employee data is going to stay in the database for many months or years. Thus, you would use permanent segments to house that data in your database. Along that same line of thinking, you would want to house your permanent segments inside a permanent tablespace. In fact, Oracle requires that permanent segments be housed in permanent tablespaces.

In contrast, some forms of data in Oracle are stored only temporarily for the duration of a particular database operation. An example of such an operation is a disk sort, when a user queries Oracle for a very large set of records that must be returned sorted in alphabetical order to the user. A sort operation can require a lot of memory temporarily. Sometimes the sort operation may require more memory than Oracle has available to use. To cope with the lack of memory, Oracle starts writing records to disk in a temporary segment. When Oracle is finished with the sort, Oracle no longer needs the data housed in the temporary segment, so Oracle deletes the temporary segment automatically behind the scenes from both the user and the DBA. You should understand that permanent tablespaces in Oracle are designed to house temporary segments for backward compatibility purposes. However, the space allocation and deallocation required to handle disk sorts take place within a matter of seconds and could be very disruptive to other permanent objects housed in a tablespace, so Oracle also offers a special type of tablespace called a *temporary tablespace*. The temporary tablespace is only used for housing temporary objects. No permanent database objects are allowed.

Default Temporary Tablespaces

Because it is possible for any user in Oracle to issue a long-running query to return data in sorted order, every user in Oracle must be assigned a tablespace where Oracle can write temporary segments in case Oracle must perform a disk sort on behalf of that user. Prior versions of Oracle handled this assignment when the user was created using the optional but highly recommended `temporary tablespace` *tablespacename* clause in the `create user` command. For now, understand that this approach has one tragic flaw. If you didn't specify a `temporary tablespace` clause in your `create user` command, Oracle assigned the user to the SYSTEM tablespace for temporary segment storage needs. This is very bad, because as you will certainly recall, temporary segment storage allocations can be very disruptive to permanent segments stored in the database. In Oracle9*i*, you can create a default temporary tablespace when creating a database by including the `default temporary tablespace` clause in your `create database` command. If you do not create one, then SYSTEM will become the default temporary storage location. However, you will be warned in the alert log about the missing default temporary tablespace. Let's take a quick look at the `create database` command we saw in Chapter 1; however, this time, we've revised it to include a default temporary tablespace:

```
CREATE DATABASE orgdb01
CONTROLFILE REUSE
LOGFILE
  GROUP 1 ('/u01/oradata/oracle/redo1a.log',
           '/u02/oradata/oracle/redo1b.log') SIZE 5M,
  GROUP 2 ('/u02/oradata/oracle/redo2a.log',
           '/u01/oradata/oracle/redo2b.log') SIZE 5M
MAXLOGFILES 40
DATAFILE '/u03/oradata/oracle/sys01.dbf'
  SIZE 50M AUTOEXTEND ON NEXT 30M MAXSIZE 150M
MAXDATAFILES 240
CHARACTERSET WE8IS08859P1
DEFAULT TEMPORARY TABLESPACE temp
TEMPFILE '/u04/oradata/oracle/temp01.dbf' SIZE 100M;
```

TIP
The default temporary tablespace can also be allocated after the database has been created using the `create default temporary tablespace` *command.*

For Review

1. Oracle supports three types of logical disk storage resources—tablespaces, segments, and extents. Underlying these logical structures are the physical structures on the host machine that make up the physical Oracle database: datafiles and Oracle blocks. Tablespaces can have many datafiles, but each datafile must be assigned to only one tablespace.

2. Oracle handles storage management of a tablespace either by storing records in the data dictionary or locally in the headers of each datafile in the tablespace. This difference produces two types of tablespaces: dictionary-managed and locally managed tablespaces, respectively. Starting with Oracle9*i*, Oracle creates non-SYSTEM tablespaces to be locally managed by default.

3. With the creation and dropping of database objects, tablespaces end up with noncontiguous chunks of free space that need coalescing periodically. SMON takes care of this task for us.

4. In Oracle9*i*, you can create a default temporary tablespace to prevent from making the SYSTEM tablespace the temporary tablespace. The default temporary tablespace is created when the database is created.

Exercises

1. **You are conceptualizing the logical to physical mapping of disk storage components of your Oracle database. Which of the following physical database components maps to the tablespace logical component of Oracle?**

   A. Datafile

   B. Segment

   C. Extent

   D. Block

2. You are configuring Oracle to handle space management tasks. Which of the following background processes coalesces free space in datafiles when locally managed tablespaces are in use?

   A. PMON

   B. SMON

   C. ARCH

   D. RECO

3. You haven't configured default temporary storage management on your Oracle database. You then issue the `create user smithers identified by associate`, along with the appropriate privileges. As his first act, SMITHERS issues `select * from emp order by ename` against the EMP table, which contains over 8 million rows. Which of the following choices identifies where temporary segments will be created?

   A. TEMP

   B. UNDO

   C. DATA

   D. SYSTEM

4. You are configuring space management on your Oracle database. Which of the following choices identifies the location where free space information can be found when locally managed tablespaces are in use?

   A. The SYSTEM tablespace

   B. Datafile headers in the SYSTEM tablespace

   C. The local tablespace

   D. Datafile headers in the local tablespace

5. You are configuring locally managed tablespaces for your Oracle database. Which of the following choices identifies the location where free space information can be found for the SYSTEM tablespace when locally managed tablespaces are in use?

   A. The SYSTEM tablespace

   B. Datafile headers in the SYSTEM tablespace

   C. The local tablespace

   D. Datafile headers in the local tablespace

Answer Key

1. A. **2.** B. SMON handles coalescing free space regardless of how you configure tablespace free space management. **3.** D. **4.** D. **5.** A.

Creating Tablespaces

Historically in Oracle, the SYSTEM tablespace was the only tablespace you could create during the creation of the database. This done by explicitly specifying the location of the SYSTEM tablespace datafile in the `create database` command. You can still do things this way, but starting with Oracle9*i*, you can also create two other types of tablespaces at the same time. We've already seen one example, where we created a default temporary tablespace in the `create database` command. The other example is the *undo segment tablespace*. For those of you approaching Oracle9*i* with experience as an Oracle DBA on prior versions, you should make a mental note that undo is the same as rollback. You can create your SYSTEM, temporary, and UNDOTBS tablespaces when you create the Oracle database in Oracle9*i*.

What Are Some Tablespaces You Might Want to Create?

On a typical database, you'll want to segregate different types of data into different tablespaces. At a minimum, you will typically want to create the following tablespaces:

- **SYSTEM**   Every database must have a SYSTEM tablespace. This tablespace is created when you create the database.

- **DATA**   A DATA tablespace is used to house table data.

- **INDEX**   An INDEX tablespace is used to house indexes separate from other types of objects.

- **UNDOTBS**   An UNDOTBS tablespace houses undo segments (called *rollback segments* in prior versions of Oracle). These need to be kept separate from other types of objects due to volatility in allocating extents.

- **TEMP**   A TEMP tablespace houses temporary segments. These also need to be kept separate from other types of objects due to volatility in allocating extents.

- **TOOLS**   A TOOLS tablespace houses objects that support administrative or other tools you might use in conjunction with your database, such as Oracle Enterprise Manager.

TIP
We'll focus on the creation of a tablespace to house object data for the rest of the chapter. Keep in mind that the principles you will learn also apply to the manual creation of these other types of tablespaces.

Creating Tablespaces to House Permanent Segments

All other tablespaces must be created using the `create tablespace` command after the database has been created. Let's look at an example, where we create a locally managed tablespace for a database hosted in a Windows environment that we will probably use to hold table data in our database. How do we know this tablespace will hold table data? Because of the nomenclature—notice that the name of the tablespace is DATA. This typically indicates that the tablespace will be used for housing table data. Let's now look at the actual command:

```
SQL> CREATE TABLESPACE DATA DATAFILE
   2  'E:\oradata\Oracle\data01.dat' SIZE 20M,
   3  'F:\oradata\Oracle\data02.dat' SIZE 30M
   4  AUTOEXTEND ON NEXT 10M MAXSIZE 50M
   5  MINIMUM EXTENT 150K
   6  EXTENT MANAGEMENT LOCAL
   7  PERMANENT ONLINE;
```

TIP
The creation of a tablespace can take a long time, depending on how large you specified your tablespace datafiles to be. This is because Oracle has to physically allocate itself a file of whatever size you specify on the host system. You should be patient during this operation, particularly if you've specified your tablespace to be quite large.

As you can see, there are several components to the `create tablespace` statement. First, you specify the datafiles your tablespace will own, using absolute pathnames. (If you are using an operating system like UNIX to host your Oracle database, be sure the pathnames you specify for your datafiles are ones Oracle has permission to write.) Notice that one of our datafiles has an `autoextend` clause defined for it. This feature enables the datafile to grow past its originally defined size automatically in order to accommodate data growth.

The next step is to specify the `default storage` clause to set options that will be applied to database object creation if the object created does not have storage parameters defined for it. If an object placed in this tablespace has its own `storage` clause defined, then the object's `storage` clause settings will override the tablespace's `default storage` clause settings, with one exception. There is one storage option that when defined in a tablespace cannot be overridden. That option is `minimum extent`, which ensures that every extent size used in the tablespace is a multiple of the specified integer value. The other details of the `default storage` parameters will be explained shortly.

TIP

Permanent tablespaces like the one created in the previous code block can house both permanent segments and temporary segments. This functionality is provided by Oracle for backward compatibility purposes. However, you should put temporary segments in temporary tablespaces.

After that, notice that we define this tablespace to be locally managed using the `extent management local` clause. This is the default space management setting for tablespaces in Oracle9*i* and later releases, so we didn't need to specify the clause in order to achieve local extent management. If we wanted to specify dictionary-managed tablespaces, we would have used the `extent management dictionary` clause instead. You can specify that the tablespace houses permanent database objects with the `permanent` keyword; however, Oracle assumes that the tablespace is a permanent tablespace if the `permanent` keyword is omitted. Finally, we instruct Oracle to bring the tablespace online after creating it using the `online` keyword. This is the default availability status of your tablespace after you create it: online. If you omit the `online` keyword from your `create tablespace` statement, it will still be online. You can also ensure that it is online later by issuing `alter tablespace` *name* `online`.

NOTE

If no specification is made in a `create tablespace` *command whether it is locally managed or dictionary-managed, Oracle9*i *will create it as a locally managed tablespace.*

Creating Tablespaces for Temporary Segments

Most of your tablespaces on the database will house permanent objects that will stick around in your database for a long time. However, remember that you will also want a special tablespace for housing temporary segments. If you have not created a default temporary tablespace during the database creation, then you can create a tablespace to store temporary objects. You should do so for two reasons. The first is to take advantage of Oracle's more efficient usage of sort segments compared to temporary segments. The second reason is to prevent anyone from creating a permanent database object, such as a table or index with data, in the tablespace used for temporary segments. There are some important keywords you should be aware of that are different for creating temporary tablespaces. Take a moment to review the following code block, paying special attention to the keywords in bold:

```
SQL> CREATE TEMPORARY TABLESPACE temp
  2    TEMPFILE '/u06/oradata/oracle/temp01.dbf' SIZE 300M
  3    extent management local;
Tablespace created.
```

Another way to create a temporary tablespace is to include the `temporary` keyword at the end of the `create tablespace` command. Note that we use the `datafile` keyword rather than `tempfile` when we create a temporary tablespace in this manner. The following code block illustrates:

```
SQL> CREATE TABLESPACE temp
  2    DATAFILE '/u06/oradata/oracle/temp01.dbf' SIZE 300M
  3    extent management local TEMPORARY;
Tablespace created.
```

Like permanent tablespaces, your temporary tablespace will be brought online automatically after Oracle creates it. You can view the status of your temporary tablespaces in the data dictionary view DBA_TEMP_FILES. You can also view whether a tablespace is temporary or not by viewing the CONTENTS column of the DBA_TABLESPACES data dictionary view.

NOTE
All tablespaces in the database will use the standard block size defined for the database. A standard block size is the size of the Oracle block that is defined by the parameter DB_BLOCK_SIZE. However, you may also create a tablespace with a nonstandard block size. This could be useful when transporting tablespaces between databases of different block sizes. To use nonstandard block sizes, you must configure subcaches within the buffer cache of System Global Area (SGA) for all the nonstandard block sizes that you intend to use. There are platform-specific restrictions and some platforms may not support it.

Default Storage Options Defined

The `default storage` clause defines storage options that will be applied to newly created database objects if the `create` statement does not have storage parameters defined for it. The initial and next options specify the size of the object's initial segment and next allocated extent, respectively. If `minimum extent` is defined for the tablespace you put your object in, and the value specified for `next` on your database object is less than `minimum extent`, Oracle rounds up to the next highest multiple for `minimum extent` and creates the initial or next extent as that size. This feature can reduce the amount of fragmentation in a tablespace.

TIP

This is really the old way of doing things. You'll want to use locally managed uniform extent allocation in order to take advantage of the new technology. However, you should be familiar with the old way to do this as well in case there's a question on the OCP exam.

The `minextents` and `maxextents` options specify the minimum and maximum number of extents the object can allocate in the tablespace. If you specify `minextents` greater than one and the tablespace has more than one datafile, Oracle will tend to spread extents over multiple datafiles, which can improve performance if those datafiles are also located on different disk resources.

Finally, `pctincrease` enables you to specify a percentage increase in the amount of space allocated for the next extent in the object. For example, if `next` is set to 200KB and `pctincrease` is 50, the second extent would be 200KB in size, the third extent would be 300KB (50 percent more than the second extent), the fourth extent would be 450KB (50 percent more than the third extent), and so on. The minimum value is 0, and the default value is 50. The calculated value is rounded up to the next data block, which is a multiple of five times DB_BLOCK_ SIZE. To make all extents the same size, specify `pctincrease` to be zero.

For Review

1. Non-SYSTEM tablespaces in Oracle are created through the `create tablespace` command.

2. You can specify to autoextend the datafile as the data grows and you can specify the default storage parameters for objects that are created in it. The `default storage` parameters could be the sizes of initial and next extents, and the minimum and maximum number of extents for the object being created.

3. If an object is being created in this tablespace with no storage option, then Oracle takes the default storage parameters of the tablespace while creating the object.

4. Permanent tablespaces can store both permanent and temporary objects in them. Temporary tablespaces, in contrast, can house only temporary segments.

Exercises

1. **You are preparing to create a temporary tablespace for housing a particular type of segment. Which of the following choices identifies the keyword that begins the clause where you will define the absolute path and filename of datafiles associated with this tablespace?**

   A. `permanent`

   B. `temporary`

   C. `datafile`

   D. `tempfile`

2. **You are managing tablespaces to house your data. Which of the following statements is true regarding tablespaces in an Oracle database?**

   A. Permanent tablespaces can house permanent and temporary segments, whereas temporary tablespaces can house only temporary segments.

   B. Permanent tablespaces can house only permanent segments, whereas temporary tablespaces can house only temporary segments.

   C. Permanent tablespaces can house permanent and temporary segments, and temporary tablespaces can also house permanent and temporary segments.

   D. Permanent tablespaces can house temporary segments, and temporary tablespaces can house permanent segments.

3. **You issue the following statement on the Oracle database:**

```
create tablespace tbs_temp
datafile '/u05/oradata/oracle/tbs_temp01.dbf' size 600M
extent management dictionary online;
```

   Which of the following choices correctly describes the tablespace you just created?

   A. You created a locally managed temporary tablespace.

   B. You created a dictionary-managed temporary tablespace.

    C. You created a locally managed permanent tablespace.

    D. You created a dictionary-managed permanent tablespace.

4. **You are creating tablespaces in Oracle. Which of the following keywords or clauses permits the datafiles of a tablespace to grow automatically in order to accommodate data growth?**

    A. `default storage`

    B. `extent management`

    C. `autoextend`

    D. `datafile`

5. **You are creating tablespaces in Oracle with the `create database` command. Which three of the following tablespaces can be created with this command in Oracle9_i_ and later releases?**

    A. SYSTEM

    B. DATA

    C. UNDO

    D. TEMP

Answer Key

1. D. **2.** A. **3.** D. Although the name implies that it is temporary, the tablespace is actually permanent because you omitted the `temporary` and `tempfile` keywords. **4.** C. **5.** A, C, and D.

Changing Tablespace Size

Once a tablespace is created, there are a few different ways to modify the size of a tablespace. The first is by adding new datafiles to the tablespace. This task is accomplished with the `alter tablespace add datafile` statement. You can add as many datafiles to your tablespace as you want, subject to two restrictions. First, you cannot add datafiles that will exceed the physical size of your disk resources (that restriction is pretty straightforward). Let's look at an example of increasing the size of your tablespace by adding datafiles:

```
SQL> ALTER TABLESPACE data ADD DATAFILE
  2  'G:\oradata\Oracle\data03.dat' SIZE 50M;
```

TIP
The length of time Oracle requires to complete this operation depends directly on the size of the datafile you want to add.

The other restriction relates to the following point about `maxdatafiles`. If you have added the maximum number of datafiles permitted for your database as specified by this parameter, and you still need more room, you can increase the size of existing datafiles in your tablespace with the `resize` keyword. Resizing a datafile upward is rarely met with difficulty, unless there is not enough space in the file system. Usually, you can also resize a datafile to be smaller, either through dropping datafiles with `alter database datafile` *filename* `offline drop` or by resizing a datafile to be smaller. This is not always safe, however, especially if the datafile contains segments or extents owned by database objects. Be careful when attempting this sort of activity. Resizing a datafile upward is an operation you perform on individual datafiles, not at the tablespace level. To do so, issue the following statement:

```
SQL> ALTER DATABASE DATAFILE
  2  'G:\oradata\Oracle\data03.dat'
  3  RESIZE 1088M;
```

A third way to expand the size of your existing datafiles is through the use of the `autoextend` feature in Oracle. We've already seen an example of how this is used. As with resizing datafiles, enabling the `autoextend` feature is an operation you perform on individual datafiles, not on the tablespace to which the datafile belongs. To enable automatic extension of your datafile, execute the following statement:

```
SQL> ALTER DATABASE DATAFILE
  2  'G:\oradata\Oracle\data03.dat'
  3  AUTOEXTEND ON NEXT 100M MAXSIZE 1988M;
```

Notice a few important features of the `autoextend` clause. First, you define the size of the next block of space Oracle will acquire for the datafile using the `next` clause. In this case, we tell Oracle to acquire another 100MB whenever it needs to extend the size of the datafile. Second, we tell Oracle the maximum size we want the datafile to be able to grow to using the `maxsize` clause. The value specified for this clause must be larger than the datafile's current size. In this case, we tell Oracle we want this datafile to grow to a size of just under 2GB.

For Review

1. You can grow a tablespace by enabling auto extension of the datafile. By doing so, that datafile will automatically grow when space is needed. You can specify how large it can grow and how big each growth can be.

2. Secondly, you can resize the tablespace to either grow or shrink.

3. Finally, you can grow a tablespace by adding more datafiles.

Exercises

1. **You are increasing the size of your tablespace. Which of the following choices does not identify a command that can be used for this purpose?**

   A. `alter datafile resize`

   B. `alter datafile autoextend`

   C. `alter database add datafile`

   D. `alter tablespace add datafile`

2. **You are resizing a datafile in your Oracle database. Which of the following choices represents an issue you may face when doing so to adjust the size of a datafile in the downward direction?**

   A. SMON may have trouble coalescing free space later.

   B. A segment assigned to a database object may restrict the operation.

   C. Adjusting a datafile size too often may cause Oracle to drop the datafile automatically.

   D. There are no restrictions about adjusting datafiles in the downward direction.

3. **You are increasing the size of your Oracle tablespace by adding more datafiles. Which of the following choices describes a restriction you may encounter in this process?**

   A. The maximum number of datafiles defined for the database could be exceeded.

   B. You might run out of space on disk if the datafile is sized too large.

   C. Choices A and B are both correct.

   D. None of the above

Answer Key
1. C. The add datafile clause is not valid for the alter database command.
2. B. **3.** C.

Allocating Space for Temporary Segments

Recall that temporary segments can be housed in both permanent tablespaces and temporary tablespaces. This functionality is provided for backward compatibility; however, you should always design your databases so that temporary segments are housed in temporary tablespaces and permanent segments are housed in permanent tablespaces. You cannot put a permanent database object (a table, for example) in a temporary tablespace. You can switch a tablespace between being permanent and temporary, provided the permanent tablespace does not contain permanent database objects when you try to switch it to a temporary tablespace. The following code block illustrates this:

```
SQL> create tablespace test01 datafile 'D:\ORACLE\test01.dat'
  2   size 1M default storage ( initial 10K
  3   next 10K pctincrease 0
  4   minextents 1 maxextents 5 ) temporary;
Tablespace created.
SQL> create table dummy3 (dummy varchar2(10)) tablespace test01;
create table dummy3 (dummy varchar2(10)) tablespace test01;
ERROR at line 1:
ORA-02195: Attempt to create PERMANENT object in a TEMPORARY
tablespace
SQL> alter tablespace test01 permanent;
Command completed successfully;
SQL> create table dummy3 (dummy varchar2(10)) tablespace test01;
Table created.
SQL> alter tablespace test01 temporary;
alter tablespace test01 temporary
ERROR at line 1:
ORA-01662: tablespace 'TEST01' is non-empty and cannot be made temporary
```

Temporary Segments in Permanent Tablespaces

A user may be assigned to either a permanent or temporary tablespace for sorting. Users create temporary segments in a tablespace when a disk sort is required to support their use of select statements containing the group by, order by, distinct, or union clauses, or the create index statement, as mentioned earlier. Users can be assigned to either permanent or temporary tablespaces for creating temporary segments. If the user is assigned to a permanent tablespace for creating temporary segments, the temporary segment will be created at the time the disk sort is required. When the disk sort is complete, the SMON process drops the temporary segment automatically to free the space for other users. Because this activity causes high fragmentation, it is advisable to create a separate temporary tablespace to store the temporary segments for all users.

Temporary Segments in Temporary Tablespaces

Temporary space is managed differently in temporary tablespaces. Instead of allocating temporary segments on-the-fly, only to have them be dropped later by SMON, the Oracle instance allocates one sort segment for the first statement requiring a disk sort. All subsequent users requiring disk sorts can share that segment. There is no limit to the number of extents that can be acquired by the sort segment either. The sort segment is released at instance shutdown. Management of temporary segments in this manner improves performance in two ways. First, Oracle saves time by assigning transactions to temporary segments that have been preallocated. Second, Oracle does not deallocate the primary temporary segment once the sorting operation is complete. Rather, Oracle simply eliminates the extents and keeps the primary segment available for the next transaction requiring a sort. All space management for the sort segment in a temporary tablespace is handled in a new area of the SGA called the *sort extent pool*. A process needing space for disk sorts can allocate extents based on information in this area.

Using Locally Managed Temporary Tablespaces

Your temporary tablespaces should be locally managed. This is because Oracle needs fast access to free space information when performing a disk sort, and because disk sorts are notoriously poor performers anyway, there's no sense in making your data dictionary yet another bottleneck in the process. The following is an example for how to create a locally managed temporary tablespace:

```
CREATE TEMPORARY TABLESPACE temp
TEMPFILE '/DISK2/temp_01.dbf' SIZE 500M
EXTENT MANAGEMENT LOCAL
UNIFORM SIZE 10M;
```

You've already seen the use of the `tempfile` and `temporary` keywords to define temporary tablespaces in this manner. However, the `uniform extent size` clause is new to you. Uniform extent sizing is a feature in the world of tablespace management designed to simplify how extents are allocated to objects. Rather than having every object define its own extent allocation via a `storage` clause, or having the tablespace assign objects a storage allocation via the `default storage` clause, `uniform extent management` simplifies the process by assigning every object in the tablespace the exact same extent management configuration. When an object is placed in a tablespace using `uniform extent management`, the tablespace's `uniform extent management` setting overrides any storage configuration included in the object's creation statement.

Space Allocation in Temporary Tablespaces

Temporary tablespaces offer improved performance for disk sorts and better multiuser space management. If you use the `default storage` clause to govern how temporary segments and extents are sized in this tablespace, there are some special rules you should know when defining values for these storage options. Because, by the definition of a disk sort, the data written to disk will equal SORT_AREA_SIZE, your extents must be at least that large. Size your initial sort segment according to the `formula` $num \times$ SORT_AREA_SIZE + DB_BLOCK_SIZE, where num is a small number of your choice used as a multiplier of SORT_AREA_SIZE. This sizing formula allows for header block storage as well as multiple sort data to be stored in each extent. Next, as with undo segments, sort segments should acquire extents that are all the same size, so set `initial` equal to `next`. Also, `pctincrease` should be zero. Finally, the `maxextents` storage option is not used in temporary tablespaces.

You can also create multiple temporary tablespaces to support different types of disk sorts required by your users. For example, you might have an extremely large temporary tablespace for long-running `select order by` statements in report batch processes or for the creation of an index on a large table that is periodically reorganized. In addition, you might include a smaller temporary tablespace for disk sorts as the by-product of ad hoc queries run by users. Each of these temporary tablespaces can then be assigned to users based on their anticipated sort needs.

Obtaining Temporary Segment Information from Oracle

There are several data dictionary views available for obtaining information about temporary segments. The views in the dictionary displaying this information base their content either on temporary segments that exist in the database or on dynamic performance information about temporary segments collected while the instance is running. The views you should remember for viewing temporary segment information include the following:

- **DBA_SEGMENTS**   This gives information about the name, tablespace location, and owner of both types of temporary segments in Oracle. Note that you will only see information on temporary segments in permanent tablespaces while those segments are allocated, but you will see information about temporary segments in temporary tablespaces for the life of the instance.

- **V$SORT_SEGMENT** This gives information about the size of the temporary tablespaces, current number of extents allocated to sort segments, and sort segment high-water mark information.

- **V$SORT_USAGE** This gives information about sorts that are happening currently on the database. This view is often joined with V$SESSION, described earlier in the chapter.

You can obtain the name, segment type, and tablespace storing sort segments using the DBA_SEGMENTS view. Note that this segment will not exist until the first disk sort is executed after the instance starts. The following code block is an example:

```
SQL> select owner, segment_name, segment_type, tablespace_name
  2  from dba_segments;
OWNER SEGMENT_NAME SEGMENT_TYPE TABLESPACE_NAME
----- ------------ ------------ ----------------
SYS   13.2         TEMPORARY    TEST01
```

You can get the size of sort segments allocated in temporary tablespaces by issuing queries against V$SORT_SEGMENT, which you will find useful in defining the sizes for your temporary tablespaces on an ongoing basis. The following query illustrates how to obtain this sort segment high-water mark information from V$SORT_SEGMENT:

```
SQL> select tablespace_name, extent_size,
  2  total_extents, max_sort_blocks
  3  from v$sort_segment;
TABLESPACE_NAME EXTENT_SIZE TOTAL_EXTENTS MAX_SORT_SIZE
--------------- ----------- ------------- -------------
TEST01              3147776            14      44068864
```

Finally, you can see information about sorts currently taking place on the instance by joining data from the V$SESSION and V$SORT_USAGE views. The following code block displays an example:

```
SQL> select a.username, b.tablespace,
  2  b.contents, b.extents, b.blocks
  3  from v$session a, v$sort_usage b
  4  where a.saddr = b.session_addr;
USERNAME TABLESPACE  CONTENTS   EXTENTS BLOCKS
-------- ----------- ---------- ------- ------
SPANKY   TEST01      TEMPORARY       14  21518
```

Dictionary Views for Temporary Tablespace Management

There are a couple of new dictionary views for managing temporary tablespaces:

- **DBA_TEMP_FILES** This dictionary view gives you information about every datafile in your database that is associated with a temporary tablespace.

- **V$TEMPFILE** Similar to DBA_TEMP_FILES, this performance view gives you information about every datafile in your database that is associated with a temporary tablespace.

For Review

1. For the performance of sorting, the extent size of the temporary tablespace should be properly sized. It should be equal to multiple of SORT_AREA_SIZE × DB_BLOCK_SIZE. This is because Oracle always sorts in sizes of SORT_AREA_SIZE.

2. Also, make sure that all extents in temporary tablespace are equal in size, the percentage increase is always zero, and are not coalesced. It is also advisable to have multiple temporary tablespaces for different kinds of sorting needs.

3. Oracle provides many data dictionary views to know about the temporary segments. DBA_SEGMENTS is one static view and V$SORT_SEGMENT and V$SORT_USAGE give dynamic information about the sort segments in existence and how they are being utilized.

4. To know about the temporary tablespaces, Oracle provides DBA_TEMP_FILES and V$TEMPFILE views.

Exercises

1. **You want to find out more information about the space usage allocations for temporary segments. Which of the following dictionary views would assist you in this task?**

   A. V$SORT_SEGMENT

   B. V$TEMPFILE

   C. DBA_TEMP_FILES

   D. DBA_SEGMENTS

2. **You want to convert a temporary tablespace into a permanent tablespace. Which of the following statements is true regarding this operation?**

    A. Temporary tablespaces can be converted into permanent tablespaces when only temporary segments are stored in the tablespace.

    B. Temporary tablespaces can be converted into permanent tablespaces when permanent segments are housed in the tablespace.

    C. Temporary tablespaces can be converted into permanent tablespaces only when the tablespace is not in use.

    D. Temporary tablespaces can be converted into permanent tablespaces with no restrictions.

3. **You want to configure space allocation in temporary tablespaces. Which of the following choices identifies a feature in Oracle that, when implemented, will force the tablespace segment allocations to all be the same size regardless of storage allocations defined on objects placed in the tablespace?**

    A. `default storage`

    B. `storage`

    C. `uniform extent management`

    D. `autoextend`

Answer Key

1. A. **2.** C. **3.** C.

Changing Tablespace Status

One of the `create tablespace` code blocks from a previous lesson describes how to create the tablespace so that it is online and available for use as soon as it's created. Recall also that the `alter tablespace` *name* `online` statement enables you to bring a tablespace online after creation. You can also take a tablespace offline using the `alter tablespace` *name* `offline` statement. You might do this if you were trying to prevent access to the data in that tablespace while simultaneously leaving the rest of the database online and available for use. Individual datafiles can be taken online and offline as well, using the `alter database datafile` *filename* `online` or `alter database datafile` *filename* `offline` statements.

    A tablespace can be taken offline with one of several priorities, including `normal`, `temporary`, and `immediate`. Depending on the priority used to take the tablespace offline, media recovery on that tablespace may be required. A tablespace taken offline with normal priority will not require media recovery, but a tablespace taken offline with immediate priority will. A tablespace taken offline with temporary priority will not require media recovery if none of the datafiles were offline prior to taking the tablespace offline. However, if any of the datafiles were offline before the tablespace was taken offline temporarily due to read or write errors, then media recovery will be required to bring the tablespace back online. The following code block demonstrates taking a tablespace offline with each of the three possible priorities. Note that if you leave off a priority specification, normal priority is assumed.

```
ALTER TABLESPACE data OFFLINE;
ALTER TABLESPACE data OFFLINE NORMAL;
ALTER TABLESPACE data OFFLINE IMMEDIATE;
ALTER TABLESPACE data OFFLINE TEMPORARY;
```

On occasion, you may also have situations that make use of Oracle's capability to specify tablespaces to only be readable. The following code block demonstrates both the code required to make a tablespace readable but not writable, and then to change it back to being writable again:

```
ALTER TABLESPACE data READ ONLY;
ALTER TABLESPACE data READ WRITE;
```

Finally, if you want to eliminate a tablespace, use the `drop tablespace` command. This command has a few additional clauses, such as `including contents` for removing all database objects contained in the tablespace as well as the tablespace itself, and the `cascade constraints` keywords to remove any constraints that may depend on database objects stored in the tablespace being dropped. The following code block demonstrates a `drop tablespace` command:

```
DROP TABLESPACE data INCLUDING CONTENTS CASCADE CONSTRAINTS;
```

TIP
You can now use the same command and take the datafiles out of the operating system with statement `drop tablespace name including contents cascade constraints and datafiles`.

Making a Tablespace Read-Only Online

Recall that a tablespace is the logical view of disk storage and that it may be composed of multiple datafiles. Oracle uses relative datafile numbering conventions that make the datafile number unique to the tablespace, as opposed to earlier versions of Oracle prior to Oracle8, where datafile number is absolutely unique throughout the entire database. A read-only tablespace is one where no user can make a data change to any of the objects stored in that tablespace. There are a few exceptions to this rule. For example, you can drop items, such as tables and indexes, from a read-only tablespace, because these commands only affect the data dictionary, but you cannot create or alter items such as tables or index in read-only tablespaces. This is possible because the `drop` command only updates the data dictionary, not the physical files that make up the tablespace.

In order to make a tablespace read-only, certain conditions have to be met. The tablespace has to be online, the tablespace must not contain any active undo segments, and the tablespace must not be in online backup mode.

In versions of Oracle prior to Oracle8*i*, to make a tablespace read-only, you had to ensure that no user was currently making changes to any of the objects in that tablespace before issuing the `alter tablespace read only` statement. If any active transactions were processing data in the tablespace you wanted to make read-only, an error would occur when you attempted to issue the statement. In Oracle8*i* and later, this is no longer the case. Instead, you can issue the `alter tablespace read only` statement, and Oracle will wait until all active transactions complete, and then make the tablespace read-only. While Oracle waits for the transactions to complete, the tablespace is placed in a transitional read-only mode during which no further write transactions are allowed against the tablespace while the existing transactions are allowed to commit or rollback.

TIP
*In Oracle8*i *and later releases, we do not have to wait for transactions to finish in order to make a tablespace read only. Also, a tablespace must be read-only before you transport it to another database.*

For Review

1. Tablespaces could be in many states. They could be online or offline and read-only or read-write only. Under normal situations where tablespaces are actively used, they are in an online and read-write state. However, under certain conditions, you may want to bring a tablespace in an offline mode (to rename the datafiles) or read-only (to preserve the data in the tablespace).

2. There are many ways a tablespace can brought offline—normal, immediate, and temporary.

3. In order to make a tablespace read-only, certain conditions have to be met. The tablespace should be online and there should be no active undo segments in it. For this reason, the SYSTEM tablespace can never be made read-only as it contains system undo segment in it. Also, the tablespace should not be in online backup mode.

Exercises

1. **You want to make the tablespaces of your Oracle database read-only. Which of the following tablespaces cannot be taken offline due to active undo segments?**

   A. SYSTEM

   B. DATA

   C. INDEX

   D. TEMP

2. **You are about to drop a tablespace. Which of the following statements can be used for dropping tablespaces that contain parent tables in foreign key relationships?**

   A. `alter database datafile offline drop`

   B. `alter tablespace offline immediate`

   C. `drop tablespace cascade constraints`

   D. `drop tablespace including contents`

Answer Key
1. A. 2. C.

Changing Tablespace Storage Settings

Now, consider again the `default storage` parameters you set for a tablespace when you create it. They have no bearing on the tablespace itself, but rather are used as default settings when users issue `create table`, `create index`, or `create undo segment` statements that have no storage parameter settings explicitly defined. You can change the default settings for your tablespace by issuing the `alter tablespace` command, as shown in the following block:

```
SQL> ALTER TABLESPACE data DEFAULT STORAGE ( INITIAL 2M NEXT 1M );
```

You needn't specify all the `default storage` parameters available—only the ones for which you want to change values. However, keep in mind that changing the `default storage` settings has no effect on existing database objects in the tablespace. It only affects storage settings on new database objects and only when those new database objects do not specify their own storage settings explicitly.

Relocating Tablespace Datafiles

Depending on the type of tablespace, the database administrator can move datafiles using one of two methods: the `alter tablespace` command or the `alter database` command. Relocating datafiles underlying a tablespace in Oracle offers tremendous value, particularly when you were trying to eliminate hot spots in the database or distribute I/O load or disk use more evenly across the host machine. When relocating or renaming the datafiles within a single tablespace, use the `alter tablespace` command and when relocating the datafiles for many tablespaces, use the `alter database` command. In either case, executing these commands only modifies the pointers to the datafiles as recorded in the control file. They do not physically rename or move the files in the operating system. The actual renaming or relocation of the datafiles has to be done on the operating system level. The following discussion gives detailed steps how to do the relocation.

NOTE
Even though you may rename the datafiles underlying the tablespaces, you cannot rename the tablespace names using Oracle commands. In order to rename a tablespace, you have to delete the tablespace and re-create it with the new name.

Relocating Datafiles with `alter database`

To relocate datafiles with the `alter database` command, you execute the following steps:

1. Shut down the database.

2. Use an operating system command to move the files.

3. Mount the database.

4. Execute the `alter database rename file` command.

5. Open the database.

6. Back up the database and the control file.

The following code block illustrates these steps in Windows:

```
D:\ORACLE\DATABASE\> sqlplus
Oracle SQL*Plus Release 9.0.1.0.0 - Production
(c)1999, Oracle Corporation. All Rights Reserved.
Enter user-name: sys as sysdba
Enter password:
Connected to:
Oracle9i Enterprise Edition Release 9.0.1.0.0 - Production
With the Partitioning and Objects options
PL/SQL Release 9.0.1.0.0 - Production
SQL> shutdown immediate
Database closed.
Database dismounted.
ORACLE instance shut down.
SQL> host move tmp1jsc.ora temp1jsc.ora
        1 file(s) moved.
SQL> startup mount pfile=initjsc.ora
Total System Global Area          14442496 bytes
Fixed Size                           49152 bytes
Variable Size                     13193216 bytes
Database Buffers                   1126400 bytes
Redo Buffers                         73728 bytes
Database mounted.
SQL> alter database rename file
    2> 'D:\ORACLE\DATABASE\TMP1JSC.ORA'
    3> to
    4> 'D:\ORACLE\DATABASE\TEMP1JSC.ORA';
Statement Processed.
SQL> alter database open;
Statement processed.
```

Relocating Datafiles with `alter tablespace`

Use the following process to rename a datafile with the `alter tablespace` command:

1. Take the tablespace offline.

2. Use an operating system command to move or copy the files.

3. Execute the `alter tablespace rename datafile` command.

4. Bring the tablespace online.

5. Back up the database and the control file.

Limitations in Oracle9*i*

In general, you will experience the following limitations in Oracle9*i* with respect to tablespaces:

- The maximum number of tablespaces per database is 64,000.

- The operating system-specific limit on the maximum number of datafiles allowed in a tablespace is typically 1,023 files; however, this number varies by operating system.

For Review

1. When creating database objects such as tables and indexes, if no storage parameters are specified, Oracle takes the tablespace storage parameters as the defaults and uses them for creating these objects.

2. These default storage parameters of a tablespace can be modified after the tablespaces are created using `alter tablespace` command. The modified default storage parameters of a tablespace take effect only on the new objects that will be created but not the existing ones.

3. Very often you would need to rename or relocate the tablespace datafiles. Depending on how many datafiles you need to rename or relocate, you have the option to use two Oracle commands—`alter tablespace` and `alter database`.

4. When using the `alter database` command, you need to shut down the database, move the datafiles, mount the database, give the Oracle command, and then bring up the database.

5. When using the `alter tablespace` command, you can either shut down the database or bring the tablespace offline, move the datafiles, mount the database, give the Oracle command, and open the database.

6. After relocating or renaming the datafiles, it is highly advisable to back up the database and the control file.

Exercises

1. **You are moving a datafile from one location on disk to another. After copying the physical file to the new location, which of the following steps would be appropriate to continue the task?**

   A. Bring the tablespace online.

   B. Bring the database online.

   C. Issue the appropriate `alter database` command to inform Oracle of the move.

   D. Issue the appropriate `alter system` command to inform Oracle of the move.

2. **You alter a tablespace's `default storage` settings in the Oracle database to increase the size of initial extents. Which of the following choices identifies when the change will take effect for tables that already exist in that tablespace?**

   A. The change takes effect immediately.

   B. The change takes effect when data is added to the table.

   C. The change takes effect when data is removed from the table.

   D. The change will not take effect for existing tables.

Answer Key
1. C. 2. D.

Oracle-Managed Files (OMF)

By this time, you have been introduced to Oracle-Managed Files (OMF) at least three times: once as an introduction in the first chapter and twice to introduce Oracle-managed redo log files and Oracle-managed control files. We will not spend too much time in this section on the functionality of this feature except to introduce how they are used while creating or dropping tablespaces. OMF is not intended for production systems but more for development or test databases to simplify the datafile management while managing the tablespaces. To create Oracle-managed datafiles for tablespaces or tempfiles or UNDOTBS tablespaces, you need to define the parameter DB_CREATE_FILE_DEST in the `init.ora` file. This parameter should point to the default location where all Oracle-managed datafiles or tempfiles need to be created. The following is an example of defining this parameter in Windows:

```
DB_CREATE_FILE_DEST = 'C:\Oracle\oradata\DB1'
```

Creating OMF Datafiles for Tablespaces

OMF datafiles can be created for regular tablespaces and UNDOTBS tablespaces. (UNDOTBS tablespaces will be discussed further in Chapter 4.) When creating the tablespace, the `datafile` clause is optional. If you include the `datafile` clause, then the datafile name is optional. If the `datafile` clause is omitted entirely or does not include a filename, then your datafile is created in the location specified by the DB_CREATE_FILE_DEST parameter. The following code block contains an example of how OMF datafiles can be created or altered:

```
SQL> show parameter db_create_file_dest
NAME                      TYPE         VALUE
---------------------     ----------   --------------------
db_create_file_dest       string       C:\oracle\oradata\DB1
SQL> create tablespace data datafile size 25M;
Tablespace created.
SQL> select file_name, tablespace_name, bytes/1024/1024 as megs
  2  from dba_data_files
  3  where tablespace_name = 'DATA';
FILE_NAME                                          TABLESPACE MEGS
--------------------------------------------       ---------- ----
C:\ORACLE\ORADATA\DB1\ORA_DATA_ZVSRKH00.DBF        DATA         25
```

The previous code shows the creation of tablespace with no filename specification or the location it has to be created except for the size. When you query the location of the datafile for the tablespace created, you will find it created at the location specified by the parameter DB_CREATE_FILE_DEST. Note the name of the file and the size. When you drop a tablespace containing Oracle-managed datafiles, the datafiles are automatically removed from the underlying operating system.

Creating OMF Tempfiles for Temporary Tablespaces

When creating the temporary tablespace with OMF, the `tempfile` clause is optional. If you include the `tempfile` clause, then the filename is optional. If the `tempfile` clause or the filename is not specified, then the datafile will be created at the location specified by DB_CREATE_FILE_DEST parameter. The following code block contains an example of how OMF tempfiles can be created or altered.

```
SQL> create temporary tablespace temptbs;
Tablespace created.
```

```
SQL> select tablespace_name, contents from dba_tablespaces
  2  where tablespace_name = 'TEMPTBS';
TABLESPACE CONTENTS
---------- ---------
TEMPTBS    TEMPORARY
SQL> select file_name, tablespace_name
  2  from dba_temp_files;
FILE_NAME                                         TABLESPACE
------------------------------------------------- ----------
C:\ORACLE\ORADATA\DB1\TEMP01.DBF                  TEMP
C:\ORACLE\ORADATA\DB1\ORA_TEMPTBS_ZVSRZ200.TMP    TEMPTBS
```

For Review

1. Oracle-Managed Files (OMF) is a new feature of Oracle9*i* that eases the administration of datafiles for tablespaces, control files, and redo log files. Defining the parameter DB_CREATE_FILE_DEST in `init.ora` file activates OMF for tablespaces. This parameter should point to a location on the machine where the OMF datafiles will be created by default.

2. With OMF active, you do not need to specify the `datafile` clause or even the datafile name while creating the tablespaces. The same holds true while creating the temporary tablespaces where you don't have to specify the `tempfile` clause. By skipping these clauses, Oracle creates the datafiles in the default location specified by the previous `init.ora` parameter. If no filename is specified, then Oracle uses a default naming convention that keeps the datafiles unique from each other.

Exercises

1. **You are creating a tablespace on a database where OMF is enabled. Which of the following choices identifies how Oracle determines what the name of the file will be?**

   A. Oracle must use the contents of the mandatory `datafile` clause to name the file.

   B. Oracle must use the contents of the mandatory `tempfile` clause to name the file.

   C. Oracle will name the file according to its own default settings in all cases.

   D. Oracle will name the file according to its own default settings if no `datafile` or `tempfile` clause is specified.

2. **You are implementing OMF on your Oracle database. When OMF is enabled, Oracle manages creation and removal of datafiles from the host system for which of the following tablespaces?**

   A. SYSTEM tablespace only

   B. UNDOTBS tablespaces only

   C. TEMP tablespace only

   D. All tablespaces in the database

Answer Key

1. D. **2.** D.

Chapter Summary

In this chapter, you learned the core concepts of Oracle related to tablespaces and their management. We covered the physical mapping of datafiles and blocks to their logically associated counterparts: the tablespace, segment, and extent. We also covered how to create tablespaces. You learned about the different types of free space management that Oracle supports, including dictionary-managed tablespaces and locally managed tablespaces. You also learned about the differences between permanent tablespaces and temporary tablespaces with respect to the types of segments each can store. You learned how to change the size of tablespaces using various methods, such as adding more datafiles or increasing the size of datafiles. The use of the `autoextend` feature for datafiles was also discussed in some detail. We then discussed temporary tablespaces in some detail, including the different methods for creating them. You learned how to alter tablespace availability status and `default storage` settings. Finally, we covered implementation of Oracle-Managed Files (OMF) with respect to tablespace management.

Two-Minute Drill

■   Understand how tablespaces and datafiles relate to one another. A tablespace can have many datafiles, but each datafile can associate with only one tablespace.

■   At database creation, there is one tablespace—SYSTEM. In Oracle9*i*, it is possible to create a default temporary tablespace for the database and an UNDOTBS tablespaces as well.

- All other tablespaces are created with the `create tablespace` command.

- There are two methods Oracle uses for free space management in a tablespace. Dictionary-managed tablespaces have all their free space information stored and managed via the Oracle data dictionary. Locally managed tablespaces have all their free space information stored and managed in the datafile headers of all tablespace datafiles.

- The DBA should *not* place all database objects into that tablespace, because often their storage needs conflict with each other. Instead, the DBA should create multiple tablespaces for the different segments available on the database and place those objects into those tablespaces.

- The SMON process handles periodic coalescence of noncontiguous free space in dictionary-managed tablespaces into larger, contiguous blocks of free space. No coalescence takes place in locally managed tablespaces, however.

- Permanent segments store data in permanent database objects, such as tables.

- Temporary segments store data in temporary segments, generated whenever Oracle performs a disk sort.

- Temporary tablespaces differ from permanent tablespaces in that only temporary segments can be stored in them. In contrast, permanent tablespaces can house both permanent and temporary segments. However, for practical purposes you learned about in the chapter, temporary segments should be kept out of permanent tablespaces.

- Tablespaces are brought online by Oracle automatically after they are created by default.

- In Oracle9*i*, all tablespaces use local extent management by default unless you specify otherwise at tablespace creation time.

- Temporary tablespaces should use local extent management because of performance reasons.

- A new memory area called the sort extent pool manages how user processes allocate extents for disk sorts in temporary tablespaces.

- SMON handles deallocation of temporary segments in permanent tablespaces when the transaction no longer needs them.

- You cannot create permanent database objects, such as tables, in temporary tablespaces. You also cannot convert permanent tablespaces into temporary ones unless there are no permanent objects in the permanent tablespace.

- You can get information about temporary segments and sort segments from the DBA_SEGMENTS, V$SORT_SEGMENT, V$SESSION, and V$SORT_USAGE dictionary views.

- A sort segment exists in the temporary tablespace for as long as the instance is available. All users share the sort segment.

- The size of extents in the temporary tablespace should be set to a multiple of SORT_AREA_SIZE, plus one additional block for the segment header, in order to maximize disk sort performance.

- Know what dictionary views are used to find information about storage structures, including DBA_SEGMENTS, DBA_TABLESPACES, DBA_TS_QUOTAS, V$TABLESPACE, DBA_EXTENTS, DBA_FREE_SPACE, and DBA_FREE_SPACE_COALESCED.

- You can change the availability status of tablespaces using the `alter tablespace` command. Review the chapter to understand all the different statuses available.

- You can use the Oracle-Managed Files (OMF) feature in conjunction with tablespace management. When OMF is used, you do not need to specify the name or location of datafiles related to the tablespaces you want to create.

Fill-in-the-Blank Questions

1. The Oracle background process that handles periodic coalescence of free space in a tablespace is _____.

2. The status of a tablespace as soon as it is created is _____.

3. This tablespace cannot be brought offline as long as the database is open: _____.

4. You should configure temporary segments/extents to be a multiple of this `init.ora` parameter value: _____.

Chapter Questions

1. **The keyword that prevents you from creating a table in a tablespace marked for use when you run `select order by` statements on millions of rows of output is which of the following choices?**

   A. `lifespan`

   B. `permanent`

   C. `online`

   D. `offline`

   E. `temporary`

   F. `read only`

2. **When no storage options are specified in a `create table` command, what does Oracle use in order to configure the object's storage allocation?**

   A. The default options specified for the user in the tablespace

   B. The default options specified for the table in the tablespace

   C. The default options specified for the user in the database

   D. The default options specified for the table in the database

3. **To determine the space allocated for temporary segments, the DBA can access which of the following views?**

   A. DBA_TABLESPACES

   B. DBA_TABLES

   C. DBA_SEGMENTS

   D. DBA_FREE_SPACE

4. **The process that most directly causes fragmentation in a tablespace storing temporary segments because it deallocates segments used for disk sorts is which of the following choices?**

   A. Server

   B. DBWR

   C. SMON

   D. LGWR

5. **Which of the following choices best describes the methodology for sizing extents for the sort segments on your Oracle database?**

   A. DB_BLOCK_SIZE + 6

   B. X * SORT_AREA_SIZE + DB_BLOCK_SIZE

   C. (avg_row_size - init_row_size) * 100 / avg_row_size

   D. 100 - pctfree - (*avg_row_size* * 100) / *avail_data_space*

6. **Each of the following choices identifies an event in a series of events that are run from SQL*Plus. If A is the first event and D is the last event, which of the following choices identifies the event that will cause an error?**

   A. create tablespace TB01 datafile '/oracle/tb01.dbf' default storage

   B. (initial 10K next 10K pctincrease 0 minextents 4 maxextents 20) temporary;

   C. create table my_tab (my_col varchar2(10)) tablespace TB01;

   D. alter tablespace TB01 permanent;

   E. create table my_tab (my_col varchar2(10)) tablespace TB02;

7. **You are trying to determine how many disk sorts are happening on the database right now. Which of the following dictionary tables would you use to find that information?**

   A. V$SESSION

   B. V$SYSSTAT

   C. DBA_SEGMENTS

   D. V$SORT_USAGE

Fill-in-the-Blank Answers

 1. SMON

 2. Online

 3. SYSTEM

 4. SORT_AREA_SIZE

Answers to Chapter Questions

 1. E. `temporary`

Explanation Oracle enforces the intended use of a temporary tablespace through the use of the `temporary` keyword. There is no `lifespan` keyword, although the concept of a life span is very important in understanding tablespace fragmentation, eliminating choice A. Choices C, D, and F are incorrect because the tablespace availability status is not the factor that is being tested in this situation. Finally, although there is a difference between permanent and temporary tables, `permanent` is not an actual keyword used anywhere in the definition of your tablespace.

 2. B. The default options specified for the table in the tablespace

Explanation All `default storage` parameters for table objects are specified as part of the tablespace creation statement. A default tablespace can be named for a user on username creation, along with a maximum amount of storage in a tablespace for all objects created by the user. However, there are no `default storage` parameters on a table-by-table basis either in the database or for a user. Refer to the discussion of tablespace creation.

 3. C. DBA_SEGMENTS

Explanation Choices A and D are incorrect because they are not actual views in the data dictionary. Choice B is incorrect because DBA_TABLES only lists information about the tables in the database, not the temporary segments created as part of a sort operation. Refer to the discussion of viewing storage information in Oracle.

 4. C. SMON

Explanation The SMON process automatically drops temporary segments from the permanent tablespace as soon as they are no longer needed by the transaction. The server process can only retrieve data from disk, eliminating choice A. DBWR handles writing data changes to disk, but does not drop the temporary segment, eliminating choice B. Choice D is also incorrect because LGWR handles writing redo log entries to disk, as explained in Chapter 7.

5. B. `X * SORT_AREA_SIZE + DB_BLOCK_SIZE`

Explanation   If the data to be sorted was any smaller than the `initsid.ora` parameter SORT_AREA_SIZE, then the sort would take place in memory. Thus, you can be sure that all disk sorts will write data at least as great as SORT_AREA_SIZE to disk, so you should size your sort segment to be a multiple of that parameter. Because the sort segment will need a header block, adding in DB_BLOCK_SIZE is required to make the extra room for the header. Choices C and D are formulas for determining `pctfree` and `pctused`, respectively, so they are wrong. Choice A is used to determine the number of undo segments your database needs, making that one wrong as well.

6. B. `create table my_tab (my_col varchar2(10))`
        `tablespace TB01;`

Explanation   Because tablespace TB01 is temporary, you cannot create a permanent object like a table in it, making choice B correct. Incidentally, if the tablespace created in choice A had been permanent, then choice C would have been the right answer because an error occurs when you try to convert a permanent tablespace into a temporary one when the tablespace contains a permanent object. Choice D could be correct in that scenario, too, because your MY_TAB table would already exist.

7. D.   V$SORT_USAGE

Explanation   The V$SORT_USAGE view shows the sessions that are using sort segments in your database. Although you may want to join that data with the data in choice A, V$SESSION, to see the username corresponding with the session, V$SESSION by itself gives no indication about current disk sorts. V$SESSTAT or DBA_SEGMENTS do not either, eliminating those choices as well.

CHAPTER
4

Storage Structures
and Undo Data

n this chapter, you will learn about and demonstrate knowledge in the following areas:

- Storage structures and relationships
- Managing undo data

As a DBA, part of your daily job function is to create database objects. This is especially true for database administrators who manage development and test databases. However, even DBAs working on production systems will find that a good deal of their time is spent exploring the depths of setting up database objects. In this chapter, you will cover what you need to know about the underlying storage structures like segments and extents that house database objects like tables and indexes in Oracle. You will also learn about undo segments, which are important data structures used for managing transactions and read-consistency in Oracle. The contents of this chapter lay the foundation for management of tables, indexes, and integrity constraints, which are topics covered in Chapter 5. The information covered in this chapter comprises about 14 percent of material tested on the OCP DBA Fundamentals I exam.

Storage Structures and Relationships

In this section, you will cover the following topics concerning storage structures and relationships:

- Different segment types and their uses
- Using block space utilization parameters
- Obtaining information about storage structures
- Criteria for separating segments

The storage of database objects in Oracle can often become a cantankerous matter, because each of the different types of database objects has its own storage needs and typical behavior. What's more, the behavior of one type of database object often interferes with the behavior of other objects in the database. As the Oracle DBA, your job is to make sure that all objects "play well together." To help you with OCP and in being a DBA, this section will discuss the different segment types and their uses. You'll also learn how to control Oracle's use of extents, the management of space at the block level, where to go for information about your database storage allocation, and how to locate segments by considering fragmentation and lifespan.

TIP
Refer to the discussion titled "Describing the Logical Structure of the Database" listed as a subtopic for the "Storage Structures and Relationships" section, which is covered in Chapter 3. The OCP Candidate Guide for the Oracle9i DBA track has the same discussion topic listed for both sections. For brevity's sake, we'll only cover it once.

Different Segment Types and Their Uses

For a quick review, the logical structure of your database consists of the following components: tablespaces, segments, and extents. Tablespaces are logical structures that house Oracle database objects and are comprised of one or more datafiles. Segments are collections of physical data blocks that are used for housing the data in database objects (for example, a table). When Oracle runs out of room in the segment used for housing data in that object, Oracle acquires another set of physical data blocks to house the data being added. This next set of physical data blocks is called an extent.

In the previous chapter, we said that different types of objects need different types of tablespaces to store them. In contrast, Oracle usually creates a database with only one tablespace—the SYSTEM tablespace. This tablespace should only be used for housing Oracle data dictionary and SYSTEM undo segments. Oracle9i permits you to create undo and temporary tablespaces when you create the database, so at a minimum, in addition to the SYSTEM tablespace, you will have separate tablespaces for your tables, indexes, undo segments, and temporary segments.

In order to understand the different types of tablespaces (and why it is a bad idea to ever try to store all your database objects in the SYSTEM tablespace), you must understand the different types of objects that a tablespace may store. Every database object, such as tables or undo segments, ultimately consists of segments and extents. For this reason, the discussion focuses on the different types of segments available on the Oracle database and how they are used.

Table Segments and Their Usage

The first type of segment is the table segment. Each segment contains data blocks that store the row data for that table. The rate at which the table fills and grows is determined by the type of data that table will support. For example, if a table supports an application component that accepts large volumes of data insertions (sales order entries for a popular brand of wine, for example), the segments that comprise that table will fill at a regular pace and rarely, if ever, reduce in size. Therefore, the DBA managing the tablespace that stores that segment will want to plan for regular growth. If, however, this table is designed for storing a small amount of validation data, the size requirements of the table may be a bit more static. In this case, the DBA may want to focus more on ensuring that the entire table fits comfortably into one segment, reducing the potential fragmentation that extent allocation could cause. Still another factor to consider when planning table segments is whether or not you intend to use parallel processing on your Oracle database. Under those circumstances, you would actually want your table divided into several segments and extents, or even to use partitioning. We'll consider this topic in more detail shortly.

Index Segments and Their Usage

Another type of segment is the index segment. As with table segments, index segment growth is moderated by the type of role the index supports in the database. If the table to which the index is associated is designed for volume transactions (as in the wine example mentioned previously), the index also should be planned for growth. However, the index will almost invariably be smaller than the tables in your database, because it only houses one or a few columns from the table in an easy-to-search format, along with the ROWID information for the associated rows from the table.

What does an index consist of exactly? An index consists of a list of entries for a particular column (the indexed column) that can be easily searched for the values stored in the column. Corresponding to each value is the ROWID for the table row that contains that column value. The principle behind index growth is the same as the growth of the corresponding table. If an index is associated with a table that rarely changes, the size of the index may be relatively static. However, if the index is associated with a table that experiences high `insert` activity, then plan the index for growth as well. Again, however, if you plan to use parallel processing in your database, you might actually want your index data stored in a few segments or even to use partitioning. Again, we'll discuss the criteria for separating index segments shortly.

Undo Segments and Their Usage

Undo segments are different from the table and index segments just discussed. Undo segments store data changes from transactions to provide read consistency and transaction concurrency. The segments used to store data for tables and indexes are generally for ongoing use, meaning that once data is added to a table or index segment, it generally stays there for a while. Undo segments aren't like that. Instead, once a user process has made its database changes and `commits` the transaction, the space in the undo segment that held that user's data is released for reuse in support of another user's transaction. Oracle's undo segment architecture is designed to allow the undo segment to reuse that space. Usually, an undo segment has some extents allocated to it at all times to store uncommitted transaction information.

As the number of uncommitted transactions rises and falls, so, too, does the amount of space used in the undo segment. Where possible, the undo segment will try to place uncommitted transaction data into an extent that it already has allocated to it. For example, if an undo segment consists of five extents, and the entire initial extent contains old data from committed transactions, the undo segment will reuse that extent to store data from new or existing uncommitted transactions once it fills the fifth extent. However, if the undo segment fills the fifth extent with data from a long uncommitted transaction, and the first extent still has data from uncommitted transactions in it, the undo segment will need to allocate a new extent. Various long- and short-running transactions on your Oracle database can cause undo segments to allocate and deallocate dozens of extents over and over again throughout the day, which can adversely affect the growth of other database objects because of tablespace fragmentation. Thus, it is wise to keep undo segments by themselves, in their own undo tablespace.

TIP

You can create an undo tablespace when you issue the `create database` *command by including the* `undo tablespace` *name* `datafile` `'filename' size` *number*`[K|M]` *clause in that command. If you don't create an undo tablespace when you create the database, you should create one later using the* `create tablespace` *command.*

Temporary Segments and Their Usage

Next, consider the temporary segment. True to its name, the temporary segment is allocated to store temporary data for a user transaction that cannot all be stored in memory. One popular use for temporary segments in user processes is for sorting data into a requested order. These segments are allocated on-the-fly and dismissed when their services are no longer required. Their space utilization is marked by short periods of high storage need followed by periods of no storage need. Because you have no idea when a temporary segment could come in and use all the available space in a tablespace, you can't make an adequate plan to accommodate the growth of other database objects—you really need to keep temporary segments in their own tablespace as separate from other database objects as possible.

TIP
You can create a default temporary tablespace along with your Oracle database using the default temporary tablespace *clause in the* create database *command. If you don't create a temporary tablespace when you issue the* create database *command, you should create them later using the* create default temporary tablespace *command.*

Beyond the Basics: LOB, Cluster, and IOT Segments

The final types of segments that may be used in your Oracle database are LOB segments, cluster segments, and IOT segments. LOB stands for large object, and a large object in Oracle will use a special type of segment to house its data. If your database uses large objects frequently, you may want to create a separate tablespace to hold these objects. Otherwise, don't bother to create the extra tablespace.

You may have heard of clustered tables—a physical grouping of two or more tables in the same segment around a common index. Cluster segments support the use of clusters on the database. The sizing of cluster segments and planning for their growth is complex and should be performed carefully, as each segment will essentially be storing data from two different tables in each block.

Finally, IOT stands for index-organized table, in which essentially the entire table is stored within the structure. This was historically reserved only for use by indexes. Obviously, these segments have storage needs that are similar to indexes. However, your use of cluster and IOT segments will probably be so limited that you don't need to worry about any potential conflict between these objects and your other database objects.

A Note about Database Tools

Database administrative tools like Oracle Enterprise Manager operate based on a set of tables, indexes, and other database objects that collect data about your database. This set of database objects is often called a *repository*. Although the segments that house repository objects are the same as those segments that house your data, you should create a separate tablespace to store repository objects for several reasons. One reason is that this will keep a logical division between your organization's data and the tool's data. Another reason is that, although it is not likely, the repository may have a table or other object with the same name as an object in your database, causing a conflict. By using a special TOOLS tablespace to store objects used by your database administrative tools, you will ease your own efforts later.

Why Separate Segments into Different Tablespaces?

In order to answer that question, let's consider the fragmentation potential for the different segments (and thus tablespaces) you may store in your database. This will help you understand why it is so important to store these different types of segments in different tablespaces. First, consider the following question: What makes fragmentation happen? A tablespace gets fragmented when objects stored in the tablespace are truncated or dropped and then re-created (or, for undo segments, when extents the object has acquired are deallocated). The amount of time a segment or extent will stay allocated to a database object is known as its *lifespan*. The more frequently an extent is deallocated, the shorter the extent's lifespan. The shorter the lifespan, the more fragmented your tablespace can become. The SMON background process continuously looks for smaller fragments of free space left over by `truncate` or `drop` operations, and pieces or coalesces them together to create larger chunks of free space.

Now, consider the potential for tablespace fragmentation on different tablespaces. The SYSTEM tablespace houses the system undo segment and the data dictionary. Oracle manages its SYSTEM tablespace effectively, and extents have a long lifespan, so you are likely to see very little or no fragmentation in this tablespace. Your TOOLS tablespace will likely have little fragmentation, because you won't (and shouldn't) typically go into your TOOLS tablespace and manage things yourself—your best bet is to let the administrative tool manage the repository itself. Again, extents have a long lifespan.

The next two tablespaces to consider are DATA and INDEX. The amount of fragmentation that may happen with these tablespaces will depend completely on how often you truncate or drop tables. In your production system, you may never, or hardly ever, do this, so extents will have a long lifespan, and fragmentation may be low. In development, however, you may do this all the time, potentially making extent lifespan very short and fragmentation in the tablespace very high. You are your own best judge for interpreting fragmentation for these tablespaces, which is based on how long or short the extent lifespan is in those systems.

The other two types of tablespaces, UNDOTBS for undo segments and TEMPORARY for temporary segments (you can have more than one tablespace for sorting and temporary segments), will experience high to very high fragmentation. This is true in the UNDOTBS tablespace because undo segments have potentially a very short lifespan, and Oracle can allocate and deallocate extents as necessitated by long-running transactions. In the next chapter, you will learn more about undo segment extent allocation and deallocation. Finally, the lifespan of segments and extents in the TEMPORARY tablespace is incredibly short. Temporary segments are used to handle sort operations (a sort might be caused by issuing a `select ... order by` statement) that manipulate too much data to be stored in memory. Oracle automatically allocates the space when needed. Once the sort operation is finished, Oracle again automatically deallocates the space. Thus, by definition of usage and lifespan, the TEMPORARY tablespace will have the highest amount of fragmentation of any tablespace on your database.

TIP

Extent lifespan and tablespace fragmentation are inversely proportional—the shorter the lifespan, the higher the potential for tablespace fragmentation.

Thus, although the SYSTEM tablespace can store any database object, it is not recommended that you put objects in it other than the dictionary objects and the system undo segment. To avoid problems with your database, you will need to prepare a few other tablespaces to store types of segments. By placing these objects in other databases designed to fit their storage needs, the DBA prevents a number of potential storage problems.

Creating the Necessary Tablespaces for Housing Different Segments

One of your first database activities should be to create separate tablespaces to store tables, indexes, undo segments, temporary segments, and segments associated with database administrative tools such as Oracle Enterprise Manager. The tablespaces necessary for your Oracle database can be created with statements like the following:

```
CREATE TABLESPACE UNDOTBS datafile '/u05/oradata/oracle/undo01.dbf'
SIZE 300M EXTENT MANAGEMENT LOCAL ONLINE;

CREATE TABLESPACE data datafile '/u06/oradata/oracle/data01.dbf'
SIZE 300M EXTENT MANAGEMENT LOCAL ONLINE;

CREATE TABLESPACE index datafile '/u07/oradata/oracle/index01.dbf'
SIZE 300M EXTENT MANAGEMENT LOCAL ONLINE;

CREATE TABLESPACE tools datafile '/u08/oradata/oracle/tools01.dbf'
SIZE 300M EXTENT MANAGEMENT LOCAL ONLINE;

CREATE temporary TABLESPACE temp tempfile '/u09/oradata/oracle/temp01.dbf'
SIZE 300M EXTENT MANAGEMENT LOCAL online;
```

Each of these different types of database objects has its own unique behavior, and sometimes the behavior of one type of object conflicts with another. The section on storage structures and relationships helped you learn more about the various types of segments that exist in Oracle and why it is important to put them in their own tablespaces. When identifying default storage parameters for these tablespaces, you should attempt to set parameters that work well for the type of database object that will be stored in this tablespace, or simply use uniform extent allocation, which is the default allocation type in Oracle9*i*. You don't need to specify default storage in your `create tablespace` commands in Oracle9*i* because of this fact. We covered this feature in Chapter 3 and also in the next discussion.

For Review

1. Be sure you can identify the types of segments available for storing database objects.

2. Know that it is important not to store all the segments in your Oracle database inside the SYSTEM tablespace. Oracle9*i* offers clauses in the `create database` statement such as `default temporary tablespace` and undo tablespace that permit you to create tablespaces specifically for temporary and undo segments when you create your database. This is used to prevent Oracle from dumping these segments into the SYSTEM tablespace, which should be used only to house data dictionary and SYSTEM undo segments.

3. You can also create the different tablespaces you will need for separating different types of segments by using the `create tablespace` command, as we showed by example in the discussion.

4. Be able to distinguish the following types of segments in an Oracle database and describe why they should be stored in their own tablespaces: DATA, INDEX, UNDOTBS, TEMP, and TOOLS.

Exercises

1. **You are configuring your Oracle database to handle different types of segments. Which of the following statements is true regarding the separation of segments and extents?**

   A. A segment used for housing different types of data in Oracle is comprised of data blocks, making most types of segments fundamentally the same; thus, they can all be placed in the SYSTEM tablespace to minimize DBA time and effort.

   B. A segment used for housing table data will likely be referenced immediately after Oracle accesses the segment housing associated index data; thus, it is desirable to house table and index segments in separate tablespaces.

   C. A segment used for housing temporary data can be frequently allocated and deallocated; thus, it should be housed in the same tablespace as that used by volatile table data, but separate from the SYSTEM tablespace.

D. The SYSTEM tablespace is used for housing SYSTEM undo segments, and because all undo segments have the same volatile nature, the SYSTEM tablespace is where you should house all undo segments in the Oracle database.

2. **Examine the following code block:**

```
create database mydb
controlfile reuse
character set US7ASCII
national character set US7ASCII
datafile '/u01/oradata/mydb/mydb01.dbf' size 400M
logfile group 1 ('/u02/oradata/mydb/redo01.log') size 10M,
        group 2 ('/u03/oradata/mydb/redo02.log') size 10M
default temporary tablespace temp
  tempfile '/u04/oradata/mydb/temp01.dbf' size 1024M
undo tablespace undotbs
 datafile '/u05/oradata/mydb/undo01.dbf' size 1024M
noarchivelog;
```

Which of the following choices identifies a tablespace that will not be created by the command shown in the previous code block?

A. SYSTEM

B. UNDOTBS

C. DATA

D. TEMP

3. **You are evaluating the placement of segments in tablespaces for the Oracle database. Which of the following segments has the shortest lifespan?**

A. Temporary segments

B. Undo segments

C. Index segments

D. Data dictionary segments

Answer Key

1. B. **2.** C. **3.** A.

Controlling the Use of Extents by Segments

Growth in a data segment is generally handled with extents. If the segment runs out of space to handle new record entries for the object, then the object will acquire an extent from the remaining free space in the tablespace. In general, a logical database object such as a table or index can have many extents, but all those extents (plus the original segment) must all be stored in the same tablespace. There are, however, some exceptions. For example, a table containing a column defined as a large object datatype (BLOB, CLOB, NCLOB) can store its nonLOB data in one tablespace while storing LOB data in a different tablespace. However, generally speaking, you should remember that most database objects will have all their extents stored in the same tablespace.

TIP
The fact that all extents for a database object should be stored in the same tablespace shouldn't be taken to mean that all extents for a database object will be stored in the same datafile. For example, a partitioned table may have its partitions or extents spread across datafiles on different disks to improve parallel processing performance. Oracle may also run out of room in one tablespace datafile and thus be forced to allocate an extent in another datafile. This fact is important to remember for OCP.

Uniform Space Allocation in Tablespaces

The default method for managing segment and extent size allocation in your tablespace in Oracle9*i* is uniform space allocation. To configure this option, you would use the `uniform size n[K|M]` keywords, where *n* is the size of the extent allocated in KB or MB, in place of `autoallocate`, when you issue the `create tablespace` command. When `uniform size` is specified, Oracle still manages all extent allocation and sizing automatically. The difference is that, when `uniform size` is specified, whatever you defined for *n* is the size Oracle uses for later extents allocated to the object in the tablespace, regardless of the settings of the other storage settings in the `create table` statement. Let's look at an example of creating a tablespace in which all extents will be sized by Oracle as 10KB:

```
SQL> create tablespace lmtab5 datafile
  2  'c:\oracle\oradata\orcl\lmtab501.dbf'
  3  size 10M reuse
  4  extent management local
  5  uniform size 10K online;
Tablespace created.
```

TIP
*When uniform extent allocation is used, Oracle
calculates the number of bits to use in the storage
allocation bitmap as the number of uniformly sized
extents that would fit in the tablespace. Otherwise,
the number of bits used for the bitmap is the same
as the number of blocks that would fit in the
tablespace.*

Explicitly Defined Object Storage and Locally Managed Tablespaces

When specified, Oracle always uses the value specified for `uniform size`
when sizing extents in locally managed tablespaces. That said, you will see some
conflicting information in your dictionary views when it comes to objects placed
in locally managed tablespaces with uniform extent management if you explicitly
ask for extents to be a different size than what Oracle wants to give you through
automatic extent management. To demonstrate what I mean by this remark, let's
create a table in the LMTAB5 tablespace:

```
SQL> create table mytab01
  2    (col1 number)
  3    tablespace lmtab5
  4    storage (initial 20K) online;
Table created.
```

Using the previous code in bold, I'm attempting to override the uniform extent
management size in LMTAB5 for table MYTAB01 by specifying an initial extent size
of 20KB with my own `storage` clause. Remember, Oracle is supposed to create
every object in LMTAB5 with an extent size of 10KB. So, of course, Oracle ignored
our attempted override of uniform storage management, right? Let's take a look at
the DBA_TABLES view to see:

```
SQL> select table_name, initial_extent
  2    from dba_tables
  3    where table_name = 'MYTAB01';
TABLE_NAME INITIAL_EXTENT
---------- --------------
MYTAB01             20480
```

Wait a minute, I hear you say. Oracle's supposed to make the initial extent
10KB. So, why is DBA_TABLES telling us the initial extent is 20KB? This is strange
behavior indeed. What's more, the same thing seems to happen when we use the
`alter table allocate extent` command as well. Take a look:

```
SQL> alter table mytab01 allocate extent (size 30K);
Table altered.
SQL> select table_name, initial_extent, next_extent
  2  from dba_tables
  3  where table_name = 'MYTAB01';
TABLE_NAME INITIAL_EXTENT NEXT_EXTENT
---------- -------------- -----------
MYTAB01             20480       30720
```

Does this mean that Oracle's uniform extent management feature can be overridden by use of a storage clause when creating the table or by explicitly allocating extents of a larger size than that permitted by uniform extent management. No, not really. Take a look at the DBA_EXTENTS view to get a picture of what's really going on here:

```
SQL> select segment_name, extent_id, bytes
  2  from dba_extents
  3  where segment_name = 'MYTAB01';
SEGMENT_NA EXTENT_ID  BYTES
---------- ---------  -------
MYTAB01            0  10240
MYTAB01            1  10240
MYTAB01            2  10240
MYTAB01            3  10240
MYTAB01            4  10240
5 rows selected.
```

So, in reality, the data dictionary satisfies both your specified space allocation in the storage clause and in the allocate extent clause as well as its own rules about uniform extent sizes by simply allocating more extents of the same size. What do you think Oracle would do if we asked it to allocate an extent of 15KB in this context? Well, Oracle would simply allocate more space than you asked for by grabbing two more extents of 10KB each.

Extent Allocation in Dictionary-Managed Tablespaces

When you create a database object in a dictionary-managed tablespace, Oracle allocates it a single initial segment in the tablespace unless you specify otherwise, based on the database object's storage clause parameters if there are any. If the object creation command lacked a storage clause, then Oracle uses the default storage clause settings for the tablespace you place your object in. Usually, the object is initially created with only one segment of space allocated. As new rows are added to tables, the space of the segment is used to store that new data. When the segment storing the table data is full and more data must be added to the table, the table must allocate another extent to store that data in. Figure 4-1 illustrates an extent being acquired on an Oracle database.

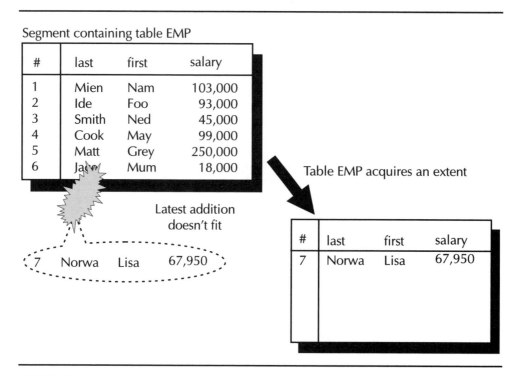

Segment containing table EMP

#	last	first	salary
1	Mien	Nam	103,000
2	Ide	Foo	93,000
3	Smith	Ned	45,000
4	Cook	May	99,000
5	Matt	Grey	250,000
6	Ja...	Mum	18,000

Latest addition doesn't fit

7	Norwa	Lisa	67,950

Table EMP acquires an extent

#	last	first	salary
7	Norwa	Lisa	67,950

FIGURE 4-1. *Acquiring extents*

A new extent will be acquired for a database object only if there is no room in any of the object's current segments or extents for the new data. Once acquired, an extent will only be relinquished if the DBA truncates or drops and re-creates the table.

Acquiring Extents in Dictionary-Managed Tablespaces: An Example

The size of an acquired extent is based on the value specified for the `next` parameter inside the `storage` clause provided in the object creation clause. If the object is acquiring its third or greater extent, the size of the extent will equal `next` multiplied by `pctincrease`. This concept is a little tricky, so let's take a look at what we mean. Let's say you create a table called EMPLOYEE with the following command:

```
SQL> create table employee
  2  (empid number primary key,
  3   name varchar2(20),
```

```
  4    salary number)
  5    storage (initial 100K next 2K pctincrease 25
  6    minextents 1 maxextents 100)
  7    tablespace DATA;
Table created.
```

TIP

You'll learn more about table `storage` *clauses in the next chapter.*

Once you issue this command, Oracle immediately allocates a single segment 100KB in size inside the DATA tablespace. We don't know which datafile Oracle will place the segment into, just that it will be a datafile associated with the DATA tablespace. We know the initial segment will be 100KB in size because that's the value specified for the `initial` setting inside the `storage` clause. Now, let's pretend that a user adds several employees to the table, filling that initial segment. The initial segment is now full, so the next user who comes along to add an employee to the table will force Oracle to allocate another extent to the EMPLOYEE table. This extent will be allocated inside the DATA tablespace and will be 2KB in size. Again, we know the second extent will be 2KB in size because the `next` setting in the `storage` clause tells us so.

If you want to specify a different size for that next extent, you should issue the `alter table storage (next nextval)` statement before that next extent gets allocated, where `nextval` is the size of the next extent (in KB or MB). Oracle applies the value you specify for this setting to the next extent it acquires. The following statement gives an example:

```
SQL> ALTER TABLE employee STORAGE (NEXT 100K);
Table altered.
```

TIP

You'll learn more about altering table definitions in the next chapter.

Now, instead of allocating only 2KB for the next extent, Oracle allocates 100KB, so that the next extent is as big as the first one. Let's move on by pretending that the second user adds several employees such that the second extent is now full. What happens next? Well, Oracle has to do some calculating to determine how large to make the third extent. How do we know? We know because a value greater than zero was specified for the `pctincrease` setting. Whenever this happens, Oracle multiplies the value you specified for `next` in the `storage` clause by the percentage increase specified. Thus, because we specified 25 for the `pctincrease` setting and 100KB for `next` in our `storage` clause, Oracle will allocate 100KB×1.25, or 125KB, for the third extent.

Whenever Oracle allocates a new extent for an object where `pctincrease` is greater than zero, Oracle recalculates the value for `next` that is stored in the data dictionary record associated with this object. This could be dangerous because the size of subsequent extents allocated will increase exponentially. To understand what we mean by this, consider what will happen when Oracle allocates the fourth extent for the EMPLOYEE table. The size of the third extent was 125KB, so Oracle bases the size of the fourth extent on the size of the third extent, increased by the value specified for `pctincrease`. In other words, Oracle allocates 100KB×1.25×1.25, or 156.25KB, of space for the fourth extent. So you see, setting `pctincrease` to a value greater than zero is meant to slow down the extent allocation process for growing database objects by allocating progressively more space each time a new extent is required.

TIP

If you don't want your database objects to grow exponentially, set `pctincrease` *to zero in the* `storage` *clause when you first create the object. That way, all extents allocated will be the same size as the value you specified for* `next`*.*

Extents and Parallel Processing

If you don't use parallel processing on your Oracle database, you will get the best performance from a database object, such as a table or index, if all the data for that object is housed in only one segment or in a set of contiguous blocks. This is especially true when you use dictionary-managed tablespaces to house Oracle data and less true when when you use locally managed tablespaces to house Oracle data.

However, when you use parallel processing, you'll want your data stored in multiple extents (preferably spread across several disks), so that parallel processes accessing the same table won't contend with each other. If you use partitioned tables and the parallel query option, obviously you'll want to have as many different segments for your table as there are parallel I/O slave processes utilized by Oracle to search that table. Furthermore, certain trade-offs exist in deciding how much space to allocate, particularly for tables you know will grow quickly.

The Preallocation Balancing Act

Recall that in the `storage` clause defined for the EMPLOYEE table we created previously, we defined two other settings for this table. They were `minextents`, the number of extents Oracle allocates to the table when it's first created, and maxextents, the maximum number of extents Oracle will ever allocate for that object. Once Oracle has allocated the maximum number of extents you identified via the maxextents setting, that's it—the table cannot grow any larger (unless you change the value for maxextents, of course!).

Many inexperienced DBAs fall prey to the trap of preallocation. They want to preallocate as much space as possible to avoid problems later with hitting the limit set by maxextents. Sometimes that's a good thing—especially if you believe that users are going to fill the object with data quickly or if you need to keep all the data in one segment. However, there are a couple of drawbacks to be aware of. First, the host machine has limited space. Second, and more importantly, your database could suffer from poor backup performance because of the excessive time required to compress a tablespace containing mostly empty segments for storage on tape. A third drawback is also evident sometimes. If the tablespace has vast wastelands of empty segment space, then tables are placed far away from one another on disk. This could cause your database to experience the poor performance seen on databases with huge tables, even though your tables are mostly empty. On the other hand, don't fall victim to the miserly approach to storage allocation either. Every additional extent your database object has to allocate to store its information contributes to poorer performance on data queries and changes, although this problem is attributed mainly to the use of dictionary-managed tablespace and can be solved usually through the use of locally managed tablespaces. The trick, then, is to balance the following considerations:

- Using locally managed tablespaces instead of dictionary-managed tablespaces

- Leaving a generous percentage of additional space, both in the tablespace and the object's initial segment, to accommodate growth

- Planning disk purchases for the host machine or leaving extra space to add new tablespaces and datafiles in order to alleviate a space crunch

- If possible, setting up a monthly or quarterly maintenance schedule with your users so that you can have some downtime to reorganize your tablespaces to avert those potential sizing issues before they become headaches

For Review

1. Extents are allocated whenever a database object runs out of space for incoming data.

2. The size of an extent allocated depends on the storage settings defined when the object was created. This information comes either from the storage clause in the object creation statement or from the `default` storage clause present on the tablespace the object is stored in.

3. Understand the use of uniform extent allocations in Oracle9*i*. Remember that uniform extent management is the default for locally managed temporary tablespaces, whereas automatic allocation is the default for locally managed permanent tablespaces.

4. Know what the `initial`, `next`, and `pctincrease` settings mean in the context of segments in dictionary-managed tablespaces. Pay particular attention to the exponential growth factor present whenever `pctincrease` is set to a value greater than zero.

5. Understand the balancing act required when considering how large to make your segments and extents. Too much preallocation leads to wasted space, whereas too little leads to too many extents. It's a tightrope that ultimately every DBA walks, and the right answer often depends on the needs of a particular system. For OCP, understand how to define these parameters, while for real life, you'll need a lot of experience with a particular system (or a lot of meetings with users to figure out how quickly they add data) before the numbers start seeming intuitive.

Exercises

1. **You create a locally managed tablespace with the following statement:**

```
SQL> create tablespace DATA datafile
  2   'c:\oracle\oradata\orcl\DATA01.dbf'
  3   size 150M reuse
  4   extent management local
  5   uniform size 500K online;
Tablespace created.
```

   After creating the tablespace, you create a table with the `initial` set to 100KB and `minextents` set to 3 in the `storage` clause. After the table is created, how much space will the table occupy in the tablespace?

   A. 100KB

   B. 300KB

   C. 500KB

   D. 1,500KB

2. **You want to create a locally managed tablespace for housing sort segments in Oracle. Which of the following statements would be appropriate for the purpose with respect to allocation of segments and extents?**

A. ```create temporary tablespace temp01 datafile
'/u01/oradata/orcl/temp01.dbf' size 100M extent
management local;```

B. ```create temporary tablespace temp01 tempfile
'/u01/oradata/orcl/temp01.dbf' size 100M extent
management local;```

C. ```create tablespace temp01 datafile
'/u01/oradata/orcl/temp01.dbf' size 100M extent
management local temporary;```

D. ```create tablespace temp01 tempfile
'/u01/oradata/orcl/temp01.dbf' size 100M extent
management local temporary;```

3. **You define a locally managed tablespace using the following syntax:**

```
SQL> create tablespace DATA datafile
  2  'c:\oracle\oradata\orcl\DATA01.dbf'
  3  size 150M reuse
  4  extent management local online;
Tablespace created.
```

Which of the following choices indicates the storage allocation clause left out but implied by Oracle when this tablespace was created?

A. `autoallocate`

B. `autoallocate size 1M`

C. `uniform`

D. `uniform size 1M`

4. **You create a table with the following command:**

```
SQL> create table tester
  2  (col1 varchar2 primary key)
  3  tablespace testdata
  4  storage (initial 50M next 100M pctincrease 20
  5  minextents 1 maxextents 200);
```

Which of the following choices indicates how large the fifth extent Oracle allocates will be?

A. 120MB

B. 144MB

    C. 173MB

    D. 207MB

5. **A table was just created on your Oracle database with six extents allocated to it. Which of the following factors most likely caused the table to have so many extents allocated?**

    A. The value for `minextents` setting.

    B. The value for `pctincrease` setting.

    C. The value for `maxextents` setting.

    D. By default, Oracle allocates six extents to all database objects.

Answer Key

1. D. This is because `minextents` tells Oracle to allocate three extents, and Oracle uses uniform storage allocation to determine how large to make the extents. **2.** B. **3.** A. **4.** C. **5.** A.

Using Block Space Utilization Parameters

In addition to overall storage allocation for extents on objects in the database, Oracle enables you to manage how the objects use the space inside each data block they are given. Space usage is determined at the block level with the `pctfree` and `pctused` options. By controlling space allocation at the block level, you can manage how a database object utilizes the space allocated to it more effectively according to the type of data change activity the object is likely to be subjected to. Database objects are subjected to data changes in different ways by different applications: for example, a database that supports high online transaction-processing (OLTP) activity where later data changes expand the size of existing rows by populating columns initially set to NULL when the row was added to the table need space preallocated at the block level to let the row grow. In contrast, a decision support system (DSS) such as a data warehouse will likely not see its data changed once rows are loaded for query access. In this case, you'll want to pack as much data into every block allocated to a row as possible.

    Why do DBAs manage space allocation at the block level? Because the objects themselves are utilized differently by different application data manipulation language (DML) activities. For example, if a table experiences a high `update` activity that increases the size of rows in the table, the block space allocation for that database object should allow for additional growth per row. If data change activity on the object consists of a lot of `insert` statements entering rows mostly the same size, then the space usage goal within each block should be to place as many rows as possible into each block before allocating another one. This same approach may work if a table's size is static and rows are infrequently added to the table.

Leaving Extra Space for Row Growth: pctfree

The pctfree clause is specified at the database object level. It tells Oracle how much free space to leave in a block when that block initially gets populated with row data. This leftover space remains free in each block to accommodate the growth of existing rows in the block. For example, if a table has pctfree specified to be 10 percent, Oracle will stop adding new rows to the block when there is 10 percent free space left over in the block. That remaining space is used by existing rows when users set NULL columns to a non-NULL value.

You should use the following general approach when deciding how to set pctfree. If rows added to a table will be updated often and each update will add to the size in bytes of the row, then set pctfree to a high value. You'll see some examples of values that are considered high for pctfree in a moment. For now, understand that setting pctfree high prevents performance killers such as row migration (where Oracle moves an entire row to another block because the original block doesn't have the room to store it anymore). Conversely, if the rows in the block will not be updated frequently, or if the updates that will occur will not affect the size of each row, set the value for pctfree low on that database object.

TIP

A high value for pctfree *is about 20 to 25, which means that 20 or 25 percent of space in a block is left free for later updates that might increase the size of an existing row in the block. Conversely, a low value for* pctfree *would be 4 or 5, which you might use for static or read-only tables.*

Ongoing Management of Free Space in Blocks: pctused

The other option for managing free space in blocks is pctused. It is also defined at the database object level. The pctused option specifies the percent usage threshold by which Oracle will determine if it is acceptable to add new rows to a block. To understand what we mean, consider the situation where data is added to a table. As new rows are added, Oracle fills the block with inserted rows until reaching the cutoff set by pctfree. Later, as data is deleted from the table, that table's space utilization at the block level falls. When the space used in a data block falls below the threshold limit set by pctused, Oracle adds the block to a *freelist* maintained for that table. A freelist is a list of data blocks that are currently accepting new data rows.

When setting `pctused`, be mindful that Oracle incurs some performance overhead by marking a block free and adding it to a freelist for that database object. Thus, there is a trade-off inherent in specifying `pctused` that you should understand for OCP and beyond. You must temper your interest in managing space freed by row removal as efficiently as possible against that overhead incurred by each block. To prevent the block from making its way to the freelist when only one or two rows can even be added to the block, you should set the `pctused` option relatively low.

TIP
Unless you're really concerned about managing free space actively, don't set `pctused` *higher than 40 or 50. A situation where you might be concerned about managing free space actively would be when you have very little free space on the disks in your host system.*

Setting Actual Values for `pctfree` and `pctused`

These two options are defined at the database object level, and the values assigned must always be considered in tandem. You can specify a value for each option between 0 and 100. However, when determining values for `pctfree` and `pctused`, do not assign values for these space utilization options that exceed 100 when added together. In fact, you should not set values for these options that even approach 90, because this causes Oracle to spend more time managing space utilization than is necessary. The following bullets identify some values for `pctfree` and `pctused` that would likely be considered appropriate. Following each value is a description of the scenario in Oracle where this setting might be appropriate, along with an indication of whether this is considered a high or low value for either option:

- **`pctfree 5, pctused 40`**   Good for static or read-only tables, such as those loaded periodically for data warehouse and/or query-only applications

- **`pctfree 10, pctused 40`**   Good for all-around OLTP situations especially when existing rows won't be increased by update activity after the row is inserted

- **`pctfree 20, pctused 40`**   Good for OLTP activity where existing rows will be increased by updates after the row is inserted (20 is a high value for `pctfree`)

Setting `pctfree` and `pctused`: An Example

You'll learn more about storage options for creating database objects in later chapters. For now, to give you the opportunity to see `pctfree` and `pctused` in action, the following code block contains a `create table` statement with `pctfree` and `pctused` specified. Notice that these clauses are not defined as part of the `storage` clause—they are their own clauses in a `create table` command:

```
SQL> CREATE TABLE FAMILY
  2  ( NAME VARCHAR2(10) primary key,
  3    RELATIONSHIP VARCHAR2(10))
  4  storage (initial 100K next 100K
  5          pctincrease 0 minextents 1 maxextents 200)
  6  PCTFREE 20 PCTUSED 40;
Table created.
```

For Review

1. Understand the use of `pctfree` and `pctused` with respect to space management in a table.

2. The `pctfree` option tells Oracle how much space should be left over when new rows are added to a block in order to leave room for growth in existing rows.

3. The `pctused` option tells Oracle the space usage threshold below which Oracle should place a block on the table's freelist so new rows can be added to that block.

4. The values for these options are set in tandem when the database object is created, so that they never add up to a value close to 100.

Exercises

1. **User CAROLYN issues some statements in her SQL*Plus session against an Oracle database with a 4KB block size. The transcript from her session is shown in the following block:**

```
SQL> describe records
 Name                            Null?    Type
 ------------------------------- -------- ------------
 RECORDNO                        NOT NULL NUMBER(4)
 RECNAME                                  VARCHAR2(10)
 RECDESC                                  VARCHAR2(4000)
 RECDATE                                  DATE
SQL> insert into records (recordno) values (1000);
```

```
1 row inserted.
SQL> select vsize(*) from records where recordno = 100;
VSIZE(*)
--------
      12
```

Later, another user populates the description for this record, which consists of a 100-word block of text. When Carolyn issues the **select vsize(*)** statement shown previously again, Oracle returns a value of 3,215. Which of the following choices identifies appropriate settings for **pctfree** and **pctused**?

A. pctfree 5, pctused 80

B. pctfree 10, pctused 50

C. pctfree 15, pctused 20

D. pctfree 80, pctused 5

2. You are configuring block space utilization on an Oracle table. Which of the following choices identifies block space utilization settings that are never appropriate under any circumstances?

A. pctfree 5, pctused 90

B. pctfree 15, pctused 80

C. pctfree 20, pctused 70

D. pctfree 10, pctused 40

Answer Key
1. D. 2. B.

Obtaining Information about Storage Structures

You can determine storage information for database objects from many sources in the data dictionary. There are several data dictionary views associated with tracking information about structures for storage in the database, such as tablespaces, extents, and segments. In addition, there are dictionary views for the database objects that offer information about space utilization settings. The names of dictionary views are usually taken from the objects represented by the data in the dictionary view, preceded by classification on the scope of the data. Each segment has its own data dictionary view that displays the storage information. Assuming that you want to know the storage parameters set for all objects on the database, you may use the following views to determine storage information for the segment types already discussed:

- **DBA_SEGMENTS**   This summary view contains all types of segments listed by the data dictionary views and their storage parameters.

- **DBA_TABLESPACES**   You can use this view to see the default storage settings for the tablespaces in the database.

- **DBA_TS_QUOTAS**   You can use this view to identify the tablespace quotas assigned for users to create objects in their default and temporary tablespaces.

- **V$TABLESPACE**   This gives a simple listing of the tablespace number and name.

- **DBA_EXTENTS**   You use this view to see the segment name, type, owner, name of tablespace storing the extent, ID for the extent, file ID storing the extent, starting block ID of the extent, total bytes, and blocks of the extent.

- **DBA_FREE_SPACE**   This view identifies the location and amount of free space by tablespace name, file ID, starting block ID, bytes, and blocks.

- **DBA_FREE_SPACE_COALESCED**   This view identifies the location of free space in a tablespace that has been coalesced by tablespace name, total extents, extents coalesced, and the percent of extents that are coalesced, as well as other information about the space in the tablespace that SMON has coalesced.

- **DBA_DATA_FILES**   This view gives information about datafiles for every tablespace.

- **V$DATAFILE**   This view gives information about datafiles for every tablespace.

TIP
Coalescing is the act of putting small chunks of free space in a tablespace, that are contiguous, and merging them into larger chunks of free space. The SMON process takes care of coalescing the tablespace on a regular basis. If you want to take care of coalescing the tablespace yourself, issue the `alter tablespace` *tblspc* `coalesce` *command. Also, when using locally managed tablespaces free space is monitored in datafile header bitmaps, so SMON doesn't need to coalesce.*

For Review

Know the different views in the data dictionary that give you information about storage.

Exercises

1. You need to find information about the total amount of space that has been allocated to a table in Oracle. Which of the following choices identifies a view you would look in?

   A. DBA_OBJECTS

   B. DBA_SEGMENTS

   C. DBA_EXTENTS

   D. DBA_FREE_SPACE_COALESCED

2. You want to determine the amount of space that has been allocated to the EMP table owned by SCOTT in Oracle, stored in tablespace DATA. Which of the following choices identifies the SQL statement you might use for this purpose?

   A. `select blocks from dba_tables where table_name = 'EMP' and owner = 'SCOTT';`

   B. `select sum(bytes) from dba_free_space where tablespace_name = 'DATA';`

   C. `select sum(bytes) from dba_extents where segment_name = 'EMP' and owner = 'SCOTT';`

   D. `select * from dba_objects where object_name = 'EMP' and owner = 'SCOTT';`

3. You want to identify the space utilization settings for tables owned by SMITHERS in Oracle. Which of the following SQL statements would be useful for this purpose?

   A. `select * from dba_objects where owner = 'SMITHERS';`

   B. `select * from dba_segments where owner = 'SMITHERS';`

   C. `select * from dba_extents where owner = 'SMITHERS';`

   D. `select * from dba_indexes where owner = 'SMITHERS';`

Answer Key
1. C. 2. C. 3. B.

Managing Undo Data

Oracle**9i**
and higher In this section, you will cover the following topics related to management of undo segments in Oracle9*i*:

- The purpose of undo segments

- Implementing automatic undo management

- Creating and configuring undo segments

- Dictionary views for undo data

Experienced Oracle DBAs may be familiar with the term "undo" in its prior form —rollback. Rollback segments have existed in Oracle for a long time as a resource that DBAs had to manage actively and manually. In Oracle9*i*, the database makes management of rollback segments much simpler than a mere name change might suggest. In addition to renaming rollback segments undo segments, Oracle9*i* offers several options for the simplified management of these occasionally problematic resources. This section will define the purpose of undo segments and the data they contain. It will also introduce you to implementing automatic undo segment management in Oracle9*i*. You will learn how to create and configure undo segments as well. Finally, you will cover where to look in the Oracle data dictionary for information about your undo segments.

TIP
If you're an experienced Oracle DBA and you're having trouble with the concept of undo segments, just substitute undo for rollback and you'll know exactly the role these objects handle!

The Purpose of Undo Segments

Often, the DBA spends part of any given day "fighting fires." Many times, these fires involve a group of database objects that in prior versions of the Oracle database were called rollback segments. In Oracle9*i*, these objects are referred to as undo segments. Undo segments store the old data value when a process is making changes to the data in a database. The undo segment stores data and block information, such as file and block IDs, for data from a table or index as that block existed before being modified. This copy of data changes made to the database is available to other users running queries until the user making changes `commits` his or her transaction. The undo segment stores the changes after the `commit` as well, but Oracle will eventually and systematically overwrite the data in an undo segment from committed transactions whenever a user process initiates a new transaction and therefore needs room in the undo segment to store data for its uncommitted changes. Undo segments serve three purposes:

- They provide transaction-level read consistency of data to all users in the database.

- They permit users to roll back, or discard, changes that have been made in a transaction in favor of the original version of that data.

- They provide transaction recovery in case the instance fails while a user is making a data change.

Undo segments are probably the most useful database objects in data processing, but they can be troublesome for DBAs to maintain. In prior versions of Oracle, you had to master the management of these fussy objects very quickly if you were going to survive as a DBA for long. However, Oracle9*i* has simplified administrative tasks related to undo segments greatly by automating many of the aspects of their management.

The contents of an undo segment are manifold. Each undo segment contains a table in the segment header. This table lists the transactions and users currently using this undo segment to store data changes for the purpose of read-consistency. Each undo segment also has several extents allocated to it. The extents store original versions of data from tables and indexes. Whenever a user issues an `update` or `delete` statement in Oracle, the server process writes the original version of the data being changed or removed to the undo segment. Later, if the user decides to roll back his or her transaction, Oracle can easily copy the old version of the data in the undo segment back into its proper place. Or, if the user decides to `commit` his or her transaction, Oracle simply leaves the original data in the undo segment. Later, the space in the undo segment can be reused for storing original data for another transaction that is needed by another user.

TIP

A new feature in Oracle9i called Flashback Query uses undo data stored in an undo segment to permit users to view data as it existed in the database at some point in the past.

Designing and administering undo segments manually is one of the most challenging tasks for DBAs. If the undo segments were not properly designed, users would experience the dreaded ORA-15555: Snapshot too old (rollback segment too small) error. This error message is misleading. This error could be caused not just due to small rollback segmetn but due to many other reasons. If this problem is not taken care you may face a situation where a batch process running for many hours had to be rerun just because it fails in the middle due to this error.

In order to understand and solve this problem one has to understand how Oracle supports read consistency. In a multi-user environment many transactions are writing or modifying rows. Before a transaction commits the changes it made, the changed data is visible to all statements within this transaction that is making the changes but not to other statements or transactions. Once committed the changes are visible to all subsequence transactions. Statements that began prior to the commit will continue to show the old data because those changes were not present at the start of this transaction. This is called Read Consistency.

How is this made possible by Oracle? We will consider two transactions - the changing transaction that is making the changes in the table and reading transaction that is reading the data that is being changed by changing transaction. As discussed before the changing transaction keeps the before-image of the data being changed in an undo segment. The reading transaction that started before the changing transaction committed the changes will read the before-image of the data from the undo segment. Once the changing transaction commits, the undo segments containing the before-image are marked free and can be used by any transaction or could be cleaned up due to shrinking of undo segment. If the reading transaction continues to exist and comes back to read the before-image data from the undo segment and finds it missing, it returns the 'ORA-1555' error message and rolls back all the changes it made since it started. This could be quite a disruption if this transaction was a long running one.

So what causes this to happen? It could be many reasons. It could be caused due to inadequate number of undo segments or inadequately sized undo segments or data buffer cache being too small or large and small transactions using the same undo segments or improperly sized optimal parameter (that could be shrinking too often) or sometimes committing too often in a transaction. One sure way of preventing this is making sure the undo tablespace is large enough, preventing too many shrinks (set larger Optimal value) and making sure the buffer cache has a high hit ratio. Oracle9i helps you prevent this situation by allowing you to specify how long to retain undo data after it is committed. The parameter is UNDO_RETENTION.

Oracle9*i* administers undo data in two ways—automatic undo management and manual undo management. For the purpose of passing the OCP DBA Fundamentals I exam, we'll look at how to implement both automatic undo management and manual management of undo segments. If you're an experienced DBA, rest assured —Oracle hasn't taken away your ability to configure undo segments manually.

Manual configuration of undo segments is still available in Oracle9*i* for backward compatibility. The OCP DBA Fundamentals Exam I may or may not test manual management of undo segments, so this book will cover how to manage undo segments automatically as well as manually.

For Review

1. Be sure you can define the threefold purpose of an undo segment in Oracle, including the usage of undo segments for read consistency, transaction recovery, and instance recovery.

2. Know the causes of the Snapshot too old error in Oracle.

Exercises

1. **You are administering the Oracle database. A user approaches you to inform you that he has just received the ORA-1555 error. Which of the following choices describes the reason this user has received the error?**

   A. The user remained connected overnight, and his connection has timed out.

   B. The user has queried a read-inconsistent view of data in the process of being changed by a long-running transaction.

   C. The OPTIMAL value of the undo segments is very small.

   D. The user's `drop table` command took too long, and the database needs time to acquiesce.

2. **A user is executing a transaction in an Oracle database. Which of the following choices correctly identifies all the statements that will generate undo information within the transaction?**

   A. `delete` statements only

   B. `insert` statements only

   C. `update` and `insert` statements only

   D. `delete` and `update` statements only

   E. `delete`, `insert`, and `update` statements only

Answer Key

1. C. 2. E.

Implementing Automatic Undo Management

Oracle**9i** and higher Implementing automatic undo management is by far the easiest way to configure the management of undo segments in an Oracle database, especially for less-experienced DBAs. It is quick and easy, and it pushes the dirty work back on Oracle. Even if you're an experienced DBA, automatic undo management could be a good option to reduce the time you spend on mundane administrative tasks. This is because automatic undo management enables you to focus your attention on more interesting aspects of your work like strategic planning for data growth or architecture of new database systems just coming online. In addition, automatic undo management works well in Oracle systems that aren't transaction intensive, such as development or testing environments. Configuration and deployment of automatic undo management consists of three important steps:

1. You define an undo tablespace that Oracle can use for allocation and deallocation of undo segments.

2. You instruct Oracle to run in automatic undo management mode.

3. You instruct Oracle how long it should retain undo information in undo segments.

Step 1: Creating and Configuring Undo Segments

In order to use automatic undo management in an Oracle9i database, you must first create an undo tablespace. The undo tablespace houses undo segments, and it can be created in two different ways. You can create it when you create the database. The following code block shows an example of how to create an undo tablespace automatically during database creation in a Windows environment:

```
CREATE DATABASE DB1
CONTROLFILE REUSE
LOGFILE GROUP 1 ('C:\Oracle\oradata\DB1\redo01.log') SIZE 100K,
        GROUP 2 ('C:\Oracle\oradata\DB1\redo02.log') SIZE 100K,
        GROUP 3 ('C:\Oracle\oradata\DB1\redo03.log') SIZE 100K;
DATAFILE 'C:\Oracle\oradata\DB1\system01.dbf'
  SIZE 100M REUSE AUTOEXTEND ON NEXT 10240K MAXSIZE UNLIMITED
UNDO TABLESPACE UNDOTBS
  DATAFILE 'C:\Oracle\oradata\DB1\undotbs01.dbf'
   SIZE 50M REUSE AUTOEXTEND ON NEXT  5120K MAXSIZE UNLIMITED
NOARCHIVELOG
CHARACTER SET US7ASCII
;
```

Or, you can create the undo tablespace manually with the `create tablespace` command, as shown in the following code block:

```
SQL> CREATE UNDO TABLESPACE undotbs_2
  2  DATAFILE 'c:\oracle\oradata\DB1\undotbs2.dbf' SIZE 1M;
Tablespace created.
```

Step 2: Instruct Oracle to Run in Automatic Undo Management Mode

This step is accomplished by setting the UNDO_MANAGEMENT initialization parameter in your `init.ora` file. This parameter has two settings: MANUAL and AUTO. When set to MANUAL (this is the default setting when the UNDO_MANAGEMENT parameter isn't present in the `init.ora` file), then Oracle will permit you to manage undo segments manually, as you would have managed rollback segments in versions of Oracle prior to Oracle9*i*. To place the Oracle database into automatic undo management node, you set UNDO_MANAGEMENT to AUTO in the `init.ora` file, as shown in the following block:

```
UNDO_MANAGEMENT = AUTO
```

When a database is defined to run in automatic undo management mode, you have to have at least one undo tablespace created and online. If you have more than one undo tablespace in the tablespace, Oracle will use only one of them. You can explicitly specify which one to use by specifying it in the `init.ora` parameter UNDO_TABLESPACE.

```
UNDO_TABLESPACE = undotbs
```

This parameter can also be dynamically altered using the following command:

```
ALTER SYSTEM SET undo_tablespace = UNDOTBS;
```

Finally, a caveat: If you specify automatic undo management but provide no undo tablespace for Oracle to use, Oracle will not let your database start. So, for example, if you set UNDO_MANAGEMENT to AUTO but set UNDO_TABLESPACE to a tablespace that does not exist, then Oracle will issue the ORA-01092 error when you attempt to start up and open the database. The solution to this issue is to set the UNDO_TABLESPACE parameter to a valid undo tablespace in your database. Note, however, that if you actually have an undo tablespace available and have set UNDO_TABLESPACE to that tablespace at any point when the database was running before, Oracle will keep track of the setting for that parameter using the SPFILE feature. That way, if you simply omitted the UNDO_TABLESPACE parameter setting in `init.ora`, Oracle will still run normally. It is only when you incorrectly instruct Oracle to use an invalid tablespace that you will encounter this problem.

TIP
If you choose not to use automatic undo management, then you should ensure that you set the ROLLBACK_SEGMENTS parameter to bring named undo segments when the database starts. Otherwise, Oracle will only have the SYSTEM undo segment in the SYSTEM tablespace online at database startup.

Step 3: Instructing Oracle How Long to Retain Undo Data

One significant improvement with Oracle9*i* undo segments is the ability to retain prechange data in the undo segments for a specific period of time. This functionality works in conjunction with a new feature in Oracle9*i* called Flashback Query, which enables you to view old versions of your data after changes are committed for a specified period of time. With automatic undo management, you could specify how long you want to retain the committed undo information. The number of seconds to retain this data is specified in the init.ora parameter UNDO_RETENTION. This can also be dynamically changed using the alter system set undo_retention = *n* command, where *n* is the number in seconds that Oracle9*i* will retain the prechange original copy of data in an undo segment for Flashback Query. The default value for this parameter is 900.

Administering Undo Tablespaces

Even though undo data is a new concept in Oracle9*i*, the management of undo tablespace is same as any other tablespace. The undo tablespace can be altered using the alter tablespace command to add datafiles, rename datafiles, bring a datafile online, offline, or in backup mode. For full syntax of these actions, refer to the previous chapter on tablespaces and datafiles. Similarly, the alter database command can also be used to resize undo datafiles. An undo tablespace can also be dropped using a drop tablespace command but with a main restriction. An undo tablespace cannot be dropped while active transactions are using undo segments in it. This restriction is similar to the restriction on tablespaces containing active undo segments created manually. The following code block illustrates this:

```
SQL> drop tablespace undotbs_2;
drop tablespace undotbs_2
*
ERROR at line 1:ORA-30013: undo tablespace 'UNDOTBS_2' is currently in use
```

Oracle supports multiple undo tablespaces, but only one is used per instance. However, Oracle does let you switch from one undo tablespace to the other dynamically while the database is online and available to users. The following code block shows how this could be done. In this case, we move from using one undo tablespace to another in order to drop the other undo tablespace:

```
SQL> ALTER SYSTEM SET UNDO_TABLESPACE=undotbs;
System altered.
SQL> DROP TABLESPACE undotbs_2;
Tablespace dropped.
```

Creating the Undo Segments Themselves

If you're an experienced DBA, you might be asking yourself the question, "OK, so now I know how to create the undo tablespace, but how do I create the undo segments in Oracle9*i*?" The answer is, you don't. Oracle creates and manages all undo segments for you automatically as soon as the undo tablespace is created. Thus, when automatic undo management is enabled, you do not need to ensure that the undo segments are created or that they are online, the way you had to in earlier versions of Oracle. However, you can still manage undo segments manually if you like. The next discussion will cover how this is done. The OCP DBA Fundamentals I exam may or may not test manual management of undo segments, but it will definitely test automatic management of undo segments. Be sure you understand the fundamental difference in how undo segments are managed for Oracle9*i*, especially if you already have hands-on experience with the Oracle database from prior versions.

For Review

1. For automatic undo management, you must first create undo tablespaces in Oracle. Undo tablespaces can be created using the `create undo tablespace` command or by including the `undo tablespace` clause in the `create database` command.

2. Undo tablespaces can be altered using the `alter tablespace` or `alter database` commands to add datafiles, rename data files, and bring a datafile online, offline, or in backup mode. Undo tablespaces can also be dropped provided no active transactions are in them using the `drop tablespace` command.

3. To configure Oracle9*i* to run in automatic undo management mode, you must set the parameter UNDO_MANAGEMENT to AUTO in the `init.ora` file.

4. You can have more than one undo tablespace in your database, but only one will be used at a time per instance. If you have more than one undo tablespace, then the one to be used by the instance can be specified in the parameter UNDO_TABLESPACE. If you forget to set this parameter in your

`init.ora` file, it is still possible that Oracle will bring the correct undo tablespace online for you via the SPFILE feature in Oracle9*i*.

5. You also specify how long undo data should be kept available for Flashback Query by setting the UNDO_RETENTION initialization parameter.

6. Once the undo tablespace is created and automatic undo management is enabled, you do not have to actually create the undo segments themselves. Oracle9*i* creates them for you as soon as the undo tablespace is created. Moreover, Oracle brings the undo segments online automatically when the database starts.

Exercises

I. **You are configuring automatic undo management on your Oracle database. Which of the following choices indicates what you must do to handle the situation where more than one undo tablespace is available for storage of undo segments?**

  A. Set UNDO_MANAGEMENT to MANUAL in the `init.ora` file.

  B. Set UNDO_MANAGEMENT to AUTO in the `init.ora` file.

  C. Set UNDO_TABLESPACE to one of the tablespaces in the `init.ora` file.

  D. Set UNDO_TABLESPACE to both of the tablespaces in the `init.ora` file.

2. **The Oracle database with undo tablespaces UNDO_TBS1 and UNDO_TBS2 was opened with undo management enabled for this database. In a prior session, the `alter system set undo_tablespace = UNDO_TBS1` command was issued. However, the appropriate parameter instructing Oracle as to which undo tablespace to use was omitted from `init.ora`. Which of the following choices correctly describes what happens when the first user connecting to Oracle initiates her first transaction?**

  A. The database will open, but only the system undo segment will be online.

  B. The database will open, but no undo segments will be online.

  C. The database will open and all undo segments in UNDO_TBS1 will be online.

  D. Oracle will return errors and the database will not open.

3. **The Oracle database with undo tablespaces UNDO_TBS1 and UNDO_TBS2 was opened with undo management enabled for this database. In a prior session, the `alter system set undo_tablespace = UNDO_TBS1` command was issued. In the `init.ora` file, the UNDO_TABLESPACE parameter was set to UNDOTBS1. Which of the following choices correctly describes what happens when the first user connecting to Oracle initiates her first transaction?**

   A. The database will open, but only the system undo segment will be online.

   B. The database will open, but no undo segments will be online.

   C. The database will open and all undo segments in UNDO_TBS1 will be online.

   D. Oracle will return errors and the database will not open.

Answer Key
1. C. 2. C. 3. D.

Creating and Configuring Undo Segments Manually

Experienced DBAs might be wondering if they can still configure undo segments manually the way they configured rollback segments. The answer is emphatically yes! To understand undo segment manual configuration, let's start with a quick refresher on the types of undo segments. These objects can be broken into two categories: the system undo segment and non-SYSTEM undo segments. As you know, the system undo segment is housed by the SYSTEM tablespace and handles transactions made on objects in the SYSTEM tablespace. The other type of undo segments, non-SYSTEM undo segments, handles transactions made on data in non-SYSTEM tablespaces in the Oracle database. These non-SYSTEM undo segments are housed in a non-SYSTEM tablespace, such as the UNDOTBS tablespace. In order for Oracle to start when the database has one or more non-SYSTEM tablespaces, there must be at least one non-SYSTEM undo segment available for the instance to acquire outside the SYSTEM tablespace.

Non-SYSTEM undo segments come in two flavors: private and public undo segments. A *private* undo segment is one that is only acquired by an instance explicitly naming the undo segment to be acquired at startup via the ROLLBACK_SEGMENTS parameter in `initsid.ora`, or via the `alter rollback segment` *undo_seg* `online` statement issued manually by you, the DBA. *Public* undo segments are normally used when Oracle9*i* Real Application Clusters is running, but can also be used in a single instance. Public undo segments are acquired by Oracle automatically using a calculation of the TRANSACTIONS and the TRANSACTIONS_PER_ROLLBACK_SEGMENT init.ora parameters from a pool of undo segments available on the database.

How Transactions Use Undo Segments

Transactions occurring on the Oracle database need undo segments to store their uncommitted data changes. Transactions are assigned to undo segments in one of two ways. You can assign a transaction to an undo segment explicitly with the set transaction use rollback segment *undo_seg* statement. Or, if no undo segment is explicitly defined for the transaction, Oracle assigns the transaction to the undo segment that currently has the lightest transaction load, in round-robin fashion. Thus, more than one transaction can use the same undo segment, but each block in the undo segment houses data from one and only one transaction.

Undo segments are used as follows. An undo segment usually has several extents allocated to it at any given time, and these extents are used sequentially. After the database is started, the first transaction will be assigned to the first undo segment, and it will store its data changes in extent #1 of the undo segment. As the transaction progresses (a long-running batch process with thousands of update statements, let's say), it places more and more data into undo segment extent #1. An extent containing data from a transaction in progress is called an *active* extent. More and more transactions are starting on the database, and some of those other transactions may be assigned to this undo segment. Each transaction will fill extent #1 with more and more change data until the transactions commit.

If extent #1 fills with data changes before the transactions commit, the transactions will begin filling extent #2 with data. Transactions with data changes spilling over to a new extent are said to be performing a *extend*. A special marker called an undo segment *head* moves from extent #1 to extent #2 to indicate to the extent where new and existing transactions assigned to the undo segment can write their next data change. As soon as the transaction commits its data changes, the space in extent #1 used to store its data changes is no longer required. If extent #1 is filled with data change information from only committed transactions, extent #1 is considered *inactive*. Figure 4-2 displays this type of undo segment behavior.

To effectively use undo segment space, the undo segment allocates only a few extents, and those extents are reused often. The ideal operation of an undo segment with five extents is as follows: Transactions assigned to the undo segment should fill extent #5 a little after transactions with data changes in extent #1 commit. Thus, extent #1 becomes inactive just before transactions in extent #5 need to *wrap* into it. However, this behavior is not always possible. If a transaction goes on for a long time without committing data changes, it may eventually fill all extents in the undo segment. When this happens, the undo segment acquires extent #6, and wraps data changes from the current transaction into it. The undo segment head moves into

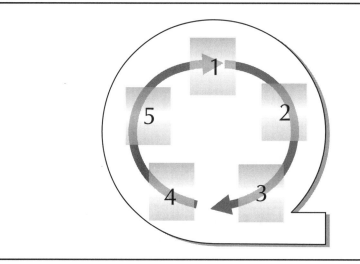

FIGURE 4-2. *Undo segment containing five reusable extents*

extent #6 as well. Figure 4-3 illustrates how Oracle obtains or allocates more extents for an undo segment.

If a transaction causes the undo segment to allocate the maximum number of extents for storing the long transaction's data changes—as determined by the `maxextents` storage option defined when the undo segment is created—the undo segment becomes enormously stretched out of shape. Oracle has an `optimal` option available in undo segment storage that permits undo segments to deallocate extents after long-running transactions cause them to acquire more extents than they really need. The `optimal` clause specifies the ideal size of the undo segment in KB or MB. This value tells Oracle the ideal number of extents the undo segment should maintain. If `optimal` is specified for an undo segment, that object will deallocate space when the undo segment head moves from one extent to another, if the current size of the undo segment exceeds `optimal` and if there are contiguous adjoining inactive extents. Figure 4-4 illustrates undo segment extent deallocation.

TIP

Extent deallocation as the result of `optimal` *has nothing whatsoever to do with transactions committing on the database. The deallocation occurs when the undo segment head moves from one extent to another. Oracle does not deallocate extents currently in use (even if the total size exceeds* `optimal`*) and always attempts to deallocate the oldest inactive extents first.*

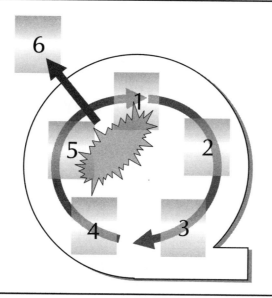

FIGURE 4-3. *How an undo segment acquires more extents*

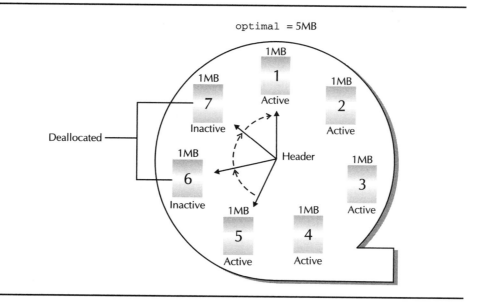

FIGURE 4-4. *Undo segment extent deallocation*

The Rule of Four to Plan Undo Segment Numbers for OLTP Systems

Oracle's recommended strategy for planning the appropriate number of undo segments for most online transaction-processing (OLTP) systems is called the *Rule of Four*, for easy recollection. Take the total number of transactions that will hit the database at any given time and divide by 4 to decide how many undo segments to create. Consider this example. You have a database that will be used for a small user rollout of an OLTP application. About 25 concurrent transactions will happen on the database at any given time. By applying the Rule of Four, you determine that about six undo segments are required. Shortly, you will see the additional calculation required for determining undo segment size.

Two exceptions exist to the Rule of Four. The first is, if the quotient is less than 4, round the result of the Rule of Four up to the nearest multiple of 4 and use that number of undo segments. In this case, the result would be rounded from 6 to 8. The second exception to the Rule of Four is that Oracle generally doesn't recommend more than 50 undo segments for a database, although that exception has faded somewhat in the face of massive database systems requiring more than 2,000 concurrent users. Thus, if the Rule of Four determines that more than 50 undo segments are needed, the DBA should start by allocating 50 and spend time monitoring the undo segment wait ratio to determine whether more should be added later.

Planning Undo Segment Numbers for Batch System Processing

When planning the number of undo segments required on the batch transaction-processing system, you need to make a small number of large undo segments available to support long-running processes that make several data changes. You should monitor the database to see how many transactions your batch processes execute concurrently and apply the Rule of Four to determine the number of undo segments needed, just as you would with an OLTP application. The next topic will demonstrate how to calculate the size of undo segments supporting both OLTP and batch transactions.

Sizing OLTP and Batch Undo Segments

There are two components to determining undo segment size, and the first is the overall size of the undo segment. The size of your undo segments, in turn, depends on two main factors: the type of DML statement used to perform the data change and the volume of data being processed. Different DML statements that change data require different amounts of data storage; the order from the least amount of data change information stored in an undo segment to greatest is `insert` (stores new ROWID in undo segment only), `update` (stores ROWID plus old column values), and `delete` (stores ROWID and all row/column data). Incidentally, data change information stored in an undo segment is called *undo*. So, if your transactions primarily `insert` data, your undo segments would be smaller than if your transactions primarily `delete` data.

The second component involved in undo segment size is the number of extents that will comprise the undo segment. Bigger is often better in determining the number of extents to have in your undo segment. By using more extents in the initial undo segment allocation—determined by the `minextents` storage option—you reduce the probability of your undo segment extending. Oracle recommends 20 (or more) extents as part of the initial undo segment allocation.

Creating Undo Segments with Appropriate Storage Settings

Undo segments are created with the `create rollback segment` statement. All extents in the undo segments of an Oracle database should be the same size. Commit this fact to memory—it's on the OCP exam in one form or another. To partially enforce this recommendation, Oracle disallows the use of `pctincrease` in the `create rollback segment` statement. (The `pctincrease` option is available for other objects, such as tables, to increase the size of subsequent extents that may be allocated to the object in order to reduce the overall number of extents allocated.) Sizes for undo segments and their included extents are determined by the options in the `storage` clause.

The following list of options is available for setting up undo segments:

- ■ **initial** The size in KB or MB of the initial undo segment extent.

- ■ **next** The size in KB or MB of the next undo segment extent to be allocated. Ensure that all extents are the same size by specifying `next` equal to `initial`.

- ■ **minextents** The minimum number of extents on the undo segment. The value for `minextents` should be 2 or greater.

- ■ **maxextents** The maximum number of extents the undo segment can acquire. Be sure to set this to a number and not to `unlimited`; this will prevent runaway transactions from using all your available tablespace. This is especially important if your UNDOTBS tablespace has datafiles using the `autoextend` feature.

- ■ **optimal** The total size in KB or MB of the undo segment, optimally. Assuming `initial` equals `next`, the value for `optimal` cannot be less than `initial * minextents`.

The following code block demonstrates the creation of a non-SYSTEM private undo segment in your database, according to the guidelines Oracle recommends. On OCP questions in this area, you should base your answers on the Oracle guidelines.

```
CREATE ROLLBACK SEGMENT rollseg01
TABLESPACE orgdbrbs
STORAGE ( INITIAL    10K
          NEXT       10K
          MINEXTENTS 20
          MAXEXTENTS 450
          OPTIMAL    300K );
```

TIP
The previous command is designed for use with a dictionary-managed tablespace.

In the code block, notice the `public` keyword was not used. Undo segments are private unless you create them with the `create public rollback segment` command. After creating your undo segment, you must bring it online so it will be available for user transactions. This is accomplished with the `alter rollback segment` *undo_seg* `online` command. The number of undo segments that can be brought online can be limited at instance startup by setting MAX_ROLLBACK_SEGMENTS `init`*sid*`.ora` parameter to 1 plus the number of non-SYSTEM undo segments you want available in Oracle.

TIP
You can create undo segments using the Storage Manager administrative utility in Oracle Enterprise Manager, as well as from within SQL*Plus.

Bringing Undo Segments Online at Instance Startup

Once you issue the `shutdown` command, any undo segments you created or brought online while the database was up are now offline as well. They will only be brought back online in two ways. The first is if you issue the `alter rollback segment` *undo_seg* `online` command again for every undo segment you want online.

The other way is through a multistep process engaged by Oracle at instance startup. Oracle first acquires any undo segments at instance startup named by you in the ROLLBACK_SEGMENTS `init`*sid*`.ora` parameter, specified as ROLLBACK_SEGMENTS = (*rollseg01,rollseg02* . . .). Then, Oracle performs a calculation of the undo segments required for the proper operation of the database, based on values set for the TRANSACTIONS, TRANSACTIONS_PER_ROLLBACK_SEGMENT, and `init`*sid*`.ora` parameters. The calculation performed is TRANSACTIONS / TRANSACTIONS_PER_ROLLBACK_SEGMENT. Thus, if TRANSACTIONS is 146 and TRANSACTIONS_PER_ROLLBACK_SEGMENT is 18, then Oracle knows it needs to acquire eight undo segments. If eight undo segments were named, Oracle brings the private undo segments online. If there weren't eight undo segments named, then Oracle attempts to acquire the difference from the pool of public undo segments available. If there are enough public undo segments available in the pool, Oracle acquires the difference and brings all its acquired undo segments online. Note, however, that the calculation step is required primarily for public undo segments where Oracle Parallel Server is being used.

TIP

If not enough public undo segments are available for Oracle to acquire, the Oracle instance will start, and the database will open anyway, with no errors reported in trace files or the ALERT log.

Maintaining Undo Segments Manually

Several statements are available in Oracle for maintaining undo segments. The first is the `alter rollback segment` statement. You have already seen this statement used to bring the undo segment online, as in `alter rollback segment` *undo_seg* `online`. You can bring an undo segment offline in this way also, with `alter rollback segment` *undo_seg* `offline`. However, you can only bring an undo segment offline if it contains no active extents supporting transactions with uncommitted data changes. This statement is used to change any option in the `storage` clause as well, except for the size of the `initial` extent. However, note that changing the `next` extent size will alter the size of the next extent the undo segment acquires, not the size of any extent the undo segment already has acquired, and furthermore, doing this is not recommended for reasons already explained.

```
ALTER ROLLBACK SEGMENT rollseg01
STORAGE ( MAXEXTENTS 200
          OPTIMAL    310K );
```

The `alter rollback segment` statement has one additional clause for you to use, and that clause is `shrink to`. This clause enables you to manually reduce the storage allocation of your undo segment to a size not less than that specified for `optimal` (if `optimal` is specified). As with `optimal`, Oracle will not reduce the size of the undo segment if extents over the size specified are still active. If no value is specified, Oracle will attempt to shrink the undo segment to the value specified for `optimal`. Finally, Oracle will ignore the `alter rollback segment` *undo_seg* `shrink [to` *x*`[K|M]]` statement if the value specified for *x* is greater than the current undo segment allocation. The following code block shows appropriate use of the `shrink to` clause:

```
ALTER ROLLBACK SEGMENT rollseg01 SHRINK;
ALTER ROLLBACK SEGMENT rollseg01 SHRINK TO 220K;
```

Finally, once brought offline, an undo segment can be dropped if you feel it is no longer needed, or if you need to re-create it with different `initial`, `next`, and `minextents` extent size settings. The statement used for this purpose is `drop rollback segment` *undo_seg*.

```
DROP ROLLBACK SEGMENT rollseg01;

CREATE ROLLBACK SEGMENT rollseg01
TABLESPACE orgdbrbs
STORAGE ( INITIAL     12K
          NEXT        12K
          MINEXTENTS 25
          MAXEXTENTS 400
          OPTIMAL    300K )
```

TIP

If you want to manage undo segments manually while Oracle9i is running in automatic undo management mode, then you must change the UNDO_SUPPRESS_ERRORS `init.ora` *parameter to true. This parameter is false by default, meaning that any manual attempt to manage undo segments while Oracle automatically manages them will result in errors.*

For Review

1. What happens to database performance if Oracle has to allocate extents to its undo segments frequently without giving them up? What storage option can be used to minimize this occurrence?

2. How are `minextents` and `maxextents` used in sizing undo segments? What is the Rule of Four? What rules can you apply to sizing undo segments on batch applications? Why is it important to use many extents in your undo segment?

3. How are extents of an undo segment deallocated?

4. Identify the options available for the undo segment storage clause, and describe their general use. How does Oracle attempt to enforce equal sizing of all extents in undo segments?

5. How are undo segments brought online after creation? At instance startup?

6. What storage option cannot be modified by the `alter rollback segment` statement? How might you manually make an undo segment unavailable for transaction usage, and what might prevent you from doing so?

7. What is the `shrink to` clause of the `alter rollback segment statement`, and how is it used? When is it appropriate (or possible) to eliminate an undo segment, and what statement is used to do it?

Exercises

1. **You are attempting to manage undo segments manually while automatic undo management is enabled on your system. Which of the following choices identifies what will happen when you issue the `alter rollback segment` command in this context?**

   A. The undo segment will be altered as you requested.

   B. The undo segment will be altered, but Oracle will issue warnings.

   C. The undo segment will not be altered, and Oracle will issue errors.

   D. The database will fail.

2. **You are attempting to manage undo segments manually while automatic undo management is enabled in your system. Which of the following choices identifies an appropriate method to configure Oracle to allow this situation to occur?**

   A. Set UNDO_MANAGEMENT to AUTO.

   B. Set UNDO_SUPRESS_ERRORS to FALSE.

   C. Set UNDO_MANAGEMENT to MANUAL.

   D. Set UNDO_RETENTION to 1,800.

3. **You have disabled automatic undo management on your Oracle database. Which of the following choices identifies the method that must be employed in order to ensure that undo segments are available for user processes?**

   A. Set UNDO_TABLESPACE to the name of the undo tablespace.

   B. Set ROLLBACK_SEGMENTS to a list of undo segments to bring online.

   C. Bring the database online in read-only mode.

   D. Nothing—Oracle will bring undo segments online automatically.

Answer Key
1. C. 2. C. 3. B.

Obtaining Information about Undo Data

Oracle has many dictionary and dynamic performance views both old and new to track undo statistics. Both the undo as well as the undo data dictionary views have to be used to obtain full information about the undo data. The following is a list of the views to be aware of:

- **DBA_ROLLBACK_SEGS**   This is an existing view that displays the data about undo or undo segments such as the name of the undo segment, the tablespace they reside in, and their status.

- **DBA_UNDO_EXTENTS**   This data dictionary view contains the information about the `commit` time for each extent in the undo tablespace.

- **V$UNDOSTAT**   This view displays a histogram of statistical data to show the undo behavior. Each row in this view keeps statistics of undo segments in the instance for ten-minute intervals. This view can be used to estimate the amount of undo space required.

- **V$ROLLSTAT, V$ROLLNAME**   These two are old views that display the dynamic performance information of the undo segments.

For Review

Be sure you can identify the dictionary and dynamic performance views available for managing undo segments in Oracle.

Exercises

1. **This view offers performance information for Oracle-managed undo segments in the database:** _____.

2. **This view offers a listing of undo segments created by Oracle for handling undo information:** _____.

Answer Key
1. V$UNDOSTAT. 2. DBA_UNDO_EXTENTS.

Chapter Summary

In this chapter, we covered information regarding the management of segments in the Oracle database and the use of undo segments. These two topics comprise approximately 14 percent of the contents of the Oracle9i OCP DBA Fundamentals I exam. You learned about the different types of segments used in Oracle databases, along with some analysis techniques you can use for understanding the fragmentation and lifespan of segments. This information is useful because it gives you the basis for separating different types of segments into different tablespaces. You also learned about how Oracle acquires new extents for database objects when the current extent is full. The particular importance of object storage settings with respect to the size of extents allocated was covered in some detail as well. You then learned about the use of undo segments in Oracle. We discussed how to manage undo segments using automatic undo management, as well as how to manage them manually. We wrapped up our coverage of undo segments by pointing you to where you can find more information about undo segments in Oracle in the data dictionary.

Two-Minute Drill

- Every database object in Oracle is stored in a segment. Because these segments support data in Oracle that are used for different purposes, you should keep the different segments in different tablespaces.

- Understand the inverse proportional relationship between the lifespan of extents and fragmentation in the tablespace—the shorter the lifespan, the higher the potential for fragmentation in the tablespace.

- Remember that the method by which you can control the allocation of extents by database objects is determined by the storage settings for a database object. These can either be set at the object level or inherited from the default settings for the tablespace. The storage settings are

  - **initial**   First segment in the object

  - **next**   Next segment allocated (not simply the second one in the object)

  - **pctincrease**   Percentage increase of next extent allocated over `next` value

  - **minextents**   Minimum number of extents allocated at object creation

  - **maxextents**   Maximum number of extents the object can allocate

- **pctfree** How much of each block stays free after insert for row update

- **pctused** Threshold that usage must fall below before a row is added

- Understand how Oracle enables the DBA to control space usage at the block level with pctfree and pctused.

- Know what dictionary views are used to find information about storage structures, including DBA_SEGMENTS, DBA_TABLESPACES, DBA_TS_QUOTAS, V$TABLESPACE, DBA_EXTENTS, DBA_FREE_SPACE, and DBA_FREE_SPACE_COALESCED.

- Undo segments used to be called rollback segments in prior versions of Oracle.

- Undo segments enable transaction processing to occur by storing the old version of data that has been changed but not committed by the users.

- Oracle9i offers a new feature for undo segments—automatic undo management. To use automatic undo management, you must execute the following steps:

  1. Create undo tablespaces either when you create the database using the undo tablespace clause or by using the create undo tablespace command.

  2. Set the UNDO_MANAGEMENT parameter to AUTO and the UNDO_TABLESPACE parameter to the undo tablespace you created.

  3. Set the UNDO_RETENTION parameter to the length of time you want to retain undo information in the segments in support of Flashback Query.

- You can also manage undo segments manually, as you did in previous versions of Oracle. If you do so, set UNDO_MANAGEMENT to MANUAL. You might also want to set UNDO_SUPPRESS_ERRORS to TRUE in order to avoid the chance that your database running in automatic undo management will return errors if you try to manage undo segments manually.

- If you decide to manage undo segments manually, make sure that undo segments consist of equally sized extents.

- The pctincrease option is not permitted on undo segments if you create them manually.

- Undo segments must be brought online in order to use them. Oracle will take care of this automatically if you use automatic undo management, but if you use manual undo management, you have to bring them online yourself.

■ An undo segment cannot be taken offline until all active transactions writing undo entries have completed. This same restriction applies to tablespaces containing active undo segments.

■ Entries are associated with transactions in the undo segment via the use of a system change number (SCN).

■ Specific private undo segments can be allocated at startup if they are specified in the ROLLBACK_SEGMENTS parameter in init*sid*.ora when you're using manual undo management.

■ Monitor performance in undo segments with V$ROLLSTAT and V$WAITSTAT when using manual undo management.

■ Know the new dictionary views in support of automatic undo management.

Fill-in-the-Blank Questions

1. The storage option for database objects that can cause exponential growth in the size of each extent acquired for a database object is _____.

2. The type of segment in an Oracle database that stores the original data in a record being changed by a user process is _____.

3. This type of database segment stores data for the duration of a disk sort: _____.

4. This initialization parameter is used for enabling automatic undo management in Oracle: _____.

5. The value set for this parameter determines whether the `alter rollback segment` command will encounter errors when automatic undo management is enabled in Oracle: _____.

Chapter Questions

1. **When determining the number of undo segments in a database, which of the following choices identifies a factor to consider?**

   A. Concurrent transactions

   B. Size of typical transactions

   C. Size of rows in table most frequently changed

   D. Number of anticipated disk sorts

2. **How many undo segments will be required if the value set for TRANSACTIONS is 20 and the value set for TRANSACTIONS_PER_ROLLBACK_SEGMENT is 4?**

   A. Two

   B. Four

   C. Eight

   D. Nine

3. When an undo segment is created manually by you, its availability status is set to which of the following automatically by Oracle?

   A. Online

   B. Pending online

   C. Offline

   D. Stale

4. All of the following choices indicate a way to resolve the ORA-1555 Snapshot too old (rollback segment too small) error, except one. Which choice is it?

   A. Create undo segments with a higher optimal value.

   B. Create undo segments with higher maxextents.

   C. Create undo segments with larger extent sizes.

   D. Create undo segments with higher minextents.

5. You are managing transaction processing in Oracle. Entries in an undo segment are bound to a transaction by which of the following Oracle components?

   A. Number of commit operations performed

   B. Number of rollback operations performed

   C. ROWID

   D. System change number

6. You are managing segments in an Oracle table with storage settings of 100KB for initial and next when the table was first created, respectively, and pctincrease is set to 50. Which of the following choices identifies the size of the table after the fourth extent has been allocated?

   A. 225KB

   B. 325KB

   C. 350KB

   D. 575KB

7. You are setting block space utilization parameters for a table in a data warehouse. The table is loaded weekly with data and then made available to users for query-only access. Which of the following choices identifies an appropriate setting for block space utilization?

   A. `pctfree 5`

   B. `pctfree 40`

   C. `pctused 5`

   D. `pctused 40`

8. You just added an undo tablespace to the database and now want to configure automatic undo management in your Oracle database. Which of the following parameters is required for configuring this feature?

   A. UNDO_MANAGEMENT

   B. UNDO_TABLESPACE

   C. UNDO_RETENTION

   D. UNDO_SUPPRESS_ERRORS

Fill-in-the-Blank Answers

1. pctincrease

2. Undo

3. Temporary

4. UNDO_MANAGEMENT

5. UNDO_SUPPRESS_ERRORS

Answers to Chapter Questions

1. A. Concurrent transactions

Explanation The number of concurrent transactions is used in part to determine the number of undo segments your database should have. Had the question asked for which choice played a role in determining the size of extents or total undo segment size, then choices B or C would have been correct. Because disk sorts have little to do with undo segments, under no circumstances should you have chosen D.

2. C. Eight

Explanation Refer to the Rule of Four in creating undo segments. Remember, the equation is TRANSACTIONS/TRANSACTIONS_PER_ROLLBACK_SEGMENT. In this case, the result is five. This is a special case in the Rule of Four, which gets rounded up to eight.

3. C. Offline

Explanation Once created, an undo segment status is offline and must be brought online in order to be used. Refer to the discussion of undo segments. In order to bring it online, you must issue the `alter rollback segment online` statement, eliminating choice A. Pending online is not a valid status for undo segments in Oracle, eliminating choice B. Stale is a valid status for redo logs, but not for undo segments, eliminating choice D.

4. B. Create undo segments with higher `maxextents`.

Explanation Refer to the discussion of indexes created in conjunction with integrity constraints.

5. D. System change number

Explanation   SCNs are identifiers that group data-change statements together as one transaction both in undo segments and redo logs. The number of `commit` operations or `rollback` operations performed simply reduces the number of active transactions on the database, and thus the amount of active undo in an undo segment. Thus, choices A and B are incorrect. Finally, ROWIDs correspond to the location on disk of rows for a table and have little to do with grouping transactions, so choice C is incorrect.

6. D. 575KB

Explanation   The total amount of space allocated for this table is 575 because the first two extents are 100KB a piece, the third extent is 100KB×1.5, or 150KB, and the fourth is 100KB×1.5×1.5, or 225KB. Although choice A correctly identifies the size of the fourth extent, your careful reading of the chapter would tell you that the question is actually asking for the total size of the table after all four extents are allocated. Choice B indicates the total size of the first and fourth extent, whereas choice B indicates the total size of the second and third extent.

8. A. `pctfree 5`

Explanation   Because this table is loaded periodically and then accessed by users for queries only, you know that you do not need to leave much space left over for row growth. Thus, you know that you must focus on `pctfree` rather than `pctused` because `pctfree` is used for managing row growth. Thus, choices C and D can be eliminated right away. Of the two, choice A is the most correct answer because it offers the lowest setting for `pctfree`.

7. A. UNDO_MANAGEMENT

Explanation   In order to configure automatic undo management, you must set the UNDO_MANAGEMENT parameter in your `init.ora` file to AUTO. This is the only step required for initiating automatic undo management once the undo tablespace has been created because Oracle can figure out which tablespace to use if an undo tablespace exists; thus, choice B is incorrect. Choice C is incorrect because UNDO_RETENTION has a default value of 900. Finally, because you probably won't manage your undo segments manually when automatic undo management is enabled, you shouldn't need to change the setting for UNDO_SUPPRESS_ERRORS, making choice D incorrect.

CHAPTER
5

Managing
Database Objects

n this chapter, you will learn about and demonstrate knowledge in the following areas:

- Managing tables
- Managing indexes
- Managing data integrity

As a DBA, a big part of your daily job function is the creation and maintenance of database objects like tables and indexes. This is especially true for database administrators who manage development and test databases. Even DBAs working on production systems will find that at least some of their time is spent exploring the depths of setting up database objects. In this chapter, you will cover what you need to know for creating tables, indexes, and integrity constraints. Although there are other objects in Oracle, such as sequences, cluster tables, or index-organized tables (IOTs), tables and indexes are the core objects of most every Oracle database. Integrity constraints present a unique perspective on both tables and indexes. On one hand, constraints prevent bad data from entering your tables. On the other hand, sometimes integrity constraints use indexes as the underlying mechanism to support their activities. This chapter covers material that will comprise about 18 percent of the Oracle9*i* DBA Fundamentals I exam.

Managing Tables

In this section, you will cover the following topics related to managing tables:

- Various methods of storing data
- Distinguishing Oracle datatypes
- Extended and restricted ROWIDs
- Structure of a row
- Creating permanent and temporary tables
- Managing the storage structures in a table
- Reorganizing, truncating, and dropping tables
- Dropping columns in tables

Tables are used in Oracle for storing data. You already probably think of a table from a data perspective as an object similar to a spreadsheet insofar as a table has columns and rows for storing data. All information stored in a column will have the same datatype, whereas a row is considered a collection of single values defined for every column. This section will explore the table from an administrative perspective, as a collection of bits and bytes inside a file whose storage must be planned and managed carefully. We'll cover the different types of tables available in Oracle at a broad level, and also take a closer look at datatypes available in your Oracle database. You'll also take a long, hard look at ROWIDs, the mechanism Oracle uses for keeping track of where individual rows are stored in tables in files in databases. You'll look at the structure of a row and how to create tables in Oracle. Maintenance activities for tables will be covered as well.

Various Methods of Storing Data

Before beginning your exploration of tables in detail, consider the following question—how does a table differ from the data segments we already discussed in earlier chapters? After all, the data that users place in tables is actually stored in segments and extents inside datafiles. However, that's precisely what makes tables different—they offer a conceptual way to think of data inside a segment or extent that also enables us to reference that data, manipulate it, add new data, or even take data away. In other words, tables are the constructs that enable users to access the data that we as DBAs will think of as being stored in segments and extents.

Oracle supports various types of tables for storing user data in an Oracle segment. There are regular tables for housing permanent data and temporary tables for temporary data. Most DBAs will find that their organizational data needs are handled sufficiently with these two types of tables. However, there are also many exotic variations of tables that Oracle has introduced over the years, each of which serves an important niche purpose. These types of tables include partitioned tables, IOTs, and clustered tables. Let's now look at each of these table types in more detail.

Regular Tables

Regular tables are the most common types of table used storing the user data. When you execute the `create table` command, the default table that Oracle creates is a regular table. In keeping with E. F. Codd's original definition of tables in his landmark work on relational database theory, Oracle does not guarantee that row data will be stored in a particular order. This type of data storage is sometimes referred to as *heap-organized*, where data is stored in an unordered collection, or a heap. As you already know, order can be imposed later using various clauses in your SQL queries that you learned about for the OCP Oracle9*i* Introduction to SQL exam.

Temporary Tables

The users of Oracle who come to Oracle database administration from the world of Microsoft SQL Server might be familiar with the following concept. Suppose you want to create a complex report in which data must be run through a series of complex processing steps. To simplify processing, you believe it would be helpful to store data in an intermediate format using a table. The problem is that you don't want users to access that intermediate information during or after the report's execution, for fear of the confusion that may result. You could simply use a standard Oracle table, but then you have to remember to clean out the table when appropriate.

Oracle offers temporary tables as a means to enable you to create a table to retain session-private data for only the duration of the transaction or session. Although it doesn't necessarily offer functionality that isn't already available in Oracle using other means, the temporary table solves many annoying little problems associated with the alternative methods for you. First, because the data is only available to the session putting it there, there's no worry that other users will be able to see your data before you want them to. In addition, because the data stored in temporary tables is temporary in nature, there is no need for you to worry about eliminating the contents of the table when you don't need the data anymore. At the end of the transaction or session, the data will disappear, depending on how you define the temporary table.

TIP
Even though Oracle supports session privacy with respect to data in a temporary table, all temporary tables in Oracle are available for all current sessions to use, and the definition of the temporary table will continue to exist in the data dictionary even after its data gets eliminated.

Partitioned Tables
Partitioned tables are just like regular tables in Oracle except for an important small feature—they enable you to reference the individual segments that might support larger tables directly. The segment is not considered a separate database object, but rather it's considered a subobject that you happen to be able to reference directly. Partitioned tables give you more control over data distribution across multiple disks in the machine hosting the Oracle database. Every disk in a machine has a channel or hardware mechanism designed to facilitate access to that disk. However, that channel might not be able to provide enough bandwidth for many processes to access the disk fast enough to provide data for users during peak periods of activity.

This is where partitioning factors in. You can partition a large table that is accessed during peak periods and spread the data stored in that table across many disks. Because each disk spins independently and may have a channel available for direct access to it, partitioning supports a greater degree of parallel processing for busy databases than regular tables could allow. You might find partitioning used for the purposes of scaling extremely large tables, such as those found in data warehouses. In a partitioned table, data is stored in each partition according to a partition key, or column, that defines which range of row data goes into which partition. Each partition can then be stored in different tablespaces. Every partition in a table must have the same columns. There are several other facts about partitions that are worth knowing before you implement them, but because partitioning isn't a focus area for the OCP Oracle9*i* DBA core track, we won't spend a lot of time on this subject.

TIP

Several benefits are seen with partitions, including increased data availability and the potential for parallel data-change operations operating on different partitions simultaneously.

IOTs

In regular tables, data is stored in heap-organized fashion, which as you know means that data is not stored any in ordered way. Primary key indexes are typically associated with these tables in order to speed access to the unordered data in the table. These indexes are created in a B-tree structure, which is stored separately from the table. B-tree structure permits speedy retrieval of information stored within that structure.

Rather than storing data in an unstructured heap, Oracle stores data in index-organized tables in a B-tree index structure. The data is stored in the order of the primary key of the table. The rows in an index-organized table are not only sorted by their primary key values, but each row contains the primary key column values and other nonkey column values in it. There is no separate index structure to store the primary key in index-organized tables. This reduces storage overhead, especially for tables that don't have too many columns in them. Index-organized tables are particularly useful for data that is mostly retrieved based on primary key. An example of this sort of data would be a lookup table, where important terms are associated with short alphanumeric codes.

Cluster Table

Sometimes, you might have a set of tables that are all queried for data together at the same time. For example, an employee expense reimbursement system might contain two tables that are always being used together in a parent/child fashion. The parent table might contain key facts about each expense reimbursement request submitted by an employee. This table might store one row for each employee reimbursement request, containing column values defined for the employee's name or ID number, the expense request ID number, and the mailing address where the reimbursement check must be sent. The child table contains line items for each reimbursement request. For example, if the employee took a flight to Singapore for a trade show that lasted several days, the child table would store several rows, each corresponding to a particular expense (airfare, hotel, car, conference registration, meals, and so on), along with a charge-to account number for each expense.

A cluster might be handy in this business context because even though the data is stored as two separate tables, employees who want to see their particular expense reimbursement requests will almost invariably request data from both tables at the same time. Clusters enable you to store data from several tables inside a single segment so users can retrieve data from those two tables together very quickly. In order to store two or more tables together inside a cluster segment, the tables must all share at least one column in common. This column becomes the cluster key. Because clusters store related rows of different tables in the same physical data segments, it offers two benefits:

■ The disk I/O is reduced and access time improves for joins of clustered tables.

■ The common column(s) only needs to be stored once for all the tables grouped in a cluster.

TIP
Although it is a useful type of table, clusters work best when the data stored in them is primarily static or read-only. This is because the rows of one table stored in cluster segment blocks are laid out so that they are close to the associated rows from the other tables. If the size of a row increases too dramatically after Oracle performs the initial row layout in the cluster, then data could get shifted around inside the blocks of the cluster, negating the performance increase you might have otherwise enjoyed.

For Review

1. Regular tables in Oracle are great for general data storage needs. They are the most flexible type of database object in Oracle for storing data.

2. Temporary tables in Oracle are useful for housing intermediate datasets during complex processing for the duration of a transaction or session.

3. Partitioned tables in Oracle enable you to reference individual segments of data in a larger table directly, as though they were a miniature copy of the

table containing only a specific range of that table's data. These objects are handy for extremely large tables in data warehouses.

4. All the tables listed previously store data in a heap structure. To get at the data quickly, DBAs typically create indexes on the table. IOTs house data in an index structure to reduce storage overhead by not separating the table from the index. The result is that IOTs provide speedy lookups on their contents.

5. Usually, a segment houses information for only one table. However, clusters permit the storage of more than one table's data inside a single segment. This is useful for situations when users always access two or more tables together when attempting to access their data.

Exercises

1. **Your Oracle database stores data in a single table that is queried heavily by users of a data warehouse application. To speed parallel processing of data in that table, which of the following table variants might you consider switching to?**

   A. Temporary table

   B. Index-organized table

   C. Cluster table

   D. Partitioned table

2. **You have a long-running extract-transformation-load (ETL) batch process that performs extensive processing on several intermediate sets of data. At the end of processing, the intermediate sets must be eliminated in favor of the result set, which is then loaded directly into another table in the data warehouse. In order to facilitate that processing by providing a tabular disk storage mechanism, which of the following database objects might you use?**

   A. Temporary table

   B. Index-organized table

   C. Cluster table

   D. Standard Oracle table

3. **The rows inside three Oracle tables supporting a customer order entry system are frequently accessed together by means of a table join. Because**

data is always being added to the tables, you leave a lot of extra space inside each block to accommodate growth. Which of the following types of tables would be useful for storing the data in this context?

A. Temporary table

B. Index-organized table

C. Cluster table

D. Standard Oracle table

4. You are deploying some HIPAA-compliant healthcare applications supporting patient diagnosis and treatment. Every diagnosis is associated with a five-letter alphanumeric code that the application looks up dynamically as new patient records are entered. A sample of these codes is shown in the following block:

```
DIAGNOSIS      CODE
------------   ----------------
Influenza      D43I2
Chicken Pox    R501F
Sore Throat    T40AS
```

Which of the following types of tables would work best for this application?

A. Temporary table

B. Index-organized table

C. Cluster table

D. Standard Oracle table

Answer Key
1. D. 2. A. 3. D. Remember, clusters work best when the data stored in the associated tables is static or read-only. 4. B.

Distinguishing Oracle Datatypes

Recall that each column in a table stores data of a particular datatype. Each row can contain values for columns of different datatypes, but each individual column can house data of only one datatype. Although Oracle offers many different datatypes that are useful for storing data, Oracle does not have as many different datatypes as you might be used to, particularly if you come to Oracle database administration from using single-user or department-level database products. For example, Oracle does not have a currency datatype because currency is nothing more than a number with a currency format mask. Thus, rather than bog users down with many different numeric datatypes, Oracle instead provides only one datatype for numbers, NUMBER, and a robust mechanism for applying whatever format masks you might deem appropriate to give your numbers meaning. Let's look at Oracle datatypes in more detail.

Oracle Scalar Datatypes

Oracle substantially reorganized the available datatypes between versions 7.3 and 8.0. There are two basic categories of datatypes in Oracle: built-in types and user-defined types. Within the built-in types, there are three basic classes of datatypes available: scalar, collection, and relationship datatypes. Within the user-defined types, the classes of datatypes you can define for your own application uses are endless. Let's look at the scalar datatypes in detail.

CHAR(L) and NCHAR(L)   These are fixed-length text string datatypes, where the data is stored with blanks padded out to the full width of the column (represented here by L). NCHAR is CHAR's NLS multibyte equivalent type. NLS stands for National Language Set, and it is used for making Oracle available in languages other than American English. Some world languages with large character sets (such as Japanese, Chinese, or Korean) or other substantial differences from English (such as being read from right to left, like Arabic or Hebrew) need multiple bytes to store one character. English, on the other hand, requires only one byte to store a character, such as the letter *A*. Both NCHAR and CHAR columns and variables can be up to 2,000 bytes in length in Oracle. In Oracle7, the limit was 255 bytes.

VARCHAR2(L) and NVARCHAR2(L)   These are variable-length text string datatypes, where data is stored using only the number of bytes required to store the actual value, which in turn can vary in length for each row. NVARCHAR2 is VARCHAR2's NLS multibyte equivalent type. (Actually, that's not quite correct: NCHAR and NVARCHAR2 are NLS datatypes that enable the storage of either fixed-width or variable-width character sets; you can also use them for nonmultibyte character sets, but that's not common. So, for all intents and purposes, NVARCHAR2 is VARCHAR2's NLS multibyte equivalent type.) These can be up to 4,000 bytes in length in Oracle.

NUMBER(L,P)   These are always stored as variable-length data, where one byte is used to store the exponent, one byte is used for every two significant digits of the number's mantissa, and one byte is used for negative numbers if the number of significant digits is less than 38 bytes.

TIP
A mantissa is the decimal part of a logarithm.
Oracle uses the logarithm of a number to store the
binary version of the number so that it takes up less
space.

DATE   This is stored as a fixed-length field of 7 bytes. The Oracle DATE format actually includes time as well as date, and this information is stored internally as a number. You can apply whatever formatting masks you need in order to render the date in the manner appropriate for your situation. By default, Oracle shows date information as DD-MON-YY, or a two-digit date, followed by a three-letter abbreviation for the month, followed by a two-digit year. Note that Oracle stores the date internally as a number that includes four-digit year references. The two-digit default representation of year information is just a formatting mask. You can change this format at the system or session level easily using the `alter [system|session] set nls_date_format = 'mask'` command, where an actual format mask is substituted for `mask`.

RAW(L)   This datatype holds a small amount of binary data. There are no conversions performed on raw data in Oracle. The raw data is simply stored as is. Oracle can house up to 2,000 bytes in a RAW column.

ROWID   This datatype is used to store ROWID information. A ROWID is a 10-byte string that identifies the location of row data in a datafile.

Comparing LONG, LONG RAW, and LOB Datatypes

Oracle can store very large amounts of information in columns using other scalar datatypes as well. There are several datatypes to be aware of, some of which are provided mainly for backward compatibility. The datatypes available in Oracle for storing very large amounts of data in a single column are listed as follows:

- **LONG**   Stores up to 2GB of text data.

- **LONG RAW**   Stores up to 2GB of binary data.

- **BLOB**   Stores up to 4GB binary data.

- **CLOB and NCLOB**   Store up to 4GB text data; NCLOB is a large fixed-width NLS datatype.

- **BFILE**   Stores up to 4GB unstructured data in operating system files.

Several key differences between LONG and LOB types make LOB types more versatile and helpful for large object management. First, there can be only one

LONG column in a table, because the LONG column data is stored *inline,* meaning that all data in the LONG column for each row in the table is stored in contiguous data blocks inside the segment used for storing the table's data. In contrast, there can be many LOB columns in a table, because when the LOB value is over 4,000 bytes, only a locator for the LOB type is stored inline with the table data—in other words, no LOB will ever require more than 4,000 bytes of space inline with other table data. The rest of the data in the LOB columns is stored in an overflow segment. Thus, `select` statements on LONG columns return the actual data, whereas the same statement on a LOB column returns only the locator. Oracle supports the use of the LOB types in object types except NCLOB, whereas LONG does not. LOBs can also be larger than LONGs—4GB for LOBs versus 2GB for LONGs. LOB data can also be accessed piecewise, whereas LONG access is sequential; only the entire value in the LONG column can be obtained, whereas parts of the LOB can be obtained.

Collection Datatypes

A collection is a gathering of like-defined elements. There are two collection types available in Oracle. The first is called a variable-length array (VARRAY). A VARRAY can be thought of as an ordered list of objects, all of the same datatype. The VARRAY is defined to have two special attributes (in addition to those attributes within the objects the VARRAY contains). These attributes are a *count* for the number of elements in the VARRAY and the *limit* for the maximum number of elements that can appear in a VARRAY. Although the VARRAY can have any number of elements, the limit must be predefined. Each element in the VARRAY has an index, which is a number corresponding to the position of the element in the array. Constraints and default values may not be created for elements in a VARRAY, and once the VARRAY is created, the user only refers to an individual element in a VARRAY with PL/SQL (although SQL can be used to access the entire VARRAY).

The other collection type is called the nested table and can be thought of as a table within a table. The nested table architecture is exceptionally suited for applications that have parent/child tables with referential integrity. A nested table is an unordered list of row records, each having the same structure. These rows are usually stored away from the table, with a reference pointer from the corresponding row in the parent table to the child table. Like VARRAYs, nested tables can have any number of elements, with the added bonus that you don't need to predetermine a maximum limit.

Reference and User-Defined Datatypes

Finally, consider the reference type and user-defined types. Developers can use the reference type to define a foreign key relationship between two objects. The reference type can reference all columns in the table for a particular row—it is a pointer to a particular object, not the object itself. User-defined types are abstract datatypes or compositions of existing scalar or other types that you can define to serve highly specialized purposes in Oracle. They are typically composed of scalar, collection, or other user-defined types.

For Review

1. There are two general categories for datatypes—built-in and user-defined. Within built-in types, you have scalar, reference, and collection datatypes. User-defined types are specialized composite datatypes you build for yourself using existing built-in types.

2. Be sure you can describe the difference between the LONG datatype and LOB datatypes available in Oracle for the storage of very large amounts of data in a single column. LOB types offer several advantages and are the preferred type for this purpose. The LONG type is provided for backward compatibility.

Exercises

1. This datatype is capable of storing up to 2,000 bytes of character data, padded with trailing blank spaces to the entire width of the column: _____.

2. In Oracle, you can store up to _____(A)_____ bytes of data in a RAW column and up to 4,000 bytes in a _____(B)_____ column.

3. Internally, Oracle stores DATE information as a _____.

4. A ___(A)____ is a large object datatype capable of storing up to _____(B)____ GB of binary data. Similarly, a CLOB is a large object datatype capable of storing _____(C)_____ data.

Answer Key
1. CHAR. **2.** (A) 2,000; (B) VARCHAR2. **3.** Number. **4.** (A) BLOB; (B) 4; (C) text.

Extended and Restricted ROWIDs

Recall that we mentioned the use of ROWIDs in Oracle for identifying the location of a row inside the database. ROWIDs are not addresses in memory or on disk; rather, they are identifiers that Oracle can use to compute the location of a row in a table. Locating a table row using the ROWID is the fastest way to find a row in a table. Although ROWID information can be queried like other columns in a table, a ROWID is not stored explicitly as a column value. When users add new rows to a database, Oracle generates a ROWID to identify that row's unique database location. The particular ROWID Oracle generates depends on a variety of factors, including

- The datafile storing the table that particular row is added to
- The segment corresponding to the object that the row will be stored in
- The block inside the segment that will house the row
- The slot or location inside an Oracle block that the row will be stored in

The previous bullets correspond to the components of information Oracle uses to generate a ROWID using Oracle's extended ROWID format that is 16 bytes in size and contains these four components. This format was introduced in Oracle 8.0.3 to overcome a limitation in the amount of space on disk that prior versions of Oracle were capable of addressing. In versions of Oracle after 8.0.3, Oracle uses 80 bits (10 bytes) for storage of an extended ROWID. The ROWID itself consists of four components: an object number (32 bits), a relative file number (10 bits), a block number (22 bits), and a row (slot) number (16 bits). Extended ROWIDs are displayed as 18-character representations of the location of data in the database, with each character represented in a base-64 format consisting of *A* through *Z*, *a* through *z*, zero through nine, +, and /. The first six characters correspond to the data object number, the next two are the relative file number, the next five are the block number, and the last three are the row number. With the use of extended ROWIDs, Oracle is capable of addressing rows in tables such that the database can grow to a virtually limitless size. The following code block demonstrates extended ROWID format:

```
SQL> select name, ROWID from employee;
NAME        ROWID
----------  ------------------
DURNAM      AAAA3kAAGAAAAGsAAA
BLANN       AAAA3kAAGAAAAGsAAB
```

The limitation we mentioned previously was due to the restricted ROWID format Oracle used in releases of the database software prior to Oracle 8.0.3. Historically, Oracle used a 6-byte format for ROWIDs that we now consider restricted because it does not store the object number for the table the row will be stored in. This format was acceptable in older versions of Oracle because at that time Oracle required all datafiles to have a unique file number within the database, regardless of the tablespace the file belonged to. In contrast, Oracle8*i* and later releases number datafiles relative to the tablespace they belong to. Restricted ROWIDs were displayed as 18 characters in base-16 format, where the first 8 characters represent the block number, characters 10 through 13 are the row number, and characters 15 through 18 are the (absolute) file number. Characters 9 and 14 are static separator characters.

With the added functionality provided by extended ROWIDs, you may wonder why Oracle bothers with restricted ROWIDs at all. Indeed, restricted ROWIDs are rarely used anymore, with one exception. Restricted ROWID format is still used to locate rows in nonpartitioned indexes for nonpartitioned tables where all index entries refer to rows within the same segment, thus eliminating any uncertainty about relative file numbers, because a segment can be stored in one and only one tablespace.

TIP

You might think it is silly, but here's how you can remember the components of Oracle ROWIDs. In Oracle7, the components are block ID, row number, and file number, which shorten to the acronym BRF. In Oracle9i, the components are object ID, block ID, row number, and relative file number, which shorten to OBRRF. To remember the acronyms, imagine how little dogs sound when they bark.

For Review

1. ROWIDs are addresses that point to the location of a row on disk with respect to a file, block, row number, and data object number.

2. Versions of Oracle prior to 8.0.3 use a restricted ROWID format. Current versions of Oracle still use this format for very limited purposes.

3. Starting with Oracle 8.0.3, Oracle also employs an extended ROWID format enabling the database to address more space on disk than previously allowed. This dramatically increases the amount of space an Oracle database can grow to.

Exercises

1. **You can query the ROWID of a row just as you would any other column (True/False).**

2. **The extended ROWID format uses a ROWID format __(A)__ bytes in size, where each symbol in the ROWID is in base-__(B)__ format.**

3. In contrast, the restricted ROWID format uses a ROWID format __(A)__ bytes in size, where each symbol in the ROWID is in base-__(B)__ format.

4. The primary difference between extended and restricted ROWID formats arises from the fact that earlier versions of Oracle required all datafile numbers to be _____(A)_____ in the database, whereas later versions of Oracle number datafiles _____(B)_____ to the tablespace the datafile is part of.

Answer Key
1. True. **2.** (A) 10; (B) 64. **3.** (A) 6; (B) 16. **4.** (A) unique; (B) relative.

Structure of Data Blocks and Rows

A cornerstone of storage management is Oracle's capability to enable you to manage the space in a data block. The size of a block is determined when you create the database by the DB_BLOCK_SIZE initialization parameter set for the instance at the time you create the database. Data block size is almost always a multiple of operating system block size. Usually, an operating system uses a block size of either 512 or 1,024 bytes. Oracle blocks are therefore a conglomeration of operating system blocks. An Oracle block can be anywhere from 2,048 to 16,384 bytes in size (even larger for some operating system platforms), with 8,192 bytes being a popular and common size for most Oracle databases. To understand more about data blocks, let's now explore their contents in more detail. There are several different components inside every data block in your Oracle database. Figure 5-1 illustrates block and row structure in Oracle. These components are divided loosely into the following areas:

■ **Block header and directory information** Each block has a block header containing information about the block, including information about the table that owns the block and the row data the block contains.

■ **Free space** This is the space reserved for growth of existing rows in the block and is determined by the `pctfree` setting used when the object was created.

■ **Space occupied by existing rows** Every time a row is added to an object, Oracle places that row in the block. The amount of space available for rows to be added is determined by the setting for DB_BLOCK_SIZE, minus the space occupied by the block header, minus the space reserved by the setting for `pctfree`.

Looking at the Rows Themselves

Row data consists of the actual rows of each data table. Each row in a table has a row header. The *row header* stores the information about the number of columns in the row, chaining information, and the current lock status for the row. The row header is followed by actual row data. *Row data* consists of the actual rows of each data table. Row data is divided into columns, or column data. The *column data* for each row is stored in the order in which the columns were defined for the table. Additionally, a field indicating the *width* of the column is stored along with the non-NULL column data. If a column value is NULL for that row, no width field or column value will be stored in the block for that row column, and no bytes are used for the storage of NULL column values. Thus, you can see why we need to maintain some free space via `pctfree` for row growth. The column width field is 1 byte if the value for the column in this row is under 250 bytes, and it is 3 bytes if the value for the column in this row is 250 bytes or more. In both cases, Oracle stores a number identifying the width of the column value for this row only when the column value is not NULL.

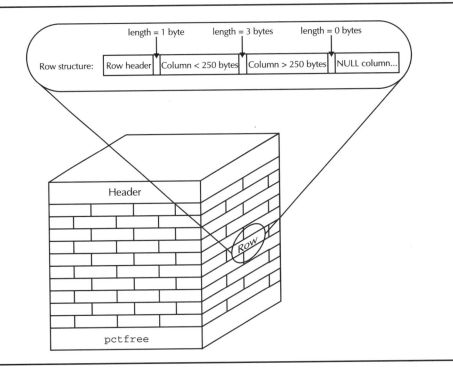

FIGURE 5-1. *The block and row structure in Oracle*

For Review

1. Blocks consist of three components—a block header, row data, and leftover free space to accommodate existing row growth.

2. Rows themselves consist of a header, column data, and a field indicating the width of each column.

3. If no data is stored in the column for a particular row, Oracle doesn't waste any space in the block indicating that fact. Instead, nothing is stored there.

Exercises

1. Every block in an Oracle database consists of a _____(A)_____, _____(B)_____, and _____(C)_____.

2. If a non-NULL value is stored for a column in a particular row, the width field will be __(A)__ byte(s) in size if the column value is less than 250 bytes wide, and __(B)__ byte(s) in size if the column value is 250 or more bytes wide.

3. A column value width field is not stored for a row with the value for the column is _____.

Answer Key
1. (A) block header; (B) row data; (C) free space. **2.** (A) 1; (B) 3. NULL.

Creating Permanent and Temporary Tables

Recall that for the OCP Oracle9*i* Introduction to SQL exam, you learned how to create permanent and temporary tables using the `create table` command. We're going to review how to do so here. However, we're also going to discuss how to manage storage considerations when doing so. Recall that in previous discussions of creating tablespaces, we discussed the use of the `default storage` clause. The settings in the `default storage` clause are applied to objects placed in that tablespace when the object itself gets created without a `storage` clause. In this discussion, we'll talk in more detail about the `storage` clause that can be defined for an object when it is created.

Creating Permanent Tables

Let's now look at creating permanent or regular tables in Oracle. You create a table in Oracle using the `create table` command. For this discussion, we'll assume you are placing your table into a dictionary-managed tablespace in order to cover the use of the `storage` clause. Later we'll discuss how locally managed tablespaces and uniform extent management factor into the `storage` clause you may define when creating your tables. The following code block shows an example of the `create table` command:

```
CREATE TABLE EMPLOYEE
(empid          NUMBER(10),
lastname        VARCHAR2(25),
firstname       VARCHAR2(25),
salary          NUMBER(10,4),
CONSTRAINT      pk_employee_01
PRIMARY KEY     (empid))
TABLESPACE data
PCTFREE     20  PCTUSED     50
INITRANS    1   MAXTRANS    255
NOCACHE         LOGGING
STORAGE  ( INITIAL 100K   NEXT   150K
           MINEXTENTS 4   MAXEXTENTS  300
           PCTINCREASE 20 );
```

The `tablespace` keyword indicates which tablespace Oracle should create the table in. If you do not specify this clause, Oracle will put the table in the default tablespace you were assigned to when your userid was created. The next two clauses are for space utilization. Recall from an earlier discussion that the `pctfree` keyword specifies space that Oracle leaves free when inserting rows to accommodate growth later via updates. The `pctused` option specifies a threshold percentage of a block that the actual contents of row data must fall below before Oracle will consider the block free for new row inserts.

The next two space utilization clauses, `initrans` and `maxtrans`, control Oracle's capability to make concurrent updates to a data block. The `initrans` option specifies the initial number of transactions that can `update` the rows in a data block concurrently, whereas `maxtrans` specifies the maximum number of transactions that can `update` the rows in a data block concurrently. For the most part, the default values for each of these options should not be changed. For `initrans`, the default for tables is 1, while for clustered tables the default is 2. For `maxtrans`, the default for tables is 255.

The `nocache` clause specifies that Oracle should not make these blocks persistent in the buffer cache if a `select` statement on the table results in a full table scan. In this case, `select * from EMPLOYEE` would have Oracle load blocks into the buffer cache so that those blocks will not persist for very long. If you wanted the table to stay cached in the buffer cache when `select * from EMPLOYEE` was issued, you would specify the `cache` keyword instead. The default is `nocache`, which specifies that the blocks retrieved for this table are placed at the least recently used end of the LRU list in the buffer cache when a full table scan is performed.

The next clause, `logging`, tells Oracle to track table creation in the redo log so that in the event of disk failure, the table could be recovered. This is the default. However, this could be changed to `nologging` so that redo is not logged, which is handy in situations like the creation of the table and certain types of bulk data loads after which the DBA plans to take a backup after loading the data into Oracle will not be logged in the redo log file. Finally, you can specify `storage` clauses for table creation that will override the default storage settings of the tablespace you create the object in. The only tablespace default that your `storage` clause will not override is `minimum extent`.

Rules of Thumb about Table Storage for OCP

Observe the following rules of thumb when creating tables, and remember them for the OCP Oracle9*i* DBA Fundamentals I exam:

- Tables do not go in the same tablespace as undo segments, temporary segments, index segments, or into the SYSTEM tablespace.

- In order to make sure there is as little fragmentation in the tablespace as possible, have a collection of standard extent sizes that are complementary for your tables or use uniform extent allocation. This latter feature is used in Oracle9*i* by default, although Oracle will allocate multiple extents of uniform size in order to adhere to the allocation settings for `initial` or `next` in the `storage` clause of your `create table` command.

- Recall that the `cache` statement makes blocks read into the buffer cache via full table scans persist for much longer than they otherwise would. If you have a small lookup table accessed frequently, you may want to keep it in memory by specifying the `cache` clause or by issuing `alter table lookup_tblname` cache.

TIP
In Oracle9i, all tables are by default created as locally managed tables unlike pre-Oracle9i where tables were by default created dictionary-managed tables.

Creating Temporary Tables

Temporary tables are created with the `create global temporary table name ( tbldef ) on commit [delete|preserve] rows` statement. Your *tbldef* table definition can use any of the column or constraint definitions that a permanent table might, and associated temporary indexes will be generated in support of primary or unique keys. The data in a temporary table is stored in memory, inside the sort area. Thus, if more space is required, temporary segments in your temporary tablespace are used. When on commit delete rows is specified, the data in a temporary table (along with data in any associated index) is purged after the transaction completes. When on commit preserve rows is specified, rows will be stored in the table until the user who created the temporary table terminates the session. For that period, you can use the temporary table in the same way you would use any other table. If you do not specify an on commit clause, Oracle will use on commit delete rows by default. Let's look at an example where user SCOTT creates and uses a temporary table:

```
SQL> connect scott/tiger
Connected.
SQL> create global temporary table mytemptab
  2  (col1 number,
  3    col2 varchar2(30));
Table created.
SQL> insert into mytemptab values (1,'JUNK');
1 row created.
SQL> select * from mytemptab;
      COL1 COL2
--------- ---------------------------
         1 JUNK
SQL> commit;
Commit complete.
SQL> select * from mytemptab;
no rows selected
```

Now, let's look at the use of a temporary table where we want the data to persist for the duration of the session:

```
SQL> connect scott/tiger
Connected.
SQL> create global temporary table T_TABLE
  2  (col1 number,
  3    col2 varchar2(20))
  4  on commit preserve rows;
Table created.
SQL> insert into t_table values (1, 'JUNK');
1 row created.
SQL> select * from t_table;
      COL1 COL2
--------- --------------------
```

```
        1 JUNK
SQL> commit;
Commit complete.
SQL> select * from t_table;
    COL1 COL2
--------- --------------------
        1 JUNK
SQL> connect turner/ike
Connected.
SQL> connect scott/tiger
Connected.
SQL> select * from t_table;
no rows selected
```

Considerations When Using Temporary Tables

As I said a moment ago, other users can utilize the temporary table SCOTT created, too. They just won't see SCOTT's data. Likewise, SCOTT won't see their data. Furthermore, if SCOTT issues the truncate table MYTEMPTAB, only SCOTT's data will be removed. Other users' data will still be in the table. You may join the temporary table with permanent tables and create objects like views, indexes, and triggers that form object dependencies on the temporary table. However, no view can be created that contains a join between temporary and permanent tables. The `create global temporary table` statement does not log any redo, so temporary table data changes are not recoverable. However, data changes made to temporary tables will generate rollback information to enable Oracle to roll back the transaction and thus, the temporary table data, in the event the instance crashes. The TEMPORARY and DURATION columns in the DBA_TABLES view indicate whether a table is a temporary table and how long the data in the table will persist.

Temporary Tables and Storage

Oracle stores temporary table data in temporary segments in a temporary tablespace. Because temporary tablespace segment allocations are managed uniformly by Oracle, you typically do not need to worry about specifying a `storage` clause when creating your temporary tablespace. Instead, focus your attention as DBA on the question of whether or not the data in the temporary table should persist for the duration of a transaction or session.

For Review

1. Be sure you can create tables with appropriate storage settings in Oracle.

2. Be able to describe the concept underlying temporary tables in Oracle. Know the purposes they serve with respect to session-private storage of

information, global availability for all users, and retention of data for either the length of the transaction or the length of the session.

3. Understand how to create temporary tables in Oracle9*i*, including how to define the period of time the data in the temporary table will be retained. Know also where to find information about temporary tables in Oracle9*i*.

Exercises

1. **Your DATA tablespace is locally managed and uses uniform extent allocation. You issue the following statement:**

```
CREATE TABLE EMPLOYEE
(empid          NUMBER(10),
lastname        VARCHAR2(25),
firstname       VARCHAR2(25),
salary          NUMBER(10,4),
CONSTRAINT      pk_employee_01
PRIMARY KEY     (empid))
TABLESPACE data
PCTFREE   20  PCTUSED    50
INITRANS   1  MAXTRANS   255
NOCACHE       LOGGING
STORAGE ( INITIAL 100K  NEXT  150K
          MINEXTENTS 4  MAXEXTENTS  300
          PCTINCREASE 20 );
```

Which of the following statements is true about the table you just created?

   A. The table is created in the same tablespace where the temporary segments will be housed.

   B. The first segment allocated for this table will be 100KB of contiguous blocks.

   C. Redo information will be generated for the creation of this table.

   D. When full table scans are issued on the EMPLOYEE table, blocks from the table will persist in the buffer cache for a long time after the statement executes.

2. **User FITZPATRICK creates a temporary table using the following statement:**

```
SQL> create global temporary table FITZTEMPTAB
  2  (name varchar2(10), value number, use_date date)
  3  on commit delete rows;
Table created
```

FITZPATRICK then informs users MCGILLICUDDY and OBRYAN of his temporary table. While each user is connected to Oracle8*i* and populating table FITZTEMPTAB, OBRYAN issues `truncate table FITZTEMPTAB`. Which of the following users had their records removed temporary table by this action?

A. FITZPATRICK only

B. OBRYAN only

C. OBRYAN and FITZPATRICK only

D. OBRYAN, FITZPATRICK, and MCGILLICUDDY

3. User FITZGERALD issues the following statement to the FITZTEMPTAB table created in the code shown in Question 1: `update fitztemptab set name = 'MYCHANGE' where value = 55`. Which of the following aspects of the database will Oracle definitely not utilize as part of this operation?

A. The sort area

B. The TEMP tablespace

C. The LGWR process

D. The rollback segment assigned to the transaction

4. User OBRYAN adds a record to FITZTEMPTAB, defined using the code block shown in Question 1. At what point will the data added to FITZTEMPTAB by OBRYAN be removed from the temporary table?

A. When FITZPATRICK `commits` the transaction

B. When OBRYAN `commits` the transaction

C. When OBRYAN logs off of Oracle8*i*

D. When FITZPATRICK issues `truncate table FITZTEMPTAB`

Answer Key
1. C. 2. B. 3. C. 4. B.

Managing Storage Structures in a Table

Recall from earlier chapters that Oracle allocates new extents for a table automatically when more data is added than the current allocation will hold. You can add more extents manually with the `alter table allocate extent (size num[K|M] datafile 'filename')` statement, where *num* is the size of the extent you want to allocate (subject to the tablespace limit set by `minimum extent`) and *filename* is the absolute path and filename of the datafile you want the extent stored in. Both the `size` and `datafile` clauses are optional. If `size` is not used, Oracle uses the size specified in the `next` storage option for the table. If `datafile` is excluded, Oracle manages placement itself. You would use this command to control the distribution of extents before performing bulk data loads.

```
ALTER TABLE EMPLOYEE ALLOCATE EXTENT;
ALTER TABLE EMPLOYEE ALLOCATE EXTENT ( SIZE 200K );
ALTER TABLE EMPLOYEE ALLOCATE EXTENT
  (DATAFILE '/u10/oradata/oracle/data05.dbf' );
```

Table High-Water Marks and Unused Space

Now, consider how Oracle maintains knowledge about table size. A special marker called the *high-water mark* is used by Oracle to indicate the last block used to hold the table's data. As `insert` statements fill data blocks, Oracle moves the high-water mark farther and farther out to indicate the last block used. The high-water mark is stored in a table segment header and is used to determine where to stop reading blocks during full table scans. You can find the high-water mark for your table using the `unused_space( )` procedure from the DBMS_SPACE Oracle-supplied package or in the DBA_TABLES dictionary view after the `analyze` command has been run on your table. There is more information about `analyze` and the dictionary views housing table information later in this section.

Finally, if you want to eliminate the unused space allocated to your table, you can issue the `alter table tblname deallocate unused keep num [K|M]` statement, where `keep` is an optional clause that lets you retain *num* amount of the unused space. The `keep` clause specifies the number of bytes above the high-water mark that should be retained. If the command is used without the `keep` clause, the Oracle server will deallocate all unused space above the high-water mark. If the high-water mark is at an extent less than the value of `minextents`, the Oracle server will release extents above `minextents`.

```
ALTER TABLE EMPLOYEE DEALLOCATE UNUSED;
ALTER TABLE EMPLOYEE DEALLOCATE UNUSED KEEP 10K;
```

Row Migration and Chaining

If `pctfree` is too low for blocks in a table, `update` statements may increase the size of that row, only to find there is not enough room in the block to fit the change. Thus, Oracle has to move the row to another block in which it will fit. Row migration degrades performance when the server process attempts to locate the migrated row, only to find that the row is in another location.

Chaining is also detrimental to database performance. *Chaining* is when data for one row is stored in multiple blocks. This is a common side effect in tables with columns defined to be datatype LONG, because the LONG column data is stored inline with the rest of the table. The server process must piece together one row of data using multiple disk reads. In addition, there is performance degradation by DBWR when it has to perform multiple disk writes for only one row of data.

Analyzing Tables to Check Integrity and Migration

Typically, Oracle automatically handles validation of the structure of every data block used whenever the block is read into the buffer cache for user processes. However, there are two things you can do to validate the structural integrity of data blocks. The first is to use the `initsid.ora` parameter DB_BLOCK_CHECKSUM. Setting this parameter to TRUE makes the DBWR process calculate a checksum on every block it writes, regardless of tablespace, as a further measure to protecting the integrity of blocks in the database. In addition, Oracle calculates checksums for blocks written to the online redo logs as well. When this parameter is set to FALSE, the DBWR process calculates checksums only when writing blocks to the SYSTEM tablespace. The process of calculating checksums adds some overhead to normal database processing. You must balance that additional performance overhead with the need for ensuring that data blocks aren't corrupt.

The second method for checking integrity can be performed at any time using the `analyze table` *tblname* `validate structure` command. The optional `cascade` clause in this statement further validates the structure of blocks in indexes associated with the table. The `analyze` command is issued from SQL*Plus on one table at a time.

Using `analyze` to Detect Row Migration

The main use of the `analyze` command is determining performance statistics for cost-based optimization of how Oracle processes SQL statements. An added benefit of the `analyze` command is that it will also detect row migration on your table. There are two basic clauses for this command: `estimate statistics` and `compute statistics`. The former estimates statistics collection for the table based on a sample size of data that you can optionally specify with the `sample` *num* `[rows|percent]` clause. If you don't specify a `sample` clause, Oracle uses 1,064 rows. The `compute statistics` clause calculates statistics collection for the table based on every row in the table. Oracle suggests you use `estimate statistics` rather than `compute statistics` because the former is almost as accurate and takes less time.

Once statistics are generated, the CHAIN_CNT column in the DBA_TABLES dictionary view contains the number of chained and migrated rows estimated or found in the table. If you feel this number is high, you might want to save the table data, drop the table, re-create it, and reload the data to eliminate the problem. Remember, some chaining is to be expected, especially when your rows are wide (for example, if you have many VARCHAR2(4000) columns or a LONG column). Finally, if you want to validate integrity on an ongoing basis as part of a PL/SQL application, you can develop code that calls the `analyze_schema( )` procedures in the DBMS_UTILITY package or the `analyze_object` procedure in DBMS_DDL. The scope of these procedures should be self-evident.

TIP
The DBMS_STATS package can be used in place of the `analyze` *command for gathering statistics. This package offers some advantages over the use of the* `analyze` *command, particularly when you want to save statistics and reuse those statistics in different databases.*

Retrieving Data Dictionary Information about Tables

There are several data dictionary views available for obtaining information about tables. The views in the dictionary displaying this information base their content either on tables that exist in the database or on dynamic performance information about tables collected while the instance is running. The views you should remember for viewing table information include the following:

■ **DBA_SEGMENTS**   Gives information about the name, tablespace location, and owner of segments containing table data in Oracle

■ **DBA_OBJECTS**   Gives information about the object ID number used in part to determine ROWID for rows in the table, as well as the table creation timestamp for determining dependencies

■ **DBA_TABLES**   Gives information about all storage settings for the table, as well as the statistics collected as part of the `analyze` operation on that table

■ **DBA_EXTENTS**   Gives information about the number of extents allocated to a table, the datafiles in which they are stored, and how large each extent is

- **DBA_TAB_COLUMNS**   Gives information about every column in every table, including datatype, size, precision, column position in each row, and nullability

- **DBA_TAB_COMMENTS**   Gives comment information for every table, if any comment information is stored

- **DBA_COL_COMMENTS**   Gives comment information for every column in every table, if any comment information is stored

Because the possibilities for combining this data are vast, no example SQL statements will be shown here. Instead, consider the possible matchups. For example, if you wanted to determine whether an extremely large table was clumped in one datafile, you could query the DBA_EXTENTS view to find out. If you wanted to determine what rows were chained or migrated in your table, you could query the DBA_TABLES view to find out. If you were looking to see if there is a great deal of unused space in a table, you could query the DBA_TABLES view as well. Be aware that the columns you would query from DBA_TABLES in these cases will only be populated if `analyze` has been run on that table. If these columns are NULL, run `analyze` to tabulate the data you need.

For Review

1. Be sure you understand the process for manually allocating more extents to a table.

2. Know the name of the view can you use to find out the date/time a table was created and where you can look to see if there were rows chained or migrated in the table.

3. Be sure you understand what a high-water mark is and how it is set.

4. Understand what is meant by fragmentation. Fragmentation can manifest in many ways and row migration is one of the serious fragmentation problems.

Exercises

1. **Row migration in Oracle is detected using the _____ command.**

2. **Additional extents are allocated for a table using the _____ command.**

Answer Key
1. `analyze`. 2. `alter table allocate extent`.

Reorganizing, Truncating, and Dropping Tables

Moving a table into a different tablespace used to not be an easy task. To do so, you had to use the EXPORT tool to create a dump file containing the rows of the table, along with that table's definition. If there were indexes or constraints involved, you had to dump those objects to file using EXPORT, too. Generating the export dump was generally not too troublesome, but loading the table back into another tablespace via IMPORT might have been. You had to drop the table from the Oracle database after exporting it, and then you had to re-create the table in another tablespace. You then ran IMPORT with the IGNORE parameter set to Y so that IMPORT wouldn't fail when it saw that the table already existed. If you didn't perform this step, IMPORT would simply load the table right back into the tablespace it was stored in before. Worse, if that tablespace didn't exist, IMPORT would load the object into the default tablespace for the user you ran IMPORT as—which could have accidentally loaded the table into the SYSTEM tablespace if you weren't careful. You could have used SQL*Loader or the `create table as select` command with the `storage` and `tablespace` clauses explicitly defined instead, but both options would have required a long time to execute.

Relocating Tables in Oracle: Concept

Oracle now offers a great feature with respect to relocating and reorganizing tables. You can relocate a table to another tablespace or reorganize a table to resize the initial segment without the use of EXPORT and IMPORT and without the `create table as select` statement. Instead, these actions can be performed in Oracle through the use of the `move` option in the `alter table` command. The `alter table move` command supports the following clauses:

- **`tablespace` *name*** The `tablespace` clause enables you to identify the tablespace location where you want the table placed. If omitted, Oracle8*i* rebuilds the table in a new segment in the same tablespace.

- **`storage` (*storage_attributes*)** The `storage` clause enables you to reconfigure aspects of the table's storage, such as the `initial` extent or percentage increase of subsequent extents. If no `storage` clause is specified, then Oracle8*i* will re-create the table with the same storage attributes used when the table was initially created. Note that this aspect of table creation is useful only for placement in dictionary-managed tablespaces, not locally managed tablespaces.

- **`logging` or `nologging`** Use of the `logging` keyword explicitly states that you would like Oracle to write the changes made by `alter table move` to the online redo logs for recoverability purposes. This is the default behavior Oracle takes in this context. The `nologging` keyword is used to tell Oracle not to write the changes made by `alter table move` to the online redo log.

TIP
In Oracle Enterprise Edition, the `alter table move` *command also enables use of the* `online` *keyword to permit movement or reorganization of the table while the old version is still available for use.*

Relocating Tables in Oracle: Implementation

Now that we've explored the concepts underlying use of the `alter table move` command, let's explore how to use that command in action. The first example is where we move a table called WORK_TABLE from the USER_DATA tablespace to the LMTAB tablespace:

```
SQL> select owner, table_name, tablespace_name
  2  from dba_tables
  3  where table_name = 'WORK_TABLE';
OWNER       TABLE_NAME TABLESPACE_NAME
----------  ---------- ---------------
SCOTT       WORK_TABLE USER_DATA
SQL> alter table mytab move tablespace lmtab;
Table altered.
SQL> select owner, table_name, tablespace_name
  2  from dba_tables
  3  where table_name = 'WORK_TABLE';
OWNER       TABLE_NAME TABLESPACE_NAME
----------  ---------- ---------------
SCOTT       WORK_TABLE LMTAB
```

You can see where this command would be handy, especially for situations where a table must be moved out of the SYSTEM tablespace into a tablespace more appropriate for user-defined tables. However, although Oracle preserves the table's associated constraints, object privileges, and triggers when the table is moved from one tablespace to another, the `alter table name move tablespace tblspcname` command does not move any indexes associated with the table. Check out the following code block and you'll see what I mean:

```
SQL> create table TAB_W_INDEXES
  2  (col1 number primary key)
  3  tablespace system;
Table created.
```

```
SQL> select owner, table_name, index_name, tablespace_name
  2  from dba_indexes
  3  where table_name = 'TAB_W_INDEXES';
OWNER       TABLE_NAME     INDEX_NAME    TABLESPACE_NAME
----------  -------------- ------------  ---------------
SCOTT       TAB_W_INDEXES  SYS_C00953        SYSTEM
SQL> alter table tab_w_indexes
  2  move tablespace user_data;
Table altered.
SQL> select owner, table_name, index_name, tablespace_name
  2  from dba_indexes
  3  table_name = 'TAB_W_INDEXES';
OWNER       TABLE_NAME     INDEX_NAME    TABLESPACE_NAME
----------  -------------- ------------  ---------------
SCOTT       TAB_W_INDEXES  SYS_C00953        SYSTEM
```

The capabilities of this command far surpass similar functionality provided by the `create table as select` statement. Let's take a look at this functionality in action:

```
SQL> alter index sys_c00953 rebuild tablespace user_data;
Index altered.
SQL> select owner, table_name, index_name, tablespace_name
  2  from dba_indexes
  3  where table_name = 'TAB_W_INDEXES';
OWNER       TABLE_NAME     INDEX_NAME    TABLESPACE_NAME
----------  -------------- ------------  ---------------
SCOTT       TAB_W_INDEXES  SYS_C00953        USER_DATA
```

TIP
Just like creating a table in a locally managed tablespace, these parameters will show up in DBA_TABLES, but may not be in effect. You should check the actual size of the extents, listed in the BYTES or BLOCKS in the DBA_EXTENTS view.

Finally, let's look at the situation where we use the `alter table` move clause to reorganize an existing table in its original tablespace. Remember, Oracle places the table in a new segment within the original tablespace in order to rebuild the storage allocation according to your specifications. The following code block illustrates this usage:

```
SQL> alter table tab_w_indexes
  2  move storage (initial 20K next 20K);
```

```
Table altered.
SQL> select owner, table_name, initial_extent, next_extent
  2  from dba_tables
  3  where table_name = 'TAB_W_INDEXES';
OWNER       TABLE_NAME     INITIAL_EXTENT NEXT_EXTENT
----------  -------------  -------------- -----------
SCOTT       TAB_W_INDEXES         20480        20480
```

TIP

If you are performing reorganization on a large table and want to improve performance on the operation, you can also specify the nologging *keyword as part of the* alter table move *command. You will improve performance because the changes made by Oracle8i will not be written to the online redo log, but beware—the changes will not be recoverable later.*

Space Considerations for Relocating Tables

The operation of the alter table *name* move statement requires enough space for two copies of the table to exist in Oracle8*i* until the operation completes and Oracle8*i* can drop the table. During the period of moving the table, users can still issue select statements to see data in the table, but they cannot make any changes to data in the table.

Truncating and Dropping Tables

Now, consider a favorite tidbit from the archives of Oracle minutiae. You issue a delete statement on a table with many hundreds of thousands or millions of rows and commit it. Feeling smug with your accomplishment, you issue a select count(*) statement. A few minutes later, you get your count of zero rows. What happened? Oracle didn't reset the high-water mark after the delete statement, and what's more, it never does! To get rid of the extents allocated that are now empty and reset the high-water mark while still preserving the table definition, the truncate table command (with optional drop storage clause) is used. Note that this is a data definition language (DDL) operation, not data manipulation language (DML), meaning that once the table is truncated, you cannot issue a rollback command to magically get the data back. Recall also that any change made to minextents after table creation will now be applied to the table, unless you specify the optional reuse storage clause, which preserves the current storage allocation and does not reset the high-water mark. A final word of note—any associated indexes will also be truncated, and any optional drop storage or reuse storage clauses will also be applied to associated indexes.

```
TRUNCATE TABLE EMPLOYEE;
TRUNCATE TABLE EMPLOYEE DROP STORAGE;
TRUNCATE TABLE EMPLOYEE REUSE STORAGE;
```

TIP

Here's an interesting fact about `truncate table` *that may or may not find its way to OCP Exam. Despite your inability to* `rollback` *a table truncation, Oracle does acquire a rollback segment for the job. Why? Because if you terminate the* `truncate table` *command, or if some failure occurs, the rollback segment stores the changes made for the duration of the truncate operation to enable crash recovery.*

Finally, to rid yourself of the table entirely and give all allocated space back to the tablespace, issue the `drop table` statement. There is an optional clause you must include to handle other tables that may have defined referential integrity constraints into this table: the `cascade constraints` clause. The following code block demonstrates this command:

```
DROP TABLE EMPLOYEE;
DROP TABLE EMPLOYEE CASCADE CONSTRAINTS;
```

For Review

1. Know the statement that is used for moving a table to another tablespace. Understand how is this statement similar in function to the `create table as select` statement.

2. Understand the limitation to alter table move with respect to movement of supporting indexes. Be sure you know that the `alter index rebuild tablespace` command can be used for moving the associated indexes.

3. Be sure you know the space considerations involved in relocating or reorganizing a table, and also be sure you know the trade-offs inherent in use of the `nologging` keyword in the `alter table move` command.

Exercises

1. **You need to move table EMP from the DATA tablespace to the LARGE_DATA tablespace. This table was created with a unique constraint on the GOVT_ID column, with the associated index placed in the IDX tablespace. You want to move this index to the LARGE_INDX tablespace as**

well. Which of the following commands can be used for moving the corresponding index on the GOVT_ID column to the appropriate tablespace?

A. `alter index myidx rebuild tablespace large_index;`

B. `alter table emp move tablespace large_data index tablespace large_index;`

C. `alter table emp move tablespace large_index;`

D. `alter index myidx move tablespace large_index;`

2. You move the EMP table from the DATA tablespace to the LARGE_DATA tablespace. Which of the following statements about Oracle8*i*'s behavior regarding corresponding objects in this context is not true?

A. The object privileges granted to users on this table are preserved through the move.

B. A new segment in the LARGE_DATA tablespace now houses EMP's data.

C. Code for the triggers associated with the table is moved from the DATA tablespace to the LARGE_DATA tablespace.

D. The associated primary key continues to enforce uniqueness on the key column through the move.

3. You issue the following statement in Oracle8*i*: `alter table EMP move storage (initial 50K next 100K) nologging`. Which of the following statements made about this command is not true?

A. Table EMP has been moved to a new segment.

B. Table EMP has been moved to a new tablespace.

C. The change to table EMP was made without acquiring the redo allocation latch.

D. The change to table EMP will not be recoverable.

Answer Key

1. A. 2. C. Trigger code is stored in dictionary tables in the SYSTEM tablespace. 3. B.

Dropping Unused Columns from Tables

Try to envision the following scenario in versions of Oracle prior to Oracle9*i*. You have a table called EMPLOYEE that stores employee data. One of the columns stored a text string corresponding to the name of the subsidiary company the employee worked within. A reorganization of the company takes place where all subsidiary companies are now consolidated within the parent company, making it unnecessary to store subsidiary information as its own column. If you wanted to eliminate the unnecessary column, you would have to dump the contents of the table to a flat file, drop the table, re-create the table without the subsidiary column, and use SQL*Loader to reload the table records to your newly created table. Depending on how many employees there were in your company, this process could take a long time. Alternately, you could use Pro*C instead of SQL*Loader to load the records into the table more quickly using array fetches, but there would still be several steps involved in executing this task. You would likely need some downtime in order to accomplish the task as well.

Dropping Unused Columns: Concept

Instead of requiring that you execute this potentially arduous task, Oracle9*i* permits you to drop unused columns from tables simply by using the `alter table` command. There are two ways to drop a column in Oracle9*i*. The first is a logical method that removes no data but otherwise behaves as if the column has been removed. This option is known as marking the column as unused. The second is physically removing the column from the table. Let's look at the concepts behind each in more detail.

Marking a Column Unused   Users of the table cannot see an unused column. Information about the unused column does not appear in the output of the `describe table` command, nor can you query data in an unused column. Marking a column as unused is like deleting a column logically because the data is still in the table, but it cannot be used. The syntax for marking a column as unused is `alter table name set unused column colname`. To see which tables have unused columns, you can query the dictionary view in Oracle9*i* known as DBA_UNUSED_COL_TABS, and all tables with unused columns will be listed. The COUNT column in that view indicates how many unused columns there are for each table. If you wanted to drop the columns after marking them unused, you could use the `alter table name drop unused column` statement instead. Marking a column as unused and then using the `alter table name drop unused column` statement is useful because it enables you to take away column access quickly and immediately. Later on, during a DBA maintenance weekend or after business hours, you can then remove the column with `alter table name drop unused column` to reclaim the space.

Physically Removing the Column The other method for dropping a table column is through the use of the `alter table` *name* `drop column` *colname* statement. This statement actually removes all data from the column and eliminates the column from the table definition. This operation may take more time to complete than marking the column as unused because Oracle has to go through all blocks of the table and actually remove the column data in order to reclaim the space used by that column.

Dropping Columns in Oracle9*i*: Implementation

Let's take a look at some examples where you drop columns in Oracle9*i* using the `alter table` statement. The first example instructs Oracle to ignore the column by using the `set unused column` clause. In this situation, no information is removed from the table column. Oracle simply pretends the column isn't there. Later, we can remove the column using the `drop unused columns` clause. Both steps are shown in the following block:

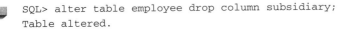

```
SQL> alter table employee set unused column subsidiary;
Table altered.
SQL> alter table employee drop unused columns;
Table altered.
```

The second option is to remove the column and all contents entirely from the table immediately. This statement is shown in the following block:

```
SQL> alter table employee drop column subsidiary;
Table altered.
```

Other Syntax for Removing Columns

There are a few optional clauses for the `alter table` *name* `drop column` *colname* statement, which are all added on after *colname* in the statement:

- **cascade constraints** Any foreign keys referring to the column to be dropped, or any constraints on the column itself, will be eliminated along with the column.

- **invalidate** Any objects related to the table whose column is being dropped will be marked invalid. Recall that objects that relate to a table in this fashion include PL/SQL blocks that refer to a table, triggers, and views.

- **checkpoint** *num* This enables you to reduce the amount of space used in a rollback segment by having Oracle9*i* perform a checkpoint every *num* number of rows. For the duration of the `alter table drop column` operation, the table shows a status of INVALID. If the operation terminates abnormally (if, for example, the session or instance crashed), Oracle would be able to roll back only to the most recent checkpoint and the table would remain in an INVALID state. However, you can resume the removal of the column after instance recovery is made or when you reconnect using the `alter table` *name* `drop columns continue` statement.

For Review

1. Be sure you know how to add columns using the `alter table` statement with the `add` clause.

2. Know how to modify column datatype definition using the `alter table` statement with the `modify` clause.

3. Understand both uses of the alter table command for dropping columns— one using the `set unused column` and `drop unused columns` syntax and the other with the `drop column` syntax.

Exercises

1. **You just issued the following statement: `alter table sales drop column profit`. Which of the following choices identifies when the column will actually be removed from Oracle?**

   A. Immediately following statement execution

   B. After the `alter table drop unused columns` command is issued

   C. After the `alter table set unused column` command is issued

   D. After the `alter table modify` command is issued

2. **The Acme Sales Company reorganizes to consolidate its entire sales force into one region, eliminating the need for a SALES_REGION column. You issue the following statement in Oracle9*i*: `alter table sales set unused column sales_region`. At what point will data actually be removed from the table?**

   A. When the `alter table sales drop unused columns` statement is issued.

   B. When the `alter table sales set unused column sales_region` statement finishes executing.

C. When you dump the contents of the table to flat file, re-create the table without the SALES_REGION column, and reload the data using SQL*Loader.

D. Never—a column is only removed when you use the `alter table sales drop column sales_region` statement.

3. **You want to determine how many columns in the EMPLOYEE table are marked unused for later removal. Which of the following methods would be appropriate for the purpose?**

   A. Querying the DBA_TABLES view

   B. Using the `describe` command

   C. Querying the DBA_UNUSED_COLS view

   D. Querying the DBA_UNUSED_COL_TABS view

Answer Key
1. A. 2. A. 3. C.

Managing Indexes

In this section, you will cover the following topics on managing indexes:

- Different index types and their use
- Creating B-tree and bitmap indexes
- Reorganizing indexes
- Dropping indexes
- Getting index information from the data dictionary
- Monitoring use of an index

Tables can grow quite large, and when they do, it becomes difficult for users to quickly find the data they need. For this reason, Oracle offers indexes as a method of speeding database performance when accessing tables with a lot of data. Oracle provides different types of indexes for different uses, and you will learn about them here. You will also learn about the specific procedures for creating B-tree and bitmap indexes and what sorts of situations may cause you to choose one over the other. The methods used to reorganize and drop indexes are shown here as well. Finally, you will learn where to look in the data dictionary for information about your indexes and how to monitor the use of an index.

Different Index Types and Their Uses

An index in Oracle can be compared to the card catalog in a library. When you want to find a book, you go to the card catalog (or computer) and look up the book under author, title, or subject. When you find the card for that book, it lists the location of the book in the library according to a classification system. Looking for a book in this way reduces the time you spend looking for a book on fly-fishing in the section where autobiographies are kept. Oracle indexes work the same way. You find row data that matches your search criteria in the index first, and then use the ROWID for that row from the index to get the entire row quickly from the table.

Several criteria are used to determine what kind of index you're looking at. The first criterion is how many columns the index has. *Simple* indexes contain only one column of data through which you can search plus the ROWID of the corresponding row in the table. *Composite* indexes store more than one column of data for you to search plus the ROWID of the corresponding row in the table. You can put up to 32 columns in a composite index, but you may be restricted from including that many if the total size of all the columns you want in the index exceeds DB_BLOCK_SIZE / 3. Other criteria for identifying indexes are whether the indexed column(s) contains all unique (composite) values, whether an index is partitioned or nonpartitioned, and whether it is a traditional B-tree or a bitmap index, or whether the data in the index is stored in reverse order.

TIP
When composite indexes are in place on a table, Oracle will only use that index if the leading column(s) of the composite index are referenced in the where *clause of the query against the table.*

Oracle maintains indexes whenever user processes make data changes to tables. For example, if you `insert` a new row in a table, an associated entry is made in the index for that row's indexed column. That entry is not made to the last leaf block of the index, but, rather, the appropriate leaf block is located according to index sort order, and the entry is made there. The `pctfree` setting has no effect on the index except at the time of creation. When data is removed from the table, the corresponding index entry is marked for removal. Later, when all other rows corresponding to all index entries in the leaf node are removed, then and only then is the entire block purged of index entries. Thus, the structure of the index is preserved. An `update` statement that changes the value of a row's indexed column value is treated as a marked removal followed by an `insert`. Finally, index entries can be added to a block even past the `pctfree` threshold.

Nonpartitioned B-Tree Indexes

The B-tree index is the traditional indexing mechanism used in Oracle. It stores data in a treelike fashion, as displayed in Figure 5-2. At the base of the index is the *root node*, which is an entry point for your search for data in the index. The root node contains pointers to other nodes at the next level in the index. Depending on the value you seek, you will be pointed in one of many directions. The next level in the index consists of *branch nodes*, which are similar to the root node in that they, too, contain pointers to the next level of nodes in the index. Again, depending on the value you seek, you will be pointed in one of many directions. Branch nodes point to the highest level of the index: the *leaf nodes*. In this highest level, *index entries* contain indexed column values and the corresponding ROWIDs of rows storing those column values. Each leaf node is linked to both the leaf node on its left and on its right, in order to make it possible to search up and down through a range of entries in the index.

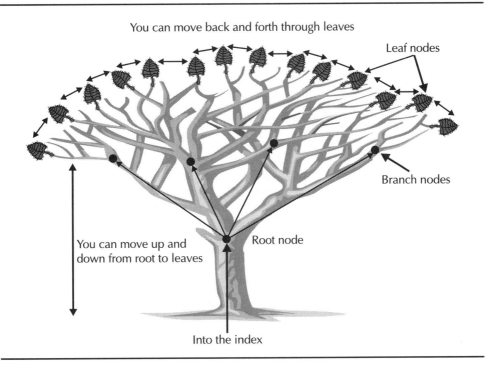

FIGURE 5-2. *The B-tree index structure*

Within a single index entry, there are several elements, some of which have already been covered. The first is the *index entry header*, containing the number of columns in the entry. Following that, the entry stores the values for the column(s) in the index. Preceding each column value is a length byte that follows the same rules that length bytes follow in row entries. Finally, the index entry stores the ROWID. No length byte is needed for this value because all ROWIDs are the same length.

There are a few special cases of data stored in index entries that you should understand:

- If the index is nonunique and several rows contain the same value for the column, then each row with that value will have its own index entry to store each unique ROWID.

- If a row has a NULL value for the column(s) being indexed, there will be no corresponding index entry for that row.

- For nonpartitioned indexes only, because the index stores data for only one table and because all tables can be stored in only one tablespace, the object ID number is not required to locate the row from the index. Thus, nonpartitioned B-tree indexes use restricted ROWIDs to point to row data.

B-tree indexes are used most commonly to improve performance on `select` statements using columns of unique or mostly distinct values. It is relatively easy and quick for Oracle to maintain B-tree indexes when data is changed in an indexed column, too, making this type of index useful for online transaction-processing applications. However, these indexes do a bad job of finding data quickly on `select` statements with `where` clauses containing comparison operations joined with `or` and in situations where the values in the indexed column are not very distinct.

Bitmap Indexes

Although all indexes in Oracle are stored with the root-branch-leaf structure illustrated in Figure 5-2, bitmap indexes are conceptualized differently. Instead of storing entries for each row in the table, the bitmap index stores an entry containing each distinct value, the start and end ROWIDs to indicate the range of ROWIDs in this table, and a long binary string with as many bits as there are rows in the table.

For example, say you are looking at a representation of a bitmap index for a table such as the one in Figure 5-3. The APPLE_TYPE column indexed has only three distinct values. The bitmap index would have three entries, as you see in the figure. The start and end restricted ROWIDs for the object are also shown, so that you know what the potential ROWID range is. Finally, you see a binary string representing a bitmap. A position will be set to 1 for the entry if the column for that row contains the associated value; otherwise, the bit is set to 0. If an entry contains a bit set to 1, the corresponding bit in every other entry will always be set to 0.

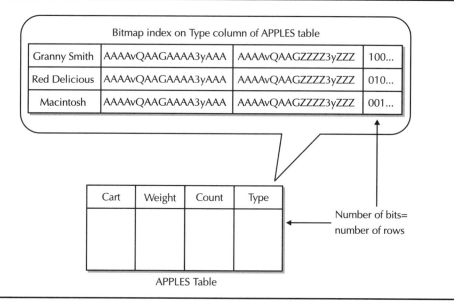

FIGURE 5-3.   *A logical representation of a bitmap index*

Actually, this binary entry is also compressed, which means you cannot see the bitmap with 0 and 1, but this is how the information is represented internally.

Bitmap indexes improve performance in situations where you `select` data from a column whose values are repeated often, as is the case with employee status (for example, active, LOA, or retired). They also improve performance on `select` statements with multiple `where` conditions joined by `or`.

Bitmap indexes improve performance where data in the column is not distinct and is infrequently or never changed. By the same token, it is a somewhat arduous process to change data in that column. This is because changing the value of a column stored in a bitmap index requires Oracle to lock the entire segment storing the bitmap index to make the change. Locking occurs to the whole bitmap index. In other words, when changes are made to the key column in the table, bitmaps must be modified. This results in locking of the relevant bitmap segments.

```
SQL> create bitmap index idx_emp_bmp_01 on table emp (gender);
Index created.
```

Reverse-Key Indexes

Finally, consider the use of reverse-key indexes. This type of index is the same as a regular B-tree index except for one thing—the data from the column being indexed is stored in reverse order. Thus, if the column value in a table of first names is

JASON, the reverse-key index column will be NOSAJ. Typically, users see the most benefit from reverse-key indexes when their `select` statements contain `where` clauses that use equality comparisons, such as `where X = 5`, but not in situations where range comparisons are used, such as `where X between 4 and 6`. The value or benefit to reverse-key indexes is to assist performance in Oracle Real Application Cluster environments.

```
SQL> create index idx_emp_rev_01 on table emp (lastname) reverse;
Index created.
```

Function-Based Indexes

The function-based index is a new type of index in Oracle8*i* that is designed to improve query performance by making it possible to define an index that works when your `where` clause contains operations on columns. Traditional B-tree indexes won't be used when your `where` clause contains columns that participate in functions or operations. For example, suppose you have table EMP with four columns: EMPID, LASTNAME, FIRSTNAME, and SALARY. The SALARY column has a B-tree index on it. However, if you issue the `select * from EMP where (SALARY*1.08) > 63000` statement, the relational database management system (RDBMS) ignores the index, performing a full table scan instead. Function-based indexes are designed to be used in situations like this one, where your SQL statements contain such operations in their `where` clauses. The following code block shows a function-based index defined:

```
CREATE INDEX idx_emp_func_01
ON emp(SALARY*1.08);
```

By using function-based indexes like this one, you can optimize the performance of queries containing function operations on columns in the `where` clause, like the query shown previously. As long as the function you specify is repeatable, you can create a function-based index around it. A repeatable function is one whose result will never change for the same set of input data. For example, 2 + 2 will always equal 4, and will never change one day so that it equals 5. Thus, the addition operation is repeatable. To enable the use of function-based indexes, you must issue two `alter session` statements, as follows:

```
SQL> alter session set query_rewrite_enabled = true;
Session altered.
SQL> alter session set query_rewrite_integrity=trusted;
Session altered.
```

TIP
Bitmap indexes can also be function-based indexes.
Function-based indexes can also be partitioned.

Descending Indexes

Another new type of index instituted in Oracle8*i* is the descending index. Recall
that the order by clause is used in SQL statements to impose sort order on data
returned from the database to make it more readable. Oracle does not typically
store data in any particular order, a common practice in relational database systems.
However, a B-tree index does store information in a particular order. In versions of
Oracle before Oracle8*i*, the order used by B-tree indexes has been ascending order,
ordered from the lowest column value to the highest.

In Oracle8*i*, you can now categorize data in a B-tree index in descending order
as well. This feature can be useful in applications where sorting operations are
required in conflicting ways. For example, say you have the EMP table with four
columns: EMPID, LASTNAME, SALARY, and DEPT. As part of a departmental
performance comparison, you may have to query this table by department code in
ascending order and salary in descending order, using the following query:

```
SQL> select dept, salary, empid, lastname
  2    from emp
  3    order by dept asc, salary desc;
```

If the EMP table is large, then prior versions of Oracle may have required
enormous amounts of sort space to obtain DEPT data in one sort order and SALARY
data in another. Descending indexes can be used to change that. For example, you
could define separate, simple indexes for DEPT and SALARY data, where the DEPT
data used the traditional ascending method in its B-tree index, while the SALARY
column used descending order in the index. To create the simple indexes, you could
use the following code block:

```
-- Regular ascending index
CREATE INDEX emp_dept_idx_01
ON EMP(DEPT);

-- Descending index
CREATE INDEX emp_sal_idx_01
ON EMP(SALARY DESC);
```

Different sort orders can be specified for columns in a composite index as well.
Using the previous example, you could define a composite index containing two

columns with different sort orders specified for each column, such as the index definition shown in the following code block:

```
CREATE INDEX emp_dep_sal_idx_01
ON EMP(dept ASC, salary DESC);
```

TIP
You can also combine function-based indexes with descending-index features to create function-based descending indexes. Descending indexes can also be partitioned.

For Review

1. Be sure you know what a unique index is and how it compares with a nonunique index. Know the differences between composite and simple indexes, as well as the differences between B-tree and bitmap index structure.

2. Know what the other types of indexes are in Oracle, including descending indexes, function-based indexes, reverse-key indexes, and so on.

Exercises

1. Your Oracle EMPLOYEE table contains many unique values in the FIRSTNAME column. You want to index that column to take advantage of this fact in query access. Which of the following indexes might you use?

   A. Bitmap index

   B. Function-based index

   C. Simple B-tree index

   D. Composite B-tree index

2. You want to employ bitmap indexes in your Oracle database. Which of the following statements is true regarding bitmap indexes?

   A. Bitmap indexes are useful where a table column contains few unique values, and those values are changed frequently.

   B. Bitmap indexes are useful where a table column contains many unique values, and those values are changed frequently.

C. Bitmap indexes are useful where a table column contains few unique values, and those values are changed infrequently.

D. Bitmap indexes are useful where a table column contains many unique values, and those values are changed infrequently.

Answer Key
1. C. 2. C.

Creating B-Tree and Bitmap Indexes

The create index statement is used to create all types of indexes. To define special types of indexes, you must include various keywords, such as create unique index for indexes on columns that enforce uniqueness of every element of data or create bitmap index for creating bitmap indexes. The following code block shows the statement for creating a unique B-tree index. The statement also includes options for data storage and creation:

```
CREATE UNIQUE INDEX employee_lastname_indx_01
ON employee (lastname ASC)
TABLESPACE INDEXES
PCTFREE 12
INITRANS 2 MAXTRANS 255
LOGGING
NOSORT
STORAGE ( INITIAL 900K
          NEXT 1800K
          MINEXTENTS 1
          MAXEXTENTS 200
          PCTINCREASE 0 );
```

There are several items in the storage definition that should look familiar, such as pctfree, tablespace, logging, and the items in the storage clause. Other than pctfree, these options have the same use as they do in create table statements. Oracle uses pctfree only during the creation of the index to reserve space for index entries that may need to be inserted into the same index block.

There are a few other items that may look unfamiliar, such as unique, asc, and nosort. You specify unique when you want the index to enforce uniqueness for values in the column. The asc keyword indicates ascending order for this column in the index, and desc (descending) can be substituted for this clause.

The `nosort` keyword is for when you have loaded your table data in the proper sort order on the column you are indexing. In this case, it would mean that you have loaded data into the EMPLOYEE table sorted in ascending order on the LASTNAME column. By specifying `nosort`, Oracle will skip the sort ordinarily used in creating the index, thereby increasing performance on your `create index` statement. You might use this option if your operating system offered a procedure for sorting that was more efficient than Oracle's. Finally, `pctused` is not used in index definitions. Because all items in an index must be in the right order for the index to work, Oracle must put an index entry into a block, no matter what. Thus, `pctused` is not used.

You can create bitmap indexes with several storage specifications as well, but remember that they are used to improve search performance for low-cardinality columns, so bitmap indexes may not be unique. The following code block creates a bitmap index:

```
CREATE BITMAP INDEX employee_lastname_indx_01
ON employee (lastname)
TABLESPACE ORGDBIDX
PCTFREE 12
INITRANS 2 MAXTRANS 255
LOGGING
NOSORT
STORAGE ( INITIAL 900K
          NEXT 1800K
          MINEXTENTS 1
          MAXEXTENTS 200
          PCTINCREASE 0 );
```

The performance of commands that use bitmap indexes is heavily influenced by an area of memory specified by the CREATE_BITMAP_AREA_SIZE init*sid*.ora parameter. This area determines how much memory will be used for storing bitmap segments. You need more space for this purpose if the column on which you are creating the bitmap index has high cardinality. For a bitmap index, high cardinality might mean a dozen or so unique values out of 500,000 (as opposed to B-tree indexes, for which high cardinality might mean 490,000 unique values out of 500,000). So, in this situation, you might stick with the Oracle default setting of 8MB for your CREATE_BITMAP_AREA_SIZE initialization parameter.

An example of low cardinality for a column would be having two distinct values in the entire table, as is the case for a column indicating whether an employee is male or female. In this case, you might size your initialization parameter considerably lower than the Oracle default, perhaps around 750KB.

Sizing and Other Index-Creation Issues

Searching a large table without the benefit of an index takes a long time because a full table scan must be performed. Indexes are designed to improve search performance. Unlike full table scans, whose performance worsens as the table grows larger, the performance of table searches that use indexes gets exponentially better as the index (and associated table) gets larger and larger. In fact, on a list containing 1 million elements, a binary search tree algorithm similar to the one used in a B-tree index finds any element in the list within 20 tries—in reality, the B-tree algorithm is actually far more efficient.

However, there is a price for all this speed, which is paid in the additional disk space required to store the index and the overhead required to maintain it when DML operations are performed on the table. To minimize the trade-off, you must weigh the storage cost of adding an index to the database against the performance gained by having the index available for searching the table. The performance improvement achieved by using an index is exponential over the performance of a full table scan, but there is no value in the index if it is never used by the application. You should also consider the volatility of the data in the table before creating an index. If the data in the indexed column changes regularly, you might want to index a more static column.

Also, consider how you are sizing `pctfree` for your index. Oracle only uses `pctfree` to determine free space when the index is first created. After that, the space is fair game, because Oracle has to keep all the items in the index in order. So, after creation, Oracle will put index records in a block right down to the last bit of space available. To determine the best value for `pctfree` on your index, consider the following. If the values in the column you are indexing increase sequentially, such as column values generated by sequences, you can size `pctfree` as low as 2 or 3. If not, you should calculate `pctfree` based on row-count forecasts for growth over a certain time period (12 months, for example) with the following formula: $((max\_\#\_rows\_in\_period - initial\_\#\_rows\_in\_period) / max\_\#\_rows\_in\_period) \times 100$.

For Review

1. Be sure you can describe the settings that can and cannot be used in a storage clause for an index and know the reason why this is the case.

2. Know that you cannot create unique bitmap indexes—this is a contradiction in terms. Also, understand how Oracle uses the SORT_BITMAP_AREA_SIZE parameter with respect for creating bitmap indexes.

Exercises

1. You are defining the storage allocation settings for an index. Which of the following choices identifies an aspect of index storage allocation that is not present for tables?

   A. `pctfree`

   B. `pctincrease`

   C. `pctused`

   D. `initial`

2. You plan to use the text file shown in the following code block as the source for loading data into the EMPLOYEE table:

```
0193 FLOM         BETSY
4302 BUTTERWORTH  LORNA
6302 GUPTA        RAJIV
1201 FLOM         TOM
```

   Which of the following choices identifies a method that you could use when creating an index on the LASTNAME column that would improve performance without sacrificing recoverability?

   A. Create the index before loading the table with low `storage` clause settings.

   B. Use the `nosort` keyword when creating the index after loading the table.

   C. Use the `nologging` keyword when creating the index after loading the table.

   D. Create the index before loading the table with high `storage` clause settings.

Answer Key
1. C. 2. B.

Reorganizing Indexes

Reorganizing indexes is handled with the `alter index` statement. The `alter index` statement is useful for redefining storage options, such as `next`, `pctincrease`, `maxextents`, `initrans`, or `maxtrans`. You can also use the `alter index` statement to change the `pctfree` value for new blocks in new extents allocated by your index. You can also add extents manually to an index much like you do for tables, with the `alter index allocate extent` statement, specifying `size` and `datafile` optionally. You can also rid yourself of unused space below the index high-water mark with the `alter index deallocate unused` statement, optionally reserving a little extra space with the `keep` clause.

Another option for reorganizing your index is to rebuild it. This operation enables you to create a new index using the data from the old one, resulting in fewer table reads while rebuilding, tidier space management in the index, and better overall performance. This operation is accomplished with the `alter index idxname rebuild tablespace tblspcname` statement. The `tablespace` clause in this statement also moves the index to the tablespace named, which is handy for situations where you want to accomplish this task easily. All the storage options you can specify in a `create index` statement can be applied to `alter index rebuild` as well. You would rebuild an index in situations where you want to move the index to another tablespace or when many rows have been `deleted` from the table, causing index entries to be removed as well. Queries can continue to use the existing index while the new index is being built.

TIP

You can use the `analyze index validate structure` *command as you would with tables to check for block corruption. The INDEX_STATS dictionary view shows you the number of index entries in leaf nodes in the LF_ROWS column compared to the number of deleted entries in the DEL_LF_FOWS column. Oracle recommends that if the number of deleted entries is over 30 percent, you should rebuild the index.*

Building or Rebuilding Indexes Online

Indexes are maintained by Oracle behind the scenes whenever you make a change to data on the indexed column in the table. As time goes on, the values in an indexed column may change such that Oracle has to rearrange the contents of the index to make room for the new values in the indexed column. If enough column values are changed over that time to skew the overall number of elements in the index from the configuration Oracle initially made when it created the index, the index may become stale. A stale index does a poor job of retrieving data quickly, which causes users to notice degraded performance when running their queries even though the statement execution plan shows that the index is being used.

You can rebuild indexes in order to correct index staleness using the `alter index rebuild` statement. In order to rebuild the index, Oracle places a DML lock on the base table whose index is about to be rebuilt. During the time Oracle holds this DML lock, you cannot make any changes to data in the base table. Thus, if you had to build or rebuild an index for any reason, you usually had to plan when you would perform the maintenance operation around the needs of users needing to make changes to the tables. If the table being indexed was both large and had to be available to users, downtime at night or over the weekend was required, because Oracle had to prevent DML operations to data in the table while building or rebuilding the index. However, for e-business applications requiring 24×7 availability, downtime is simply not possible.

Oracle provides a method for building or rebuilding indexes using less-restrictive locking mechanisms. This less-restrictive locking method permits other users to make changes to data in the table while you continue to build or rebuild the index. These changes are also recorded in the new or rebuilt index as well. Oracle performs the work for an online index rebuild in the following way. First, Oracle obtains locks on the table for a very short time to define the structure of the index and to update the data dictionary. This step is illustrated in Figure 5-4. During this time, the table and the index are not available for data queries or changes.

When the first step is complete, Oracle releases the lock required to obtain index structure, and users can once again make data changes to the table. The index as it currently exists is made available for queries only, while Oracle starts rebuilding a copy of the index. Oracle simultaneously maintains a small copy of the

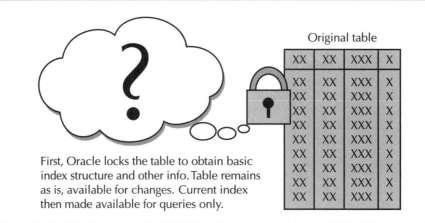

FIGURE 5-4. *The first step of rebuilding indexes online*

index called a *journal table*. This journal table is built exclusively for housing new information added to the table column. This step is illustrated in Figure 5-5.

Next, Oracle incorporates new data added to the table column previously stored in the smaller index copy into the larger index copy. An even smaller copy of the index exists for capturing any new data added to the table during the time that the other copy is added to the index being rebuilt. Once changes from the small copy are added to the rebuilt index, Oracle begins incorporating the new data found in the even smaller copy. Oracle then repeats the process, creating the smallest copy of the index for housing the few new records added while Oracle incorporated new data from the smaller copy, as shown in Figure 5-6.

This process cannot continue forever, so after Oracle integrates the changes from the smaller copy, it locks a few rows of the table at a time, so that no users can change data. The smallest index copy is then incorporated into the index being rebuilt. When finished, Oracle discards the original index in favor of the rebuilt version, releases all locks, and users are once again given access to the table. This is shown in Figure 5-7.

Building or Rebuilding Indexes Online: Syntax

To build an index on a table while continuing to leave the table online and available for user changes in this fashion, you can use the `create index` *name* `on` `table(`*columns*`) online` statement. To rebuild an existing index, you can use the `alter index` *name* `rebuild online` statement. The following code block shows the use of the `online rebuild` command in a SQL*Plus session:

```
SQL> alter index idx_emp_01 rebuild online;
Index altered.
```

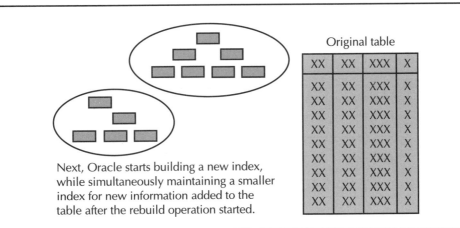

Next, Oracle starts building a new index, while simultaneously maintaining a smaller index for new information added to the table after the rebuild operation started.

FIGURE 5-5. *The second step of rebuilding indexes online*

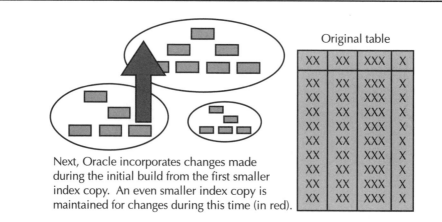

Next, Oracle incorporates changes made during the initial build from the first smaller index copy. An even smaller index copy is maintained for changes during this time (in red).

FIGURE 5-6. *The third step of rebuilding indexes online*

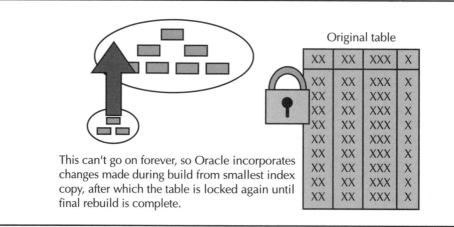

This can't go on forever, so Oracle incorporates changes made during build from smallest index copy, after which the table is locked again until final rebuild is complete.

FIGURE 5-7. *The final step in rebuilding indexes online*

TIP

Depending on the size of the table being indexed and how much data is changed by users while the index is being rebuilt, the `online rebuild` *operation could take a long time to complete. Unfortunately, there is little that can be done to tune*

*the process. That's just one of the trade-offs you
have to make when you want 24×7 data
availability. You can minimize impact on end users
by scheduling the* `online rebuild` *during off-
peak times.*

Building or Rebuilding Indexes Online: Restrictions

You cannot use this method for building or rebuilding any kinds of bitmap or cluster
indexes. This method works mainly for B-tree indexes and their variants, such as
function-based, descending, and reverse-key indexes, and for partitioned indexes.
You also cannot use this indexing method on secondary indexes in IOTs.

For Review

1. Be sure you know what situations you would want to rebuild an index and
   the statement for doing so. Know what storage parameters cannot be
   changed as part of the `alter index` command as well.

2. Know what the usage of the INDEX_STATS dictionary table is and how it
   relates to the `analyze` command.

3. Be sure you can describe the process in which indexes are built or rebuilt
   by default. Understand why this operation requires downtime. Know how
   this operation can be performed online in Oracle.

4. Be sure you can identify the syntax used to rebuild an index online. Know
   the performance implications and other restrictions for doing so as well.

Exercises

1. **You want to rebuild an index in Oracle. Which of the following choices
   identifies the reason why rebuilding indexes online is possible in Oracle?**

   A. Less restrictive locks on underlying base tables

   B. More restrictive locks on the index rebuilt

   C. Use of a standby database for temporary storage

   D. Use of a temporary table for temporary storage

2. **You are examining use of rebuilding indexes online for your 24×7 Oracle database. Which of the following choices identifies an index that cannot be rebuilt online?**

   A. Partitioned B-tree indexes

   B. Bitmap indexes

   C. Reverse key indexes

   D. Secondary IOT indexes

Answer Key
1. A. 2. D.

Dropping Indexes

What happens when you want to expand your index to include more columns or to get rid of columns? Can you use `alter index` for that? Unfortunately, the answer is no. You must drop and re-create the index to modify column definitions or change column order from ascending to descending (or vice versa). This is accomplished with the `drop index idxname` statement.

You may want to get rid of an index that is used only for specific purposes on an irregular basis, especially if the table has other indexes and volatile data. You may also want to drop an index if you are about to perform a large load of table data, perhaps preceded by purging all data in the table. In this way, your data load runs faster, and the index created later is fresh and well organized. You may have to re-create your index if it has a status of INVALID in the DBA_OBJECTS view, or if you know the index is corrupt from running DBVERIFY on the tablespace housing the index or the `analyze` command on the index itself.

For Review

Know why you might want to drop an index and how to do so.

Exercises

1. The statement for dropping an index is _____.

Answer Key
1. drop index.

Getting Index Information
from the Data Dictionary

You may find yourself looking for information about your indexes, and the Oracle data dictionary can help. The DBA_INDEXES view offers a great deal of information about indexes, such as the type of index (normal or bitmap), its current status (valid, invalid, and others), and whether the index enforces uniqueness or not. You also get information about which table is associated with the index. Another view that contains information about the columns that are stored in an index is called DBA_IND_COLUMNS. The most valuable piece of information this view can give you (in addition to telling you which columns are indexed) is the order in which the columns of the index appear. This is a crucial factor in determining whether the index will improve performance in selecting data from a table. For example, if you were to issue select * from EMPLOYEE where LASTNAME = 'SMITH' and a composite index existed in which LASTNAME was the first column in the index order, then that index would improve performance. However, if the index listed FIRSTNAME as the first column, then the index would not help. Figure 5-8 illustrates this concept.

Finally, a note on finding information about reverse-key indexes. You might notice, if you have reverse-key indexes in your database, that there is no information in the DBA_INDEXES view telling you specifically that the index is reverse key. To see this information, you must execute a specialized query that uses a SYS-owned table called IND$, as well as the DBA_OBJECTS view. The following code block shows the query:

```
SELECT object_name FROM dba_objects
WHERE object_id IN (SELECT obj#
FROM ind$
WHERE BITAND(property,4) = 4);
```

For Review

1. Identify some dictionary views and tables that contain information about indexes.

2. Understand the significance of column position in a composite index and where you can look in the data dictionary to find this information.

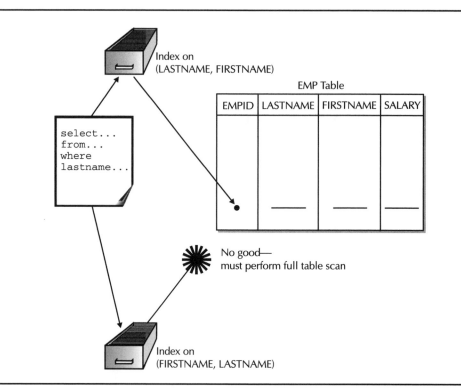

FIGURE 5-8. *The effect of column position in composite indexes*

Exercises

1. This is the view you would look into in order to determine the columns on a table that have been indexed: _____.

2. This is the view you would use to determine what indexes exist for certain tables: _____.

Answer Key
1. DBA_IND_COLUMNS. 2. DBA_INDEXES.

Monitoring Use of Indexes

As said repeatedly, the purpose of indexes is to speed performance in users' ability to access data in a large table. However, an index isn't doing its job if no one uses the index. In order to make sure your users are utilizing the indexes you've generated, Oracle provides a means of monitoring indexes to determine if they are being used or not used. Although you might be tempted to provide as many indexes as possible to improve performance in as many query situations as possible, each index you create takes up space that could have been used for other purposes. Even though disk space isn't very expensive anymore, if you determine that an index is not being used, then you can drop that index, eliminating unnecessary statement overhead, if only to make room for a new index that stands a better chance of being utilized.

Oracle's mechanism for monitoring disk usage is activated with the `alter index` *name* `monitoring usage` command, where *name* is the name of the index you intend to monitor. You then let users access the Oracle database for a while. During this time, Oracle gathers information about which indexes are used and which aren't. For accuracy purposes, try to ensure that usage of the Oracle database during this period realistically reflects typical use of the database. For example, you wouldn't want to monitor index disk usage from late on a Friday evening to early Saturday morning if you knew that most of your users would be at home during that time and that no batch processes would be running either. Later, you issue the `alter index` *name* `nomonitoring usage` statement to have Oracle stop monitoring index usage.

Once Oracle's done with gathering the usage statistics, you can look in the V$OBJECT_USAGE dynamic performance view to figure out whether your index is being employed by users in a meaningful way. Records for every index that has been monitored during the life of the instance will be kept in this view, listed by the name of the index and its associated table. As soon as you start monitoring the index for the first time, a corresponding record is added to V$OBJECT_USAGE. Subsequent attempts to monitor the index will not add new records to V$OBJECT_USAGE, but the MONITORING column will contain YES for this index whenever monitoring is turned on for the index and any previous monitoring information for that index in V$OBJECT_USAGE will be cleared and reset. This view also contains a column called USED. Possible values for this column include YES or NO, making its interpretation fairly easy as well. If the index was used during the monitoring period, Oracle lists YES; otherwise, Oracle lists NO. The view also contains the start and stop times of the monitoring period.

TIP
You must be logged into Oracle as the user owning the index in order to see index statistics in the V$OBJECT_USAGE. For example, if the index being monitored is owned by SCOTT and you log in as SYS to query V$OBJECT_USAGE, you won't see info for SCOTT's index.

Monitoring Object Usage: Scenario

The USED column in V$OBJECT_USAGE only changes when the index being monitored has been used, so it is worth noting when indexes are used and when they are not. For this scenario, we'll employ the standard DEPT table owned by that ever-popular Oracle user, our old friend SCOTT. SCOTT is concerned that the index on the DEPTNO column in the DEPT table, PK_DEPT, is not being utilized effectively by other users in Oracle, so he logs into the database and starts monitoring the PK_DEPT index. He also queries the V$OBJECT_USAGE table to make sure everything is in place for Oracle to start monitoring use of the index. These activities are shown in the following code:

```
SQL> connect scott/tiger
Connected.
SQL> alter index pk_dept monitoring usage;
Index altered.
SQL> select * from v$object_usage;
INDEX_NAME      TABLE_NAME      MONI USED START_MONITORING END_MONITORING
--------------  --------------  ---- ---- ---------------- --------------
PK_DEPT         DEPT            YES  NO   10/21/2001 13:21
```

At this point, SCOTT is convinced that index monitoring is turned on. The SYSTEM user then logs into Oracle9*i* and issues the following query on the DEPT table:

```
SQL> select * from dept;
    DEPTNO DNAME        LOC
---------- ------------ --------------
        10 ACCOUNTING   NEW YORK
        20 RESEARCH     DALLAS
        30 SALES        CHICAGO
        40 OPERATIONS   BOSTON
```

Later, SCOTT queries the V$OBJECT_USAGE view again to see how things have progressed:

```
INDEX_NAME      TABLE_NAME      MONI USED START_MONITORING END_MONITORING
--------------  --------------  ---- ---- ---------------- --------------
PK_DEPT         DEPT            YES  NO   10/21/2001 13:21
```

"But how can that be?" I hear you saying. SYSTEM logged in and queried the DEPT table, yet Oracle tells us that the index on the DEPTNO column isn't being used. That's exactly how it should be, because SYSTEM didn't query the DEPT table based on the contents of the DEPTNO table—SYSTEM simply asked for all the data, which resulted in Oracle executing a full table scan to retrieve all data from the DEPT table. Had SYSTEM issued `select * from dept where deptno = 10` instead, SCOTT would have seen the following output:

```
INDEX_NAME      TABLE_NAME      MONI USED START_MONITORING END_MONITORING
--------------  --------------  ---- ---- ---------------- --------------
PK_DEPT         DEPT            YES  YES  10/21/2001 13:21
```

For Review

1. Know how to use the `alter index monitoring usage` and `alter index nomonitoring usage` command, and that the purpose these commands serve is to enable you to detect whether an index is being used in the database.

2. Understand the contents of the V$OBJECT_USAGE view. It is populated with records pertaining to indexes being monitored only after that index is being monitored for the first time. The record will persist after monitoring is turned off, and later attempts to monitor that index's usage will clear and reset values from the previous attempt.

3. Generally speaking, understand when indexes will and will not be used in a database. An index will likely be used when the indexed column is referenced in a `where` clause. An index will not be used when the query has no `where` clause or references columns that aren't indexed.

Exercises

1. Use the following information to answer the question. You have a table called ODDS_AND_EVENS containing two columns: THE_NAME and THE_NUMBER. The column THE_NUMBER has an index on it. Your users issue the following query on this table: `select * from ODDS_AND_EVENS where mod(THE_NUMBER,2) = 0`. What sort of index on the column THE_NUMBER will be used in support of executing the previous query?

    A. Bitmap index

    B. B-tree index

    C. Function-based index

    D. Descending index

2. **You issue the `alter index my_idx monitor usage` command on your Oracle database. This is the second time you've monitored this index since creating your database, and the instance has been shut down only once since the last time you monitored this index. Which of the following statements is true regarding the contents of the V$OBJECT_USAGE view?**

    A. V$OBJECT_USAGE will be populated with a new record corresponding to MY_IDX when the previous command is issued.

    B. V$OBJECT_USAGE will be populated with a second record corresponding to MY_IDX when the previous command is issued.

    C. The information in the existing MY_IDX record in V$OBJECT_USAGE will be cleared and reset when the previous command is issued.

    D. The information in the existing MY_IDX record in V$OBJECT_USAGE will be cleared but not reset when the previous command is issued.

3. **You terminate monitoring the MY_IDX index after monitoring its use for several hours. Which of the following statements is correct regarding V$OBJECT_USAGE in this context?**

    A. Oracle removes the record corresponding to MY_IDX from V$OBJECT_USAGE.

    B. Oracle fills in the END_MONITORING column in the record corresponding to MY_IDX in the V$OBJECT_USAGE view.

    C. Oracle fills in the USED column in the record corresponding to MY_IDX in the V$OBJECT_USAGE view.

    D. Oracle clears all values in the record corresponding to MY_IDX in the V$OBJECT_USAGE view.

Answer Key

1. C. **2.** A. **3.** B.

Managing Data Integrity

In this section, you will cover the following topics related to managing data integrity constraints:

- Implementing data integrity constraints
- Maintaining integrity constraints
- Obtaining constraint information from Oracle

The goal of an integrity constraint is to enforce business rules of some kind. For example, in an organization that wants to be sure every employee has a last name, there are three ways to accomplish the goal. The one most commonly employed in Oracle databases is using a declarative integrity constraint. The LASTNAME column of the EMPLOYEE table can have a not NULL constraint that prevents any row of information from being added without that LASTNAME column populated. The popularity of integrity constraints relates to the fact that they are easy to define and use, they execute quickly, and they are highly flexible. This section explains how to use, maintain, and manage your integrity constraints in Oracle.

Implementing Data Integrity Constraints

As you should recall from taking the Oracle9*i* OCP Introduction to SQL exam, there are five types of declarative integrity constraints in Oracle: primary keys, foreign keys, unique keys, check constraints, and not NULL constraints. Each will be described here to refresh your memory.

Primary Keys

The primary key of a database table is the unique identifier for that table that distinguishes each row in the table from all other rows. A primary key constraint consists of two data integrity rules for the column declared as the primary key. First, every value in the primary key column must be unique in the table. Second, no value in the column declared to be the primary key can be NULL. Primary keys are the backbone of the table. You should choose the primary key for a table carefully. The column or columns defined to be the primary key should reflect the most important piece of information that is unique about each row of the table.

Foreign Keys

The creation of a foreign key constraint from one table to another defines a special relationship between the two tables that is often referred to as a parent/child relationship, as illustrated in Figure 5-9. The parent table is the one referred to by the foreign key, whereas the child table is the table that actually contains the foreign key.

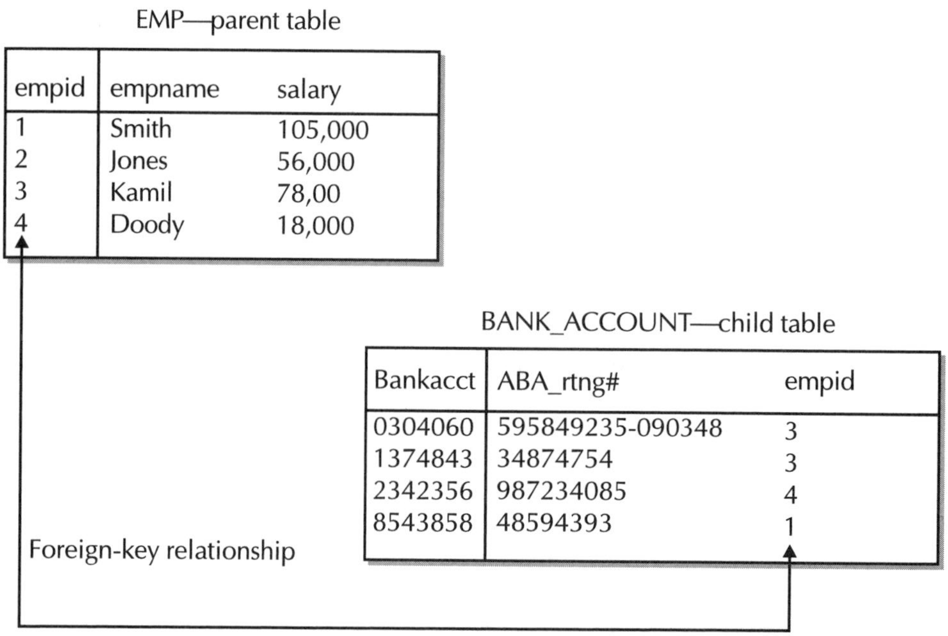

EMP—parent table

empid	empname	salary
1	Smith	105,000
2	Jones	56,000
3	Kamil	78,00
4	Doody	18,000

BANK_ACCOUNT—child table

Bankacct	ABA_rtng#	empid
0304060	595849235-090348	3
1374843	34874754	3
2342356	987234085	4
8543858	48594393	1

Foreign-key relationship

FIGURE 5-9. *Creating parent/child table relationships using foreign keys*

The DBA should ensure that foreign keys on one table refer only to primary keys on other tables. Unlike primary key constraints, a foreign key constraint on a column does not prevent user processes from setting the value in the foreign key column of the child table to NULL. In cases where the column is NULL, there will be no referential integrity check between the child and the parent.

Unique Constraints

Like the primary key, a unique constraint ensures that values in the column on which the unique constraint is defined are not duplicated by other rows. In addition, the unique constraint is the only type of constraint other than the primary key constraint that has an associated index created with it when the constraint is named.

Not NULL Constraints

NULL cannot be specified as the value for a column on which the not NULL constraint is applied. Often, the DBA will define this constraint in conjunction with another constraint. For example, the not NULL constraint can be used with a foreign key constraint to force validation of column data against a valid value table.

Check Constraints

Check constraints enable the DBA to specify a set of valid values for a column, which Oracle will check automatically when a row is inserted with a non-NULL value for that column. This constraint is limited to hard-coded valid values only. In other words, a check constraint cannot look up its valid values anywhere, nor can it perform any type of SQL or PL/SQL operation as part of its definition.

TIP
Primary keys and unique keys are created with an associated unique index. This index preserves uniqueness in the column(s) and also facilitates high-performance searches on the table whenever the primary key is named in the where *clause.*

Creating an Integrity Constraint

Constraint definitions are handled at the table-definition level, either in a create table or alter table statement. Whenever a constraint is created, it is enabled automatically unless a condition exists on the table that violates the constraint. If the constraint condition is violated, Oracle will create the constraint with disabled status and the rows that violated the constraint are optionally written to a special location. Alternatively, you can specify your constraint to be disabled on creation with the disable clause or force the constraint to be created and enabled by not validating the data with the novalidate clause. Some general guidelines for creating constraints are as follows:

■ Put indexes associated with constraints in a tablespace separate from table data.

■ Disable constraints before loading tables with lots of row data, and then reenable the constraints afterward.

■ Make constraints deferrable when using self-referencing foreign key constraints.

Creating Primary Keys and Not NULL Constraints

The primary key is defined with the constraint clause. A name should be given to the primary key in order to name the associated index. The type of constraint is defined on the next line; it will either be a primary key, foreign key, unique, or check constraint. For indexes associated with primary and unique keys, the tablespace used for storing the index is named in the using tablespace clause. You should specify a separate tablespace for indexes and the tables, for performance reasons. The code block here illustrates the creation of a table with constraints defined:

```
CREATE TABLE emp
( empid          NUMBER            NOT NULL,
  empname        VARCHAR2(30)      NOT NULL,
  salary         NUMBER            NOT NULL,
  CONSTRAINT pk_emp_01
  PRIMARY KEY (empid)
  NOT DEFERRABLE
  USING INDEX TABLESPACE indexes_01 DISABLE)
TABLESPACE data_01;
```

The preceding example displays a `create table` statement defining constraints after the columns are named. This is called *out-of-line* constraint definition because the constraints are after the columns. You must do this if you plan to use two or more columns in your primary or unique keys. A different way to use `create table` with inline constraint definitions is shown here, but remember that if you use inline constraint definition, your constraint can only apply to the column it is inline with. Also, remember that not NULL constraints must always be defined inline.

```
CREATE TABLE emp
( empid          NUMBER
  CONSTRAINT pk_emp_01
  PRIMARY KEY NOT DEFERRABLE
  USING INDEX TABLESPACE indexes_01 ENABLE NOVALIDATE,
  empname        VARCHAR2(30)      NOT NULL,
  salary         NUMBER            NOT NULL )
TABLESPACE data_01;
```

Creating Foreign Keys

A foreign key is also defined in the `create table` or `alter table` statement. The foreign key in one table refers to the primary key in another, which is sometimes called the parent key. Another clause, `on delete cascade`, is purely optional. When included, it tells Oracle that if any deletion is performed on EMP that causes a bank account to be orphaned, the corresponding row in BANK_ACCOUNT with the same value for EMPID will also be deleted. Typically, this relationship is desirable because the BANK_ACCOUNT table is the child of the EMP table. If the `on delete cascade` option is not included, then deletion of a record from EMP that has a corresponding child record in BANK_ACCOUNT with the EMPID defined will not be allowed. Additionally, in order to link two columns via a foreign key constraint, the names do not have to be the same, but the datatype for each column must be identical.

```
CREATE TABLE bank_account
(bank_acct      VARCHAR2(40)      NOT NULL,
 aba_rtng_no    VARCHAR2(40)      NOT NULL,
 empid          NUMBER            NOT NULL,
 CONSTRAINT pk_bank_account_01
 PRIMARY KEY (bank_acct)
 USING INDEX TABLESPACE indexes_01,
 CONSTRAINT fk_bank_account_01
 FOREIGN KEY (empid) REFERENCES (emp.empid)
 ON DELETE CASCADE)
TABLESPACE data_01;
```

TIP
In order for a foreign key to reference a column in the parent table, the datatypes of both columns must be identical.

Creating Unique and Check Constraints

Defining a unique constraint is handled as follows. Suppose the DBA decides to track telephone numbers in addition to all the other data tracked in EMP. The `alter table` statement can be issued against the database to make the change. As with a primary key, an index is created for the purpose of verifying uniqueness on the column. That index is identified with the name given to the constraint.

```
alter table emp
add (home_phone varchar2(10)
constraint ux_emp_01 unique
using index tablespace indexes_01);
```

The final constraint considered is the check constraint. The fictitious company using the EMP and BANK_ACCOUNT tables places a salary cap on all employees of $110,000 per year. In order to mirror that policy, the DBA issues the following `alter table` statement, and the constraint takes effect as soon as the statement is issued. If a row exists in the table whose column value violates the check constraint, the constraint remains disabled.

```
ALTER TABLE emp
ADD CONSTRAINT ck_emp_01
CHECK (salary < 110000);
```

Constraint Deferability

Oracle furthers the success of declarative integrity constraints with new features for their use. The first change made to the declarative integrity constraints in the Oracle database is the differentiation between deferred and immediate constraints. *Immediate* constraints are those integrity constraints that are enforced immediately, as soon as the statement is executed. If the user attempts to enter data that violates the constraint, Oracle signals an error and the statement is rolled back. Up until Oracle8*i*, all declarative integrity constraints in the database were immediate constraints. However, Oracle8*i* and later releases also offer the DBA an option to defer database integrity checking. *Deferred* integrity constraints are those that are not enforced until the user attempts to commit the transaction. If, at that time, the data entered by statements violates an integrity constraint, Oracle will signal an error and roll back the entire transaction.

The user can defer any and all constraints that are deferrable during the entire session using the alter session set constraints=deferred statement. Alternatively, the user can defer named or all constraints for a specific transaction, using the set constraint *name* deferred or set constraint all deferred. This form of lazy evaluation temporarily enables data to enter the database that violates integrity constraints. For example, in Oracle7, there was no way to insert data into a child table for which there wasn't also data in the parent. In Oracle8*i*, the user can conduct the insert on the child table before inserting data into the parent simply by deferring the foreign key constraint. The user may also set constraints for immediate enforcement, using the set constraint *name* immediate or set constraint all immediate statement. You can define constraints as either deferrable or not deferrable, and either initially deferred or initially immediate. These attributes can be different for each constraint. You specify them with keywords in the constraint clause, as described next.

Deferrable or Not Deferrable   The definition of a constraint determines whether the constraint is deferrable by users. Two factors play into that determination. The first is the overall deferability of the constraint. If a constraint is created with the deferrable keyword, the constraint is deferrable by user processes until the time the transaction is committed. In contrast, if the constraint is created with the not deferrable keywords, then user process statements will always be bound by the integrity constraint. The not deferrable status is the default for the constraint. If a constraint has been created with the not deferrable status, then the alter session and set statements for deferring integrity constraints, mentioned previously, cannot be used.

Initially Deferred or Initially Immediate   The second factor is the default behavior of the constraint. The first option is to have the constraint deferred, defined with the initially deferred keyword. This option and the not deferrable keyword option described previously are mutually exclusive. The other option is to have the integrity constraint enforced unless explicitly deferred by the user process, which is specified by the initially immediate keywords.

```
CREATE TABLE employees
(empid      NUMBER(10)      NOT NULL,
 name       VARCHAR2(40)    NOT NULL,
 salary     NUMBER(10)      NOT NULL,
 CONSTRAINT pk_employees_01
 PRIMARY KEY (empid) NOT DEFERRABLE);
```

TIP

If you do not include an indication about whether the constraint can be deferrable, Oracle will assume the constraint cannot be deferrable. Later attempts to issue `alter table modify constraint name deferrable` *will return an error. To make the constraint deferrable, you will have to drop and re-create the constraint.*

For Review

1. Understand what declarative data integrity means, and be sure you can name the five types of integrity constraints used on the Oracle database. Know how to use the `alter table` command or `create table` command to generate constraints.

2. Be sure you remember that Oracle creates indexes in support of primary keys and unique constraints in the database.

3. Remember that when defining foreign key constraints between two columns in two different tables, those two columns must be defined with the exact same datatype. The column names do not have to be the same, however.

Exercises

1. **You implement an integrity constraint in an Oracle database using the following command:** `alter table EMP add constraint PK_EMP_01 primary key (EMPNO)`. **Which of the following statements is true about the constraint you just added?**

   A. The constraint will cause Oracle to generate a bitmap index to support its activities.

   B. The constraint will reference back to the primary key in another table for valid values.

C. The constraint will be created but will remain disabled unless all values in the EMPNO column are unique and not NULL.

D. The constraint will enforce uniqueness, but NULL values will be permitted.

2. **You create a table with the following command:**

```
CREATE TABLE employees
(empid      NUMBER(10)     NOT NULL,
 name       VARCHAR2(40)   NOT NULL,
 salary     NUMBER(10)     NOT NULL,
 CONSTRAINT pk_employees_01
 PRIMARY KEY (empid) NOT DEFERRABLE);
```

Several rows are then added to the table. Which of the following choices indicates a statement that if issued, will result in Oracle returning an error?

A. `alter table employees disable novalidate pk_employees_01;`

B. `alter table employees modify constraint pk_employees_01 deferrable;`

C. `alter employees enable novalidate pk_employees_01;`

D. `alter employees enable validate pk_employees_01;`

Answer Key
1. C. 2. B.

Maintaining Integrity Constraints

Historically, there have been two basic statuses for the integrity constraints: `enable` and `disable`. In more recent versions of Oracle, the database offers variations on the theme. For example, the `enable` status has been modified to include an `enable validate` status, whereby the current contents of the constrained column are checked for violations. Another status for integrity constraints, `enable novalidate`, enables Oracle to enforce the constraint on new data entering the table (enabling), but not on data that already exists on the table (no validating). These statuses can be used by issuing the `alter table` *table_name* `enable novalidate constraint` *constraint_name* statement or `alter table` *name* `enable validate constraint` *constraint_name* statement.

Also, Oracle can support unique constraints being enforced with nonunique indexes. The columns indexed as part of the unique constraint should be the first columns in the nonunique index, but as long as those columns are the leading columns of the index, they may appear in any order. Other columns can also be present in the index to make it nonunique. This feature speeds the process of enabling primary key or unique constraints on the table. The nonunique index supporting the unique or primary key constraint cannot be dropped.

TIP

In Oracle8i and later releases, there is a fourth status for integrity constraints called DISABLE VALIDATE. *If a constraint is in this state, any modification of the constrained columns is not allowed. In addition, the index on the constraint is dropped and the constraint is disabled. That is useful for a unique constraint; the* DISABLE VALIDATE *state enables you to load data efficiently from a nonpartitioned table into a partitioned table using the* EXCHANGE PARTITION *option of the* alter table *command.*

Constraints perform their intended operation when enabled, but do not operate when they're disabled. The alter table *tblname* enable constraint command enables a constraint. You can use the optional validate or novalidate keywords to have Oracle validate or not validate data currently in the constrained column for compliance with the constraint. Using validate means Oracle will check the data according to the rules of the constraint. If Oracle finds that the data does not meet the constraint's criteria, Oracle will not enable the constraint. Using novalidate causes Oracle to enable the constraint automatically without checking data, but users may later have trouble committing their changes if the changes contain data that violates the deferred constraint.

```
ALTER TABLE emp ENABLE NOVALIDATE CONSTRAINT pk_emp_01;
ALTER TABLE emp ENABLE VALIDATE CONSTRAINT pk_emp_01;
ALTER TABLE emp ENABLE CONSTRAINT pk_emp_01;  -- automatic validate
```

Disabling a constraint is much simpler—just use the alter table *tblname* disable constraint command. If you want to remove a constraint from the table, use the alter table *tblname* drop constraint statement. If you want to remove a table from your database that is referenced by foreign keys in other tables, use the drop table *tblname* cascade constraints statement.

```
ALTER TABLE emp DISABLE CONSTRAINT pk_emp_01;
ALTER TABLE emp DROP CONSTRAINT ux_emp_01;
DROP TABLE emp CASCADE CONSTRAINTS;
```

TIP

When using novalidate *to enable or*
deferrable *to defer a primary or unique key,*
your associated index must be nonunique to store
the potential violator records for a short time while
the transaction remains uncommitted.

Using the EXCEPTIONS Table

The only foolproof way to create a constraint without experiencing violations on
constraint creation is to create the constraint before any data is inserted. Otherwise,
you must know how to manage violations using the EXCEPTIONS table, which is
created by running a script provided with the Oracle software distribution called
utlexcpt.sql. This file is usually found in the rdbms/admin subdirectory under
the Oracle software home directory. You can alternatively use a table you name
yourself, so long as the columns are the same as those created by the
utlexcpt.sql script for the EXCEPTIONS table. This table contains a column for
the ROWID of the row that violated the constraint and the name of the constraint it
violated. In the case of constraints that are not named explicitly (such as not NULL),
the constraint name listed is the one that was automatically created by Oracle at the
time the constraint was created. The exceptions into clause also helps to
identify those rows that violate the constraint you are trying to enable.

The following code block demonstrates a constraint violation being caused and
then resolved using the EXCEPTIONS table. First, you create the problem:

```
SQL> truncate table exceptions;
Table truncated.
SQL> alter table emp disable constraint ux_emp_01;
Table altered.
SQL> desc emp
 Name                                   Null?     Type
 ----------------------------------- -------- ----
 EMPID                                  NOT NULL NUMBER
 EMPNAME                                NOT NULL VARCHAR2(30)
 SALARY                                 NOT NULL NUMBER
 HOME_PHONE                                      VARCHAR2(10)
SQL> insert into emp (empid, empname, salary, home_phone)
  2  values (3049394,'FERRIS',110000,'1234567890');
1 row created.
SQL> insert into emp (empid, empname, salary, home_phone)
```

```
  2  values(40294932,'BLIBBER',50000,'1234567890');
1 row created.
SQL> commit;
Commit complete.
SQL> alter table emp enable validate constraint ux_emp_01
  2  exceptions into exceptions;
alter table emp enable validate constraint ux_emp_01
*
ERROR at line 1:
ORA-02299: cannot enable (SYS.UX_EMP_01) - duplicate keys found
```

Once you come up against a problem like this, you can use the EXCEPTIONS table to resolve it. Note that EXCEPTIONS shows you every row that violates the constraint. You could easily have simply deleted the offending data as well, and then added it after enabling the constraint:

```
SQL> select rowid, home_phone from emp
  2  where rowid in (select row_id from exceptions);
ROWID              HOME_PHONE
------------------ ----------
AAAA89AAGAAACJKAAA 1234567890
AAAA89AAGAAACJKAAB 1234567890
SQL> update emp set home_phone = NULL where rowid =
  2  chartorowid('AAAA89AAGAAACJKAAB');
1 row updated.
SQL> commit;
Commit complete.
SQL> select * from emp;
    EMPID EMPNAME                            SALARY HOME_PHONE
--------- ------------------------------ ---------- ----------
  3049394 FERRIS                             110000 1234567890
 40294932 BLIBBER                             50000
SQL> alter table emp enable validate constraint ux_emp_01;
Table altered.
SQL> truncate table EXCEPTIONS;
Table truncated.
```

TIP
Remember to clean up the EXCEPTIONS table before and after you use it to avoid being confused by rows violating constraints from different tables.

For Review

1. Understand that whether Oracle enforces the constraints on a table depends on whether those constraints are enabled or not. If a constraint is enabled, Oracle validates incoming data. If not enabled, Oracle does not validate incoming data.

2. You can use the `validate` and `novalidate` keywords to determine whether or not Oracle will check the existing data in a table for violations.

Exercises

1. You are managing integrity constraints in Oracle. Which of the following choices identifies the command you would use if you wanted to disable a primary key integrity constraint?

   A. `alter table`

   B. `alter constraint`

   C. `alter index`

   D. `alter system`

2. You want to determine what rows in a table violate an integrity constraint you are trying to enable. Which of the following scripts would you use to generate the database objects supporting this activity?

   A. `utlfile.sql`

   B. `utlxplan.sql`

   C. `catalog.sql`

   D. `utlexcpt.sql`

Answer Key
1. A. 2. D.

Obtaining Constraint Information from Oracle

There are several ways to access information about constraints. Many of the data dictionary views present various angles on the constraints. Although each of the views listed are prefixed with DBA_, the views are also available in the ALL_ or

USER_ versions, with data limited in the following ways. ALL_ views correspond to the data objects, privileges, and so on that are available to the user who executes the query, whereas the USER_ views correspond to the data objects, privileges, and so on that were created by the user.

DBA_CONSTRAINTS

This view lists detailed information about all constraints in the system. The constraint name and owner of the constraint are listed, along with the type of constraint it is, the status, and the referenced column name and owner for the parent key, if the constraint is a foreign key constraint. One weakness lies in this view—if trying to look up the name of the parent table for the foreign key constraint, the DBA must try to find the table whose primary key is the same as the column specified for the referenced column name. Some important or new columns in this view for Oracle8*i* include the following:

- **CONSTRAINT_TYPE** Displays *p* for primary key, *r* for foreign key, *c* for check constraints (including checks to see if data is not NULL), and *u* for unique constraints

- **SEARCH_CONDITION** Displays the check constraint criteria

- **R_OWNER** Displays the owner of the referenced table, if the constraint is foreign key

- **R_CONSTRAINT_NAME** Displays the name of the primary key in the referenced table if the constraint is foreign key

- **GENERATED** Indicates whether the constraint name was defined by the user creating a table or if Oracle generated it

- **BAD** Indicates whether the check constraint contains a reference to two-digit years, a problem for millennium compliance

DBA_CONS_COLUMNS

This view lists detailed information about every column associated with a constraint. The view includes the name of the constraint and the associated table, as well as the name of the column in the constraint. If the constraint is composed of multiple columns, as can be the case in primary key, unique, and foreign key constraints, the position or order of the columns is specified by a 1, 2, 3, . . . *n* value in the POSITION column of this view. Knowing the position of a column is especially useful in tuning SQL queries to use composite indexes when there is an index corresponding to the constraint.

For Review

Know where you would look in the data dictionary to find out whether a constraint's status is enabled or disabled and where to determine what columns have integrity constraints on them.

Exercises

1. **This is the view you would use to determine whether a constraint existed on a particular column in Oracle tables:** _____.

2. **This is the view you would use in order to determine the constraints associated with a particular table in Oracle:** _____.

Answer Key
1. DBA_CONS_COLUMNS. 2. DBA_CONSTRAINTS.

Chapter Summary

We covered a lot of ground in this chapter with respect to preparation for the OCP DBA Fundamentals 1 exam. In this chapter, we started off by covering a lot of information about the administrative aspects of managing tables in an Oracle database. You learned about various types of tables and the relative advantages and disadvantages of each for storing data in your Oracle database. You reviewed the different datatypes available in Oracle as well. We covered the purpose and structure of restricted and extended ROWIDs, along with a brief history of each in the Oracle database. From there, we went on to discuss the internal structure of blocks in Oracle, along with the structure of row data inside those blocks. You also learned how to create regular and temporary tables from an administrative perspective. The management of storage structures (that is, segments and extents) within tables was discussed at length as well. You learned how to maintain tables, including table reorganization, truncation, and removal, along with how to drop unused columns. From there, we moved on to cover indexes in Oracle. You learned the administrative aspects of indexes, such as how to create, maintain, rebuild online, and drop indexes. You learned how to find out whether an index is being used and where to look in the data dictionary for information about indexes. Finally, we discussed integrity constraints in Oracle. You learned how to create them, manage them, and find information about them in your data dictionary.

Two-Minute Drill

- There are four types of tables: regular tables, partitioned tables, cluster tables, and index-organized tables.

- There are two categories of datatypes: user-defined and built-in.

- There are three classes of built-in types: scalar, collection, and relationship types.

- The regular-size scalar types include CHAR, NCHAR, VARCHAR2, NVARCHAR2, DATE, RAW, ROWID, and NUMBER.

- The large-size scalar types include LONG and LONG RAW from Oracle7, and CLOB, NCLOB, BLOB, and BFILE.

- The collection types include VARRAY, which is a variable-length array, and TABLE, which is a nested table type.

- The relationship type is REF, and it is a pointer to other data in another table.

- Collection and relationship types require the object option installed on your Oracle database.

- To remember the components of a ROWID, think of the BRF and OBRRF acronyms (and a little dog barking).

- Remember how to use each of the options for defining storage and table creation. They are as follows:

  - `initial` First segment in the table

  - `next` Next segment allocated (not simply the second one in the table)

  - `pctincrease` Percentage increase of next extent allocated over `next` value

  - `minextents` Minimum number of extents allocated at table creation

  - `maxextents` Maximum number of extents the object can allocate

  - `pctfree` How much of each block stays free after `insert` for row `update`

  - `pctused` Threshold that usage must fall below before a row is added

  - `initrans` Number of concurrent changes that can happen per block

  - `maxtrans` Maximum number of transactions that can perform the same function

- ■ **logging/nologging** Whether Oracle will store redo for the `create table` statement

- ■ **cache/nocache** Whether Oracle lets blocks stay in the buffer cache after full table scans

■ Row migration is when an `update` makes a row too large to store in its original block.

■ Chaining is when a row is broken up and stored in many blocks. Both require multiple disk reads/writes to retrieve/store, and therefore, are bad for performance.

■ Indexes are used to improve performance on database objects in Oracle. The types of indexes in Oracle are bitmap, B-tree, descending, function-based, and reverse-key.

■ Bitmap indexes are best used for improving performance on columns containing static values with low cardinality or few unique values in the column.

■ B-tree indexes are best used for improving performance on columns containing values with high cardinality.

■ The decision to create an index should weigh the performance gain of using the index against the performance overhead produced when DML statements change index data.

■ The `pctused` parameter is not available for indexes, because every index block is always available for data changes as the result of Oracle needing to keep data in order in an index.

■ DBA_INDEXES and DBA_IND_COLUMNS are dictionary views that store information about indexes.

■ Data integrity constraints are declared in the Oracle database as part of the table definition.

■ There are five types of integrity constraints:

  - ■ **Primary key** Identifies each row in the table as unique

  - ■ **Foreign key** Develops referential integrity between two tables

  - ■ **Unique** Forces each non-NULL value in the column to be unique

  - ■ **Not NULL** Forces each value in the column to be not NULL

  - ■ **Check** Validates each entry into the column against a set of valid value constants

■ There are different constraint states in Oracle8*i*, including deferrable constraints or nondeferrable constraints.

■ In addition, a constraint can be enabled on a table without validating existing data in the constrained column using the `enable novalidate` clause.

■ Oracle uses unique indexes to enforce unique and primary key constraints when those constraints are not deferrable. If the constraints are deferrable, then Oracle uses nonunique indexes for those constraints.

■ When a constraint is created, every row in the table is validated against the constraint restriction.

■ The EXCEPTIONS table stores rows that violate the integrity constraint created for a table.

■ The EXCEPTIONS table can be created by running the `utlexcpt.sql` script.

■ The DBA_CONSTRAINTS and DBA_CONS_COLUMNS data dictionary views display information about the constraints of a database.

■ Constraints can be enabled or disabled. If enabled, constraints will be enforced. If disabled, constraints will not be enforced.

Fill-in-the-Blank Questions

1. The keyword used in order to cause a table DDL operation not to log any redo log entry: _____.

2. The datatype that allows for up to 4GB of text data to be stored in a table column: _____.

3. A term used to describe what Oracle must do when users attempt to add more data to an existing row in the database, but the block housing the row has no room for the row to grow: _____.

4. The scope of availability used whenever defining temporary tables in Oracle: _____.

5. A type of index that would store a listing of numbers from highest to lowest, rather than from lowest to highest: _____.

6. A block space clause that is not relevant for defining indexes: _____.

7. A declarative integrity constraint that prevents duplicate values from entering a column: _____.

8. A dictionary view that contains a listing of all columns that are part of declarative integrity constraints: _____.

Chapter Questions

1. You want to compute statistics for cost-based optimization on all rows in your EMPLOYEE table using Oracle default settings. Which of the following choices contains the statement you will use?

   A. `analyze table EMPLOYEE validate structure;`

   B. `analyze table EMPLOYEE compute statistics;`

   C. `analyze table EMPLOYEE estimate statistics;`

   D. `analyze table EMPLOYEE estimate statistics sample 10 percent;`

2. The DBA suspects there is some chaining and row migration occurring on the database. Which of the following choices indicates a way to detect it?

   A. `select CHAIN_CNT from DBA_SEGMENTS`

   B. `select CHAIN_CNT from DBA_TABLES`

    C. `select CHAIN_CNT from DBA_OBJECTS`

    D. `select CHAIN_CNT from DBA_EXTENTS`

3. **Which of the following datatypes are used in situations where you want an ordered set of data elements, where every element is the same datatype, and where you predefine the number of elements that will appear in the set?**

    A. REF

    B. TABLE

    C. CLOB

    D. VARRAY

4. **Using the `nologging` clause when issuing `create table as select` has effects described by which of the following choices?**

    A. Slows performance in creating the table

    B. Ensures recoverability of the table creation

    C. Improves performance in creating the table

    D. Makes blocks read into memory during full table scans persistent

5. **The largest size a table has ever reached is identified by which of the following items stored in the segment header for the table?**

    A. ROWID

    B. High-water mark

    C. Session address

    D. None of the above

6. **The DBA is designing the data model for an application. Which of the following statements is not true about primary keys?**

    A. A primary key cannot be NULL.

    B. Individual or composite column values combining to form the primary key must be unique.

    C. Each column value in a primary key corresponds to a primary key value in another table.

    D. A primary key identifies the uniqueness of that row in the table.

    E. An associated index is created with a primary key.

7. **In working with developers of an application, the DBA might use the POSITION column in DBA_CONS_COLUMNS for which of the following purposes?**

    A. To indicate the position of the constraint on disk

    B. To relate to the hierarchical position of the table in the data model

    C. To improve the scalability of the Oracle database

    D. To identify the position of the column in a composite index

8. **The DBA is evaluating what type of index to use in an application. Bitmap indexes improve database performance in which of the following situations?**

    A. `select` statements on a column indicating employee status, which has only four unique values for 50,000 rows

    B. `update` statements where the indexed column is being changed

    C. `delete` statements where only one or two rows are removed at a time

    D. `insert` statements where several hundred rows are added at once

9. **The DBA is developing an index creation script. Which of the following choices best explains the reason why indexes do not permit the definition of the `pctused` storage option?**

    A. Indexes have a preset `pctused` setting of 25.

    B. Oracle must keep index entries in order, so index blocks are always being updated.

    C. Indexes are not altered unless they are re-created.

    D. Indexes will not be modified after the `pctfree` threshold is crossed.

10. **The DBA is designing an architecture to support a large document-scanning and cross-referencing system used for housing policy manuals. The architecture will involve several tables that will house in excess of 30,000,000 rows. Which of the following table designs would be most appropriate for this architecture?**

A. Partitioned tables

B. Index-organized tables

C. Clustered tables

D. Regular tables

11. **In order to design a table that enforces uniqueness on a column, which three of the following choices are appropriate?**

   A. Unique constraint

   B. Bitmap index

   C. Primary key

   D. Foreign key

   E. Not NULL constraint

   F. Partitioned index

   G. Unique index

   H. Check constraint

12. **In designing a database architecture that maximizes performance on database `select` statements, each of the following would enhance performance except _____.**

   A. Using indexes on columns frequently used in `where` clauses

   B. Using bitmap indexes on frequently updated columns

   C. Putting indexes in a separate tablespace from tables on a different disk resource

   D. Designing index-organized tables around `select` statements used in the application

13. **When attempting to reenable the primary key after a data load, the DBA receives the following error: "ORA-02299: cannot enable (SYS.UX_EMP_01) - duplicate keys found." Where might the DBA look to see what rows caused the violation?**

   A. DBA_CONS_COLUMNS

   B. DBA_CONSTRAINTS

    C. DBA_CLU_COLUMNS

    D. EXCEPTIONS

14. **The DBA notices that the system-generated indexes associated with integrity constraints in the Oracle database have been defined to be nonunique. Which of the following choices accurately describes the reason for this?**

    A. Nondeferrable primary key constraints

    B. Deferrable unique constraints

    C. Internal error

    D. Incomplete data load

Fill-in-the-Blank Answers

1. `nologging`

2. CLOB

3. Migration

4. GLOBAL

5. Descending

6. `pctused`

7. Unique

8. DBA_CONS_COLUMNS

Answers to Chapter Questions

1. B. `analyze table EMPLOYEE compute statistics;`

Explanation   The tip-off in this question is that you are being asked to compute statistics for all rows in the table. In this situation, you would never estimate, because you are processing all rows in the table, not just some of them. Thus, choices C and D are both incorrect. Also, because the `validate structure` clause only verifies structural integrity of data blocks, choice A is also incorrect.

2. B. `select CHAIN_CNT from DBA_TABLES`

Explanation   The CHAIN_CNT column is found in the DBA_TABLES dictionary view, making choice B correct. The trick of this question is identifying not where the data comes from, for it obviously comes from the CHAIN_CNT column, which is populated by the `analyze` command. The trick is knowing where to look in the dictionary for information. Before taking OCP Exam 2, be sure you go through each of the dictionary views identified in this chapter and run the `describe` command on them to get a feel for which columns show up where.

3. D. VARRAY

Explanation   The content in the question, namely that you want an ordered set of data elements, where every element is the same datatype, and where you predefine the number of elements that will appear in the set, describes the features available in a VARRAY. A nested table is not correct because the nested table is an unordered set, eliminating choice B. Choice A, REF, is a relationship type that stores a pointer to data, not data itself, and is therefore wrong. Finally, a CLOB is a text large object, eliminating choice C.

4. C.   Improves performance in creating the table

Explanation   Because `nologging` causes the `create table as select` statement to not generate any redo information, performance is improved somewhat for the overall operation. This is the logical opposite of choice A, and given these other facts, choice A is wrong. Choice B is also wrong because disabling redo generation means your operation is not recoverable. Finally, choice D is wrong because the `cache` option is used to make blocks read into memory for full table scans persistent, not `nologging`.

5. B.   High-water mark

Explanation   ROWID information is simply a locator for rows in a table. It does nothing to determine the size of that table. Thus, choice A is incorrect. Choice C is incorrect because the session address is dynamic information about the user processes currently connected to Oracle. This has nothing to do with the size of any table anywhere in the database. Because choice B is correct, choice D is logically wrong as well.

6. C.   Each column value in a primary key corresponds to a primary key value in another table.

Explanation   All other statements made about primary keys are true. They must be not NULL and unique in order to enable them to represent each row uniquely in the table. An associated index is also created with a primary key. Refer to the discussion of primary keys as part of integrity constraints.

7. D.   To identify the position of a column in a composite index

Explanation   Constraints are stored with the data definition of a table, without regard to the value stored in POSITION. Therefore, choice A is incorrect. POSITION also has nothing to do with parent/child hierarchies in the data model or with scalability, thereby eliminating choices B and C. Refer to the discussion on using dictionary views to examine constraints.

8. A.   `select` statements on a column indicating employee status, which has only four unique values for 50,000 rows

Explanation   Bitmap indexes are designed to improve performance on a table whose column contains relatively static data of low cardinality. This means there are very few unique values in a large pool of rows. Four unique values out of 50,000 definitely qualify. Choice B is incorrect because of the point made about the column values being relatively static. Because it is a relatively processor-intensive activity to change a value in a bitmap index, you should use bitmap indexes mainly on column values that are static.

9. B.   Oracle must keep index entries in order, so index blocks are always being updated.

Explanation   Recall from the discussion of how an index works that in order for Oracle to maintain the index order, all blocks are always available for update. Thus, choice B is the correct answer to this question. Besides, there is no default `pctused` value for indexes.

10. A.   Partitioned tables

Explanation   30,000,000 rows is a lot of data to manage in an ordinary table. Thus, you should eliminate choice D immediately. A smart DBA will want to maximize data availability by ensuring that the table is partitioned and that the partitions are spread across multiple drives to make it possible to use parallel processing. Although IOTs are designed for text scanning, they also cannot be partitioned, making them a poor candidate for storing this much data. Thus, eliminate choice B. Finally, because no mention of table joins is made, you have no reason to choose choice C.

11. A, C, and G.   Unique constraint, primary key, unique index

Explanation   Unique indexes enforce uniqueness of values in a column or columns. They are used by Oracle as the underlying logic for primary keys and unique keys as well. This fact makes A, C, and G the correct answers. Choices D and E are eliminated because neither of these declarative integrity constraints have unique indexes nor any other mechanism to support uniqueness. Bitmap indexes cannot be unique either, eliminating choice B.

12. B.   Using bitmap indexes on frequently updated columns

Explanation   Bitmap indexes should never be used on columns that are frequently updated, because those changes are very costly in terms of maintaining the index. Using indexes on columns frequently used in `where` clauses, putting indexes in a separate tablespace from tables on a different disk resource, and designing index-organized tables around `select` statements used in the application are all good methods for performance enhancement.

13. D.   EXCEPTIONS

Explanation   When a constraint fails upon being enabled, you would not look in the data dictionary at all. This fact eliminates choices A, B, and C. Instead, you look in the EXCEPTIONS table. Recall that the `exceptions into EXCEPTIONS` clause in the `alter table enable constraint` statement enables you to put the offending records into the EXCEPTIONS table for review and correction later.

14. B.   Deferrable unique constraints

Explanation   The entire rationale behind the situation described in this question, namely that the system-generated indexes associated with integrity constraints in the Oracle database have been defined to be nonunique, is completely a product of deferrable integrity constraints. Because the constraint is deferrable, the index cannot be unique, because it must accept new record input for the duration of the transaction. The user's attempted `commit` causes the transaction to roll back if the constraints are not met.

CHAPTER
6

Managing Database Users

In this chapter, you will learn about and demonstrate knowledge in the following areas:

- Managing users
- Managing password security and resources
- Managing privileges
- Managing roles

This chapter focuses on the functionality Oracle provides for limiting database access. There are several different aspects to limiting database use. In many larger organizations, you may find that a security administrator handles security—the functionality provided by Oracle for security might not be handled by the DBA at all. As the resident expert on Oracle software, it helps to familiarize yourself with this subject in order to better manage the Oracle database. Bear in mind that this discussion will use the terms *DBA* and *security administrator* interchangeably and that the main reason it is covered here is that there will be questions about security on the OCP Exam 2. Approximately 16 percent of the content of this exam focuses on database security.

Managing Users

In this section, you will cover the following topics related to managing users:

- Creating new database users
- Altering and dropping existing users
- Monitoring information about existing users

The safest database is one with no users—but take away the users, and there's little reason to have a database! This section of the chapter focuses on the prudent creation of users in Oracle. You will learn the basic syntax for user creation and how to avoid problems with user creation. We're covering this section before discussing password security and resources because inherent in the discussion of password security and resources is an understanding of how to create users. Thus, it makes sense to talk about user creation first.

Creating New Database Users

One of your primary tasks early on in the creation of a new database is adding new users. However, user creation is an ongoing task. As users enter and leave the organization, so too must you keep track of access to the database granted to those users. When using Oracle's own database authentication method, new users are created with the `create user` statement:

```
CREATE USER spanky
IDENTIFIED BY first01
DEFAULT TABLESPACE users_01
TEMPORARY TABLESPACE temp_01
QUOTA 10M ON users_01
PROFILE app_developer
PASSWORD EXPIRE
ACCOUNT UNLOCK;
```

This statement highlights several items of information that comprise the syntax and semantics of user creation, and these areas will be covered in the following subtopics:

create user

This is the user's name in Oracle. If you're using operating system authentication to enable users to access the database, then the usernames should by default be preceded with OPS$. In no other case is it recommended that a username contain a nonalphanumeric character, although both _ and # are permitted characters in usernames. The name should also start with a letter. On single-byte character sets, the name can be from 1 to 30 characters long, while on multibyte character sets, the name of a user must be limited to 30 bytes. In addition, the name should contain one single-byte character according to Oracle recommendations. The username is not case sensitive and cannot be a reserved word.

identified by

This is the user's Oracle database password. This item should contain at least three characters, and preferably six or more. Generally, it is recommended that users change their password once they know their username is created. Oracle enforces this with the `password expire` clause. Users should change their passwords to something that is not a word or a name that preferably contains a numeric character somewhere in it. As is the case with the username, the password can be a maximum length of 30 bytes and cannot be a reserved word. If operating system authentication is being used, you would use the keywords `identified externally`. This is the only aspect of a user's ID in Oracle that the user is allowed to change with the `alter user` command.

default tablespace

Tablespace management is a crucial task in Oracle. The `default tablespace` names the location where the user's database objects are created by default. This clause plays an important role in protecting the integrity of the SYSTEM tablespace. If no `default tablespace` is named for a user, objects that the user creates may be placed in the SYSTEM tablespace. Recall that SYSTEM contains many database objects, such as the data dictionary and the SYSTEM rollback segment, that are critical to database use. Users should not be allowed to create their database objects in the SYSTEM tablespace.

temporary tablespace

As you may recollect from the discussions on creating databases early in this book, Oracle9*i* enables you to create a *default temporary tablespace* either during the creation of the database or altering it using the `create temporary tablespace` command. By creating default temporary tablespaces, you need not specify the `temporary tablespace` clause for every user created. You can, however, assign users to a different temporary tablespace than the default temporary tablespace for all users, using the `temporary tablespace` option in the `create user` or `alter user` commands.

NOTE
If a default temporary tablespace is not defined and if `temporary tablespace` *is not explicitly specified by the DBA when the username is created, the location for all temporary segments for that user will be the SYSTEM tablespace. SYSTEM, as you already know, is a valuable resource that should not be used for user object storage.*

quota

A `quota` is a limit on the amount of space the user's database objects can occupy within the tablespace. If a user attempts to create a database object that exceeds that user's `quota` for that tablespace, then the object creation script will fail. A `quota` can be specified either in kilobytes (KB) or megabytes (MB). A `quota` clause should be issued separately for every tablespace other than the temporary tablespace on which the user will have access to create database objects. If you want a user to have the ability to use all the space in a tablespace, `quota unlimited on` *tblspcname* can be specified.

TIP
Users need `quotas` *on tablespaces to create database objects only. They do not need a* `quota` *on a tablespace to* `update`, `insert`, *or* `delete` *data in an existing object in the tablespace, so long*

as they do have the appropriate privilege on the
object for data being inserted, updated, or deleted.

profile

`profiles` are a bundled set of resource-usage parameters that the DBA can set in
order to limit the user's overall host machine utilization. A driving idea behind their
use is that many end users of the system only need a certain amount of the host
machine's capacity during their session. To reduce the chance that one user could
affect the overall database performance with, say, a poorly formulated ad hoc report
that drags the database to its knees, you may assign profiles for each user that limit
the amount of time they can spend on the system.

password expire

This clause enforces the requirement that a user change his or her password on first
logging into Oracle. This extra level of password security guarantees that not even
you, the DBA, will know a user's password. If this clause is not included, the user
will not have to change the password on first logging into Oracle.

account unlock

This is the default for the user accounts created. It means that the user's account is
available for use immediately. The DBA can prevent users from using their accounts
by specifying `account lock` instead.

Creating an Operating System Authenticated User

An Oracle database user can be authenticated at various levels—by Oracle itself, by
an operating system, or by a remote service. We already discussed in the previous
section how to create Oracle users authenticated by Oracle. The following
command shows how to create a user authenticated by an operating system:

```
CREATE USER sam
   IDENTIFIED EXTERNALLY
   DEFAULT TABLESPACE users;
```

The previous command creates a user called SAM who will be authenticated
by the operating system. This means the user SAM must have an operating system
account on the machine the Oracle is executing, and once logged into the machine,
the user SAM should give the following command to log into the database:

```
sqlplus /
```

Before creating an operating system-authenticated user, the OS_AUTHENT_PREFIX initialization parameter has to be defined. This parameter specifies the format of the username of operating system-authenticated users. This value defaults to OPS$ to make it backward compatible, but it can now be defined as a NULL as follows:

```
OS_AUTHENT_PREFIX = " "
```

To permit operating system-authenticated users to log into Oracle from a remote machine, you can set the REMOTE_OS_AUTHENT parameter to TRUE. Doing so specifies that the user can be authenticated by a remote operating system. The default value of this parameter if FALSE. However, be aware that using this parameter opens a security hole in the database, whereby operating system-authenticated users on rogue systems may be able to gain access to your Oracle database.

Guidelines for User-Account Management

The following list identifies several new guidelines to follow when managing user accounts. In many cases, these items are new for Oracle8*i* and enhance the management of user accounts:

- Use a standard password for user creation, such as `123abc` or `first1`, and use `password expire` to force users to change this password to something else the first time they log into Oracle.

- Avoid operating system authentication unless all your users will access Oracle while connected directly to the machine hosting your database (this second part is also not advised).

- Always create a default temporary tablespace. Then you don't have to worry about assigning one during user creation. But in case you don't have a default temporary tablespace, be sure to always assign `temporary tablespace` and `default tablespace` to users with the ability to create database objects, such as developers.

- Give few users `quota unlimited`. Although it's annoying to have users asking for more space, it's even more annoying to reorganize tablespaces carelessly filled with database objects.

- Become familiar with the user-account management and other host machine limits that can be set via profiles. These new features take Oracle user-account management to new levels of security.

For Review

1. Understand how to set up new users in Oracle using the `create user` command. Know each of the components of that statement as well. In particular, pay attention to the `default tablespace` and `temporary tablespace` clauses.

2. Be aware of the clauses that force users to change their password regularly and after they first login.

Exercises

1. The following tablespace information was taken from an Oracle database:

```
SQL> select tablespace_name, contents from dba_tablespaces;
TABLESPACE_NAME     CONTENTS
------------------  -------------
SYSTEM              PERMANENT
DATA                PERMANENT
INDEXES             PERMANENT
UNDOTBS             UNDO
TEMP                TEMPORARY
USERS               PERMANENT
```

You create a user in this database with the following command: `create user serena identified by tranquill`. Which of the following choices identifies the location where Oracle will place SERENA's data required for disk sorts?

   A. SYSTEM

   B. DATA

   C. TEMP

   D. UNDOTBS

2. The security administrator for YourCo., a Fortune 500 user of Oracle database software, has issued a mandate that all users in the organization must have a password that no one, not even the DBA, must know. User BETTYBOOP just joined the firm today, and your job as DBA is to create her a new user ID on the Oracle database. Which of the following `create user` clauses would you use to ensure that BETTYBOOP has to change her password the first time she logs into Oracle?

   A. `identified by`

   B. `quota`

    C. `password expire`

    D. `account unlock`

3. **The following tablespace information was taken from your Oracle database:**

```
SQL> select tablespace_name, contents from dba_tablespaces;
TABLESPACE_NAME    CONTENTS
-----------------  ------------
SYSTEM             PERMANENT
DATA               PERMANENT
INDEXES            PERMANENT
UNDOTBS            UNDO
TEMP               TEMPORARY
USERS              PERMANENT
```

    You create a user in this database with the following command: `create user serena identified by tranquill`. Which of the following choices identifies the location where Oracle will place SERENA's new table that she creates with the `create table mytab (col1 number primary key)` command?

    A. SYSTEM

    B. DATA

    C. TEMP

    D. UNDOTBS

Answer Key

1. C. SYSTEM is not used because this database has a default temporary tablespace. **2.** C. **3.** A. If no `default tablespace` clause is included in a `create user` command, tables and indexes for that user are placed in the SYSTEM tablespace if no `tablespace` clause is included in the `object creation` command.

Altering and Dropping Existing Users

Once a user is created, there are a few reasons you'll need to modify that user. One is to expire the password if a user forgets it, so that the next time the user logs in, the password can be changed by the user. The `alter user identified by` statement is used to change the user's password:

```
ALTER USER athena
IDENTIFIED BY forgotpassword
PASSWORD EXPIRE;
```

TIP

Users themselves can also issue the `alter user`
`identified by` *command to change their own
passwords. However, this is the only aspect of a
user's ID that the user can change.*

In certain situations, as the result of user profiles, a user's account may become
locked. This may occur if the user forgot his or her password and tried to log in
using a bad password too many times. To unlock a user's account while also making
it possible for the user to change the password, the following `alter user`
statement can be used:

```
ALTER USER athena
IDENTIFIED BY forgotpassword
ACCOUNT UNLOCK
PASSWORD EXPIRE;
```

TIP

*You'll learn more about account locking in the
password management section later in this chapter.*

Other situations abound. In an attempt to prevent misuse, you may want to lock
an account that has been used many times unsuccessfully to gain access to Oracle
with the following statement:

```
ALTER USER athena
ACCOUNT LOCK;
```

TIP

*You should remember that changes to passwords,
account lock status, or password expiration are
applied only to subsequent user sessions, not the
current one.*

Changing User Tablespace Allocation

You may want to reorganize tablespaces to distribute the input/output (I/O) load and
make more effective use of the hardware running Oracle. Perhaps this effort involves
dropping some tablespaces and creating new ones. If the DBA wants to change a
user's default tablespace, the `alter user default tablespace` statement can
be used. As explained earlier, this change is good for preserving the integrity of the
SYSTEM tablespace. Only newly created objects will be affected by this statement.

Existing objects created in other tablespaces by that user will continue to reside in those tablespaces until they are dropped. Additionally, if the user specifies a tablespace in which to place a database object, that specification will override the default tablespace.

```
ALTER USER spanky
DEFAULT TABLESPACE overflow_tabspc01;
```

By the same token, you may want to reorganize the tablespace used for disk sorts as you move from permanent tablespaces to temporary tablespaces, and this is done using `alter user temporary tablespace`. Only the DBA can make these changes; the users cannot change their own temporary or default tablespaces.

```
ALTER USER spanky
TEMPORARY TABLESPACE temp_overflow_01;
```

TIP

You only need to specify the `temporary`
`tablespace` *clause for users if no default
temporary tablespace exists for the database, or if
you want to assign users to a temporary tablespace
other than the default temporary tablespace for the
database.*

A tablespace accessible to the user at user creation can have a quota placed on it. A quota can be altered by the DBA with the `alter user quota` statement. For example, the DBA may want to reduce the quota on the USERS_01 tablespace from 10MB to 5MB for user SPANKY. If the user has already created over 5MB worth of database objects in the tablespace, no further data can be added to those objects and no new objects can be created. Only the DBA can change a user's tablespace quota; the users cannot change their own quotas.

```
ALTER USER spanky
QUOTA 5M ON users_01;
```

TIP

Specifying `quota 0` *on SYSTEM for a user will
prevent him or her from creating any object in the
SYSTEM tablespace, even if that user still has his or
her* `default tablespace` *set to SYSTEM.
However, this restriction does not include the
creation of packages, stored procedures, and
functions.*

Aspects of User Accounts Changeable by Users

All aspects of the user's account covered already are the components that can be modified by the DBA. However, the aspects of the account that can be changed by the actual user are far more limited. A situation may arise in regular database use where a user wants to change his or her password. This is accomplished with the following:

```
ALTER USER athena
IDENTIFIED BY mynewpassword;
```

TIP

Except for altering the password, the user can change nothing about his or her own user account, except in certain situations where the alter any user *privilege has been granted to that user.*

Dropping User Accounts

As users come and go, their access should be modified to reflect their departure. To drop a user from the database, you execute the drop user statement. If a user has created database objects, the user cannot be dropped until the objects are dropped as well. In order to drop the user and all related database objects in one fell swoop, Oracle provides the cascade option.

```
DROP USER spanky CASCADE;
```

TIP

If you want to remove a user but assign his or her table(s) to another user, you should use the EXPORT tool to dump the user's table(s), and then use IMPORT with the FROMUSER and TOUSER parameters to import the tables as that other user.

For Review

1. Understand how to use the alter user statement to change a user's ID configuration. Also, be aware that the only aspect of a user's ID that can be changed with the alter user statement that cannot also be set with the create user statement is the default role clause. We'll discuss roles in more detail later in this chapter.

2. Users can only change their own passwords. All other aspects of changing a person's user ID must be completed by you, the DBA.

Exercises

1. User BETTYBOOP logs onto Oracle. Which of the following statements can she herself execute to change an aspect of her own user ID?

   A. `alter user bettyboop identified by boop2edoop;`

   B. `alter user bettyboop default tablespace users;`

   C. `alter user bettyboop quota 100M on tablespace SYSTEM;`

   D. `alter user bettyboop default role none;`

2. User BOBSMITH has been asked to leave YourCo. The department director asks you to drop his user ID from the Oracle database. In your analysis, you discover that BOBSMITH has about 60 tables in his schema, all of which are housed in the USERS tablespace, along with tables for many other users. Which of the following choices identifies the command that will eliminate BOBSMITH's user and schema contents in the fewest number of steps?

   A. Issue `drop table` for all 60 tables and then `drop user bobsmith;`.

   B. Issue `spool genscrpt.sql`, followed by `select 'drop table ' || table_name || ';' from dba_tables where owner = 'BOBSMITH'` to generate a script, then issue `@genscrpt`, and then `drop user BOBSMITH`.

   C. Issue the `drop user bobsmith cascade` command.

   D. Issue the `drop tablespace users including contents` command.

3. You issue the following command in Oracle: `alter user JOSEPHINE default tablespace SYSTEM quota 0 on SYSTEM`. Assuming JOSEPHINE has the appropriate privileges to do so, which of the following commands will JOSEPHINE not be able to issue as a result of this action?

   A. `create table mytab (col1 number primary key);`

   B. `create procedure myproc begin null; end;`

   C. `create function myfunc return null begin null; end;`

   D. `create table mytab2 (col1 number primary key) tablespace data;`

Answer Key
1. A. 2. C. 3. A.

Monitoring Information about Existing Users

As the DBA, you may periodically want to monitor information about users. Several data dictionary views may be used for the purpose of obtaining information about users. Some information you may want to collect includes default and temporary tablespace information, objects created by that user, and what the current account status for that user account is. The following data dictionary views can be used to determine this information:

- **DBA_USERS** Contains the username, Oracle-generated ID number, encrypted password, default and temporary tablespace information, and user profile that was specified in the ID creation statements or any alteration that may have followed. Also, the view offers ACCOUNT_STATUS, which may be locked, open, or expired; LOCK_DATE, which is the date on which the account was locked (NULL for open accounts); and EXPIRY_DATE, which is the date for account expiration.

- **DBA_OBJECTS** Contains the specific information about every object in the database. The DBA can determine which objects belong to which users by using the OWNER column of this view.

- **DBA_SEGMENTS** Similar to DBA_OBJECTS. Contains information about various segments (tables, indexes, and so on) created by users, where they reside, and their space allocation information.

- **DBA_TS_QUOTAS** Names all users and any tablespace quotas that have been created for them.

TIP
A value of -1 in MAX_BYTES or MAX_BLOCKS means that the user has an unlimited space quota for that tablespace.

For Review

1. Know the views you might use to find information about users in your Oracle database: DBA_USERS and DBA_TS_QUOTAS.

2. Understand where to look in the data dictionary for information about where a user's database objects may reside: DBA_OBJECTS and DBA_SEGMENTS.

Exercises

1. **You issue the following command in Oracle, and Oracle responds with the following information:**

```
SQL> select username, tablespace_name, max_bytes from dba_ts_quotas
  2  where username = 'CAPTAINCRUNCH';
USERNAME       TABLESPACE_NAME  MAX_BYTES
-------------  ---------------- ----------
CAPTAINCRUNCH  SYSTEM            1048576
CAPTAINCRUNCH  DATA             -1
CAPTAINCRUNCH  TEMP             -1
CAPTAINCRUNCH  INDEXES          10485760
```

Which of the following choices correctly describes an aspect of CAPTAINCRUNCH's tablespace allocation quota?

A. CAPTAINCRUNCH can allocate up to 1MB worth of space in the SYSTEM tablespace for procedure source code.

B. CAPTAINCRUNCH can perform disk sorts that generate enough temporary segments to fill the TEMP tablespace.

C. CAPTAINCRUNCH can allocate up to 10MB of storage in the DATA tablespace.

D. CAPTAINCRUNCH can allocate up to 1MB of storage in the INDEXES tablespace.

2. **You issue the following command in Oracle, and Oracle responds by providing the following information:**

```
SQL> select * from dba_users where username = 'SYS';
USERNAME                                    USER_ID PASSWORD
----------------    ------------------------------- ----------------
ACCOUNT_STATUS      LOCK_DATE                        EXPIRY_DATE
----------------    ------------------------------- ----------------
DEFAULT_TABLESPACE  TEMPORARY_TABLESPACE             CREATED
----------------    ------------------------------- ----------------
PROFILE             INITIAL_RSRC_CONSUMER_GROUP      EXTERNAL_NAME
----------------    ------------------------------- ----------------
SYS                                               0 D4C5016086B2DC6A
OPEN
SYSTEM              TEMP                             06-JUN-01
DEFAULT             SYS_GROUP
```

Which of the following statements is true regarding the user information shown previously?

A. No user may log into Oracle as SYS.

B. If SYS creates a table without specifying a `tablespace` clause, the table will be placed into the TEMP tablespace.

C. The password for the SYS user on this database is D4C5016086B2DC6A.

D. If SYS performs a disk sort, the temporary segments will be placed in the TEMP tablespace.

3. **You are attempting to find information in the DBA_USERS view about a given username. Which of the following informational components about the SYS user cannot be found in the DBA_USERS view?**

A. Default role

B. Default tablespace

C. Default temporary tablespace

D. Default profile

Answer Key
1. B. 2. D. 3. A.

Managing Password Security and Resources

In this section, you will cover the following topics related to managing resource use:

- Controlling resource use with profiles
- Administering profiles
- Managing passwords using profiles
- Obtaining profile information from the data dictionary

Profiles are objects in the Oracle database that limit a user's ability to utilize the resources of the system hosting the Oracle database. In other words, if you wanted to restrict a group of users from abusing the central processing unit (CPU) utilization on the machine hosting the Oracle database, you would use profiles in order to do so. Oracle's use of the host machine on behalf of certain users can be managed by creating specific user profiles to correspond to the amount of activity anticipated by typical transactions generated by those different types of users. The principle of user profiles is not to force the user off the system every time an artificially low resource-usage threshold is exceeded. Rather, resource-usage thresholds should enable the users to do everything they need to on the Oracle database, while also limiting unwanted or unacceptable use. If users make a mistake, or try to do something that hurts database performance, profiles can stop them short, helping to reduce problems. Let's now explore how to use profiles in the Oracle database.

Controlling Resource Use with Profiles

The main purpose behind user profiles is to control the use of host system resources by the Oracle database with respect to the user. Before proceeding into a full-fledged discussion of profiles, however, you must make a change to your `init.ora` file so that Oracle will enforce host system resource limits set in profiles. To use resource limits, you must first change the RESOURCE_LIMIT `init.ora` parameter to TRUE on your Oracle database. To enable resource restrictions to be used in conjunction with profiles on the current database session, you can also issue the following statement:

```
ALTER SYSTEM
SET RESOURCE_LIMIT = TRUE;
```

Once resource limits are enabled, there are three different aspects of resource usage and limitation to consider when setting up profiles. This discussion will cover all three. They are session-level resource limits for individuals, call-level resource limits, and the assignment of resource cost to enable composite limits.

Setting Individual Resource Limits: Session Level

The following resource-usage areas can have limits assigned for them within the profiles you create. If a session-level resource limit is exceeded, the user gets an error and the session is terminated automatically. At the session level, the resource limits are as follows:

- **sessions_per_user**   The number of sessions a user can open concurrently with the Oracle database.

- **cpu_per_session**   The maximum allowed CPU time in $1/100$ seconds that a user can utilize in one session.

- **logical_reads_per_session**   The maximum number of disk I/O block reads that can be executed in support of the user processing in one session.

- **idle_time**   The time in minutes that a user can issue no commands before Oracle times out his or her session.

- **connect_time**   The total amount of time in minutes that a user can be connected to the database.

- **private_sga**   The amount of private memory in KB or MB that can be allocated to a user for private storage. This is only used when MTS is in use on your Oracle database.

TIP
You'll see examples of profiles with these limits set in the next discussion.

Individual Resource Limits: Call Level

At the call level, the resource-usage areas can have limits assigned for them within the profiles you create. If the user exceeds the call-level usage limits he or she has been assigned, the SQL statement that produced the error is terminated, any transaction changes *made only by the offending statement* are rolled back, previous statements remain intact, and the user remains connected to Oracle. Call-level usage limits are identified as follows:

- **logical_reads_per_call**   The maximum number of disk I/O block reads that can be executed in support of the user's processing in one session.

- **cpu_per_call**   The maximum allowed CPU time in $1/100$ seconds that any individual operation in a user session can use.

TIP
You'll see examples of profiles with these limits set in the next discussion.

Setting Composite Limits and Resource Costs

In some cases, you may find individual resource limits inflexible. The alternative is setting composite limits on the principle of resource cost. Resource cost is an arbitrary number that reflects the relative value of that resource based on the host machine's capabilities. For example, on a host machine with few CPUs and many disk controllers, you might consider `cpu_per_session` more valuable than `logical_reads_per_session`. The statement used for assigning a resource cost is `alter resource cost`. Resource costs only apply to the `cpu_per_session`, `logical_reads_per_session`, `connect_time`, and `private_sga` resources. The default value for each resource cost is zero. Resource costs are not necessarily monetary costs. Cost is specified as an abstract unit value, not a monetary resource price. For example, setting the resource cost of CPU cycles per session equal to 1.5 does not mean that each CPU cycle costs a user process $1.50 to run.

```
ALTER RESOURCE COST
CPU_PER_SESSION 10
LOGICAL_READS_PER_SESSION 2
PRIVATE_SGA 6
CONNECT_TIME 1;
```

TIP
You'll see an example of a profile with composite limits set in the next discussion.

Resource Consumer Groups and Host System Resource Management

In Oracle8*i*, Oracle introduced a new feature for host system resource management —the use of resource consumer groups. This feature uses built-in PL/SQL procedures and functions to control the use of host system resources by users. Although not tested extensively on the OCP DBA Fundamentals I exam, it's worth taking some time to explore this feature on your own. For more information, consult the database resource management section of the Oracle9*i* Database Administrators Guide that comes as part of your Oracle Generic Documentation.

For Review

1. Know that you must set the RESOURCE_LIMIT initialization parameter before Oracle will enforce resource limits according to your profile settings.

2. Be sure you can identify the different levels of host system resource settings: session-level, call-level, and composite limits. To set composite limits, you use the `alter resource cost` command to define cost values for resources.

Exercises

1. You want to use composite resource limits in the Oracle database. Which of the following commands must be issued so that composite resources are assigned a value for composite limits?

   A. `alter system`

   B. `alter resource cost`

   C. `alter profile`

   D. `alter user`

2. You issue the following command in the Oracle database: `alter system set resource_limit = true;`. Which of the following statements describes the purpose this command serves?

   A. This command is meant to set composite resource limit costs in your Oracle database.

   B. This command is meant to enable the use of profiles to limit host system resource utilization.

   C. This command is meant to create profiles for use in Oracle.

   D. This command is meant to assign users to profiles in Oracle.

3. You are defining resource limits for use with profiles. Which of the following is not a resource limit that can be set in conjunction with composite limits on your Oracle database?

   A. IDLE_TIME

   B. CPU_PER_SESSION

   C. PRIVATE_SGA

   D. CONNECT_TIME

Answer Key
1. B. 2. B. 3. A.

Administering Profiles

Profiles are assigned to users with the create user or alter user command. You've already seen some examples of the create user command in previous discussions. A special user profile exists in Oracle at database creation called DEFAULT. If you do not assign a profile to a user with the profile clause in the create user statement, Oracle assigns the DEFAULT profile to that user automatically. The DEFAULT profile isn't very restrictive of host system resources; in fact, DEFAULT gives users unlimited use of all resources definable in the database. You might create a user profile that has some host system usage restrictions on it, such as the one in the following code block:

```
CREATE PROFILE developer LIMIT
SESSIONS_PER_USER 1
CPU_PER_SESSION 10000
CPU_PER_CALL 20
CONNECT_TIME 240
IDLE_TIME 20
LOGICAL_READS_PER_SESSION 50000
LOGICAL_READS_PER_CALL 400
PRIVATE_SGA 1024;
```

This code block is a good example of using profiles to set *individual resource limits*. You don't need to define limits for all available resources, because any resources not explicitly assigned limits when you create a profile will be assigned the default value for that limit, specified in the DEFAULT profile. Thus, if you change the value for a resource limit in the DEFAULT profile, you may be making changes to other profiles on your system as well. Once profiles are created, they are assigned to users with the profile clause in either the create user or alter user statement. The following code block contains some examples of each statement:

```
CREATE USER spanky
IDENTIFIED BY orange#tabby
TEMPORARY TABLESPACE temp_01
QUOTA 5M ON temp_01
PROFILE developer;

ALTER USER athena
PROFILE developer;
```

Altering and Dropping Profiles

Once created, you can alter the host system resource limit settings in your profile using the alter profile command. Changing a user profile may be required if user profiles in the database rely on default values set in the DEFAULT profile. For example, if the resource limit `cpu_per_session` in DEFAULT is changed from `unlimited` to 20,000, then `cpu_per_session` in any user profile that didn't explicitly set one for itself will also be affected. You may not want this to happen, but only by explicitly setting its own value for `cpu_per_session` will the profile not depend on the DEFAULT profile for the `cpu_per_session` limit. You issue the following statement to change a resource limit in a profile:

```
ALTER PROFILE developer LIMIT
CPU_PER_SESSION UNLIMITED;
```

> **TIP**
> *Any option in any profile can be changed at any time; however, the change will not take effect for users assigned to that profile until the user logs out and logs back in.*

If you want to drop a user profile from the database, do so by executing the `drop profile` statement. A question you might have is, what happens if you try to drop a profile that has already been assigned to users? Well, in that case, you must use the `drop profile cascade` command. After issuing the `drop profile cascade` command, Oracle switches users assigned to the dropped profile back to the DEFAULT profile instead. For obvious reasons, the DEFAULT profile cannot be dropped. Let's look at an example of the `drop profile` command to understand the syntax:

```
DROP PROFILE developer CASCADE;
```

> **TIP**
> *To gather information about how users are utilizing the host machine in database sessions to set resource limits properly, use the* `audit session` *command. You'll learn more about auditing in a later discussion. Resource limits you can gather information for include* `connect_time`, `logical_reads_per_session`, *and* `logical_reads_per_call`.

Creating Profiles with Composite Limits Set

Once resource costs are set, you assign composite limits to your users. Composite limits restrict database use by specifying a limit of how much a host machine resource can be used per session. Each time the session uses a resource, Oracle tallies the total resource use for that session. When the session hits the composite_limit, the session is terminated. Profiles are altered to include a composite_limit with the alter profile statement.

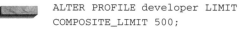

```
ALTER PROFILE developer LIMIT
COMPOSITE_LIMIT 500;
```

For Review

1. Be sure you understand the basic purpose behind profiles. They prevent misuse of underlying host system resources by setting limits on those resources at the user level.

2. Know the purpose of the DEFAULT profile. It is assigned to users when you do not specify a profile clause in the create user command. It isn't very restrictive, however—all host resource-usage limits are set to unlimited.

3. You create profiles with the create profile command. If you don't set an aspect of host system limits in your profile, Oracle defaults that host system limit to whatever setting is present for that limit in the DEFAULT profile.

4. If you drop a profile that has been assigned to a user, you must use the cascade option in the drop profile command. Oracle switches the user back to the DEFAULT profile in this situation.

Exercises

1. **The following output was taken from a session with your Oracle database:**

```
SQL> select username, profile from dba_users;
USERNAME          PROFILE
--------------    --------------
SYS               SYS_PROFILE
SYSTEM            SYS_PROFILE
MARYANN           DATA_ADMIN
MARYSUE           DEVELOPER
MARYJANE          MANAGER
```

   If you issue the drop profile DATA_ADMIN cascade command, which of the following profiles will MARYANN be assigned to?

   A. DEVELOPER

   B. MANAGER

   C. SYS_PROFILE

   D. DEFAULT

2. **You create a profile using the following command:**

```
CREATE PROFILE myprofile LIMIT
SESSIONS_PER_USER 1
CPU_PER_CALL 20
CONNECT_TIME 240
IDLE_TIME 20
PRIVATE_SGA 1024;
```

Which of the following choices best identifies how Oracle will determine what the value for the CPU_PER_SESSION limit will be?

A. Oracle uses the same value as CPU_PER_CALL from this `create profile` command.

B. Oracle uses the value for CPU_PER_SESSION from the SYS_PROFILE profile.

C. Oracle uses the value for CPU_PER_SESSION from the DEFAULT profile.

D. Oracle sets CPU_PER_SESSION to `unlimited`.

3. **You have created three profiles on your Oracle database at YourCo., a Fortune 500 user of Oracle database software: DEVELOPER for your Oracle developers, MANAGEMENT for IT managers, and ORACLE_USERS for the end users of your Oracle database. BETTYBOOP's first day at YourCo. is today, and your job is to create a user ID for her. You issue the following in Oracle: `create user bettyboop identified by changeme password expire account unlock`. Which of the following choices identify the resource profile BETTYBOOP will be assigned?**

A. DEVELOPER

B. ORACLE_USERS

C. MANAGEMENT

D. DEFAULT

E. None—no `profile` clause was specified in the `create user` command.

Answer Key

1. D. 2. C. 3. D.

Administering Passwords Using Profiles

We've already hinted that advanced password management features are available in Oracle through the use of profiles. These features include *account locking, password aging and expiration, password history,* and *password complexity requirements.* These features are designed to make it harder than ever to hack the Oracle database as an authorized user without knowing the user's password. This protects the integrity of assigned usernames as well as the overall data integrity of the Oracle database.

Though not required to enable password management, the DBA can run the `utlpwdmg.sql` script as SYS to support the functionality of password management. This script can be found in the `rdbms/admin` subdirectory under the Oracle software home directory. This script makes some additions to the DEFAULT profile, identified earlier in the chapter, for use with password management. When the password management script is run, all default password management settings defined in the DEFAULT profile are enforced at all times on the Oracle database. This is unlike other resource limits, which still require that RESOURCE_LIMIT be set to TRUE before the instance starts.

Account Management

Account locking enables Oracle to lock out an account when users attempt to log into the database unsuccessfully on several attempts. The maximum number of failed attempts is defined per user or by group. The number of failed attempts is specified by the DBA or security officer in ways that will be defined shortly, and the failed attempts are tracked by Oracle such that if the user fails to log into the database in the specified number of tries, Oracle locks out the user automatically. In addition, a time period for automatic user lockout can be defined such that the failed login attempt counter will reset after that time period, and the user may try to log into the database again. Alternatively, automatic lockout can be permanent, disabled only by the security administrator or DBA. User accounts can also be locked manually if the security administrator or DBA so desires. In this situation, the only way to unlock the account is manually. The following command shows how to set the parameters for account locking:

```
ALTER PROFILE default LIMIT
  FAILED_LOGIN_ATTEMPTS 3
  PASSWORD_LOCK_TIME unlimited;
```

In the previous example, the FAILED_LOGIN_ATTEMPTS setting defines the number of failed login attempts before the account is locked out. In this case, we've set this option to 3, meaning that after three failed attempts at logging, Oracle locks the user's account automatically. The other option, PASSWORD_LOCK_TIME, indicates the number of days the account is locked after three failed login attempts. In this case, we've specified that the user account stays locked indefinitely, until we, as DBAs, investigate the situation and unlock the account manually.

Password Aging and Rotation

A password can also be aged in the Oracle database. The DBA or security administrator can set a password to have a maximum lifetime in the Oracle database. Once a threshold time period passes, the user must change his or her password or be unable to access the Oracle database. A grace period can be defined, during which the user must change the password. If the time of the grace period passes and the user doesn't change the password, the account is then locked and only the security administrator can unlock it. A useful technique for creating new users is to create them with expired passwords, such that the user enters the grace period on first login and must change the password during that time.

A potential problem arises when users are forced to change their passwords. Sometimes users try to "fool" the system by changing the expired password to something else and then immediately changing the password back. To prevent this, Oracle8*i* supports a password history feature that keeps track of recently used passwords and disallows their use for a specified amount of time or number of changes. The interval is defined within the user profile, and information on how to set it will be presented shortly. The following is some sample code to implement password aging and rotation:

```
ALTER PROFILE default LIMIT
  PASSWORD_LIFE_TIME 60
  PASSWORD_GRACE_TIME 10
  PASSWORD_REUSE_TIME 1800
  PASSWORD_REUSE_MAX 0;
```

The PASSWORD_LIFE_TIME parameter defines the lifetime of the password in days after which the password will expire. The PASSWORD_GRACE_TIME parameter defines the grace period in days for changing the password after the first successful login once the password has expired. The PASSWORD_REUSE_TIME parameter specifies the maximum number of days before the user can reuse a previous password. Finally, the PASSWORD_REUSE_MAX parameter specifies the maximum number of times a previous password can be reused.

Password Complexity Verification

Finally, and perhaps most important to the integrity of an Oracle user's account, there is the feature of password complexity verification. There are many commonly accepted practices in creating a password, such as making sure it has a certain character length, that it is not a proper name or word in the dictionary, that it is not all numbers or all characters, and so on. Too often, however, users don't heed these mandates and create passwords that are easy to decode using any of a number of products available for decoding encrypted password information.

To prevent users from unwittingly subverting the security of the database, Oracle supports the automatic verification of password complexity with the use of a

PL/SQL function that can be applied during user or group profile creation to prevent users from creating passwords of insufficient complexity. The checks provided by the default function include making sure the minimum password length is four characters and is not the same as the username. Also, the password must contain at least one letter, number, and punctuation character, and the password must be different from the previous password defined by at least three characters.

If this level of complexity verification provided by the given PL/SQL function is not high enough, a PL/SQL function of sufficient complexity may be defined by the organization, and be subject to certain restrictions. The overall call syntax must conform to the details in the following code listing. In addition, the new routine must be assigned as the password verification routine in the user's profile or the DEFAULT profile. In the `create profile` statement, the following must be present: `password_verify_function` *user_pwcmplx_fname*, where *user_pwcmplx_fname* is the name of the user-defined password complexity function. Some other constraints on the definition of this function include that an appropriate error must be returned if the routine raises an exception or if the verification routine becomes invalid, and that the verification function will be owned by SYS and used in system context. The call to the PL/SQL complexity verification function must conform to the following parameter-passing and return-value requirements:

```
USER_PWCMPLX_FNAME
( user_id_parm      IN VARCHAR2,
  new_passwd_parm   IN VARCHAR2,
  old_passwd_parm   IN VARCHAR2
) RETURN BOOLEAN;
```

To show the coding used in a password complexity function, the following example is offered. This example is a simplified and modified block of code similar to the password verification function provided with Oracle. The function will check three things: that the new password is not the same as the username, that the new password is six characters long, and that the new password is not the same as the old one. When the DBA creates a username, the verification process is called to determine whether the password is appropriate. If the function returns TRUE, the DBA will be able to create the username. If not, the user creation will fail. This example is designed to give you some groundwork for coding your own password complexity function; bear in mind, however, that the function in the following listing is greatly simplified for example purposes only:

```
CREATE OR REPLACE FUNCTION my_pwver (
x_user    IN  VARCHAR2,
x_new_pw  IN  VARCHAR2,
x_old_pw  IN  VARCHAR2
```

```
)RETURN BOOLEAN IS
BEGIN
   IF LENGTH(x_new_pw) < 6 THEN
     RAISE_APPLICATION_ERROR(-20001, 'New password too short.');
   ELSIF x_new_pw = x_user THEN
     RAISE_APPLICATION_ERROR(-20002, 'New password same as username');
   ELSIF x_new_pw = x_old_pw THEN
     RAISE_APPLICATION_ERROR(-20003, 'New password same as old');
   ELSE
     RETURN(TRUE);
   END IF;
END;
```

The function itself can be defined in the profile as follows:

```
ALTER PROFILE default LIMIT
   PASSWORD_VERIFY_FUNCTION my_pwver;
```

Password Management Resource Limits in the DEFAULT Profile

After the `utlpwdmg.sql` script is run, default values will be specified for several password-management resource limits. An explanation of each option is listed in this section. The default value for each of these settings is `unlimited` or NULL.

- **failed_login_attempts**   The number of unsuccessful attempts at login a user can make before the account locks

- **password_life_time**   The number of days a password will remain active

- **password_reuse_time**   The number of days before the password can be reused

- **password_reuse_max**   The number of times the password must be changed before one can be reused

- **password_lock_time**   The number of days after which Oracle will unlock a user account that is locked automatically when the user exceeds `failed_login_attempts`

- **password_grace_time**   The number of days during which an expired password must be changed by the user or else Oracle permanently locks the account

- **password_verify_function**   The function used for password complexity verification

Using Password Settings for Profiles: Example

Following is a sample code of creating a new profile with all of the previous password parameters:

```
CREATE PROFILE tmp_profile LIMIT
   FAILED_LOGIN_ATTEMPTS 3
   PASSWORD_LOCK_TIME unlimited
   PASSWORD_LIFE_TIME 30
   PASSWORD_REUSE_TIME 30
   PASSWORD_VERIFY_FUNCTION my_pwver
   PASSWORD_GRACE_TIME 5;
```

For Review

1. Understand the account management features available in Oracle. You can lock and unlock user accounts using this feature.

2. Be sure you can identify the password aging and rotation features available in Oracle. You can specify it so that Oracle does not enable the reuse of passwords for a period of time, and that Oracle forces users to change their passwords periodically.

3. Know how Oracle manages password complexity verification in the database, and be sure you can describe the use of PL/SQL functions for this purpose.

Exercises

1. **You create a profile using the following code block:**

```
CREATE PROFILE tmp_profile LIMIT
   FAILED_LOGIN_ATTEMPTS 3
   PASSWORD_LOCK_TIME unlimited
   PASSWORD_LIFE_TIME 30
   PASSWORD_REUSE_TIME 180
   PASSWORD_VERIFY_FUNCTION my_pwver
   PASSWORD_GRACE_TIME 5;
```

   Which of the following choices identifies a true statement about the profile you just created?

   A. After three failed login attempts, a user assigned this profile will have to wait three days before trying to log into Oracle again.

   B. After 180 days, a user assigned this profile can reuse his or her password.

C. A user assigned this profile must change his or her password every 30 minutes.

D. A user has up to five minutes to specify a password the first time he or she logs in before Oracle automatically locks the account.

2. **You plan to run the `utlpwmg.sql` script as part of managing passwords. Which of the following directory locations can this script be found in?**

A. `$ORACLE_HOME/dbs`

B. `$ORACLE_HOME/sqlplus/admin`

C. `$ORACLE_HOME/rdbms/admin`

D. `$ORACLE_HOME/network/admin`

3. **You want to set up password management features in your Oracle database such that users may never reuse a password and that a user has three days to change his or her default password the first time he or she logs into Oracle before the account gets locked. Which of the following choices identifies the statement you will use for this purpose?**

A. `alter profile default limit failed_login_attempts 3 password_reuse_time unlimited;`

B. `alter profile default limit password_grace_time 3 password_reuse_limit unlimited;`

C. `alter profile default limit failed_login_attempts 3 password_grace_time unlimited;`

D. `alter profile default limit password_reuse_time 3 failed_login_attempts unlimited;`

Answer Key
1. B. 2. C. 3. B.

Obtaining Profile Information from the Data Dictionary

The following dictionary views offer information about the resource-usage limits defined for profiles and about the profiles that have been assigned to users:

- **DBA_PROFILES**   Contains specific information about the resource-usage parameters specified in conjunction with each profile.

- **RESOURCE_COST**   Identifies all resources in the database and their corresponding cost, as defined by the DBA. Cost determines a resource's relative importance of use.

- **USER_RESOURCE_LIMITS**   Identifies the system resource limits for individual users, as determined by the profile assigned to the users.

- **DBA_USERS**   Offers information about the profile assigned to a user, current account status, lock date, and password expiry date.

 TIP
Spend a little time on your Oracle database gaining familiarity with the contents of each of these dictionary views before taking the Oracle9i DBA Fundamentals I exam.

For Review

1. The profile assigned to a user can be found in the DBA_USERS view.

2. Resource cost and resource limit settings can be found in the RESOURCE_COST and USER_RESOURCE_LIMITS views, respectively.

3. The DBA_PROFILES view is handy for finding the resource settings in a particular profile.

Exercises

1. **You are administering profiles on your Oracle database. Which of the following queries would you use in order to determine which resource limits were in effect for user SALLY if you didn't know which profile SALLY was assigned?**

    A. `select resource_name, limit from dba_profiles where profile = (select profile from dba_users where username = 'SALLY');`

    B. `select resource_name, limit from dba_profiles where profile = (select profile from dba_users where user_id = 'SALLY');`

    C. `select resource_name, unit_cost from resource_cost where resource_name in (select resource_name from`

```
     dba_profiles where profile = (select profile from
     dba_users where username = 'SALLY'));
```

D. `select resource_name, unit_cost from resource_cost`
`where resource_name in (select resource_name from`
`dba_profiles where profile = (select profile from`
`dba_users where user_id = 'SALLY''));`

2. **You are attempting to determine which profiles have resource settings that do not impose limits on user resource utilization. Which of the following queries would be the most useful for this purpose?**

A. `select profile from dba_profiles where profile =`
`(select username from dba_users where profile =`
`'UNLIMITED');`

B. `select profile from dba_profiles where limit =`
`(select unit_cost from resource_cost where`
`resource_name = 'CPU_PER_SESSION');`

C. `select profile from dba_profiles where limit =`
`'UNLIMITED';`

D. `select distinct profile from dba_profiles where`
`limit = 'UNLIMITED';`

Answer Key

1. A. **2.** D. The question asks for the query most useful for this purpose. The query in choice C is hard to read because the output lists the profile name once for every resource limit set to `unlimited` and is therefore less useful than the query in choice D.

Managing Privileges

In this section, you will cover the following topics related to managing privileges:

- Identifying system and object privileges
- Granting and revoking privileges
- Identifying audit capabilities

All access in an Oracle database requires database privileges. Access to connect to the database, the objects the user is permitted to see, and the objects the user is allowed to create are all controlled by privileges. Use of every database object and system resource is governed by privileges. There are privileges required to create objects, to access objects, to change data within tables, to execute stored procedures, to create users, and so on. Because access to every object is governed by privileges, security in the Oracle database is highly flexible in terms of which objects are available to which users.

Identifying System and Object Privileges

There are two categories of privileges, and the first is *system privileges*. System privileges control the creation and maintenance of many database objects, such as rollback segments, synonyms, tables, and triggers. Additionally, the ability to use the `analyze` command and the Oracle database `audit` capability is governed by system privileges. The other category is object privileges. These privileges govern a user's ability to manipulate database objects owned by other users in the database.

System Privileges Identified

Generally speaking, there are several subcategories of system privileges that relate to each object. Those categories determine the scope of ability that the privilege grantee will have. The classes or categories of system privileges are listed here. In the following subtopics, the privilege itself gives you the ability to perform the action against your own database objects, whereas the `any` keyword refers to the ability to perform the action against any database object of that type in Oracle.

Admin Functions   These privileges relate to activities typically reserved for and performed by the DBA. Privileges include `alter system`, `audit system`, `audit any`, `alter database`, `analyze any`, SYSDBA, SYSOPER, and `grant any privilege`. You must have the `create session` privilege to connect to Oracle. More information about SYSDBA and SYSOPER privileges and the activities they permit you to do will be discussed in the section "The SYSDBA and SYSOPER Privileges" later in this chapter.

Database Access   These privileges control who accesses the database, when they can access it, and what they can do regarding management of their own session. Privileges include `create session`, `alter session`, and `restricted session`.

Tablespaces   You already know that tablespaces are disk resources used to store database objects. These privileges determine who can maintain these disk resources. These privileges are typically reserved for DBAs. Privileges include `create tablespace`, `alter tablespace`, `manage tablespace`, `drop tablespace`, and `unlimited tablespace`. Note that you cannot grant `unlimited tablespace` to a role. More information on roles appears in the next section.

Users   These privileges are used to manage users on the Oracle database. Typically, these privileges are reserved for DBAs or security administrators. Privileges include `create user`, `become user`, `alter user`, and `drop user`.

Undo Segments   You already know that rollback segments are disk resources that make aspects of transaction processing possible. The privileges include `create rollback segment`, `alter rollback segment`, and `drop rollback segment`. Note that you only need these privileges if you plan to administer undo segments manually. If you plan to use automatic undo management, no users need to be granted these privileges.

Tables   You already know that tables store data in the Oracle database. These privileges govern which users can create and maintain tables. The privileges include `create table`, `create any table`, `alter any table`, `backup any table`, `drop any table`, `lock any table`, `comment any table`, `select any table`, `insert any table`, `update any table`, and `delete any table`. The `create table` or `create any table` privilege also enables you to drop the table. The `create table` privilege also bestows the ability to create indexes on the table and run the `analyze` command on the table. To be able to truncate a table, you must have the `drop any table` privilege granted to you.

Clusters   You already know that clusters are used to store tables commonly used together in close physical proximity on disk. The privileges include `create cluster`, `create any cluster`, `alter any cluster`, and `drop any cluster`. The `create cluster` and `create any cluster` privileges also enable you to alter and drop those clusters.

Indexes   You already know that indexes are used to improve SQL statement performance on tables containing lots of row data. The privileges include `create any index`, `alter any index`, and `drop any index`. You should note that there is no `create index` system privilege. The `create table` privilege also enables you to alter and drop indexes that you own and that are associated with the table.

Synonyms   A synonym is a database object that enables you to reference another object by a different name. A public synonym means that the synonym is available to every user in the database for the same purpose. The privileges include `create synonym`, `create any synonym`, `drop any synonym`, `create public synonym`, and `drop public synonym`. The `create synonym` privilege also enables you to alter and drop synonyms that you own.

Views   You already know that a view is an object containing a SQL statement that behaves like a table in Oracle, except that it stores no data. The privileges include `create view`, `create any view`, and `drop any view`. The `create view` privilege also enables you to alter and drop views that you own.

Sequences   You already know that a sequence is an object in Oracle that generates numbers according to rules you can define. Privileges include `create sequence`, `create any sequence`, `alter any sequence`, `drop any sequence`, and `select any sequence`. The `create sequence` privilege also enables you to drop sequences that you own.

Database Links   Database links are objects in Oracle that, within your session connected to one database, enable you to reference tables in another Oracle database without making a separate connection. A public database link is one available to all users in Oracle, whereas a private database link is one that only the owner can use. Privileges include `create database link`, `create public database link`, and `drop public database link`. The `create database link` privilege also enables you to drop private database links that you own.

Roles   Roles are objects that can be used for simplified privilege management. You create a role, grant privileges to it, and then grant the role to users. Privileges include `create role`, `drop any role`, `grant any role`, and `alter any role`.

Transactions   These privileges are for resolving in-doubt, distributed transactions being processed on the Oracle database. Privileges include `force transaction` and `force any transaction`.

PL/SQL   You have already been introduced to the different PL/SQL blocks available in Oracle. These privileges enable you to create, run, and manage those different types of blocks. The privileges include `create procedure`, `create any procedure`, `alter any procedure`, `drop any procedure`, and `execute any procedure`. The `create procedure` privilege also enables you to alter and drop PL/SQL blocks that you own.

Triggers   You know that triggers are PL/SQL blocks in Oracle that execute when a specified DML activity occurs on the table to which the trigger is associated. Privileges include `create trigger`, `create any trigger`, `alter any trigger`, and `drop any trigger`. The `create trigger` privilege also enables you to alter and drop triggers that you own.

Profiles   You know that profiles are objects in Oracle that enable you to impose limits on resources for users in the machine hosting Oracle. Privileges include `create profile`, `alter profile`, `drop profile`, and `alter resource cost`.

Snapshots and Materialized Views   Snapshots are objects in Oracle that enable you to replicate data from a table in one database to a copy of the table in another. Privileges include `create snapshot`, `create any snapshot`, `alter any snapshot`, and `drop any snapshot`.

Directories   Directories in Oracle are objects that refer to directories on the machine hosting the Oracle database. They are used to identify a directory that contains objects Oracle keeps track of that are external to Oracle, such as objects of the BFILE type. Privileges include `create any directory` and `drop any directory`.

Types   Types in Oracle correspond to user-defined types you can create in the Oracle8i Objects Option. Privileges include `create type`, `create any type`, `alter any type`, `drop any type`, and `execute any type`. The `create type` privilege also enables you to alter and drop types that you own.

Libraries   A library is an object that enables you to reference a set of procedures external to Oracle. Currently, only C procedures are supported. Privileges include `create library`, `create any library`, `alter any library`, `drop any library`, and `execute any library`.

The `SYSDBA` and `SYSOPER` Privileges

In the beginning of this book, we introduced the system privileges `SYSDBA` and `SYSOPER` when discussing authentication using a password file. The `SYSDBA` privilege is usually assigned to DBA accounts and `SYSOPER` to database operator accounts. Only users who are assigned these privileges may log into the database using a password file with unrestricted privileges and perform operations on database and database objects. The `SYSOPER` privilege enables the user assigned this privilege to do the following:

- `STARTUP, SHUTDOWN`

- `ALTER DATABASE OPEN | MOUNT`

- `ALTER DATABASE BACKUP CONTROLFILE`

- `RECOVER DATABASE`

- `ALTER DATABASE ARCHIVELOG`

The `SYSDBA` privilege enables the user assigned this privilege to do the following:

- Receive all `SYSOPER` privileges

- `CREATE DATABASE`

■ `ALTER DATABASE [BEGIN|END] BACKUP`

■ `RESTRICTED SESSION`

■ `RECOVER DATABASE`

System Privilege Restrictions

Oracle provides an option to prevent regular database users from accessing the base tables that make up the data dictionary. Users with `UPDATE ANY TABLE` should be able to update the base tables of the data dictionary and by doing so they could jeopardize the integrity of entire database. To prevent such mishaps, Oracle provides an initialization parameter O7_DICTIONARY_ACCESSIBILITY as a dictionary protection mechanism. If the dictionary protection is enabled by setting O7_DICTIONARY_ACCESSIBILITY to FALSE, then access to objects in SYS schema (containing the data dictionary base tables) is restricted to users who connect as SYSDBA and the SYS user itself. Users with system privileges providing access to ANY SCHEMA will not be allowed access to SYS schema objects. This prevents non-DBA users from accessing the base tables that make up the data dictionary views and from modifying them. By default, this parameter is set to FALSE. By setting this parameter to TRUE, the users whose system privilege enables access to objects in any schema are also given access to SYS schema objects.

Identifying Object Privileges

The other category of privileges granted on the Oracle database is the set of *object privileges*. Object privileges permit the owner of database objects, such as tables, to administer access to those objects according to the following types of access. The eight types of object privileges are as follows:

■ **select**   Permits the grantee of this object privilege to access the data in a table, sequence, view, or snapshot.

■ **insert**   Permits the grantee of this object privilege to `insert` data into a table or, in some cases, a view.

■ **update**   Permits the grantee of this object privilege to `update` data into a table or view.

■ **delete**   Permits the grantee of this object privilege to `delete` data from a table or view.

■ **alter**   Permits the grantee of this object privilege to `alter` the definition of a table or sequence *only*. The `alter` privileges on all other database objects are considered system privileges.

- **index**   Permits the grantee of this object privilege to create an index on a table already defined.

- **references**   Permits the grantee to create or alter a table in order to create a foreign key constraint against data in the referenced table.

- **execute**   Permits the grantee to run a stored procedure or function.

TIP

A trick to being able to distinguish whether something is a system or object privilege is as follows. Because there are only eight object privileges, memorize them. If you see a privilege that is not one of the eight object privileges, it is a system privilege.

For Review

I. Be sure you can distinguish system privileges from object privileges in Oracle. The easiest way to do so is to memorize the object privileges, and assume everything else is a system privilege.

2. Know the purpose of the SYSDBA and SYSOPER privileges. These superuser privileges give users the ability to perform administrative tasks on the database.

Exercises

I. **You need to allow users on the Oracle database to create indexes on a table owned by user SCOTT. Which of the following choices identifies the appropriate means for doing so?**

   A. Grant the create table system privilege to users who need to create those indexes.

   B. Grant the create index system privilege to users who need to create those indexes.

   C. Grant the references object privilege on the table to users who need to create those indexes.

   D. Grant the index object privilege on the table to users who need to create those indexes.

2. **You grant the SYSDBA privilege to a user of the Oracle database. Which of the following abilities does this privilege bestow upon its grantee?**

A. Ability to query all tables in Oracle

B. Ability to grant the SYSDBA privilege to others

C. Ability to back up the database

D. Ability to delete information from any table in Oracle

Answer Key
1. D. 2. C.

Granting and Revoking Privileges

Giving system and object privileges to users is done with the grant command. System privileges are first given to the SYS and SYSTEM users, and to any other user with the grant any privilege permission. As other users are created, they must be given privileges, based on their needs, with the grant command. For example, executing the following grant statements provides the ability to create a table to user SPANKY and object privileges on another table in the database:

```
GRANT CREATE TABLE TO spanky;                     -- system
GRANT SELECT, UPDATE ON athena.emp TO spanky;     -- object
```

TIP
To grant object privileges to others, you must own the database object, or you must have been given the object privilege with grant option.

In addition to granting object privileges on database objects, privileges can also be granted on columns within the database object. The privileges that can be administered on the column level are the insert, update, and references privileges. However, the grantor of column privileges must be careful when administering them in order to avoid problems—particularly with the insert privilege. If a user has the insert privilege on several columns in a table but not all columns, the privilege administrator must ensure that no columns in the table that do not have the insert privilege granted are not NULL columns.

Consider the following example. Table EMP has two columns: NAME and EMPID. Both columns have not NULL constraints on them. The insert access is granted for the EMPID column to SPANKY, but not the NAME column. When SPANKY attempts to `insert` an EMPID into the table, Oracle generates a NULL for the NAME column, and then produces an error stating that the user cannot `insert` a not NULL value into the NAME column because the column has a not NULL constraint on it. Administration of `update` and `insert` object privileges at the column level must be handled carefully, whereas using the `references` privilege on a column level seems to be more straightforward.

Some special conditions relate to the use of the `execute` privilege. If a user has the ability to execute a stored procedure owned by another user, and the procedure accesses some tables, the object privileges required to access those tables must be granted *to the owner of the procedure*, and not the user to whom `execute` privileges were granted. What's more, the privileges must be granted directly to the user, not through a role. When a user executes a stored procedure, the user is able to use whatever privileges are required to execute the procedure. For example, `execute` privileges are given to SPANKY on procedure `process_deposit( )` owned by ATHENA, and this procedure performs an update on the BANK_ACCOUNT table using an `update` privilege granted to ATHENA. SPANKY will be able to perform that `update` on BANK_ACCOUNT via the `process_deposit( )` procedure even though the `update` privilege is not granted to SPANKY. However, SPANKY will *not* be able to issue an `update` statement on table BANK_ACCOUNT from SQL*Plus, because the appropriate privilege was not granted to SPANKY directly.

Giving Administrative Ability along with Privileges

At the end of execution for the two statements shown at the beginning of the discussion, SPANKY will have the ability to execute the `create table` command in her user schema and to `select` and `update` row data on the EMP table in ATHENA's schema. However, SPANKY can't give these privileges to others, nor can she relinquish them without the help of the DBA. In order to give user SPANKY some additional power to administer to other users the privileges granted to her, the owner of the object can execute the following queries:

```
GRANT CREATE TABLE TO spanky WITH ADMIN OPTION; -- system privileges
GRANT SELECT, UPDATE ON emp TO SPANKY WITH GRANT OPTION; -- object
privileges
```

The `with admin option` clause gives SPANKY the ability to give or take away the system privilege to others. Additionally, it gives SPANKY the ability to make other users administrators of that same privilege. Finally, if a role is granted to SPANKY `with admin option`, SPANKY can alter the role or even remove it. The `with grant option` clause for object privileges gives SPANKY the same kind of ability as `with admin option` for system privileges. SPANKY can `select` and update data from EMP, and can give that ability to others as well. Only privileges given with grant option or with admin option can be administered by the grantee. Additionally, there is a consolidated method for granting object privileges using the keyword all. Note that all in this context is not a privilege; it is merely a specification for all object privileges for the database object.

```
GRANT ALL ON emp TO spanky;
```

Revoking System Privileges from Users

There may also come a time when users must have privileges revoked as well. This task is accomplished with the revoke command. Revoking the create table privilege also takes away any administrative ability given along with the privilege or role. No additional syntax is necessary for revoking either a system privilege granted with admin option or an object privilege granted with grant option.

```
REVOKE CREATE TABLE FROM spanky;
REVOKE SELECT, UPDATE ON emp FROM spanky;
```

In the same way, roles can be revoked from users, even if the user created the role and thus has the admin option. The ability to revoke any role comes from the grant any role privilege, whereas the ability to grant or revoke certain system privileges comes from being granted the privilege with the admin option. When a system privilege is revoked, there are no cascading events that take place along with it. Thus, if SPANKY created several tables while possessing the create table privilege, those tables are not removed when the privilege is revoked. Only the drop table command will remove the tables.

TIP
Understand the following scenario completely before continuing: User X has a system privilege granted to her, with admin option. *User X then grants the privilege to user Y, with the administrative privileges. User Y does the same for user Z. Then X revokes the privilege from user Y. User Z will still have the privilege. Why? Because there is no cascading effect to revoking system privileges other than the fact that the user no longer has the privilege.*

Revoking Object Privileges from Users

When an object privilege is revoked, there are some cascading events. For example, if you have the update privilege on SPANKY's EMP table and SPANKY revokes it, then you will not be able to change records in the table. However, the rows you've already changed don't get magically transformed back the way they were before. There are several considerations to make when revoking object privileges. For instance, if a privilege has been granted on two individual columns, the privilege cannot be revoked on only one column—the privilege must be revoked entirely and then regranted, if appropriate, on the individual column. Also, if the user has been given the `references` privilege and used it to create a foreign key constraint to another table, then there is some cascading that must take place in order to complete the revocation of the `references` privilege.

```
REVOKE REFERENCES ON emp FROM spanky CASCADE CONSTRAINTS;
```

In this example, not only is the privilege to create referential integrity revoked, but any instances where that referential integrity was used on the database are also revoked. If a foreign key constraint was created on the EMP table by user SPANKY, and the prior statement was issued without the `cascade constraints` clause, then the `revoke` statement will fail.

> **TIP**
> *Understand this fact sequence before proceeding. User X grants user Y an object privilege,* with grant option, *and user Y then grants the same privilege to user Z. When user X revokes the object privilege user Y, user Z will also have that privilege revoked. This is because Oracle cascades the revocation of object privileges.*

Open to the Public

Another aspect of privileges and access to the database involves a special user on the database. This user is called PUBLIC. If a system privilege, object privilege, or role is granted to the PUBLIC user, then every user in the database has that privilege. Typically, it is not advised that the DBA should grant many privileges or roles to PUBLIC, because if the privilege or role ever needs to be revoked, then every stored package, procedure, or function will need to be recompiled.

Dictionary Information on Privileges

To display privileges associated with users and roles, you can use the following views:

- **DBA_SYS_PRIVS** Shows all system privileges associated with this user.
- **DBA_TAB_PRIVS** Shows all object privileges associated with this user.
- **SESSION_PRIVS** Shows all privileges available in this session for this user.

You can find information about system privileges granted to all users in the DBA_SYS_PRIVS view and the privileges available to you as the current user in the session using the SESSION_PRIVS dictionary view. You can also find information about the object privileges granted in the database with the DBA_TAB_PRIVS and DBA_COL_PRIVS dictionary views.

For Review

1. Know how to give system and object privileges to users and how to take them away as well. Also, understand which clauses are required for giving the ability to administrate other users' ability to have a privilege for both system and object privileges.

2. Understand the role of the PUBLIC user in Oracle. When privileges are given to PUBLIC, every user has the privilege.

3. Know where to look in the data dictionary for information about privileges granted to users in Oracle.

Exercises

1. User MARYANN has the `create table` privilege granted to her from IMADBA with the following command: `grant create table to maryann with admin option`. MARYANN then grants the privilege to GILLIGAN. IMADBA finds out and issues the `revoke create table from maryann` command. Which of the following statements is true regarding MARYANN, GILLIGAN, and IMADBA?

   A. IMADBA and GILLIGAN have the privilege, but MARYANN does not.

   B. IMADBA and MARYANN have the privilege, but GILLIGAN does not.

   C. IMADBA has the privilege, but GILLIGAN and MARYANN do not.

   D. IMADBA, GILLIGAN, and MARYANN all have the privilege.

2. User MARYANN has the `select` privilege granted on the EMPLOYEE table to her from IMADBA with the following command: `grant select on EMPLOYEE to maryann with grant option`. MARYANN then grants the privilege to GILLIGAN. IMADBA finds out and issues the `revoke select on EMPLOYEE from maryann` command. Which of the following statements is true regarding MARYANN, GILLIGAN, and IMADBA?

   A. IMADBA and GILLIGAN have the privilege, but MARYANN does not.

   B. IMADBA and MARYANN have the privilege, but GILLIGAN does not.

    C. IMADBA has the privilege, but GILLIGAN and MARYANN do not.

    D. IMADBA, GILLIGAN, and MARYANN all have the privilege.

3. **You would like to know which system privileges have been granted to user GINGER. Which of the following queries would be useful for this purpose?**

    A. `select privilege from dba_tab_privs where grantee = 'GINGER';`

    B. `select privilege from dba_sys_privs where grantee = 'GINGER';`

    C. `select privilege from session_privs where grantee = 'GINGER';`

    D. `select grantor from dba_sys_privs where grantee = 'GINGER';`

Answer Key
1. A. 2. C. 3. B.

Identifying Audit Capabilities

Securing the database against inappropriate activity is only one part of the total security package Oracle offers the DBA or security administrator of an Oracle database. The other major component of the Oracle security architecture is the ability to monitor database activity to uncover suspicious or inappropriate use. Oracle provides this functionality via the use of database auditing. This section will cover differentiating between database and value-based auditing, using database auditing, using the data dictionary to monitor auditing options, and viewing and managing audit results.

TIP
Auditing your database requires a good deal of additional space allocated to the SYSTEM tablespace for storing the audit data generated.

Several things about your database are always audited. They include privileged operations that DBAs typically perform, such as starting and stopping the instance and logins, as `sysdba` or as `sysoper`. You can find information about these activities in the ALERT log on your database, along with information about log switches, checkpoints, and tablespaces taken offline or put online.

You can also configure systemwide auditing with the AUDIT_TRAIL init*sid*.ora parameter. Valid values for this parameter include DB (TRUE), operating system (FALSE), or NONE. DB indicates that the database architecture will be used to store audit records. You can alternately specify TRUE for AUDIT_TRAIL to accomplish the same result DB gives. Operating system indicates that the audit trail will be stored externally to Oracle, using some component of the operating system. You can alternately specify FALSE for AUDIT_TRAIL to accomplish the same result operating system gives. Finally, NONE indicates that no database auditing will be conducted at all. After changing the value set for this parameter, the instance must be shut down and started again.

Database and Value-Based Auditing

There is a difference between *database auditing* and *value-based auditing*. Database auditing pertains to audits on database object access, user session activity, startup, shutdown, and other database activity. The information about these database events is stored in the audit trail, and the information can then be used to monitor potentially damaging activities, such as rows being removed from tables. The data can also be used by the DBA for statistical analysis of database performance over time. Value-based auditing pertains to audits on actual column/row values that are changed as the result of database activity. The Oracle audit trail does not track value-based audit information, so instead you must develop triggers, tables, PL/SQL code, or client applications that handle this level of auditing in the database.

A good example of value-based auditing in a package delivery application would be to track status changes on existing deliveries from the time the order is received to the time it is delivered. Customers can then call in or access the system via the Web to find out the package delivery status. Each time the package reaches a certain milestone, such as "picked up at local office" or "signed over to recipient," the delivery status is updated and a historical record is made of the old status, the time of status change, and the username of the person making the change. However, as you might imagine, value-based auditing is specific to an application. Thus, the DBA will focus much of his or her time managing database auditing with Oracle's audit features.

TIP

When AUDIT_TRAIL is set to operating system, your audit trail information will be stored in the directory named by your AUDIT_FILE_DEST init*sid*.ora *file, which is set to the* rdbms/audit *directory under your Oracle software home directory by default. When AUDIT_TRAIL is set to DB, your audit trail information is stored in the AUD$ table owned by SYS.*

Using Database Auditing

A database audit is most effective when the DBA or security administrator knows what he or she is looking for. The best way to conduct a database audit is to start the audit with a general idea about what may be occurring on the database. Once the goals are established, set the audit to monitor those aspects of database use and review the results to either confirm or disprove the hypothesis.

Why must an audit be conducted this way? Database auditing generates lots of information about database access. If the DBA tries to audit everything, the important facts would get mixed into a great deal of unnecessary detail. With a good idea about the general activity that seems suspicious as well as knowledge of the types of statements or related objects on the database that should be looked at, the DBA can save a lot of time sorting through excess detail later.

Using the Audit Command for Privilege or Statement Audits

You do not need to set the AUDIT_TRAIL `init.ora` parameter in order to use the `audit` SQL command to set up the auditing options you want to use. You can set auditing features to monitor database activities including starting, stopping, and connecting to the database. Or you can set up audits on statements involving the creation or removal of database objects. Additionally, you can set up audits on direct database use, such as table updates or inserts.

The general syntax for setting up auditing on statements or system privileges is as follows. State the name of the statement (such as `update`) or system privilege (such as `create table`) that will be audited. Then state which users will be monitored, either by *username*, by `session`, or by `access`. Finally, state whether or not the audit should record successful or unsuccessful executions of the activity in question. The following code block shows an example of an `audit` statement:

```
AUDIT CREATE TABLE, ALTER TABLE, DROP TABLE
BY spanky
WHENEVER SUCCESSFUL;
```

The following statement demonstrates how you can record the data-change operations that happen on particular tables:

```
AUDIT UPDATE, DELETE
ON spanky.cat_toys
BY ACCESS
WHENEVER NOT SUCCESSFUL;
```

Consider some other unique features in the `audit` syntax. The person setting up audits need not name particular users on which to monitor activity. Rather, the activities of this sort can be monitored every time the statement is issued with the by access clause. Additionally, when the `not successful` option is specified, audit records are generated only when the command executed is unsuccessful. The omission of clauses from the audit syntax causes `audit` to default to the widest scope permitted by the omission. For example, an audit can be conducted on all inserts on table PRODUCTS, regardless of user and completion status, by omitting the `by` and `whenever` clauses:

```
AUDIT INSERT ON products;
```

You can use the `default` option of the `audit` command to specify auditing options for objects that have not yet been created. Once you have established these default auditing options, any subsequently created object is automatically audited with those options. The following code block demonstrates use of the `default` keyword:

```
AUDIT INSERT
ON DEFAULT
WHENEVER SUCCESSFUL;
```

Using the `audit` Command for Object Audits

Any privilege that can be granted can also be audited. However, because there are more than 100 system and object privileges that can be granted on the Oracle database, the creation of an `audit` statement can be an excessively long task. As an alternative to naming each and every privilege that goes along with a database object, Oracle enables the administrator to specify the name of an object to audit, and Oracle will audit all privileged operations. Instead of listing all privileged operations related to the type of object that would be audited, the security administrator could name the type of object and achieve the desired result.

```
AUDIT TABLE
BY spanky
WHENEVER SUCCESSFUL;
```

Finally, the person setting up auditing can also specify that audit records are to be compiled by session. This means that `audit` will record data for audited activities in every session, as opposed to `by access`. Eliminating the `when successful` clause tells `audit` to record every table creation, alteration, or drop activity for every session that connects to the database, regardless of whether or not they were successful.

```
AUDIT TABLE
BY SESSION;
```

Using Audit Definition Shortcuts

There are other options available to consolidate the specification of database activities into one easy command for auditing. These commands are listed in the following:

- **connect**   Audits the user connections to the database. It can be substituted with session for the same effect. connect audits the login and logout activities of every database user.

- **resource**   Audits detailed information related to the activities typically performed by an application developer or a development DBA, such as creating tables, views, clusters, links, stored procedures, and rollback segments.

- **dba**   Audits activities related to "true" database administration, including the creation of users and roles, and granting system privileges and system audits.

- **all**   Is the equivalent of an on/off switch, where all database activities are monitored and recorded.

TIP

A PL/SQL procedure or SQL statement may reference several different objects or statements being audited. Thus, many audit trail entries can be produced by one single statement.

Disabling Audit Configuration

There are two methods used to disable auditing. The first method is to change the initialization parameter AUDIT_TRAIL to NONE or FALSE. On database shutdown and restart, this option will disable the audit functionality on the Oracle database. Note, however, that because you don't need to set AUDIT_TRAIL in order to use the SQL audit command, the other option used for changing the activities that audit will record is called noaudit. This option can be executed in two ways. The first is used to turn off selective areas that are currently being audited.

```
NOAUDIT INSERT ON application.products;
```

In some cases, however, the person conducting the audit may want to shut off all auditing processes going on and simply start auditing over again. Perhaps the auditor has lost track of which audits were occurring on the database. This statement can be further modified to limit turning off auditing to a particular database object.

```
NOAUDIT ALL;
NOAUDIT ALL PRIVILEGES;
NOAUDIT ALL ON application.products;
```

Finally, Remember to Protect the Audit Information!

Above all else in handling database audits for inappropriate activity is the importance of protecting the evidence. The DBA must ensure that no user can remove records from the audit logs undetected. Therefore, a key step in auditing is to audit the audit trail. This step might include write-protecting the $ORACLE_HOME/rdbms/audit directory using operating system commands (such as chmod in UNIX), and it might also include monitoring the removal of data from the SYS.AUD$ table, as demonstrated in the following code block:

```
AUDIT delete ON sys.aud$;
```

Viewing Enabled Auditing Options

The following views offer information about the enabled audit options configured in the Oracle database:

- **DBA_OBJ_AUDIT_OPTS**   A list of auditing options for views, tables, and other database objects

- **DBA_PRIV_AUDIT_OPTS**   A list of auditing options for all privileges on the database

- **DBA_STMT_AUDIT_OPTS**   A list of auditing options for all statements executed on the database

- **ALL_DEF_AUDIT_OPTS**   A list of all default options for auditing database objects

Retrieving and Maintaining Auditing Information

The following data dictionary views are used to find results from audits currently taking place in the Oracle database. These views are created by the cataudit.sql script found in rdbms/admin off the Oracle software home directory. This script is run automatically at database creation by the catalog.sql script. Some additional audit information is stored in the ALERT log, as explained earlier, and more audit information will be stored in an operating system file if operating system auditing is used:

- **DBA_AUDIT_EXISTS**   A list of audit entries generated by the exists option of the audit command

- **DBA_AUDIT_OBJECT**   A list of audit entries generated for object audits

- **DBA_AUDIT_SESSION**   A list of audit entries generated by session connects and disconnects

- **DBA_AUDIT_STATEMENT**   A list of audit entries generated by statement options of the `audit` command

- **DBA_AUDIT_TRAIL**   A list of all entries in the AUD$ table collected by the `audit` command

Managing Audit Information

Once created, all audit information will stay in the AUD$ table owned by SYS. In cases where several auditing options are used to gather information about database activity, the AUD$ table can grow to be large. In order to preserve the integrity of other tables and views in the data dictionary, and to preserve overall space in the SYSTEM tablespace (where all data dictionary objects are stored), the DBA or security administrator must periodically remove data from the AUD$ table, either by deleting or by archiving and then removing the records. Additionally, in the event that audit records on an Oracle database are being kept to determine whether there is suspicious activity, the security administrator must take additional steps to ensure that the data in the AUD$ table is protected from tampering.

TIP
You may want to move the AUD$ table outside the SYSTEM tablespace because of the volatile and high-growth nature of audit data. To do so, create another table with AUD$ data, using the `alter table move tablespace` *statement. Next, drop AUD$ and rename your other table to AUD$. Next, create one index on the new AUD$ table on the SESSIONID and SES$TID columns in the new tablespace (storing the index outside of the SYSTEM tablespace, of course). Finally, grant* `delete` *on the new AUD$ table to DELETE_CATALOG_ROLE.*

In order to prevent a problem with storing too much audit data, the general guideline in conducting database audits is to record enough information to accomplish the auditing goal without storing a lot of unnecessary information. The amount of information that will be gathered by the auditing process is related to the number of options being audited and the frequency of audit collection (namely, `by username,` `by access,` and `by session`). What if problems occur because too much information is collected? To remove records from AUD$, a user with the `delete any table` privilege, the SYS user, or a user to whom SYS has granted `delete` access to AUD$ must log onto the system and remove records from AUD$. Before doing so, however, it is generally advisable for archiving purposes to make a copy of the records being deleted. This task can be accomplished by copying all records from AUD$ to another table defined with the same columns as AUD$, spooling a `select` statement of all data in AUD$ to a flat file, or using EXPORT to place all AUD$ records into a database dump file. After this step is complete, all or part of the data in the AUD$ table can be removed using either `delete from AUD$` or `truncate table AUD$`. But remember to protect the audit trail using methods already outlined.

For Review

1. Understand the purpose served by auditing in the database and the difference between database auditing and value-based auditing.

2. Know that the auditing feature in Oracle is enabled using the `audit` command.

3. Know that all audit records are stored in the SYS.AUD$ dictionary base table in Oracle, and that there are many dictionary views that give you information from this table.

4. Auditing generates a lot of information being stored in the SYSTEM tablespace. If you plan to use this feature, it's best that you know what you're looking for first, rather than set up auditing haphazardly and have a lot of extraneous audit information fill your SYSTEM tablespace.

Exercises

1. **Auditing on the database is configured using this command:**
    _____.

2. **When auditing is enabled, records are placed in the _____(A)_____ table owned by user _____(B)_____. This table can be found in the _____(C)_____ tablespace.**

3. **To set up auditing in Oracle, the _____(A)_____ initialization parameter must be set to _____(B)_____.**

Answer Key
1. `audit`. 2. (A) AUD$; (B) SYS; (C) SYSTEM. 3. (A) AUDIT_TRAIL; (B) TRUE.

Managing Roles

In this section, you will cover the following points on managing roles:

- Creating and modifying roles
- Controlling the availability of roles
- Removing roles
- Using predefined roles
- Displaying role information from the data dictionary

Roles take some of the complexity out of administrating user privileges. A role in the database can be thought of as a virtual user. The database object and system privileges that are required to perform a group of user functions are gathered together and granted to the role, which then can be granted directly to the users. In this section, you will learn how to create and change roles, control their availability, remove roles, use roles that are predefined in Oracle, and display information about roles from the data dictionary.

Creating and Modifying Roles

As users add more objects to the database, privilege management can become a nightmare. This is where roles come in. Roles are named logical groupings of privileges that can be administered more easily than the individual privileges. Roles are created on databases in the following manner. The DBA determines which types of users exist on the database and which privileges on the database can be logically grouped together.

Creating Roles

In order to create a role that will support user privilege management, one of the following statements can be executed. Once the role is created, there are no privileges assigned to it until you explicitly grant privileges to the role. The following statement can be used to create a role in Oracle:

```
CREATE ROLE cat_priv;
```

This statement creates a role named `cat_priv`. The following code block shows a variant of the `create role` command, where we explicitly state that this role does not require a password in order to be enabled for the user. This is the default behavior for roles in Oracle.

```
CREATE ROLE cat_priv NOT IDENTIFIED;
```

The following statement shows a role created in your database called `cat_priv`. This time, we set up the role to require the user to supply a password whenever the role is to be enabled for use. This role must be enabled by the user before the privileges associated with the role can be utilized. Let's take a look at the statement now:

```
CREATE ROLE cat_priv IDENTIFIED BY meow;
```

Granting Roles

Once created, roles must have privileges granted to them. Privileges are granted to roles in the following manner. At the same time that the DBA determines the resource use of various classes of users on the database, the DBA may also want to determine which object and system privileges each class of user will require. Instead of granting the privileges directly to users on an individual basis, however, the DBA can grant the privileges to the roles, which then can be granted to several users more easily.

```
GRANT SELECT, INSERT, UPDATE ON cat_food TO cat_privs;
GRANT SELECT, INSERT, UPDATE ON litter_box TO cat_privs;
GRANT SELECT ON fav_sleeping_spots TO cat_privs;
```

Roles enable dynamic privilege management as well. If several users already have a role granted to them, and you create a new table and grant `select` privileges on it to the role, then all the users who have the role will be able to `select` data from your table. Once granted, the ability to use the privileges granted via the role is immediate. Roles can be granted to other roles as well. However, you should take care not to grant a role to itself (even via another role) or else Oracle will return an error.

Granting Roles to Users

Once you've created a role and granted some privileges to it, you must then grant the role to a user. This allows the user to have access to the privileges the role is meant to manage. You give the role to a user with the `grant` command and take it away with the `revoke` command. The following code block shows how to `grant` a role to a user:

```
GRANT cat_privs TO spanky;
```

Passwords and Roles

Using a password to authenticate users of a role is optional. If used, however, the password provides an extra level of security over the authentication process at database login. For heightened security when using roles with passwords, set the role authenticated by a password to be a nondefault role for that user. That way, if the user tries to execute a privilege granted via the role, he or she will first have to supply the role's password. Like users, roles have no owner, nor are they part of a schema. The name of a role must be unique among all roles and users of a database.

Altering Roles

Later on, you may want to change a role using the `alter role` command. All items that are definable in `create role` are also definable using `alter role`, as shown in the following code block:

```
ALTER ROLE role_name NOT IDENTIFIED;
ALTER ROLE role_name IDENTIFIED BY role_password;
```

Administrative Ability and Roles

By default, only the user who creates the role has administrative privileges over that role, including the ability to grant that role to other users. Other users can, of course, grant privileges to the role—so long as they are permitted to grant those privileges. However, like privileges, roles can be granted with an administrative ability to users. This is accomplished using the `grant rolename to username with admin option`, the same option as that used for granting administrative abilities with system privileges.

For Review

1. Understand what a role is conceptually. To use roles, you must first create a role and then grant privileges to it. Then you can consolidate the granting of those privileges to the users by simply granting the role to that user.

2. Roles can be created to enforce password authentication. When password authentication is used, the user must supply the password in order to use privileges associated with the password-authenticated role. Passwords on roles are optional in Oracle.

3. By default, the owner of the role has the ability to grant that role to others. However, roles can be granted to users along with the administrative ability over that role using the `grant rolename to username with admin option` command.

Exercises

1. You create a role in Oracle called DEVELOPER and then grant it to user SKIP. SKIP then logs into the Oracle database. You then grant the `create table` privilege to your DEVELOPER role. Which of the following statements best describes SKIP's ability to create tables in Oracle?

   A. SKIP can create tables the next time he logs into Oracle.

   B. SKIP can create tables immediately after you grant that privilege to the role.

   C. SKIP must own the role in order to create tables with it.

   D. SKIP cannot create tables in Oracle without having the role given to him as a default role.

2. You want to use roles in Oracle to manage privileges. Which of the following choices correctly describes the sequence of events required in order for users to employ roles successfully in using privileges?

   A. Create the role, grant privileges to the role, grant the role to users, and users enable the role.

   B. Create the role, users enable the role, grant privileges to the role, and grant the role to users.

   C. Grant privileges to the role, create the role, grant the role to users, and users enable the role.

   D. Users enable the role, create the role, grant the role to users, and grant privileges to the role.

Answer Key
1. B. 2. A.

Controlling Availability of Roles

A user may have several roles granted when he or she logs on. By default, all the roles assigned to a user are enabled at logon without the need of a password. Some, all, or none of these roles can be set as a default role, which means that the privileges given via the role will be available automatically when the user logs on to Oracle. There is no limit to the number of roles that can be granted to a user;

however, if there are privileges granted to a user through a nondefault role, the user may have to switch default roles in order to use those privileges.

All roles granted to a user are default roles initially. You can change which roles are default roles after granting the role to the user with the `alter user` statement. The `alter user default role all` statement sets all roles granted to SPANKY to be the default role. Other options available for specifying user roles include physically listing one or more roles that are to be the default, or specifying all roles except for the ones named using `all except (role_name [,...])` or `none`.

```
ALTER USER spanky DEFAULT ROLE ALL;
```

The previous statement sets all roles granted to user SPANKY as default roles. The following statement sets the ORG_USER and ORG_DEVELOPER roles as default roles for user SPANKY:

```
ALTER USER spanky DEFAULT ROLE org_user, org_developer;
```

In the previous statement, the roles ORG_USER and ORG_DEVELOPER are assigned as the default roles, and the rest of the granted roles are not default roles for the user SPANKY. The following statement makes the ORG_MGR role the only nondefault role SPANKY has:

```
ALTER USER spanky DEFAULT ROLE ALL EXCEPT (org_mgr);
```

The following statement makes it so that SPANKY has no default role set up at login. The only privileges that the user SPANKY has at login will be those privileges assigned directly to the user.

```
ALTER USER spanky DEFAULT ROLE NONE;
```

TIP
Note that `default role` *is only an option used for the* `alter user` *statement. You do not define a default role in* `create user` *because no roles have been granted to the user yet. Keep in mind the default roles are subsets of roles granted to the user that are enabled automatically when the user logs into Oracle.*

Enabling or Disabling Roles
When a user logs in, the user's default roles are automatically activated. However, it is possible to enable and disable roles that are not default roles using the `set role`

command. Those roles enabled or disabled using the set role command will apply as long as the user session is active. Once the user exits from the session and logs back into Oracle, only the default roles will again be active. The following code block shows an example of the set role command:

```
SET ROLE cat_privs;
```

Note that, if the cat_privs role requires a password, you must supply the password when you enable the role using the set role command. The following code block shows this syntax:

```
SET ROLE cat_privs IDENTIFIED BY meow;
```

> **TIP**
> *You can also enable many roles at once (so long as none of the roles requires a password) using the* set role all *command. You can also exclude certain roles from being enabled using the* set role all except role_name *command. Additionally, you can disable all roles granted to you using the* set role none *command.*

The DBMS_SESSION package contains a procedure called set_role( ), which is equivalent to the set role statement. It can enable or disable roles for a user and can be issued from Oracle forms, reports, anonymous blocks, or any other tool that enables PL/SQL, except for stored PL/SQL functions, procedures, and packages. Finally, note that enabling or disabling a role using the set role command does not change whether or not the role is a default role for this user. Only the alter user default role command issued by the DBA can change whether the role is a default role for the user.

For Review

1. Roles granted to users are considered default roles unless you specify otherwise. You make or do not make a role a default role using the alter user *username* default role *rolename* command.

2. When a user logs into Oracle, he or she will be able to use all privileges assigned to him or her directly and via default roles.

3. Assigning a role as a nondefault role to a user adds a level of security, especially when the nondefault role has a password. In this case, users must employ the set role *rolename* identified by *password* command in order to enable use of the role.

4. Setting a role in the way shown previously does not make the role a default role—it merely enables the role for the current session. The user will have to use the `set role` command in order to enable those role-given privileges again.

Exercises

1. **The following output shows a listing of roles granted to user KENNY:**

```
GRANTEE   GRANTED_ROLE     ADM DEF
--------  ---------------  --- ---
KENNY     APP_DEVELOPER    NO  NO
KENNY     POWER_USER       NO  YES
```

   The `create table` privilege is granted to KENNY via the APP_DEVELOPER role. Which of the following statements best describes what happens when KENNY attempts to issue the `create table mytab (col1 number primary key) tablespace data1` command?

   A. Oracle will return an error indicating KENNY's quota on tablespace DATA1 was exceeded.

   B. Oracle will return an error indicating that KENNY lacks sufficient privileges to perform this task.

   C. Oracle will return an error indicating that he needs to enable the POWER_USER role.

   D. Oracle performs the task successfully.

2. **Review the following transcript from a SQL*Plus session:**

```
SQL> connect scott/tiger
Connected.
SQL> create user smithers identified by mort1;
User created.
SQL> create role user_role identified by useme;
Role created.
SQL> grant all on scott.emp to user_role;
Grant succeeded.
SQL> grant user_role to smithers;
Grant succeeded.
SQL> grant create session to smithers;
Grant succeeded.
SQL> alter user smithers default role none;
User altered.
SQL> connect smithers/mort1
Connected.
SQL> select * from scott.emp;
```

Which of the following choices describes the command that SMITHERS will need to issue in order to see the contents of the EMP table as requested in the session transcript?

A. None—the `select` statement will execute successfully.

B. `connect smithers/useme`

C. `set role user_role identified by useme;`

D. `alter user smithers default role user_role;`

Answer Key
1. B. 2. C.

Removing Roles

Another way to restrict role use is to revoke the role from the user. This is accomplished with the `revoke` command in the same way that a privilege is revoked. The effect is immediate—the user will no longer be able to use privileges associated with the role. You can drop a role to restrict its use as well. You don't need to revoke the role from users before dropping it—Oracle handles that task for you. However, you must have the `drop any role` privilege or have been granted the role `with admin option` in order to drop it.

```
REVOKE cat_privs FROM spanky;
DROP ROLE cat_privs;
```

TIP
In order to drop a role, you must have been granted the role `with admin option` *or have a* DROP ANY ROLE *system privilege.*

For Review

1. Know that the `revoke` command is used for taking roles away from other users, and that the `drop role` command is used for removing roles from the database.

2. Roles needn't be revoked from all grantees before they are dropped, so long as you have permission to drop the role.

Exercises

1. You remove a role from the database using the _____(A)_____ command (two words). You (need to/need not) revoke the role from grantees before dropping the role from the database.

2. A role can be removed from the database either by the user who _____(A)_____ the role or by a user with the _____(B)_____ privilege (three words).

Answer Key
1. (A) `drop role`; need not. 2. (A) created (owns also acceptable); (B) `drop any role`.

Using Predefined Roles

There are some special roles available to the users of a database. The roles available at database creation from Oracle7 onward include the CONNECT, RESOURCE, DBA, EXP_FULL_DATABASE, and IMP_FULL_DATABASE roles. Additionally, Oracle8*i* adds the DELETE_CATALOG_ROLE, EXECUTE_CATALOG_ROLE, and SELECT_CATALOG_ROLE roles to the mix and much more. The use of each role is described in the following list:

- **CONNECT** Enables the user extensive development abilities within his or her own user schema, including the ability to use `create table`, `create cluster`, `create session`, `create view`, `create sequence`, and more. The privileges associated with this role are platform-specific, and therefore the role can contain a different number of privileges, but typically the role never enables the creation of stored procedures.

- **RESOURCE** Enables the user moderate development abilities within his or her own user schema, such as the ability to execute `create table`, `create cluster`, `create trigger`, and `create procedure`. The privileges associated with this role are platform-specific, and therefore the role can contain a different number of privileges.

- **DBA** Enables the user to administer and use all system privileges.

- **EXP_FULL_DATABASE** Enables the user to export every object in the database using the EXPORT utility.

- **IMP_FULL_DATABASE** Enables the user to import every object from an export dump file using the IMPORT utility.

- ■ **DELETE_CATALOG_ROLE** Extends `delete` privileges on SYS-owned dictionary tables in response to the new restriction on `delete any table` privileges that prevent grantees from removing rows from SYS-owned dictionary tables.

- ■ **EXECUTE_CATALOG_ROLE** Enables the user to receive `execute` privileges on any SYS-owned package supplied with the Oracle software.

- ■ **SELECT_CATALOG_ROLE** Enables the user to `select` data from any SYS-owned dictionary table or view.

Using Other Predefined Roles

Other optional, predefined roles are available in Oracle and are usually defined by the DBA using SQL scripts provided with the database. For example, AQ_ADMINISTRATOR_ROLE and AQ_USER_ROLE are created by the `dbmsaqad.sql` script. These roles are used with the advanced queuing feature in the Oracle database. Other roles you might find on your database include PLUSTRACE, which is created by running the `plustrce.sql` script for setup of the autotrace feature in SQL*Plus.

For Review

1. Understand the predefined roles in Oracle. CONNECT, RESOURCE, and DBA are very popular for giving users the ability to get started quickly. However, you should be careful when using these roles because they may give far more privileges to users than you care to offer them.

2. Know the purpose behind the catalog roles. These roles give users the ability to see data in the data dictionary. You don't always need to grant these roles to end users in order for the user to see certain dictionary views, but in the event a user cannot see an object in the data dictionary, the catalog roles will give the user that ability.

Exercises

1. The _____ role is useful for database administrators because it grants all the administrative privileges one needs to act as the database administrator.

2. The _____ role enables users to export the contents of an Oracle database.

3. The _____ role enables users to query the data dictionary.

Answer Key

1. DBA. 2. EXP_FULL_DATABASE. 3. SELECT_CATALOG_ROLE.

Displaying Role Information from the Data Dictionary

You can find information about the roles created in your Oracle database in the data dictionary. The following bullets list the various views available for finding information about your created roles:

- **DBA_ROLES**   Names all the roles created on the database and whether a password is required to use each role.

- **DBA_ROLE_PRIVS**   Names all users and the roles granted to them in the database.

- **ROLE_ROLE_PRIVS**   Identifies all the roles and the roles that are granted to them in the database.

- **DBA_SYS_PRIVS**   Identifies all the role and user grantees and the granted system privileges to those roles and users.

- **ROLE_SYS_PRIVS**   Identifies all the system privileges granted only to roles in Oracle.

- **ROLE_TAB_PRIVS**   Identifies all the object privileges granted only to roles in Oracle.

- **SESSION_ROLES**   Identifies all the roles available in the current session of Oracle.

Fine-Grained Access Control

Fine-grained access control enables you to implement security policies with functions and then associate those security policies with tables or views. The database server automatically enforces those security policies. You can use different policies for select, insert, update, and delete. You can also use security policies only where you need them (for example, on salary information). Finally, you can use more than one policy for each table, including building on top of base policies in packaged applications.

The function or package that implements the security policy you create returns a predicate (a where condition). This predicate controls access as set out by the policy. Rewritten queries are fully optimized and sharable. The PL/SQL package

DBMS_RLS enables you to administer your security policies. Using this package, you can add, drop, enable, disable, and refresh the policies you create.

For Review

1. The DBA_ROLES view shows you all the roles in your Oracle database. ROLE_TAB_PRIVS and ROLE_SYS_PRIVS show all object and system privileges granted to roles in Oracle.

2. DBA_ROLE_PRIVS shows roles granted to users in Oracle, whereas ROLE_ROLE_PRIVS shows you the roles granted to other roles in Oracle.

3. The SESSION_ROLES view shows all current roles active in a user's session.

Exercises

1. To determine which roles are active in your session, you can look in the _____ dictionary view.

2. To determine which system privileges have been granted to a role, use the _____(A)_____ view. To determine which object privileges have been granted to a role, use the _____(B)_____ view.

3. To determine the roles available in the database, use the _____ view.

Answer Key
1. SESSION_ROLES. 2. (A) DBA_SYS_PRIVS; (B) DBA_TAB_PRIVS. 3. DBA_ROLES.

Chapter Summary

This chapter covered the fundamentals you need to understand about users, profiles, privileges, and roles for the OCP Oracle9*i* DBA Fundamentals I exam. We discussed the creation of users and the management of created users in Oracle. You learned how to create users, maintain them, and where to look for more information. You also learned about profiles, Oracle's tool for the management of underlying host system resources accessed via Oracle by end users. We discussed how to create profiles and assign users to them. The special topic of composite resources was defined and discussed as well.

We also covered system and object privileges in Oracle. You learned that every action available on the Oracle database is governed by a privilege. You learned what system privileges were and how they differ from object privileges. You also learned how to grant and revoke privileges, with or without administrative ability. We discussed the audit capabilities available in Oracle for detecting misuse of the database as well.

Finally, we covered the particular importance that roles play in Oracle. You learned that roles act as a clearinghouse for granting privileges more efficiently, especially when there are many database objects and many users of an Oracle system. You learned how to create roles, grant privileges to roles, and how to grant roles to users. You learned the difference between a default role and a nondefault role, and how to use the `alter user default role` command to set up a user's default roles. You learned that the privileges given to users via nondefault roles are not available until users issue the `set role` command, which adds an extra layer of protection and security, especially when password-authenticated roles are used. We covered how to drop roles, use predefined roles, and where to find information about roles in the data dictionary as well. All in all, this chapter covered 16 percent of the materials tested on the OCP Oracle9*i* DBA Fundamentals I exam.

Two-Minute Drill

- New database users are created with the `create user` statement.
- A new user can have the following items configured by the `create user` statement:
  - Password
  - Default tablespace for database objects
  - Temporary tablespace
  - Quotas on tablespaces
  - User profile
  - Account lock status
  - Whether the user must specify a new password on first logging on
- User definitions can be altered with the `alter user` statement and dropped with the `drop user` statement. Users can issue the `alter user` statement only to change their password and default roles.
- Information about a database user can be found in the following data dictionary views:
  - DBA_USERS
  - DBA_PROFILES

- DBA_TS_QUOTAS

- DBA_OBJECTS

- DBA_ROLE_PRIVS

- DBA_TAB_PRIVS

- DBA_SYS_PRIVS

- Users in operating system-authenticated database environments generally have their usernames preceded by OPS$ at user-creation time.

- User profiles help to limit resource usage on the Oracle database.

- The DBA must set the RESOURCE_LIMIT parameter to TRUE in order to use user profiles.

- The resources that can be limited via profiles include the following:

  - Sessions connected per user at one time

  - CPU time per call

  - CPU time per session

  - Disk I/O per call

  - Disk I/O per session

  - Connection time

  - Idle time

  - Private memory (only for MTS)

  - Composite limit

- Profiles should be created for every type or class of user. Each parameter has a resource limit set for it in a user profile, which can then be assigned to users based on their processing needs.

- Oracle installs a special profile granted to a user if no other profile is defined. This special profile is called DEFAULT, and all values in the profile are set to `unlimited`.

- Any parameter not explicitly set in another user profile defaults in value to the value specified for that parameter in DEFAULT.

- New Oracle8*i* features in password administration are also available:

  - **`failed_login_attempts`** The number of unsuccessful attempts at login a user can make before the account locks. The default is three.

- **`password_life_time`** The number of days a password will remain active. The default is 60.

- **`password_reuse_time`** The number of days before the password can be reused. The default is 1,800 (approximately five years).

- **`password_reuse_max`** The number of times the password must be changed before one can be reused. The default is `unlimited`.

- **`password_lock_time`** The number of days after which Oracle will unlock a user account locked automatically when the user exceeds `failed_login_attempts`. The default is 1/1,440 (one minute).

- **`password_grace_time`** The number of days during which an expired password must be changed by the user or else Oracle permanently locks the account. The default is 10.

- **`password_verify_function`** The function used for password complexity verification. The default function is called `verify_function( )`.

- Database privileges govern access for performing every permitted activity in the Oracle database.

- There are two categories of database privileges: system privileges and object privileges.

- System privileges enable the creation of every object on the database, along with the ability to execute many commands and connect to the database.

- Object privileges enable access to data within database objects.

- There are three basic classes of system privileges for some database objects: `create`, `alter`, and `drop`. These privileges give the grantee the power to create database objects in their own user schema.

- Some exceptions exist to the preceding rule. The `alter table` privilege is an object privilege, while the `alter rollback segment` privilege is a system privilege. The `create index` privilege is an object privilege as well.

- Three oddball privileges are `grant`, `audit`, and `analyze`. These privileges apply to the creation of all database objects and to running powerful commands in Oracle.

- The `any` modifier gives the user extra power to create objects or run commands on any object in the user schema.

- The final system privilege of interest is the `restricted session` privilege, which enables the user to connect to a database in `restricted session` mode.

- Object privileges give the user access to place, remove, change, or view data in a table or one column in a table, as well as to alter the definition of a table, create an index on a table, and develop foreign key constraints.

- When system privileges are revoked, the objects a user has created will still exist.

- A system privilege can be granted using `with admin option` to enable the grantee to administer others' ability to use the privilege.

- When object privileges are revoked, the data placed or modified in a table will still exist, but you will not be able to perform the action allowed by the privilege anymore.

- An object privilege can be granted using `with grant option` to another user in order to make him or her an administrator of the privilege.

- The `grant option` cannot be used when granting a privilege to a role.

- Roles are used to bundle privileges together and to enable or disable them automatically.

- A user can create objects and then grant the nongrantable object privileges to the role, which then can be granted to as many users require it.

- There are roles created by Oracle when the software is installed:

  - **CONNECT**   Can connect to the database and create clusters, links, sequences, tables, views, and synonyms. This role is good for table schema owners and development DBAs.

  - **RESOURCE**   Can connect to the database and create clusters, sequences, tables, triggers, and stored procedures. This role is good for application developers. It also has unlimited tablespace.

  - **DBA**   Can use any system privilege using `with admin option`.

  - **EXP_FULL_DATABASE**   Can export all database objects to an export dump file.

  - **IMP_FULL_DATABASE**   Can import all database objects from an export dump file to the database.

  - **DELETE_CATALOG_ROLE**   Extends `delete` privileges on SYS-owned dictionary tables in response to the new restriction on `delete any` `table` privileges that prevent grantees from removing rows from SYS-owned dictionary tables.

- **EXECUTE_CATALOG_ROLE**   Enables the grantee to have `execute` privileges on any SYS-owned package supplied with the Oracle software.

- **SELECT_CATALOG_ROLE**   Enables the grantee to `select` data from any SYS-owned dictionary table or view.

- Roles can have passwords assigned to them to provide security for the use of certain privileges.

- Users can alter their own roles in a database session. Each role requires 4 bytes of space in the Program Global Area (PGA) in order to be used. The amount of space each user requires in the PGA can be limited with the MAX_ENABLED_ROLES initialization parameter.

- When a privilege is granted to the user PUBLIC, every user in the database can use the privilege. However, when a privilege is revoked from PUBLIC, every stored procedure, function, or package in the database must be recompiled.

- Auditing the database can be done either to detect inappropriate activity or to store an archive of database activity.

- Auditing can collect large amounts of information. In order to minimize the amount of searching, the person conducting the audit should limit the auditing of database activities to where he or she thinks a problem lies.

- Any activity on the database can be audited either by naming the privilege or by naming an object in the database.

- The activities of one or more users can be singled out for audit, or every access to an object or privilege, or every session on the database, can have their activities audited.

- Audits can monitor successful activities surrounding a privilege, unsuccessful activities, or both.

- In every database audit, starting and stopping the instance, as well as every connection established by a user with DBA privileges as granted by `SYSDBA` and `SYSOPER`, are monitored regardless of any other activities being audited.

- Audit data is stored in the data dictionary in the AUD$ table, which is owned by SYS.

- Several dictionary views exist for seeing data in the AUD$ table. The main ones are as follows:
  - DBA_AUDIT_EXISTS
  - DBA_AUDIT_OBJECT
  - DBA_AUDIT_SESSION
  - DBA_AUDIT_STATEMENT
  - DBA_AUDIT_TRAIL
- If auditing is in place and monitoring session connections, and if the AUD$ table fills, no more users can connect to the database until the AUD$ table is (archived and) emptied.
- The AUD$ table should be audited, whenever in use, to detect any tampering of its data.

Fill-in-the-Blank Questions

1. The name of the table in Oracle where audit data is stored: _____.

2. The name of the Oracle-defined role that lets you execute all Oracle-supplied packages: _____.

3. The Oracle database object that facilitates use of advanced Oracle password management features: _____.

4. Use of this object privilege enables you to define a foreign-key relationship: _____.

5. The name of the profile created for you by Oracle when you first create a database: _____.

Chapter Questions

1. **The DBA is considering restricting her users' use of the host machine via the Oracle database. If the DBA wants to use resource costs to limit resource usage, the first thing she must do is which of the following?**

   A. Change the value of RESOURCE_LIMIT to TRUE.

   B. Change the value of `composite_limit` in the user profile to 0.

   C. Change the value of `composite_limit` in the DEFAULT profile to 0.

   D. Change the value of the resource costs for the resources to be limited.

2. **The owner of a database table is eliminating some foreign key dependencies from the Oracle database prior to the removal of some tables. When revoking the `references` privilege, the DBA must use which option to ensure success?**

   A. `with admin option`

   B. `with grant option`

   C. `cascade constraints`

   D. `trailing nullcols`

3. **The DBA is using operating system authentication for his Oracle database. He is creating a user for that database. Which line of the following statement will produce an error?**

   A. `create user OPS$ELLISON`

   B. `identified externally`

   C. `default tablespace USERS_01`

   D. `default role CONNECT;`

   E. There are no errors in this statement.

4. **The DBA is about to enable auditing on the Oracle database in an attempt to discover some suspicious database activity. Audit trail information is stored in which of the following database object names?**

   A. SYS.SOURCE$

   B. SYS.AUD$

   C. DBA_SOURCE

   D. DBA_AUDIT_TRAIL

5. **The creator of a role is granted which of the following privileges with respect to the role she has just created?**

   A. `grant any privilege`

   B. `create any role`

   C. `with admin option`

   D. `with grant option`

   E. `sysdba`

6. **In order to find out how many database objects a user has created, which view would the DBA query in the Oracle data dictionary?**

   A. DBA_USERS

   B. DBA_OBJECTS

   C. DBA_TS_QUOTAS

   D. DBA_TAB_PRIVS

7. **The DBA is considering which settings to use for profiles in the Oracle database. Upon database creation, the value of the CONNECT_TIME parameter in the DEFAULT profile is set to which of the following choices?**

   A. 1

   B. 10

   C. 300

   D. `unlimited`

   E. None—the DEFAULT profile hasn't been created yet.

8. **A user cannot change aspects of his or her account configuration with the exception of one item. Which of the following choices identifies an area of the user's account that the user can change himself or herself using an `alter user` statement?**

   A. `identified by`

   B. `default tablespace`

   C. `temporary tablespace`

   D. `quota on`

   E. `profile`

   F. `default role`

9. **The DBA is considering implementing controls to limit the amount of host machine resources a user can exploit while connected to the Oracle database. Which of the following choices accurately describes a resource cost?**

   A. A monetary cost for using a database resource

   B. A monetary cost for using a privilege

   C. An integer value representing the importance of the resource

   D. An integer value representing the dollar cost for using the resource

10. **The DBA gets a production emergency support call from a user trying to connect to Oracle, saying that the database won't let her connect and that the audit log is full. Which of the following choices accurately describes what is happening on the Oracle database?**

A. The database is up and running.

B. The AUD$ table has been filled and `session` is being audited.

C. Restricted session has been disabled.

D. Operating system authentication is being used.

11. **The DBA needs to keep track of when the database is started due to a reported problem with Oracle being available after the host machine reboots. When auditing instance startup, the audit records are placed in which of the following locations?**

A. SYS.AUD$

B. DBA_AUDIT_TRAIL

C. ARCHIVE_DUMP_DEST

D. AUDIT_FILE_DEST

12. **In determining resource costs for defining user profiles, the DBA will assign a resource a high-resource cost to indicate which of the following?**

A. A less expensive resource

B. A lower amount of resource used per minute

C. A more expensive resource

D. A higher amount of resource used per minute

Fill-in-the-Blank Answers

1. SYS.AUD$

2. EXECUTE_CATALOG_ROLE

3. Profiles

4. References

5. DEFAULT

Answers to Chapter Questions

1. A.   Change the value of RESOURCE_LIMIT to TRUE.

Explanation   In order for any value set for a resource cost to be effective, and in order to use any user profile, the RESOURCE_LIMIT initialization parameter must be set to TRUE. Refer to the discussion of user profiles.

2. C.   `cascade constraints`

Explanation   If a foreign key constraint is defined as the result of a `references` privilege being granted, then in order to revoke the `references` privilege, the `cascade constraints` option must be used. Choices A and B are incorrect because `admin option` and `grant option` relate to the granting of system and object privileges, respectively, while this question is asking about the revocation of an object privilege. Choice D is incorrect because `trailing nullcols` refers to an option in the SQL*Loader control file covered in the next chapter. Refer to the discussion of administering object privileges.

3. D.   `default role CONNECT`

Explanation   Although a user profile can be specified as part of a user-creation statement, the individual options specified in a user profile cannot be. Therefore, the user-creation statement will error out on line D. This is because no privileges or roles have been granted to the user yet. After creating the user and granting some privileges and/or roles to him or her, you can issue the `alter user default role` statement. Refer to the section on user creation.

4. B.   SYS.AUD$

Explanation   AUD$ holds all audit trail records. It is owned by user SYS. Choice A is incorrect because SOURCE$ contains source code for all stored procedures, functions, and packages. Choices C and D are dictionary views that provide access to the underlying data dictionary tables named in choices A and B. Although they enable viewing of the data, the views themselves store nothing because they are views. Refer to the discussion of auditing.

5. D. `with grant option`

Explanation   Choice D is the correct answer because it is the appropriate administrative clause offered to the creator of a role in Oracle. The creator of a role can do anything he or she wants to with the role, including remove it. Choice C is incorrect because `with admin option` refers to the administrative clause for system privileges. Choices A, B, and E are incorrect because no privileges are given to a role on creation. Refer to the discussion of roles and the `with grant option`.

6. B.   DBA_OBJECTS

Explanation   The DBA_OBJECTS view lists all objects that are in the Oracle database as well as the owners of those objects. Choice A is incorrect because DBA_USERS contains the actual user-creation information, such as the encrypted password, default and temp tablespace, user profile, and default role. Choice C is incorrect because DBA_TS_QUOTAS identifies all the tablespace quotas that have been named for the user. Choice D is incorrect because DBA_TAB_PRIVS names all the table object privileges that have been granted and to whom they have been given. Refer to the discussion of monitoring information about existing users.

7. D.   `unlimited`

Explanation   All resource limits in the DEFAULT user profile created when Oracle is installed are set to `unlimited`. You can change them later using the `alter profile` command. Refer to the discussion of the DEFAULT profile in the managing resource-usage discussion.

8. A.   `identified by`

Explanation   There is only one user-creation option that the created user can modify. All others are managed either by a security administrator or the DBA. Although users can change the current role from the roles currently granted to them using the `set role` statement, they cannot issue the `alter user` statement to get the same result. Refer to the discussion of user creation.

9. C.   An integer value representing the importance of the resource

Explanation   The resource cost is an integer that measures the relative importance of a resource to the DBA. Its value is completely arbitrary and has nothing to do with money. Therefore, choices A, B, and D are all incorrect. Refer to the discussion of assessing resource costs in the section on user profiles.

10. B. The AUD$ table has been filled and `session` is being audited.

Explanation   If user connections are being audited and the AUD$ table fills, no user can connect until the AUD$ table is cleared. Choice A is incorrect because the database is open for everyone's use when it is up and running. By the same token, choice C is incorrect as well, because when a restricted session is disabled, the database is open for general access. Choice D is incorrect because operating system authentication is simply another means of verifying user passwords; it doesn't cut users off from accessing the database. Refer to the discussion of managing the audit trail.

11. D. AUDIT_FILE_DEST

Explanation   This is a difficult question. For instance, upon startup, `audit` places the information collected in this action into a special file that is placed where background process trace files are written. The location where background processes place their trace files is identified at instance startup with the AUDIT_FILE_DEST initialization parameter. Because the database has not started yet, the AUD$ table cannot be the location to which instance startup information is written, eliminating choice A. Because DBA_AUDIT_TRAIL is a view on AUD$, choice B is wrong, too. Choice C is the location where archive logs are written, which is closer to the spirit of the answer, but still not correct. Refer to the discussion of auditing system-level database activity.

12. C. A more expensive resource

Explanation   The higher the value set for resource cost, the more valued the resource is to the database system, increasing its relative "expense." Choice A is incorrect because the exact opposite is true. Choices B and D are incorrect because, although the DBA can track resource use on a per-minute basis, there is no value added by doing so—nor does doing so indicate the relative expense of using the resource.

PART
II

OCP Oracle9*i*
DBA Fundamentals I
Practice Exams

CHAPTER
7

OCP Database
Administration
Fundamentals I

he OCP Oracle9*i* DBA Fundamentals I exam in the Oracle DBA track covers concepts and practices regarding routine Oracle database administration. To pass this exam, you need to demonstrate an understanding of the features available in Oracle for administering your database objects and the overall database itself. In more recent editions of this exam, the focus has included understanding the use of automatic undo management, Oracle-Managed Files (OMF), and other new Oracle9*i* features. In addition, you should also be sure you understand use of National Language Support (NLS) for language control.

IMPORTANT
Do not take any of these practice exams until you have reviewed the contents of Appendix A, "Globalization Support." Although this is not a big topic, there are sure to be a few questions about globalization support on the OCP DBA Fundamentals I exam!

Practice Exam I

1. **Automatic archiving of redo information is enabled, and all redo logs are found on the same disk resource. Which background processes may conflict with one another's operation?**

    A. SMON and LGWR

    B. ARCH and RECO

    C. PMON and DBWR

    D. ARCH and LGWR

2. **You are adding redo logs to the Oracle database. Creating a new redo log adds information to which of the following Oracle resources?**

    A. Shared pool

    B. Control file

    C. SGA

    D. PGA

3. You need to find where the data dictionary tables are stored in your Oracle database. The tables that store information about the Oracle database—such as table names, users, and online undo segments—are found in which of the following tablespaces?

   A. SYSTEM

   B. TEMP

   C. UNDOTBS

   D. INDEX

4. You are performing the steps that will create your Oracle data dictionary. The objects in the Oracle data dictionary are part of which of the following schemas?

   A. SYSTEM

   B. SYS

   C. PUBLIC

   D. SCOTT

5. As the DBA, you are attempting to limit users' misuse of Oracle's capability to use host machine resources. Which of the following features of the Oracle database is useful for this purpose?

   A. Undo segments

   B. Roles

   C. Profiles

   D. Parameter files

6. You have identified a table in the database that is experiencing severe row chaining. Which of the following choices best identifies a way to correct the problem?

   A. Increase `pctused`.

   B. Increase `pctfree`.

   C. Increase `pctincrease`.

   D. Increase `next`.

7. Which of the following choices best identifies the Oracle feature enabling you to save multiple online copies of redo information on several disks to prevent problems with media failure?

   A. Multiplexing

   B. Archiving

   C. Redoing

   D. Logging

8. You have a database with thousands of tables and users. Managing complex databases with many objects and users is best handled with which of the following access methods?

   A. Granting privileges to profiles directly

   B. Granting privileges to users directly

   C. Use of profiles

   D. Granting privileges to roles directly

9. You are attempting to increase the checkpoint interval on your database. Each of the following choices will affect the duration and/or frequency of checkpoints, except one. Which is it?

   A. Size of redo logs

   B. Number of datafiles

   C. LOG_CHECKPOINT_INTERVAL

   D. LOG_CHECKPOINT_TIMEOUT

10. As the result of configuring an area of the Oracle database, the Oracle RDBMS has been spending more time managing the space utilization of blocks on a high transaction volume OLTP system. Which of the following choices identifies a potential cause for this behavior?

   A. High pctfree

   B. High pctused

   C. Low pctfree

   D. Low pctused

11. You intend to prevent excessive host machine processing by user SPANKY on the database. Which of the following choices indicates the step you must take in order for this to be possible in the current instance?

A. Issue grant LIMITER to SPANKY, where LIMITER is a profile.

B. Issue grant LIMITER to SPANKY, where LIMITER is a role.

C. Issue alter user SPANKY PROFILE LIMITER, where LIMITER is a profile.

D. Issue alter user SPANKY PROFILE LIMITER, where LIMITER is a role.

12. Your application regularly issues the following statement:

```
SELECT * FROM BANK_ACCT
WHERE ACCT_BALANCE BETWEEN 1000 AND 100000;
```

Which of the following database objects would be inappropriate for use with this statement?

A. Materialized views

B. Indexes

C. Index-organized tables

D. Hash clusters

13. The DBA needs to reorganize a tablespace. Which of the following privileges will be used in order to log into Oracle while the database is open, but not available to other users?

A. create session

B. restricted session

C. connect

D. mount

14. You are trying to alter the initial segment size given to a table in a dictionary-managed tablespace. Which of the following keywords would be used as part of this process?

A. drop table

B. alter table

C. resize

D. coalesce

15. **You are in the process of creating users in the database. Which of the following clauses in a `create user` statement prevents a user's disk sorts from conflicting with dictionary objects?**

    A. `identified by`

    B. `temporary tablespace`

    C. `default tablespace`

    D. `default role`

16. **In order to enable remote administration of users and tablespaces on an Oracle database, which of the following types of files must exist in the database?**

    A. Password file

    B. Initialization file

    C. Datafile

    D. Control file

    E. Nothing—`SYSDBA` privileges are not required for these actions.

17. **All of the following choices identify a component of Oracle's redo architecture, except one. Which of the following is not a direct component of Oracle's redo mechanism when the database is in `archivelog` mode?**

    A. DBW0

    B. Redo log buffer

    C. LGWR

    D. Online redo log

    E. CKPT

    F. Archive redo logs

18. **Examine the following statement:**

```
CREATE TABLE SPANKY.EMPLOYEE
(empid          NUMBER(10),
lastname        VARCHAR2(25),
firstname       VARCHAR2(25),
salary          NUMBER(10,4),
CONSTRAINT      pk_employee_01
PRIMARY KEY     (empid))
```

```
TABLESPACE orgdbdata
EXTENT MANAGEMENT DICTIONARY
PCTFREE     20   PCTUSED      50
INITRANS    1    MAXTRANS     255
NOCACHE          LOGGING
INITIAL 100K   NEXT   150K
MINEXTENTS 4   MAXEXTENTS   300
PCTINCREASE 20  );
```

What is wrong with this statement?

A. The primary key is declared improperly.

B. Both the index and data from the table must be stored in the same tablespace.

C. The statement will not succeed because a not NULL constraint is needed on the EMPID column.

D. The statement will succeed, but no data will be inserted.

E. The storage clause is improperly defined.

19. User ANN has `insert` privilege on the EMP table `with grant option`. ANN grants the `insert` privilege to SIMON. What is the most immediate effect of the DBA revoking ANN's privilege?

    A. ANN's records will be removed from table EMP.

    B. ANN will continue to have the ability to add records to EMP.

    C. SIMON will not be able to add records to the EMP table anymore.

    D. The DBA's ability to add records to EMP will be revoked.

20. You have a table and you are trying to determine appropriate `pctfree` and `pctused` values for it. The initial insert of new data into the table will leave most of its large columns NULL, to be filled in later by subsequent updates. Records are never removed. What is the appropriate value combination for `pctfree` and `pctused`?

    A. pctused = 99, pctfree = 1

    B. pctused = 40, pctfree = 30

    C. pctused = 40, pctfree = 10

    D. pctused = 80, pctfree = 10

21. You are configuring your index to be stored in a tablespace. Which of the following storage parameters are not appropriate for indexes?

    A. OPTIMAL

    B. INITIAL

    C. PCTINCREASE

    D. NEXT

22. You need to manage some configuration for new and existing users. Which of the following clauses are available in `alter user` statements but not in `create user` statements?

    A. `identified by`

    B. `temporary tablespace`

    C. `profile`

    D. `default role`

    E. `account lock`

    F. `password expire`

23. When you arrive at work in the morning, you have messages from several users complaining that they have received the following error when they tried logging into Oracle with their new user ID and password:

    ```
    Error accessing PRODUCT_USER_PROFILE
    Warning:  Product user profile information not loaded!
    ```

    What do you need to do in order to solve the problem?

    A. Run pupbld.sql as SYSTEM.

    B. Do a shutdown abort.

    C. Drop and re-create the users.

    D. Drop and re-create the database.

24. During regular database operation, which background process will take smaller blocks of free space in a dictionary-managed tablespace and move things around to make bigger pieces of free space?

    A. DBW0

    B. LGWR

    C. ARCH

    D. SMON

    E. PMON

25. **You are designing the physical database layout on your host machine. What is the relationship between tablespaces and datafiles in the Oracle database?**

    A. One tablespace has only one datafile.

    B. Many tablespaces can share one datafile.

    C. One tablespace can have many datafiles.

    D. One datafile can contain many tablespaces.

26. **In order to set resource cost high on CPU time, and low on the overall time a user spends connected to Oracle, which of the following would be appropriate?**

    A. Increase value of COMPOSITE_LIMIT.

    B. Increase value on CPU_PER_SESSION, and decrease value on CONNECT_TIME.

    C. Decrease value on CPU_PER_SESSION, and increase value on LOGICAL_READS_PER_SESSION.

    D. Set PRIVATE_SGA to UNLIMITED.

27. **You are attempting to take the UNDOTBS01 tablespace offline when using manually managed undo segments and receive the following error: ORA-01546 - cannot take tablespace offline. What might be causing the problem?**

    A. A table has too many extents allocated to it.

    B. Your `init.ora` file is unavailable.

    C. An uncommitted transaction is still in progress.

    D. The online redo log is being archived.

28. You are analyzing how Oracle processes user statements. SQL and PL/SQL parse information is stored in which of the following database memory areas?

    A. Library cache

    B. Row cache

    C. Dictionary cache

    D. Large area

    E. Buffer cache

29. Information in the buffer cache is saved back to disk in each of the following situations except one. In which situation does this not occur?

    A. When a timeout occurs

    B. When a log switch occurs

    C. When the shared pool is flushed

    D. When a checkpoint occurs

30. You want to set up password management on your Oracle database. Which of the following choices indicates what you should do to view an example for setting up a password management function?

    A. Set RESOURCE_LIMIT to TRUE.

    B. Run utlpwmg.sql.

    C. Drop the DEFAULT profile.

    D. Run catproc.sql.

31. Inspect the following transcript from user ATHENA's session:

    ```
    SQL>  create table obobobo (bobobo varchar2(3))
      2>    tablespace rman;
    create table obobobo (bobobo varchar2(3))
    *
    ERROR at line 1:
    ORA-01536: space quota exceeded for tablespace 'RMAN'
    ```

    Where can the DBA look to find out information to solve this problem?

    A. Looking in the DBA_TS_QUOTAS dictionary view

    B. Looking in the DBA_USERS view

C. Looking in the DBA_TAB_COLUMNS view

D. Looking in the DBA_TABLESPACES view

32. **The DBA issues the following statement:**

```
CREATE USER DBADMIN
IDENTIFIED BY DBADMIN;
```

What profile will user DBADMIN have?

A. DEFAULT

B. None

C. CONNECT

D. DBA

33. **You have several profiles in your database, each with various values set to make users stay on the database for various periods of time. Where would you look to find information about the appropriate profile to assign a user who should connect for only very short periods of time?**

A. DBA_USERS

B. DBA_PROFILES

C. RESOURCE_COST

D. RESOURCE_LIMIT

34. **You have finished creating your new database and have run scripts to create the data dictionary views. Which of the following choices identifies what you need to do next to create Oracle-supplied packages?**

A. `catproc.sql`

B. `catalog.sql`

C. `utlpwdmg.sql`

D. `utllockt.sql`

35. **You are trying to strengthen security on your database. Which of the following Oracle resources supports password-authenticated security over and above the abilities a user might be granted in accessing an application?**

    A. Profiles

    B. Tables

    C. Undo segments

    D. Roles

36. **A disk crashes that contains the only copies of all four of your online redo log files. How would you alter your Oracle database to prevent this from causing much damage in the future?**

    A. Change the CONTROL_FILES parameter in the `init.ora` file.

    B. Use the `alter database add LOGFILE GROUP 5;`.

    C. Create multiple members for each of your four groups and place them on different disks.

    D. Set LOG_BLOCK_CHECKSUM in the `init.ora` file.

37. **A table has a primary key that has been disabled. Upon reenabling it, the DBA discovers that users have entered duplicate records into the table. Which of the following database objects might play a role in rectifying the situation?**

    A. EXCEPTIONS

    B. DBA_TABLES

    C. USER_TAB_COLUMNS

    D. AUD$

38. **After creating a new user for your Oracle database, a user still complains she cannot log in because of insufficient privileges errors. Which of the following actions should you take?**

    A. Grant create table privileges to the user.

    B. Reset the user's password.

    C. Grant the CONNECT role to the user.

    D. Unlock the user's account.

39. On an Oracle server installation, which of the following reorganizations of your indexes would be appropriate in order to improve performance of queries on tables containing all words in the dictionary starting with the letter *s*?

   A. Convert your B-tree index to a bitmap index.

   B. Convert your bitmap index to a B-tree index.

   C. Convert your B-tree index to a reverse-key index.

   D. Convert your reverse-key index to a B-tree index.

40. You plan to store large blocks of text in your table. You want the column to be large enough to store about ten sentences. The column must also be fixed width. Which of the following datatypes are most appropriate?

   A. CLOB

   B. LONG

   C. VARCHAR2

   D. CHAR

41. You have enabled an audit in your database using the following statement:

```
AUDIT UPDATE, DELETE
ON spanky.cat_toys
BY ACCESS
WHENEVER NOT SUCCESSFUL;
```

   Which choice best explains how Oracle will audit data?

   A. Successful `insert` statements on CAT_TOYS performed by SPANKY will be recorded.

   B. Unsuccessful `update` and `delete` statements performed by any user on CAT_TOYS will be recorded.

   C. Unsuccessful `update` and `delete` statements performed by user ACCESS on CAT_TOYS will be recorded.

   D. Unsuccessful `update` and `delete` statements performed by SPANKY on any table will be recorded.

42. The primary key of the EMP table has three columns: EMPID, LASTNAME, and FIRSTNAME. You issue the following `select` statement:

```
SELECT * FROM EMP
WHERE LASTNAME = 'HARRIS'
AND FIRSTNAME = 'BILLI'
AND EMPID = '5069493';
```

What dictionary view could you use to verify the order of leading columns in the index associated with the primary key?

   A. DBA_IND_COLUMNS

   B. DBA_TAB_COLUMNS

   C. DBA_INDEXES

   D. DBA_CLU_COLUMNS

43. You issue the following statement:

```
DROP PROFILE LTD_PROGRAMMER;
```

The LTD_PROGRAMMER profile was granted to several users on the Oracle database. What happens to those users?

   A. The users who had the LTD_PROGRAMMER profile can no longer log in to Oracle.

   B. The users who had the LTD_PROGRAMMER profile now have the DEFAULT profile.

   C. The users who had the LTD_PROGRAMMER profile now have no profile.

   D. Nothing—You cannot drop a profile that has been granted to users.

44. You want to reduce the number of extents a segment will allocate as part of table growth. Each of the following choices indicates an action that will do so, except one. Which is it?

   A. Running EXPORT with the COMPRESS parameter set to Y

   B. Increasing the value set for `pctused` on the table

   C. Increasing the value set for `pctincrease` on the table

   D. Increasing the value set for `next` on the table

45. You are planning which segments to place in which tablespaces. Which of the following segment types usually has the lowest turnover in the Oracle database?

A. Undo segments

B. Table segments

C. Temporary segments

D. SYSTEM segments

46. You issue the shutdown command at 3 P.M. on a Friday. Two hours later, the database is still in the process of shutting down. Which of the following options did you most likely use in order to shut down the database?

A. `shutdown abort`

B. `shutdown immediate`

C. `shutdown transactional`

D. `shutdown normal`

47. The user is selecting data from the Oracle database. Which of the following processes handles obtaining data from Oracle for that user?

A. The user process obtains information on its own.

B. The DBW0 process obtains information for the user.

C. The server process obtains information for the user.

D. The listener process obtains information for the user.

48. The result of select count(*) from DBA_TABLES where TABLESPACE_NAME _ 'MY_TBLSPC' is listed as follows:

```
COUNT(*)
---------------
150
```

You then issue the **drop tablespace MY_TBLSPC** command. What happens next?

A. The `drop tablespace` command succeeds.

B. The `drop tablespace` command fails because you didn't include the cascade constraints option.

C. The `drop tablespace` command fails because you didn't include the including contents option.

D. You cannot drop a tablespace after creating it.

49. After starting SQL*Plus in line mode, you issue the **shutdown immediate** command. What will most likely happen next?

A. The database shuts down.

B. The database does not shut down because users have to disconnect.

C. SQL*Plus returns an error saying you need to connect to Oracle first.

D. Nothing happens. SQL*Plus is not a line-mode tool.

50. You need to view the initialization parameter settings for your Oracle database. Which of the following choices does not identify a method you can use to obtain values set for your initialization parameters?

A. Issue `select * from DBA_PARAMETERS;` from SQL*Plus.

B. Issue `select * from V$PARAMETER;` from SQL*Plus.

C. Issue `show parameters` from SQL*Plus.

D. Use OEM Instance Manager.

51. You issue the following statement in Oracle:

```
CREATE UNIQUE BITMAP INDEX employee_lastname_indx_01
ON employee (lastname ASC)
TABLESPACE ORGDBIDX
PCTFREE 12
INITRANS 2 MAXTRANS 255
LOGGING
NOSORT
STORAGE ( INITIAL 900K
NEXT 1800K
MINEXTENTS 1
MAXEXTENTS 200
PCTINCREASE 0 );
```

What is wrong with this statement for dictionary-managed tablespaces?

A. You cannot use the `nosort` keyword in creating an index.

B. Bitmap indexes cannot be unique.

C. The `tablespace` clause must be omitted.

D. You should omit the `asc` keyword.

52. **You manage database access privileges with roles where possible. You have granted the SELECT_MY_TABLE role to another role called EMP_DEVELOPER. To view information about other roles that may be granted to EMP_DEVELOPER, which of the following dictionary views are appropriate?**

    A. DBA_ROLE_PRIVS

    B. DBA_TAB_PRIVS

    C. USER_SYS_PRIVS

    D. ROLE_ROLE_PRIVS

53. **Your current session displays date information in the following format: 10-FEB-1999:10:15AM. Which of the following statements most likely produced this result?**

    A. alter session set NLS_DATE_FORMAT = 'DD-MON-YYYY:HH:MIAM';

    B. alter session set NLS_DATE_FORMAT = 'DD-MON-YY:HH24:MI';

    C. alter session set NLS_DATE_FORMAT = 'DD-MON-YY:HH:MIAM';

    D. alter session set NLS_DATE_FORMAT = 'DD-MON-YYYY:HH24:MI';

54. **You need to set up auditing in an order entry and product shipment application so that when the ORDER_STATUS column in the ORDERS table changes to *SHIPPED*, a record is placed in a special table associated with a part of the application that gives sales representatives a daily list of customers to call on a follow-up to make sure the customer is satisfied with the order. Which of the following choices represents the best way to perform this auditing?**

    A. Statement auditing

    B. Object auditing

    C. Audit by access

    D. Value-based auditing

55. You are in the process of granting several permissions to a role. Which of the following privileges is not a system privilege?

     A. `analyze any`

     B. `index`

     C. `create rollback segment`

     D. `create synonym`

56. When sizing temporary tablespaces, you should try where possible to make the default INITIAL storage setting for the temporary tablespace a multiple of which of the following initialization parameters?

     A. LOG_BUFFER

     B. DB_BLOCK_BUFFERS

     C. SORT_AREA_SIZE

     D. SHARED_POOL_SIZE

57. When you issue the `commit` statement in your session, which of the following things will not occur?

     A. Acquired row or table locks are released.

     B. Cached data is saved immediately to disk.

     C. Acquired undo segment locks are released.

     D. Redo entry generated for committed transaction.

58. You are processing an `update` statement. At what point in SQL statement processing is the data change actually made to block buffers?

     A. When the cursor is opened

     B. When the statement is parsed

     C. When data is fetched from the cursor

     D. When the statement is executed

59. You are defining storage for various segment types in the Oracle database. Which of the following is not a valid type of segment in Oracle?

     A. Data segment

     B. Undo segment

C. Temporary segment

D. Sequence segment

60. **You need to identify the remaining free space in a tablespace. From which of the following views would you get this information most easily?**

    A. DBA_TABLESPACES

    B. DBA_FREE_SPACE

    C. V$TABLESPACE

    D. DBA_EXTENTS

Practice Exam 2

I. **If you wanted to find the name and location of your control files, you could find that information in each of the following locations except one. Which is it?**

   A. V$CONTROLFILE_RECORD_SECTION

   B. V$CONTROLFILE

   C. V$PARAMETER

   D. init.ora file

2. **You are planning the storage requirements for your database. Which of the following is an effect of maintaining a high pctfree for a table?**

   A. Oracle will manage filling data blocks with new records more actively.

   B. Oracle will manage filling data blocks with new records less actively.

   C. Oracle will leave more space free in data blocks for existing records.

   D. Oracle will leave less space free in data blocks for existing records.

3. **The DBA has a table created with the following statement:**

```
CREATE TABLE EMPL
(EMPID NUMBER(10),
LASTNAME VARCHAR2(40),
RESUME LONG RAW);
The DBA attempts to issue the following statement:
ALTER TABLE EMPL
ADD ( PERF_APPRAISE LONG);
```

   What happens?

   A. The statement succeeds.

   B. The statement succeeds, but column is added as VARCHAR2.

   C. The statement fails.

   D. The statement adds a DISABLED constraint.

4. **User ANN has insert privilege on the EMP table. What is the most immediate effect of the DBA revoking ANN's privilege?**

   A. ANN's records will be removed from the database.

   B. ANN will not have the ability to create tables.

C. ANN will not be able to access the database anymore.

D. Users to which ANN granted `insert` privileges will not be able to `insert`.

5. **If you wished to make it so that every user in Oracle could have only one connection to the database at a time, which of the following choices identifies how you would do it?**

   A. Set LICENSE_MAX_SESSIONS = 1 in `init.ora`.

   B. Set SESSIONS_PER_USER in the DEFAULT profile to 1.

   C. Set IDLE_TIME in the DEFAULT profile to 1.

   D. Set SESSIONS_PER_USER = 2 in `init.ora`.

6. **Records from the data dictionary information are stored in which of the following database memory areas?**

   A. Library cache

   B. Row cache

   C. Session UGA

   D. Buffer cache

7. **Which of the following choices correctly describes the difference between a data load via the conventional path and the direct path?**

   A. One runs faster than the other.

   B. A conventional path data load bypasses most of the Oracle RDBMS, whereas a direct path data load is a high-speed version of the SQL `insert`.

   C. A direct path data load bypasses most of the Oracle RDBMS, whereas a conventional path data load is a high-speed version of the SQL `insert`.

   D. The conventional path runs when the `conventional` command-line parameter is set to TRUE.

8. **The location of indexes in a database and the size of those indexes is information that can be found in which of the following dictionary views?**

   A. DBA_TS_QUOTAS

   B. DBA_OBJECTS

C. DBA_SEGMENTS

D. DBA_INDEXES

9. **You have a long-running process you want to assign to a specific undo segment brought online for that express purpose. You are not using automatic undo management. What statement can be used for this task?**

   A. `alter database`

   B. `set transaction`

   C. `alter rollback segment`

   D. `alter table`

10. **In a situation where no multiplexing of redo logs takes place, what happens when Oracle cannot read data from the online redo log group for archiving?**

    A. Nothing happens.

    B. Oracle will automatically switch redo logs when detected.

    C. Oracle eventually won't allow new records to be added to the database.

    D. The instance crashes.

11. **All except one of the following will alter the number of checkpoints that occur in one hour on the database. Which is it?**

    A. Decreasing tablespace size

    B. Decreasing size of redo log members

    C. Setting LOG_CHECKPOINT_INTERVAL greater than the size of the redo log file

    D. Setting LOG_CHECKPOINT_TIMEOUT to zero

12. **You are defining profile areas on your Oracle database. Which of the following profile areas can be used to control the resource usage for the other four?**

    A. LOGICAL_READS_PER_SESSION

    B. CONNECT_TIME

    C. COMPOSITE_LIMIT

    D. CPU_PER_SESSION

    E. PRIVATE_SGA

13. User ANN has the `create any table` privilege with administrative abilities on that privilege. Which of the following statements shows how to revoke the administrative component from ANN without limiting her overall ability to create tables?

    A. `revoke admin option from create any table;`

    B. `revoke admin option from create any table; then grant create any table to ANN;`

    C. `revoke create any table from ANN; then grant create any table to ANN;`

    D. `revoke create any table from ANN with admin option; then grant create any table to ANN;`

14. The DBA is defining a default role for users. Which of the following is not an acceptable method for defining a default role?

    A. `alter user default role all;`

    B. `alter user default role all except ROLE_1;`

    C. `alter user default role none;`

    D. `alter user default role none except ROLE_1;`

15. You issue the following statement from SQL*Plus: `startup mount`. Where does Oracle obtain values for starting the instance?

    A. From your `init.ora` file

    B. From Oracle default values

    C. From the default settings for the tablespace

    D. From the default settings in your redo log file

16. You are analyzing the components of the redo log mechanisms in your Oracle database. Which of the following purposes does the CKPT process serve?

    A. Writes dirty buffers to disk

    B. Writes current redo log number to datafile headers

C. Writes redo log information to disk

D. Reads information into memory for users

17. **You are architecting the database to be used in a production OLTP environment. Which of the following choices best illustrates why you should multiplex online redo logs?**

A. To take advantage of the increase in storage space

B. To avoid degraded redo log performance

C. To reduce dependency on the redo log buffer

D. To prevent users from waiting if a redo log member cannot be archived

18. **You are configuring some new profiles for your database. Which of the following is not an area that you can specify a resource profile limit on?**

A. LOGICAL_READS_PER_SESSION

B. CONNECT_TIME

C. LOGICAL_WRITES_PER_SESSION

D. IDLE_TIME

19. **You are attempting to clear an unarchived redo log file. In order to manually enact a log switch, which of the following statements is appropriate?**

A. `alter database`

B. `alter system`

C. `alter user`

D. `alter redo log`

20. **Which of the following clauses is available in `alter user` statements but not in `create user` statements?**

A. `identified by`

B. `temporary tablespace`

C. `profile`

D. `default role`

21. Which of the following choices lists an alter user option that can be executed by the user himself?

   A. `default tablespace`

   B. `identified by`

   C. `temporary tablespace`

   D. `profile`

22. In order to set a limit on the combined resource usage for users, which of the following statements would be appropriate?

   A. `alter profile default limit COMPOSITE_LIMIT 3500;`

   B. `RESOURCE_COST=TRUE`

   C. Set `CPU_PER_SESSION = 100` in DEFAULT profile.

   D. Set `LICENSE_MAX_SESSIONS = 1` in `init.ora`.

23. To allocate another role to a user, which command is most appropriate?

   A. `alter user`

   B. `alter database`

   C. `alter system`

   D. `grant`

24. Which of the following operations does not require Oracle to store information in an undo segment as part of the transaction?

   A. `insert`

   B. `select`

   C. `update`

   D. `delete`

25. You have enabled dedicated servers to be used on your Oracle database system. Where in the Oracle database is session information when dedicated servers are being used?

   A. In the PGA

   B. In the shared pool

   C. In the buffer cache

D. In the redo log buffer

E. Large area

26. Which of the following clauses in a `create user` statement restricts the number of tables a user can add to a tablespace?

   A. `quota on`

   B. `default tablespace`

   C. `profile`

   D. `identified by`

27. You have a block space utilization identified by the following values: `pctfree 25, pctused 30`. Which of the following choices best describes the block management on your database?

   A. Little free space left for `updates` and space left free by `deletes` actively filled in by Oracle

   B. Little free space left for `updates` and space left free by `deletes` not actively filled in by Oracle

   C. Much free space left for `updates` and space left free by `deletes` actively filled in by Oracle

   D. Much free space left for `updates` and space left free by `deletes` not actively filled in by Oracle

28. You are defining the path a user process takes to get information out of the Oracle database. Which of the following purposes does the process labeled D009 serve?

   A. Writes dirty buffers to disk

   B. Writes current redo log number to datafile headers

   C. Dispatches user process access to a shared server

   D. Writes redo log entries to disk

29. You are considering using the MTS architecture on the Oracle database. Where in the Oracle database is session information stored when shared servers are being used?

   A. In the PGA

   B. In the shared pool

C. In the buffer cache

D. In the redo log buffer

E. Large area

30. **The DBA executes the following statement:**

```
CREATE OR REPLACE VIEW MY_VW AS
SELECT EMPID, LASTNAME, FIRSTNAME,
TO_CHAR(SALARY) AS SALARY FROM EMP;
```

If the SALARY column in the EMP table is datatype NUMBER(10), what will the datatype of the SALARY column be in MY_VW when the DBA queries the data dictionary?

A. ROWID

B. NUMBER

C. DATE

D. VARCHAR2

31. **You have defined your national language on the Oracle database to be English, and the text data in some tables contains German characters. In order to ensure that you can list this text data in ascending alphabetical order according to German syntax, while still ensuring the language on the database is English, which of the following parameters could be set?**

A. NLS_DATE_FORMAT

B. NLS_RULE

C. NLS_TERRITORY

D. NLS_SORT

32. **When choosing a character set and national character set, which of the following factors should not enter into consideration?**

A. Your character set must either be US7ASCII or a superset of it.

B. Your national character set and character set should be closely related where possible.

C. You can use varying-length multibyte character sets as both character sets on your database.

D. Oracle supports only English-like languages as its character set for entering SQL and PL/SQL commands.

33. You are working for the United Nations as an Oracle DBA. You maintain databases in multiple countries in multiple languages. To determine the date conventions for a database in a particular country, you might use which of the following database views?

   A. V$NLS_PARAMETERS

   B. NLS_DATE_FORMAT

   C. DBA_DATES

   D. V$NLS_VALID_VALUES

34. You are running Oracle in America in support of a financial analysis project for the government of Egypt. In order to produce reports that display monetary amounts as Egyptian pounds, rather than dollars, which of the following initialization parameters would be useful?

   A. NLS_SORT

   B. NLS_CURRENCY

   C. NLS_LANG

   D. NLS_DATE_FORMAT

35. You are trying to find the ALERT file on a host machine for a database you have never administered before. Which of the following initialization parameters is used to identify the location of the ALERT file?

   A. BACKGROUND_DUMP_DEST

   B. USER_DUMP_DEST

   C. LOG_ARCHIVE_DEST

   D. CORE_DUMP_DEST

36. You issue the `alter tablespace read only` command against an Oracle database. Which of the following choices best describes what happens next?

   A. Oracle immediately puts the tablespace into read-only mode.

   B. Oracle puts the tablespace into read-only mode after the last user logs off.

C. Oracle puts the tablespace into read-only mode after the last prior transaction against that tablespace commits while preventing subsequent DML until the change happens.

D. Oracle returns an error.

37. **You are using locally managed tablespaces in Oracle. Which of the following choices best describes the way Oracle implements this feature in the database?**

A. Using a bitmap in the space header segment

B. Using the data dictionary on the local database

C. Using a flat file in the local directory storing the datafile

D. Using the data dictionary in a distributed database

38. **You are configuring Oracle's large pool feature. Which of the following choices best describes information that gets stored in the large pool if one is defined for your database?**

A. Parse trees for SQL statements

B. Session memory for MTS configuration

C. Session memory for dedicated server configuration

D. Block buffer overflow

39. **You need to remove a column from the database. Which of the following choices best identifies how to do so if your objective is to quickly execute the task without necessarily freeing up space in your tablespace?**

A. `alter table drop column`

B. `alter table set unused column`

C. `alter table modify column`

D. `truncate table`

40. When generating global temporary tables, which of the following places in your Oracle database is the actual data used by your temporary table stored in?

A. PGA

B. Buffer cache

C. SYSTEM tablespace

D. RBS tablespace

41. You are using SQL*Loader to insert data into your database quickly. Which of the following features enables you to define a row of data in your datafile to begin at a point other than the beginning of a line?

A. `fields separated by`

B. `fields terminated by`

C. `trailing nullcols`

D. `recseparator`

42. You are rebuilding indexes in Oracle. Which of the following activities cannot be combined with rebuilding your index in an Oracle database, but must instead be performed as a separate operation?

A. Estimate statistics.

B. Compute statistics.

C. Move the index to another tablespace.

D. Rebuild online.

43. You want to maintain multiple archive log destinations in Oracle. Which of the following parameters can be used to indicate how many ARCH processes Oracle needs to run in order to manage storage of archive logs to multiple destinations?

A. LOG_ARCHIVE_PROCESSES

B. LOG_ARCHIVE_MAX_PROCESSES

C. LOG_ARCHIVE_MIN_SUCCEED_DEST

D. LOG_ARCHIVE_START

44. **You have installed Oracle and used the Database Configuration Assistant to create a database in a Windows environment. Where would you find the datafiles for the database that you just created?**

    A. %ORACLE_BASE%\admin

    B. %ORACLE_BASE%\rdbms\admin

    C. %ORACLE_BASE%\database

    D. %ORACLE_BASE%\oradata

45. **You issue the following statement on an Oracle database where DB_BLOCK_SIZE is 4KB:**

    ```
    CREATE TABLESPACE orgdbindex
    DATAFILE '/oracle/disk_8/index01.dbf'
    SIZE 300M
    EXTENT MANAGEMENT LOCAL
    UNIFORM SIZE 100K
    ONLINE;
    ```

    How many blocks will each bit represent in the bitmap area of the locally managed datafiles?

    A. 25

    B. 50

    C. 80

    D. 250

46. **You have assigned three tables to the keep pool. How should you determine the appropriate size for your keep pool?**

    A. Based on the size of your shared pool

    B. Based on the number of blocks in the table only

    C. Based on the number of blocks in the table plus the number of blocks in associated indexes

    D. Based on the number of blocks in associated indexes only

    E. None of the above

47. A DBA in Germany needs to ensure that both the German mark and the Euro will be supported in the latest currency conversion application. Which of the following NLS parameters will work best for this purpose?

   A. NLS_TERRITORY

   B. NLS_LANG

   C. NLS_COMP

   D. NLS_DUAL_CURRENCY

48. The user attempts to `insert` data into a column that would violate a nondeferrable constraint. The user has issued the `alter session set constraints = deferred` statement. What happens on `insert`?

   A. The `insert` succeeds at the time it is issued, but the transaction will roll back later.

   B. The `insert` fails at the time it is issued and the transaction will end.

   C. The `insert` succeeds at the time it is issued and the transaction will not roll back later.

   D. The `insert` fails at the time it is issued, but the transaction will continue.

49. The value stored in an index for a column is '596849'. The DBA then issues the `alter index reverse` statement. What does the data in the index now look like?

   A. '596849'

   B. '849596'

   C. '948695'

   D. '695948'

50. The best choice for decreasing size requirements for tables that need only be accessed via the primary key is which of the following?

   A. Create more indexes on the table.

   B. Create an index-organized table to store the data.

   C. Drop the primary key.

   D. Increase the `pctfree` value set for table blocks.

51. While administering passwords on an Oracle database, you discover that users are simply reusing older passwords whenever their current password expires. If you wanted to prevent the reuse of passwords for a three-year period, which of the following choices identifies a profile-related method you might use to do so?

A. Set password_reuse_time to 3.

B. Set password_reuse_time to 39.

C. Set password_reuse_time to 339.

D. Set password_reuse_time to 1095.

E. Set password_reuse_time to 3195.

52. You issue the following statement in Oracle:

```
grant create table to STARSKY with admin option;
```

After which, user STARSKY issues the following statement in Oracle:

```
grant create table to HUTCH;
```

You discover STARSKY's actions and act in the following way:

```
revoke create table from STARSKY;
```

Which of the following choices correctly describes the result?

A. HUTCH can no longer create tables, but you can.

B. STARSKY can no longer create tables, but HUTCH can.

C. You and STARSKY can no longer create tables, but HUTCH can.

D. You and HUTCH can no longer create tables, but STARSKY can.

53. You grant a nondefault password-protected role to a user that permits the user to act as an application superuser with respect to adding records to certain tables. Which of the following choices best identifies the way the grantee might use to exercise the privileges granted to him or her with this role?

A. The user issues the appropriate DML commands.

B. The user issues the `alter user` command, then issues the DML commands.

C. The user issues the `set role` command, then issues the DML commands.

D. The user requires DBA intervention to exercise these privileges.

54. You are about to alter the size of a tablespace. Which of the following choices identifies a constraint on performing this operation if the intended size of the tablespace is larger than the tablespace's current size?

    A. Presence of objects in the datafile resized

    B. Availability of space on disk where datafiles are added

    C. Whether AUTOEXTEND is in use on datafiles for the tablespace

    D. Availability of space in memory for temporary storage of blocks in tablespace

55. Developers are complaining that after a few minutes of querying the database, their session disconnects abruptly. Which of the following choices does not identify a potential cause for the disconnection?

    A. The DEVELOPER profile shows a value of 230,000 for COMPOSITE_LIMIT.

    B. The DBA is issuing the `alter system kill session` command repeatedly.

    C. The DEFAULT profile shows a value of 100 for CPU_PER_SESSION.

    D. The USERS profile shows a value of 500 for CONNECT_TIME.

56. You are granting roles to users on an Oracle database. Which of the following roles is not predefined when the Oracle database is created?

    A. CREATE_CATALOG_ROLE

    B. SELECT_CATALOG_ROLE

    C. EXP_FULL_DATABASE

    D. IMP_FULL_DATABASE

57. You are managing a 24×7 database environment and need to rebuild an index online. Which of the following choices best identifies the factor you will need to consider when determining the time to execute the `online rebuild`?

    A. Availability for downtime

    B. Performance

    C. System idleness

    D. Batch processing

58. You are concerned about row chaining as a performance degrader on your Oracle database environment. Which of the following Oracle resources cannot be used to determine how many rows are chained on a table in your database?

   A. The `analyze` command

   B. The DBMS_DDL package

   C. The DBMS_UTILITY package

   D. The `alter tablespace coalesce` command

59. You attempt to issue the `alter tablespace move datafile` command in the Oracle database. Which of the following choices indicates a step that must take place after this command is issued?

   A. Physically move the datafile to the new location.

   B. Bring the tablespace offline.

   C. Bring the tablespace online.

   D. Execute IMPORT to load the new metadata.

60. You create a user on your Oracle database with the following command:

```
create user GIANT identified by GREEN;
```

You then issue the following query:

```
SQL> select password from dba_users where username = 'GIANT';
PASSWORD
----------------------------
C55278B93918BF29
```

You then issue the following statement:

```
alter user GIANT identified by "C55278B93918BF29";
```

Which of the following choices best describes what GIANT's password is now set to?

   A. GREEN

   B. C55278B93918BF29

   C. This question is irrelevant because GIANT can't connect without `create session` privileges.

   D. This question is irrelevant because GIANT's account was locked by default.

Practice Exam 3

1. You are configuring the use of servers in your Oracle database. Which of the following statements describes what happens after the listener process detects a user attempting to connect to Oracle when dedicated servers are being used?

   A. The listener spawns a new server process.

   B. The listener passes the request to a dispatcher.

   C. The listener passes the request to LGWR.

   D. The listener passes the request to DBW0.

2. A user issues a `select` command against the Oracle database. Which of the following choices describes a step that Oracle will execute in support of this statement?

   A. Acquire locks on table queried.

   B. Generate redo for statement.

   C. Fetch data from disk into memory.

   D. Write changes to disk.

3. A user issues an `insert` statement against the Oracle database. Which of the following choices describes a step that Oracle will execute in support of this statement?

   A. Make changes to data block in memory.

   B. Parse statement if parse tree already exists in shared pool.

   C. Write changed records to undo segment.

   D. Write redo for transaction to datafile.

4. You are implementing Oracle in your organization. Which of the following identifies a feature of Optimal Flexible Architecture?

   A. OFA lumps software, database, and administrative files into one area so they are easy for DBAs to locate.

   B. Use of OFA enables DBAs to define their own filesystem layouts using proprietary naming conventions in order to facilitate management of Oracle databases.

C. Use of OFA reduces support headaches by standardizing filesystem layouts for all Oracle installations.

D. OFA lumps all database objects like tables and indexes into one tablespace so they are easy for DBAs to manage.

5. **You are creating a password file in Oracle. Which of the following choices identifies how you will specify this command if you want your password file named orapwdORCL.pwd, located in /u01/app/oracle/database, to enable up to 100 other DBAs to connect and administer the database?**

   A. `orapwd directory=/u01/app/oracle/database`
   `file5orapwdORCL.pwd`

   B. `orapwd file=/u01/app/oracle/database/orapwdORCL.pwd`
   `password=oracle entries=100`

   C. `orapwd file=/u01/app/oracle/database/orapwdORCL.pwd`
   `entries=100`

   D. `orapwd file=orapwdORCL.pwd password=oracle`
   `entries=100`

6. **You are managing the Oracle database. Which of the following choices correctly identifies when Oracle reads the contents of the `init.ora` file?**

   A. When the instance is started

   B. When the database is mounted

   C. When the database is opened

   D. When the database is closed

7. **You issue the following command in Oracle: `create tablespace BOB_TBS datafile "bob01.dbf" size 2M;`. Later queries against the database reveal that the tablespace is located in the /u01/oradata/oracle directory. Which of the following choices identifies how Oracle likely determined what directory to place bob01.dbf in?**

   A. DB_CREATE_FILE_DEST

   B. DB_CREATE_ONLINE_LOG_1

   C. DB_CREATE_ONLINE_LOG_2

   D. The directory is an operating system-specific default value in Oracle that can neither be specified manually nor changed.

8. **You have configured OMF on your Oracle database system. After careful analysis, you determine that a tablespace must be removed from the database. Which of the following choices identifies how OMF can assist you in this task?**

    A. OMF will automatically update the data dictionary to remove reference to the tablespace datafiles.

    B. OMF will automatically remove the underlying datafiles from the host environment.

    C. OMF will tell Oracle to automatically stop using the datafiles associated with the tablespace.

    D. None of the above choices identify the functionality provided by OMF.

9. **Choose the appropriate choice to complete the following statement: If you want to use OMF to handle specifying the location of your online redo logs, then you must specify at least _____ destinations for Oracle to use through the definition of OMF-related `init.ora` parameters.**

    A. One

    B. Two

    C. Three

    D. Four

10. **You are administering an instance of your Oracle database. Which of the following choices identifies a command that can be used to tell Oracle to temporarily cease database operations?**

    A. `startup nomount`

    B. `alter database open read only`

    C. `alter system suspend`

    D. `alter system resume`

11. **You need to shut down the Oracle database on short notice. Which of the following choices indicates the command you would use if you were prepared to let Oracle execute instance recovery the next time the database was opened?**

    A. `shutdown abort`

    B. `shutdown transactional`

C. `shutdown normal`

D. `shutdown immediate`

12. **The following excerpt of a trace file was taken from an Oracle database:**

```
Tue Jul 18 17:04:33 2000
alter database dismount
Completed: alter database dismount
archiving is disabled
Dump file c:\Oracle\admin\orcl\bdump\orclALRT.LOG
Tue Jul 18 17:05:00 2000
ORACLE V9.0.1.0.0 - Production vsnsta=0
vsnsql=d vsnxtr=3
Windows NT V4.10, OS V192.0, CPU type 586
Starting up ORACLE RDBMS Version: 9.0.1.0.0.
System parameters with non-default values:
  processes                = 59
  shared_pool_size         = 15728640
  java_pool_size           = 20971520
  disk_asynch_io           = FALSE
  control_files            = c:\Oracle\ORADATA\orcl\control01.ctl,
c:\Oracle\ORADATA\orcl\control02.ctl
  db_block_buffers         = 200
  db_block_size            = 2048
  compatible               = 9.0.1.0.0
  log_buffer               = 8192
  log_checkpoint_interval  = 10000
  log_checkpoint_timeout   = 0
```

Which of the following choices identifies the most likely name for that trace file?

A. `orclDBW0.trc`

B. `orclLGWR.trc`

C. `orclALRT.trc`

D. `orcl13095.trc`

13. **You are preparing to create an Oracle database. Which of the following parameters must be changed in your `init.ora` file in order to create a new database that will not interfere with any existing databases on the machine hosting Oracle when you've copied the `init.ora` file from one of those other databases for use in this one?**

A. CONTROL_FILES

B. DB_BLOCK_SIZE

C. DB_DOMAIN

D. SHARED_POOL_SIZE

14. You are using the Database Configuration Assistant to configure your Oracle database. Which of the following terms pertains to the creation of an object from which creation of other databases can be based?

A. Clone

B. Copy

C. Template

D. Terminal

15. You have just created an Oracle database using the `create database` command. To which of the following tablespaces will any datafile identified as part of the `datafile` clause for the `create database` command belong?

A. DATA

B. INDEX

C. UNDOTBS

D. SYSTEM

16. You are about to create your Oracle data dictionary for use with the database. Which of the following users would you connect to the database as for this purpose in Oracle9*i* and later releases?

A. SYSTEM

B. OUTLN

C. INTERNAL

D. SYS

17. You are identifying dictionary objects in the Oracle database. Which of the following is a view in the data dictionary?

A. V$DATABASE

B. DBA_TABLES

C. SYS.AUD$

D. EMP

18. Use the following code block to answer this question:

```
TEXT
---------------------------------------------
declare
  x varchar2(10);
begin
  x := 'hello world';
  dbms_output.put_line(x);
end;
```

Which of the following views might this data?

A. DBA_ERRORS

B. DBA_SOURCE

C. DBA_VIEWS

D. DBA_TRIGGERS

19. Use the following code block to answer this question:

```
SQL> select text from DBA_views where view_name =
  2  'DBA_TABLES';
TEXT
-------------------------------------------------------------

select u.name, o.name,
       decode(bitand(t.property, 4194400), 0, ts.name, null),
```

Which of the following choices identifies a formatting command that can be used for displaying the rest of the output?

A. set long 9999

B. column text format a9999

C. set long 50

D. column text format a50

20. Your attempts to start the Oracle database have failed. After looking in the appropriate location, you ascertain the value for the CONTROL_FILES parameter to be set to /u01/oradata/orcl/control01.ctl. Which of the following choices identifies the likely next step you would take to troubleshoot the problem?

A. Verify the actual directory location of your control file.

B. Check the hardware to see if the memory card is defective.

C. Verify the actual directory location of your SYSTEM datafile.

D. Check to see if you have created two redo logs.

21. **Examine the following excerpt from an init.ora file:**

```
DB_CREATE_ONLINE_LOG_DEST_1 = /u01/oradata/db1
DB_CREATE_ONLINE_LOG_DEST_2 = /u02/oradata/db1
DB_CREATE_ONLINE_LOG_DEST_3 = /u03/oradata/db1
DB_CREATE_FILE_DEST = /u04/oradata/db1
```

Which of the following choices does *not* identify the location where Oracle will place you control file when the database gets created?

A. /u01/oradata/db1

B. /u02/oradata/db1

C. /u03/oradata/db1

D. /u04/oradata/db1

22. **You are using OMF in conjunction with management of your Oracle database control file. Which of the following choices identifies an aspect of control file management that Oracle handles regardless of whether OMF is used or not?**

A. Placement of the control file in the appropriate directory

B. Multiplexing control files to multiple destinations

C. Updates to the contents of the control file when new tablespaces are added

D. Assigning values automatically to the CONTROL_FILES parameter

23. **You are implementing control file multiplexing. Which of the following choices identifies the method you can use in order to generate the control file copies that Oracle will maintain?**

A. Issue `alter database backup controlfile to `*`filename.`*

B. Make a copy of the control file with the database shut down.

C. Issue `alter database backup controlfile to trace.`

D. Make a copy of the control file with the database still running.

24. **You are analyzing the redo log structure of your Oracle database. Which of the following choices identifies the name of the background process**

that writes changes from online redo logs to archived copies in support of a database running in ARCHIVELOG mode?

A. LGWR

B. CKPT

C. DBW0

D. ARC0

25. You have implemented OMF for redo log management. Which of the following choices reflects a log filename that might be employed when OMF is enabled?

A. `log01.log`

B. `logORCL01.log`

C. `1_2.log`

D. `ora_1_asdf1234.log`

26. You issue the following statement on the Oracle database:

```
create tablespace tbs_temp
datafile '/u05/oradata/oracle/tbs_temp01.dbf' size 600M
extent management dictionary online;
```

Which of the following choices correctly describes the tablespace you just created?

A. You created a locally managed temporary tablespace.

B. You created a dictionary-managed temporary tablespace.

C. You created a locally managed permanent tablespace.

D. You created a dictionary-managed permanent tablespace.

27. You are creating tablespaces in Oracle. Which of the following keywords or clauses permits the datafiles of a tablespace to grow automatically in order to accommodate data growth?

A. `default storage`

B. `extent management`

C. `autoextend`

D. `datafile`

28. You want to configure space allocation in temporary tablespaces. Which of the following choices identifies a feature in Oracle that, when implemented, will force the tablespace segment allocations to all be the same size regardless of storage allocations defined on objects placed in the tablespace?

    A. default storage

    B. storage

    C. uniform extent management

    D. autoextend

29. You are about to drop a tablespace. Which of the following statements can be used for dropping tablespaces that contain parent tables in foreign key relationships?

    A. alter database datafile offline drop

    B. alter tablespace offline immediate

    C. drop tablespace cascade constraints

    D. drop tablespace including contents

30. You alter a tablespace's **default storage** settings in the Oracle database to increase the size of initial extents. Which of the following choices identifies when the change will take effect for tables that already exist in that tablespace?

    A. The change takes effect immediately.

    B. The change takes effect when data is added to the table.

    C. The change takes effect when data is removed from the table.

    D. The change will not take effect for existing tables.

31. You are implementing OMF on your Oracle database. When OMF is enabled, Oracle manages creation and removal of datafiles from the host system for which of the following tablespaces?

    A. SYSTEM tablespace only

    B. UNDO tablespace only

    C. TEMP tablespace only

    D. All tablespaces in the database

32. **Examine the following code block:**

```
create database mydb
controlfile reuse
character set US7ASCII
national character set US7ASCII
datafile '/u01/oradata/mydb/mydb01.dbf' size 400M
logfile group 1 ('/u02/oradata/mydb/redo01.log') size 10M,
        group 2 ('/u03/oradata/mydb/redo02.log') size 10M
default temporary tablespace temp
  tempfile '/u04/oradata/mydb/temp01.dbf' size 1024M
undo tablespace undotbs
 datafile '/u05/oradata/mydb/undo01.dbf' size 1024M
noarchivelog;
```

Which of the following choices identifies a tablespace that will not be created by the command shown in the previous code block?

A. SYSTEM

B. UNDOTBS

C. DATA

D. TEMP

33. **You create a locally managed tablespace with the following statement:**

```
SQL> create tablespace DATA datafile
  2   'c:\oracle\oradata\orcl\DATA01.dbf'
  3   size 150M reuse
  4   extent management local
  5   uniform size 500K online;
Tablespace created.
```

After creating the tablespace, you create a table with the `initial` set to 100KB and `minextents` set to 3 in the `storage` clause. After the table is created, how much space will the table occupy in the tablespace?

A. 100KB

B. 300KB

C. 500KB

D. 1,500KB

34. You want to create a locally managed tablespace for housing sort segments in Oracle. Which of the following statements would be appropriate for the purpose with respect to allocation of segments and extents?

A. `create temporary tablespace temp01 datafile`
`'/u01/oradata/orcl/temp01.dbf' size 100M extent`
`management local;`

B. `create temporary tablespace temp01 tempfile`
`'/u01/oradata/orcl/temp01.dbf' size 100M extent`
`management local;`

C. `create tablespace temp01 datafile`
`'/u01/oradata/orcl/temp01.dbf' size 100M extent`
`management local temporary;`

D. `create tablespace temp01 tempfile`
`'/u01/oradata/orcl/temp01.dbf' size 100M extent`
`management local temporary;`

35. You define a locally managed tablespace using the following syntax:

```
SQL> create tablespace DATA datafile
  2  'c:\oracle\oradata\orcl\DATA01.dbf'
  3  size 150M reuse
  4  extent management local online;
Tablespace created.
```

Which of the following choices indicates the `storage allocation` clause left out but implied by Oracle when this tablespace was created?

A. `autoallocate`

B. `autoallocate size 1M`

C. `uniform`

D. `uniform size 1M`

36. A table was just created on your Oracle database with six extents allocated to it. Which of the following factors most likely caused the table to have so many extents allocated?

A. The value for `minextents` setting

B. The value for `pctincrease` setting

C. The value for `maxextents` setting

D. By default, Oracle allocates six extents to all database objects.

37. You want to determine the amount of space that has been allocated to the EMP table owned by SCOTT in Oracle, which is stored in tablespace DATA. Which of the following choices identifies the SQL statement you might use for this purpose?

A. `select blocks from dba_tables where table_name 5 'EMP' and owner 5 'SCOTT';`

B. `select sum(bytes) from dba_free_space where tablespace_name 5 'DATA';`

C. `select sum(bytes) from dba_extents where segment_name 5 'EMP' and owner 5 'SCOTT';`

D. `select * from dba_objects where object_name 5 'EMP' and owner 5 'SCOTT';`

38. You are administering the Oracle database. A user approaches you to inform you that he has just received the ORA-15555 error. Which of the following choices describes the reason this user has received the error?

A. The user remained connected overnight, and his connection has timed out.

B. The user has queried a read-inconsistent view of data in the process of being changed by a long-running transaction.

C. The user's long-running transaction has taken so long that space for undo information has been exhausted.

D. The user's `drop table` command took too long, and the database needs time to quiesce.

39. The Oracle database with undo tablespaces UNDO_TBS1 and UNDO_TBS2 was opened with undo management enabled for this database. In a prior session, the `alter system set undo_tablespace _ UNDO_TBS1` command was issued. However, the appropriate parameter instructing Oracle which undo tablespace to use was omitted from `init.ora`. Which of the following choices correctly describes what happens when the first user connecting to Oracle initiates her first transaction?

A. The database will open, but only the system undo segment will be online.

B. The database will open, but no undo segments will be online.

C. The database will open and all undo segments in UNDO_TBS1 will be online.

D. Oracle will return errors and the database will not open.

40. **The Oracle database with undo tablespaces UNDO_TBS1 and UNDO_TBS2 was opened with undo management enabled for this database. In a prior session, the `alter system set undo_tablespace _ UNDO_TBS1` command was issued. In the `init.ora` file, the UNDO_TABLESPACE parameter was set to UNDOTBS1. Which of the following choices correctly describes what happens when the first user connecting to Oracle initiates her first transaction?**

A. The database will open, but only the system undo segment will be online.

B. The database will open, but no undo segments will be online.

C. The database will open and all undo segments in UNDO_TBS1 will be online.

D. Oracle will return errors and the database will not open.

41. **You are attempting to manage undo segments manually while automatic undo management is enabled in your system. Which of the following choices identifies an appropriate method to configure Oracle to enable this situation to occur?**

A. Set UNDO_MANAGEMENT to AUTO.

B. Set UNDO_SUPRESS_ERRORS to FALSE.

C. Set UNDO_MANAGEMENT to MANUAL.

D. Set UNDO_RETENTION to 1800.

42. **The rows inside three Oracle tables supporting a customer order entry system are frequently accessed together by means of a table join. Because data is always being added to the tables, you leave a lot of extra space inside each block to accommodate growth. Which of the following types of tables would be useful for storing the data in this context?**

A. Temporary table

B. Index-organized table

C. Cluster table

D. Standard Oracle table

43. **Your DATA tablespace is locally managed and uses uniform extent allocation. You issue the following statement:**

```
CREATE TABLE EMPLOYEE
(empid           NUMBER(10),
lastname         VARCHAR2(25),
firstname        VARCHAR2(25),
salary           NUMBER(10,4),
CONSTRAINT       pk_employee_01
PRIMARY KEY      (empid))
TABLESPACE data
PCTFREE    20   PCTUSED    50
INITRANS   1    MAXTRANS   255
NOCACHE         LOGGING
STORAGE ( INITIAL 100K   NEXT  150K
          MINEXTENTS 4  MAXEXTENTS  300
          PCTINCREASE 20 );
```

Which of the following statements is true about the table you just created?

A. The table is created in the same tablespace as temporary segments will be housed.

B. The first segment allocated for this table will be 100KB of contiguous blocks.

C. Redo information will be generated for the creation of this table.

D. When full table scans are issued on the EMPLOYEE table, blocks from the table will persist in the buffer cache for a long time after the statement executes.

44. **User FITZPATRICK creates a temporary table using the following statement:**

```
SQL> create global temporary table FITZTEMPTAB
  2  (name varchar2(10), value number, use_date date)
  3  on commit delete rows;
Table created
```

FITZPATRICK then informs users MCGILLICUDDY and OBRYAN of his temporary table. While each user is connected to Oracle and populating table FITZTEMPTAB, OBRYAN issues truncate table FITZTEMPTAB. Which of the following users had his or her records removed temporary table by this action?

A. FITZPATRICK only

B. OBRYAN only

    C. OBRYAN and FITZPATRICK only

    D. OBRYAN, FITZPATRICK and MCGILLICUDDY

45. **User OBRYAN adds a record to FITZTEMPTAB, defined using the code block shown in the previous question. At what point will the data added to FITZTEMPTAB by OBRYAN be removed from the temporary table?**

    A. When FITZPATRICK `commits` the transaction

    B. When OBRYAN `commits` the transaction

    C. When OBRYAN logs off of Oracle

    D. When FITZPATRICK issues `truncate table FITZTEMPTAB`

46. **You just issued the following statement: `alter table sales drop column profit`. Which of the following choices identifies when the column will actually be removed from Oracle?**

    A. Immediately following statement execution

    B. After the `alter table drop unused columns` command is issued

    C. After the `alter table set unused column` command is issued

    D. After the `alter table modify` command is issued

47. **You wish to determine how many columns in the EMPLOYEE table are marked unused for later removal. Which of the following methods would be appropriate for the purpose?**

    A. Querying the DBA_TABLES view

    B. Using the `describe` command

    C. Querying the DBA_UNUSED_COLS view

    D. Querying the DBA_UNUSED_COL_TABS view

48. **You want to rebuild an index in Oracle. Which of the following choices identifies the reason why rebuilding indexes online is possible in Oracle?**

    A. Less restrictive locks on underlying base tables

    B. More restrictive locks on the index rebuilt

    C. Use of a standby database for temporary storage

    D. Use of a temporary table for temporary storage

49. You terminate monitoring the MY_IDX index after monitoring its use for several hours. Which of the following statements is correct regarding V$OBJECT_USAGE in this context?

A. Oracle removes the record corresponding to MY_IDX from V$OBJECT_USAGE.

B. Oracle fills in the END_MONITORING column in the record corresponding to MY_IDX in the V$OBJECT_USAGE view.

C. Oracle fills in the USED column in the record corresponding to MY_IDX in the V$OBJECT_USAGE view.

D. Oracle clears all values in the record corresponding to MY_IDX in the V$OBJECT_USAGE view.

50. You implement an integrity constraint in an Oracle database using the following command: `alter table EMP add constraint PK_EMP_01 primary key (EMPNO)`. Which of the following statements is true about the constraint you just added?

A. The constraint will cause Oracle to generate a bitmap index to support its activities.

B. The constraint will reference back to the primary key in another table for valid values.

C. The constraint will not be created unless all values in the EMPNO column are unique and not NULL.

D. The constraint will enforce uniqueness, but NULL values will be permitted.

51. The following tablespace information was taken from your Oracle database:

```
SQL> select tablespace_name, contents from dba_tablespaces;
TABLESPACE_NAME     CONTENTS
------------------ -------------
SYSTEM              PERMANENT
DATA                PERMANENT
INDEXES             PERMANENT
UNDOTBS             UNDO
TEMP                TEMPORARY
USERS               PERMANENT
```

You create a user in this database with the following command: `create user serena identified by tranquil1`. Which of the following choices identifies the location where Oracle will place SERENAs new table that she creates with the `create table mytab (col1 number primary key)` command?

A. SYSTEM

B. DATA

C. TEMP

D. UNDOTBS

52. You issue the following command in Oracle: `alter user JOSEPHINE default tablespace SYSTEM quota 0 on SYSTEM`. Assuming JOSEPHINE has the appropriate privileges to do so, which of the following commands will JOSEPHINE not be able to issue as a result of this action?

A. `create table mytab (col1 number primary key);`

B. `create procedure myproc begin null; end;`

C. `create function myfunc return null begin null; end;`

D. `create table mytab2 (col1 number primary key) tablespace data;`

53. You issue the following command in Oracle, and Oracle responds by providing the following information:

```
SQL> select * from dba_users where username = 'SYS';
USERNAME                               USER_ID PASSWORD
------------------ -------------------------- ---------------

ACCOUNT_STATUS     LOCK_DATE                  EXPIRY_DATE
------------------ -------------------------- ---------------

DEFAULT_TABLESPACE TEMPORARY_TABLESPACE       CREATED
------------------ -------------------------- ---------------

PROFILE            INITIAL_RSRC_CONSUMER_GROUP EXTERNAL_NAME
------------------ -------------------------- ---------------

SYS                                          0 D4C5016086B2DC6A
OPEN
SYSTEM             TEMP                       06-JUN-01
DEFAULT            SYS_GROUP
```

Which of the following statements is true regarding the user information shown previously?

A. No user may log into Oracle as SYS.

B. If SYS creates a table without specifying a `tablespace` clause, the table will be placed into the TEMP tablespace.

C. The password for the SYS user on this database is D4C5016086B2DC6A.

D. If SYS performs a disk sort, the temporary segments will be placed in the TEMP tablespace.

54. You want to use composite resource limits in the Oracle database. Which of the following commands must be issued so that composite resources are assigned a value for composite limits?

A. `alter system`

B. `alter resource cost`

C. `alter profile`

D. `alter user`

55. You are defining resource limits for use with profiles. Which of the following is not a resource limit that can be set in conjunction with composite limits on your Oracle database?

A. IDLE_TIME

B. CPU_PER_SESSION

C. PRIVATE_SGA

D. CONNECT_TIME

56. You create a profile using the following command:

```
CREATE PROFILE myprofile LIMIT
SESSIONS_PER_USER 1
CPU_PER_CALL 20
CONNECT_TIME 240
IDLE_TIME 20
PRIVATE_SGA 1024;
```

Which of the following choices best identifies how Oracle will determine what the value for the CPU_PER_SESSION limit will be?

A. Oracle uses the same value as CPU_PER_CALL from this `create profile` command.

B. Oracle uses the value for CPU_PER_SESSION from the SYS_PROFILE profile.

C. Oracle uses the value for CPU_PER_SESSION from the DEFAULT profile.

D. Oracle sets CPU_PER_SESSION to unlimited.

57. **You create a profile using the following code block:**

```
CREATE PROFILE tmp_profile LIMIT
   FAILED_LOGIN_ATTEMPTS 3
   PASSWORD_LOCK_TIME unlimited
   PASSWORD_LIFE_TIME 30
   PASSWORD_REUSE_TIME 180
   PASSWORD_VERIFY_FUNCTION my_pwver
   PASSWORD_GRACE_TIME 5;
```

Which of the following choices identifies a true statement about the profile you just created?

A. After three failed login attempts, a user assigned this profile will have to wait three days before trying to login to Oracle again.

B. After 180 days, a user assigned this profile can reuse his or her password.

C. A user assigned this profile must change his or her password every 30 minutes.

D. A user has up to five minutes to specify a password the first time he or she logs in before Oracle automatically locks the account.

58. **You want to set up password management features in your Oracle database such that users may never reuse a password and that a user has three days to change his or her default password the first time he or she logs into Oracle before the account gets locked. Which of the following choices identifies the statement you will use for this purpose?**

A. `alter profile default limit failed_login_attempts 3 password_reuse_time unlimited;`

B. `alter profile default limit password_grace_time 3 password_reuse_limit unlimited;`

C. `alter profile default limit failed_login_attempts 3 password_grace_time unlimited;`

D. `alter profile default limit password_reuse_time 3 failed_login_attempts unlimited;`

59. You are attempting to determine which profiles have resource settings that do not impose limits on user resource utilization. Which of the following queries would be the most useful for this purpose?

    A. `select profile from dba_profiles where profile = (select username from dba_users where profile = 'UNLIMITED');`

    B. `select profile from dba_profiles where limit = (select unit_cost from resource_cost where resource_name = 'CPU_PER_SESSION');`

    C. `select profile from dba_profiles where limit = 'UNLIMITED';`

    D. `select distinct profile from dba_profiles where limit = 'UNLIMITED';`

60. You grant the **SYSDBA** privilege to a user of the Oracle database. Which of the following abilities does this privilege bestow upon its grantee?

    A. Ability to query all tables in Oracle

    B. Ability to grant the SYSDBA privilege to others

    C. Ability to back up the database

    D. Ability to delete information from any table in Oracle

Answers to Practice Exam I

I. D.   ARCH and LGWR

Explanation   The ARCH and LGWR processes may have a tendency to conflict with one another when log switches occur because both processes will attempt to access the same disk resources at the same time during this operation. Choice A is incorrect because SMON handles instance recovery and tablespace coalescence, while LGWR writes redo information from memory to disk. These two processes should not conflict because datafiles and redo log files won't usually be on the same disk, and there is little overlap between the two functions. Choice B is incorrect because the RECO process handles transaction recovery between distributed systems and will not usually interfere with ARCH's archiving of redo logs. Choice C is incorrect because PMON handles process recovery when user processes fail while DBWR handles writing dirty buffers to disk—two functions that normally will not cause I/O or other types of contention. **(Topic 7.3)**

2. B.   Control file

Explanation   Creating a new redo log on your Oracle database adds information to the control file. The shared pool is incorrect because information is added to that resource when SQL or PL/SQL statements are issued by users against Oracle. The SGA is a superset of the shared pool making it wrong as well. A Program Global Area (PGA) is a memory region containing data and control information for a single process. **(Topic 6.1)**

3. A.   SYSTEM

Explanation   Using standard tablespace naming conventions, the SYSTEM tablespace contains all Oracle data dictionary objects. TEMP is incorrect because it identifies the temporary tablespace, which is designed to hold temporary segments for disk sorts. RBS is also incorrect because that tablespace is designed to store undo segments. Finally, the INDEX tablespace is incorrect because that nomenclature is used to identify the tablespace that holds indexes. **(Topic 5.1)**

4. B.   SYS

Explanation   Objects in the Oracle data dictionary are part of the SYS schema. Although the SYSTEM user owns some important database objects, the dictionary views and their underlying tables are not one of them, making that choice incorrect. The PUBLIC user is more of an alias for granting access for various things to many users, not so much a user in and of itself, thus making that choice incorrect as well. Finally, user SCOTT is commonly found in training Oracle databases, but its existence is by no means guaranteed—nor will it ever own objects as critical as the data dictionary. **(Topic 5.1)**

5. C. Profiles

Explanation Profiles are appropriately used for the purpose of limiting a user's ability to manipulate host machine resources, making it the correct answer. Undo segments provide transaction-level read consistency, but do not limit usage of the host machine in any substantial way, making this choice incorrect. Roles limit the user's ability to perform actions based on the privileges granted to those roles, but because the user may need a certain type of access and may be able to properly handle that access using appropriate methods, this choice is incorrect because you have no accurate way to limit resource usage using roles. Finally, parameter files such as `init.ora` may contain settings that limit resource usage, perhaps through limiting the number of users that may connect at any one time, but this answer is incorrect because `init.ora` parameters will do little to restrict a user's misuse of host machine resources once connected. **(Topic 14.3)**

6. B. Increase `pctfree`

Explanation Actually, although `pctfree` isn't the complete solution, it will reduce chaining for future records added to the table. `pctused` is not a component in the solution because that parameter simply reduces the frequency a data block will spend on a freelist. Changing the value set for `pctincrease` or `next` may decrease the number of extents a table will allocate if that table is growing fast, but this parametric change does little to nothing about chaining at the block level, making both those answers incomplete and incorrect. **(Topic 9.3)**

7. A. Multiplexing

Explanation The term *multiplexing* is the correct answer because that term refers to having online copies (as opposed to archives) of redo logs. These logs are then spread across several disks to reduce I/O bottlenecks. Archiving is incorrect because this choice means that the copy of the redo log information made will not be available online. Neither redoing nor logging accurately describes what the question asks for. **(Topic 7.4)**

8. D. Granting privileges to roles directly

Explanation The choice mentioning the use of roles is the correct answer. You would first grant the privileges to roles, and then give the roles to users. Profiles are not used for granting or revoking privileges or access; they are used instead for limiting host machine processing, making those two choices incorrect. Also, granting privileges directly to users is the support nightmare you are trying to avoid. **(Topic 17.1)**

9. B.   Number of datafiles

Explanation   The size of redo logs can have an effect on checkpoint intervals, because larger redo logs usually mean less frequent log switches. Fewer log switches mean fewer checkpoints. The number of datafiles will affect the duration of a checkpoint, because although the CKPT process has to write checkpoint sequence information to each datafile header (and more datafiles means more headers), this is not a time-consuming activity and happens in parallel with other activities occurring during a checkpoint. Finally, the two init.ora parameters identified in this question have a direct correlation on the frequency of checkpoints. **(Topic 7.3)**

10. B.   High pctused

Explanation   A high setting for pctused will make Oracle fill data blocks with new records when comparatively fewer records are deleted from the block. In contrast, a low setting for pctused causes Oracle to fill data blocks only after many records have been deleted from the block. pctused identifies the threshold for Oracle to return a block to a freelist for addition of new records. Lowering pctused will make Oracle manage its block space utilization less actively, whereas pctfree simply indicates how much space should be left over for updates that make records grow. **(Topic 9.3)**

11. C.   Issue alter user SPANKY PROFILE LIMITER, where LIMITER is a profile.

Explanation   The correct method for limiting Oracle's use of the host machine on SPANKY's behalf is with a profile, not a role, eliminating half the choices right there. The next aspect to consider is how to properly assign a profile to a user. This is accomplished with an alter user statement, not a grant, making the choice indicating a grant statement where LIMITER is a profile incorrect. **(Topic 14.3)**

12. D.   Hash clusters

Explanation   Range operations do not perform well when the data is stored in a cluster. Though it is more efficient in general to use comparison operations instead of range operations, normal tables will work fine with range operations, making that choice incorrect. Indexes can process range operations just fine as well, making that choice incorrect. So can index-organized tables, which makes that choice incorrect. **(Topic 12.1)**

13. B.   restricted session

Explanation   The DBA needs the restricted session privilege to make the database open but not available for users. The DBA could simply revoke the create session privilege from all users and simply leave the database open, but this task may require issuing several revoke commands, followed by the same number of `grants` later. It's easier to use `restricted session`. The CONNECT role is similar to `create session` in that `create session` is granted to CONNECT, which is then often granted to users. There is no such thing as a `mount` privilege. **(Topic 16.1)**

14. A. `drop table`

Explanation   You cannot alter or resize the initial extent on your table using the `alter table` command, making that choice incorrect. Nor can you use the `resize` or `coalesce` keywords, as these are used as part of tablespace operations. Your only alternative is to drop and re-create the table using different storage settings. **(Topic 11.2)**

15. B. `temporary tablespace`

Explanation   By assigning a `temporary tablespace` other than SYSTEM, the DBA reduces the possibility that a user will interfere with the overall operation of the Oracle database when disk sorts are performed by users. The `identified by` clause is incorrect because that is where the password is assigned, not disk usage. The `default tablespace` is also incorrect even though that clause is used to define disk usage because the disk usage is for creating permanent objects, not temporary ones. Finally, the `default role` clause is only available in `alter user` statements, not `create user` statements, and is used to change the permissions available to the user. **(Topic 15.1)**

16. E. Nothing—`SYSDBA` privileges are not required for these actions.

Explanation   The correct answer is nothing. Because the DBA does not plan to use remote administration for startup, shutdown, backup, or recovery, there is no need for a password file. Instead, the DBA can simply connect in normal mode using the SYS or other privileged account to create and administer users and tablespaces. **(Topic 2.4)**

17. A. DBW0

Explanation   DBWR, although affected by the transaction logging mechanism— particularly during log switches and checkpoints—is not an actual part of Oracle's transaction logging mechanism. The redo log buffer, LGWR, CKPT, and archive/online redo logs are all part of the operation of Oracle's transaction logging mechanism. **(Topic 7.1)**

18. E. The `storage` clause is improperly defined.

Explanation   The correct answer to this question is that the `storage` clause is improperly defined. Instead of simply naming the different storage parameters loose in the statement, you must bundle them into a `storage` clause, which is denoted with the `storage` keyword and set inside parentheses. The primary key is declared properly, so there are no problems on that end. You never need to put index and table data in the same tablespace, and in fact there are compelling reasons not to do so, making that choice wrong as well. Finally, you do not need to define a separate not NULL constraint on the EMPID column because the primary-key index will handle it for you. For reasons of a malformed `storage` clause, the `create table statement` will not succeed, making that choice incorrect as well. **(Topic 11.1)**

19. C.   SIMON will not be able to add records to the EMP table anymore.

Explanation   When object privileges given `with grant option` are revoked from a user who has given them to other users, Oracle cascades the revocation. So, not only will ANN lose the ability to add records to EMP (making the choice stating she can continue to add records to EMP incorrect), but SIMON loses the ability as well, making that the correct answer. The DBA does not lose the ability to add records to EMP, because she is the person revoking privileges. ANN's records will stay in the EMP table, even though she cannot add new ones either, making that choice incorrect as well. **(Topic 16.2)**

20. B.   `pctused = 40`, `pctfree = 30`

Explanation   The choice where `pctused` is 99 and `pctfree` is 1 should be discarded immediately because you should never set the space allocation options in a way that the two equal 100 added together. Because rows are never removed, you can set `pctused` relatively low. This leaves you with the two choices where `pctused` is 40. Next, consider row growth. The rows in this table are going to grow substantially, which means you need a higher `pctfree` than just 10 percent. Remember, the largest columns are going to be NULL on initial insert and then populated later. To avoid row migration, you are best off choosing `pctused = 40`, `pctfree = 30`. **(Topic 9.3)**

21. A.   OPTIMAL

Explanation   The OPTIMAL `storage` clause is used primarily for storing undo segments in Oracle. You do not use it for any other database object. All the rest, namely INITIAL, PCTINCREASE, and NEXT, are valid for use. Be aware that you do not have to configure this aspect of undo segments if you use automatic undo management in Oracle. **(Topic 10.3)**

22. D.   `default role`

Explanation   You do not use the `default role` clause in `create user` statements. It is part of the `alter user` syntax because when a user is created, the user doesn't have any roles granted to it yet. `identified by` is for password definition, and is part of the `create user` statement. `temporary tablespace` keeps the user's disk sorts out of the SYSTEM tablespace and is part of the `create user` statement. `profile`, `account unlock`, and `password expire` are all aspects of a robust `create user` statement, and therefore all these choices are incorrect. **(Topic 17.2)**

23. A.   Run `pupbld.sql` as SYSTEM.

Explanation   In this situation, Oracle needs user profile information to be generated for the users. In the error output for this message, Oracle will instruct you abort what is needed to resolve the issue, which is to run `pupbld.sql` to build the product user profile information. You do not need to shut down the database with the `abort` option—moreover, you shouldn't, because that will require a database recovery. Dropping and re-creating the users will not help either—they will get the same error ten minutes later when they try logging on again. Finally, you shouldn't waste your time dropping and re-creating the database. **(Topic 4.3)**

24. D.   SMON

Explanation   SMON coalesces free space in a tablespace on a regular basis, as well as manages instance recovery after instance failure. You will learn more about instance recovery in Practice Exam 3. LGWR is wrong because that process simply handles writing log information from memory to disk. ARCH handles copying online redo logs to archive destinations and is also wrong. DBWR is incorrect because it only performs writes of data blocks from buffer cache to disk, and PMON is wrong because it handles process recovery—something you will cover on the OCP DBA Fundamentals II exam. **(Topic 8.1)**

25. C.   One tablespace can have many datafiles.

Explanation   A tablespace is a collection of one or more datafiles residing on your host machine that Oracle treats as one logical area for storing data. This fact eliminates the choice that says one tablespace has only one datafile. Also, the two other choices basically state the same thing—that one datafile can contain many tablespaces—and this is just not true. **(Topic 8.1)**

26. B.   Increase value on CPU_PER_SESSION and decrease value on CONNECT_TIME.

Explanation   The correct answer is increase value on CPU_PER_SESSION, and decrease value on CONNECT_TIME. This makes resource costs for CPU time higher, and connection time lower. The COMPOSITE_LIMIT increase is too imprecise— remember, one of the resource costs is increasing, while the other is decreasing. Increasing COMPOSITE_LIMIT will only increase a user's ability to use host system resources. PRIVATE_SGA has nothing to do with CPU time or connection time, and therefore is incorrect. **(Topic 14.2)**

27. C.   An uncommitted transaction is still in progress.

Explanation   The first thing to look at in this situation is the tablespace name: UNDOTBS01. Oracle recommends having different tablespaces for different purposes. A tablespace containing the string *RBS* or *UNDOTBS* will most likely contain undo segments. In addition, if one of the undo segments is online and in use (indicated by a session having a lock on it), you will get the ORA-01546 error when you try to take the tablespace offline. A tablespace containing overextended tables can be taken offline, so that answer is incorrect. The init.ora file being unavailable has no impact on taking a tablespace offline, but it might interfere with restarting your Oracle database. Although in some situations you might see performance degradation because of an online redo log being archived, this will not interfere with taking a tablespace offline. **(Topic 10.2)**

28. A.   Library cache

Explanation   The library cache, sometimes referred to as the shared SQL area, stores parse and execution plan information for SQL and PL/SQL statements running on your database. The row and dictionary caches are one in the same and store data dictionary information for quick retrieval, and thus are incorrect. The large pool allocation heap is used in multithreaded server (MTS) systems for session memory, by parallel execution for message buffers, and by backup processes for disk I/O buffers. Finally, the buffer cache stores data blocks for quicker retrieval by server processes, and is also incorrect. **(Topic 1.1)**

29. C.   When the shared pool is flushed

Explanation   The data in the buffer cache will not be saved to disk when you flush the shared pool. You flush the shared pool with the `alter system flush shared_pool` command. Items in the buffer cache are saved to disk when a timeout occurs and when a checkpoint occurs. Because a checkpoint happens at every log switch, buffer cache information is saved to disk when a log switch occurs, too. **(Topic 7.3)**

30. B.   Run `utlpwmg.sql`.

Explanation   Running `utlpwmg.sql` is a step you accomplish for setting up password management on your Oracle database. Unlike other areas of resource limitation, you do not need to set the RESOURCE_LIMIT parameter to TRUE, making that choice incorrect. You should also not drop the DEFAULT profile beforehand. Creating a password verification function is optional, because Oracle provides you with one in the software release. **(Topic 14.1)**

31. A. Looking in the DBA_TS_QUOTAS dictionary view

Explanation   The DBA_TS_QUOTAS view contains quota information for users and tablespaces. This is the DBA's best bet in identifying what ATHENA's limits are and how they could be set differently. DBA_USERS only identifies default and temporary tablespaces for ATHENA, which isn't useful because the `create table` statement identifies its own tablespace storage. DBA_TAB_COLUMNS won't even have information about this table or anything related to tablespace quotas, because it lists the columns in every table on the database. The DBA_TABLESPACES choice is a good distractor. To avoid choosing the wrong answer, you need to be sure you are familiar with the use of dictionary views like this one. **(Topic 15.3)**

32. A. DEFAULT

Explanation   All users are assigned the DEFAULT profile if none is identified in the `create user` statement. CONNECT and RESOURCE are both roles, so those choices are incorrect. Although there is no `profile` clause in this statement, it would be incorrect to assume that no profile gets assigned to the user because of it. **(Topic 15.1)**

33. B. DBA_PROFILES

Explanation   DBA_PROFILES is the dictionary view where you can find information about profiles and the resource settings associated with them. The DBA_USERS view is incorrect because it only identifies what profile is assigned to a user. RESOURCE_COST is incorrect because it only identifies the relative cost assigned to those resources that can be lumped together using resource costing. RESOURCE_LIMIT is incorrect because it is not a view—it is an initialization parameter that must be set in order to use profiles. **(Topic 14.4)**

34. A. `catproc.sql`

Explanation   The `catproc.sql` script must be run after running `catalog.sql` to create your Oracle-supplied packages. `utlpwdmg.sql` is a script you run later to add password management, whereas `utllockt.sql` is a script you also run later to detect whether there are lock-wait events on your database. **(Topic 4.3)**

35. D. Roles

Explanation   Roles permit you to configure password authentication to limit the use of the privileges they bestow. This is accomplished with the `identified by` clause—the same as in the `create` or `alter user` statements. Profiles don't require passwords, nor do tables or undo segments, unless you count the password you supplied to log in to the database. **(Topic 17.2)**

36. C.   Create multiple members for each of your four groups and place them on different disks.

Explanation   To solve this problem, you must create multiple members for each of your four groups and place them on different disks. The `init.ora` file has nothing whatsoever to do with multiplexing online redo logs, so you can eliminate those choices. Finally, although adding groups improves some situations, you are not looking for more redo logs—you are looking for more members in each log. **(Topic 7.4)**

37. A.   EXCEPTIONS

Explanation   The EXCEPTIONS table can be used by the DBA to identify ROWIDs for rows with duplicate primary keys. The DBA_TABLES view is not going to help, because you don't need to know the table, tablespace, or storage information to enable or fix a primary key. USER_TAB_COLUMNS is also of limited value. Finally, AUD$ is no good because that's where audit records are stored. You might be able to find the folks who did it, but that isn't going to solve the problem. **(Topic 13.1)**

38. C.   Grant the CONNECT role to the user.

Explanation   The appropriate resolution is to somehow enable the user to create a session with Oracle. This is done in two ways: either by granting `create session` privileges or by granting the CONNECT role, which has the `create session` privilege granted to it. Unlocking the user's account won't help because he or she hasn't even gotten to the point where they can successfully connect yet, while resetting the user's password and granting `create table` privileges are both incorrect for roughly the same reason. **(Topic 17.5)**

39. C.   Convert your B-tree index to a reverse-key index.

Explanation   Oracle recommends using reverse-key indexes in situations where the leading significant figures of a number or characters in a string are not unique enough to provide the lead-in differentiation required for making an index perform better. If the reverse-key index choices had not been present, the B-tree index choices would have been more correct—making for strong distractors. Any conversion between bitmap and B-tree indexes is unnecessary and detrimental because bitmap and B-tree indexes improve query performance in exactly opposite situations. **(Topic 12.3)**

40. D.   CHAR

Explanation   The CHAR datatype is the most appropriate for this given situation because you want to store data in a fixed-width column. That means the column will contain extra blanks to the full, declared size of the column. VARCHAR, CLOB, and LONG do not let you do this, because they are variable-width column datatypes. Also, ten sentences of text are probably not more than 2,000 characters, the limit for CHAR datatypes in Oracle8. **(Topic 11.2)**

41. B.   Unsuccessful `update` and `delete` statements performed by any user on CAT_TOYS will be recorded.

Explanation   The correct answer is unsuccessful `update` and `delete` statements performed by any user on CAT_TOYS will be recorded. Auditing data change activities `by access` causes Oracle to write one record for each audited statement; in comparison to this, `by session` causes Oracle to write a single record for all SQL statements of the same type issued in the same session. The `whenever not successful` clause means only unsuccessful statements will be recorded. Finally, only the CAT_TOYS table will be audited. **(Topic 16.3)**

42. A.   DBA_IND_COLUMNS

Explanation   You would look in the DBA_IND_COLUMNS to see what the column order for the primary-key index was. The DBA_TAB_COLUMNS will only tell you what columns are in the table. The DBA_INDEXES table will give you structural information about the index, but not its contents. The DBA_CLU_COLUMNS view will only obtain information about clustered columns. **(Topic 12.5)**

43. D.   Nothing—you cannot drop a profile that has been granted to users.

Explanation   The correct answer is nothing. You cannot drop a profile that has been granted to users without specifying the `cascade` option. That option is missing from the statement you issued, so nothing happens. Had you included the `cascade` option, users who had the LTD_PROGRAMMER profile might now have the DEFAULT profile, so watch out for distractors like that one. Otherwise, all other statements are incorrect. **(Topic 14.2)**

44. B.   Increasing the value set for `pctused` on the table

Explanation   You can increase the values set for `pctincrease` and `next` using the `alter table` statement to reduce the number of extents a segment will allocate as part of table growth. If you wanted, you could reorganize the table using EXPORT with the COMPRESS option. However, you couldn't use `pctused` to perform this task. **(Topic 9.3)**

45. D.   SYSTEM segments

Explanation   SYSTEM object segments typically have the lowest turnover of all database segments in Oracle. This is because SYSTEM tables are never dropped and re-created, or truncated (AUD$ table notwithstanding). Undo segments frequently allocate and deallocate extents, as do temporary segments. User-defined tables usually have more volatility than SYSTEM-owned objects. **(Topic 9.5)**

46. D. `shutdown normal`

Explanation You most likely used the `shutdown normal` option to turn off the Oracle database. `shutdown normal` will not end existing sessions; instead, it will wait for users to finish their work and disconnect, but it will not allow others to log in after the `shutdown` command is issued. `shutdown immediate` would have forced user transactions to roll back and disconnected them at the time the statement was issued, whereas `shutdown abort` would simply end database operation, terminating all uncommitted transactions in progress. `shutdown transactional` is a new option that enables users already connected to complete their current transaction, but after that disconnects them in order to speed database shutdown. **(Topic 3.3)**

47. C. The server process obtains information for the user.

Explanation Information is obtained for user processes by means of the server process. DBW0 is incorrect because that process writes data to disk, not from disk into memory. The user process certainly doesn't do this work on its own, and the listener process doesn't actually obtain data from disk for the user either. **(Topic 1.2)**

48. C. The `drop tablespace` command fails because you didn't include the `including contents` option.

Explanation In this situation, the `drop tablespace` command fails because you didn't include the `including contents` option. To drop the tablespace, you must issue `drop tablespace by_tblspc including contents`. There may be some problem with `cascading constraints`, but you don't have enough information to declare this the correct answer, so it's wrong. Obviously, the `drop tablespace` command does not succeed. Finally, you must certainly drop a tablespace after creating it. **(Topic 8.5)**

49. C. SQL*Plus returns an error saying you need to connect to Oracle first.

Explanation After starting SQL*Plus and before you start doing anything substantial with it, you must connect to Oracle as a privileged user. If you don't connect as a privileged user but try performing privileged activities anyway, SQL*Plus returns errors. The database will not shut down until after you issue `shutdown immediate` while connected to Oracle, but once issued, Oracle will disconnect users forcibly and also roll back their transactions. Finally, SQL*Plus most certainly is a command-line mode tool. **(Topic 2.1)**

50. A. Issue `select * from DBA_PARAMETERS;` from SQL*Plus.

Explanation The `select * from DBA_PARAMETERS` statement yields nothing because DBA_PARAMETERS is not a valid dictionary view in Oracle. The V$PARAMETER view is appropriate for this purpose, as is the `show parameters` command in SQL*Plus. Finally, Instance Manager will show you initialization parameters in a GUI display. **(Topic 3.1)**

51. B. Bitmap indexes cannot be unique.

Explanation When you issue this statement, Oracle will give you a syntax error, stating it was looking for the `index` keyword after unique instead of the `bitmap` keyword. Thus, you cannot create bitmap indexes as unique indexes. You certainly can use the `nosort`, `tablespace`, and `asc` keywords in this statement, and in this statement they are all used correctly. However, the `unique bitmap` bit makes it invalid, and Oracle will give you an error. **(Topic 12.2)**

52. D. ROLE_ROLE_PRIVS

Explanation ROLE_ROLE_PRIVS is the correct answer because it displays all the roles and the roles granted to the roles. DBA_ROLE_PRIVS shows only users who have roles granted to them. DBA_TAB_PRIVS shows the users with object privileges granted to them. The USER_SYS_PRIVS view shows only those system privileges granted to you, the user connected to Oracle. **(Topic 17.5)**

53. A. `alter session set NLS_DATE_FORMAT = 'DD-MON-YYYY:HH:MIAM';`

Explanation Because all the statements are roughly the same, you must look carefully at the syntax in order to know what the correct answer is. The proper date format is 'DD-MON-YYYY:HH:MIAM', which obtains you the result 10-FEB-1999:10:15AM. DD-MON-YY:HH24:MI gives you a result of 10-FEB-99:10:15, so it is incorrect, while DD-MON-YY:HH:MIAM gives you 10-FEB-99:10:15AM, which is also incorrect. Finally, DD-MON-YYYY:HH24:MI gives you a result of 10-MON-1999:10:15, which is still incorrect. **(Topic 18.2)**

54. D. Value-based auditing

Explanation Value-based auditing best describes this situation. Statement auditing is not right because you don't want to audit every statement—only those that change a particular column to a particular value. Triggers will work best for this situation. You don't want to audit every access on the ORDERS table either, so object auditing is out. Finally, many different users might have the ability to change order status in several different phases of the order entry and shipment process, so audit by access isn't necessarily appropriate. Value-based auditing is auditing done by triggers or programmatically to detect when specific values change to specific other values. **(Topic 16.3)**

55. B. index

Explanation Of the privileges mentioned, only the `index` privilege is an object privilege. The rest are system privileges. One way to ensure that you understand the difference between system and object privileges is to remember that object privileges give access to objects, whereas system privileges let you create objects. In this case, however, even this basic principle of Oracle privileges is violated in concept because even though the `index` privilege lets you create indexes off of tables, it is still an object privilege. Thus, the best way to distinguish object privileges from system privileges is simply to memorize the object privileges (there are less than a dozen of them) and simply assume everything else is a system privilege. **(Topic 16.1)**

56. C. SORT_AREA_SIZE

Explanation Your INITIAL default storage setting for the temporary tablespace should be some multiple of SORT_AREA_SIZE because this ensures a relationship between the area in memory used for sorts and the utilization of disk space for that purpose when you run out of space in memory. LOG_BUFFER is the size of the redo log buffer and has little to do with disk sorts. DB_BLOCK_BUFFERS is the number of buffers that constitutes the buffer cache, and again there is little relationship between the buffer cache and disk sorts. Finally, SHARED_POOL_SIZE is exactly that—the size of the shared pool—which, again, has little to do with disk sorts. **(Topic 8.6)**

57. B. Cached data is saved immediately to disk.

Explanation Oracle divorces transaction activity from disk I/O by having a database writer process handle writing changes to disk. This activity doesn't necessarily happen immediately, and completion of the `commit` doesn't depend on it happening. All the other activities, such as releasing locks on tables, rows, or undo segments, do happen, however, and a `commit` statement generates a redo entry. **(Topic 1.1)**

58. D. When the statement is executed

Explanation Data changes are made at the time Oracle actually executes the statement. Opening and parsing the statement all occur before the statement is executed, so the data change hasn't occurred yet. `update` statements do not have data to fetch from a cursor the way `select` statements do, so there is no `fetch` activity in a DML statement like an `update`. **(Topic 1.1)**

59. D.   Sequence segment

Explanation_Sequences are not physically stored in a tablespace as database objects. Rather, their definition is stored in the data dictionary and in memory, and called upon when values from the sequence are required. All the other choices identify valid types of segments in Oracle. **(Topic 9.2)**

60. B.   DBA_FREE_SPACE

Explanation   If you only wanted to know how much of a particular tablespace was free, you would use the DBA_FREE_SPACE view. DBA_TABLESPACES AND DBA_EXTENTS will tell you the total allocation for the tablespace and the total amount of space allocated for objects in that tablespace, respectively, and although you could calculate the free space from those two amounts, it is far easier to select the appropriate value from DBA_FREE_SPACE. V$TABLESPACE will only give you the tablespace name and number for the tablespace on the database. **(Topic 9.4)**

Answers to Practice Exam 2

1. A.   V$CONTROLFILE_RECORD_SECTION

Explanation   Information about the name and location of your control files can be found in the two database views V$CONTROLFILE and V$PARAMETER, and in the `init.ora` file. However, the V$CONTROLFILE_RECORD_SECTION will not tell you your control file locations. **(Topic 6.2)**

2. C.   Oracle will leave more space free in data blocks for existing records.

Explanation   By keeping `pctfree` high, Oracle will leave more space free in database blocks for existing records to grow via later `updates`. `pctused` is the storage option that dictates how Oracle manages filling data blocks on tables more or less actively, so those choices should be easily eliminated. **(Topic 9.3)**

3. C.   The statement fails.

Explanation   The `alter table` statement will fail because you cannot have more than one column in an Oracle table with a LONG datatype. You can, however, have multiple LOB type columns in the same table in Oracle8 and Oracle. Oracle is not programmed to create the LONG column for you using a different datatype. **(Topic 11.1)**

4. D.   Users to which ANN granted `insert` privileges will not be able to insert.

Explanation Though it doesn't say whether or not ANN had the `grant option` on this object privilege, the choice stating that users to which ANN granted `insert` privileges will not be able to `insert` is the only thing that truly happens when the DBA revokes `insert` privileges from ANN. So long as the DBA didn't revoke ANN's `create session` privilege (nothing in the question points to this conclusion), ANN can still connect. Records for a user are never removed when an object privilege is revoked either. Finally, nothing in the question pointed to the conclusion that ANN was ever able to create tables, so discard that choice as well. **(Topic 16.2)**

5. B.   Set SESSIONS_PER_USER in the DEFAULT profile to 1.

Explanation The best way to handle the job the question indicates is to make an adjustment to the user profile, not the `init.ora` file, eliminating two choices right there. After that, it's simply a matter of choosing the profile limit that looks the best. In this case, SESSIONS_PER_USER looks more like something that would limit user sessions in Oracle, more so than IDLE_TIME would. **(Topic 14.2)**

6. B.   Row cache

Explanation Data dictionary records are kept in a memory area of the shared pool. This is to improve overall performance of the Oracle database by keeping frequently accessed areas of the dictionary in memory. The library cache is where SQL statement parse trees are stored, not dictionary information. The shared area cache is a vague term, and thus has no real meaning. The buffer cache stores recently used information from SQL statements that didn't use the data dictionary. Finally, the redo log buffer stores redo information for nondata dictionary changes. **(Topic 1.1)**

7. C.   A direct path data load bypasses most of the Oracle RDBMS, whereas a conventional path data load is a high-speed version of the SQL `insert`.

Explanation The most accurate description of why these two paths differ is that the direct path data load bypasses most of the Oracle RDBMS, whereas a conventional path data load is a high-speed version of the SQL `insert`. Simply saying one is faster than the other doesn't really get to the heart of the matter. The other statements are technically invalid. **(Topic 1.1)**

8. C.   DBA_SEGMENTS

Explanation DBA_SEGMENTS is the most useful view for the purpose of finding the location of indexes in a tablespace or datafile, and the amount of space used by those indexes. DBA_TS_QUOTAS will give you information about how much space a user's objects can use in a tablespace, but that's about it. DBA_OBJECTS will tell you when the object was created, but not how big it is. DBA_INDEXES will give you information about storage configuration, but not actual storage allocation. **(Topic 12.5)**

9. B. `set transaction`

Explanation The `set transaction` statement is used to assign transactions to specific undo segments. Though not typically recommended, this can be a useful technique, particularly if you have one or two long-running batch processes and specific large undo segments that are usually offline but brought online to handle this specific need. `alter database` will not assign a transaction to a undo segment, nor will `alter table`, so those choices are wrong. Finally, you must avoid the obvious distractor in `alter rollback segment`—the question clearly indicates that the undo segment is *already* online. **(Topic 10.3)**

10. C. Oracle eventually won't allow new records to be added to the database.

Explanation In this situation, Oracle eventually won't allow new records to be added to the database, and the entire database will go into a prolonged wait state until the redo log is cleared. So, something will happen, and Oracle will not switch to a new redo log automatically. However, the instance does not crash, either—it simply freezes and won't allow changes to be made or new users to connect. **(Topic 7.4)**

11. A. Decreasing tablespace size

Explanation All choices affect the number of checkpoints on the database, except for decreasing tablespace size. Smaller redo logs cause log switches to occur more frequently, making for more frequent checkpoints. Setting LOG_CHECKPOINT_TIMEOUT to zero makes checkpoints happen less frequently, as does setting LOG_CHECKPOINT_INTERVAL greater than the size of the redo log file. However, checkpoints have nothing to do with the size of your database's tablespaces. **(Topic 8.3)**

12. C. COMPOSITE_LIMIT

Explanation In this question, you must read the choices carefully, and understand what is being asked. The real question here is whether you understand resource costs and composite limits. Each of the choices other than COMPOSITE_LIMIT can be rolled up into COMPOSITE_LIMIT with the use of resource costing. Only the resources available for profiles can be included as part of a composite limit. **(Topic 14.2)**

13. C. revoke create any table from ANN; then grant create
any table to ANN;

Explanation In a revoke command, you don't refer to the admin option at all.
However, when you revoke a privilege that was granted with administrative
capability, the entire privilege along with administrative capability is removed. As
such, you must grant the privilege back to the user without administrative
privileges in order for the user to continue using the privilege. **(Topic 16.2)**

14. D. alter user default role none except ROLE_1;

Explanation You may use the except keyword in your alter user default
role command, but only if the all keyword is also used. The none keyword in
this command must be used by itself, which makes the choice that says alter user
default role none except ROLE_1; a bad statement, and thus the correct
answer. **(Topic 17.2)**

15. A. From your init.ora file

Explanation Oracle will always prefer to use your init.ora file to determine
startup settings. You can get away without specifying the absolute path of your
init.ora file for the PFILE parameter if you have a copy of the init.ora file
for this database stored in the DBS directory under $ORACLE_HOME in UNIX
(DATABASE directory in NT). If no init.ora file is found and if a location is not
specified using PFILE, Oracle will not mount or open your database, but will use
some internal default settings to start an idle instance. Tablespace default settings
have no function in database startup, and anything regarding initialization
parameters is read from the redo log file. **(Topic 3.3)**

16. B. Writes current redo log number to datafile headers

Explanation The CKPT process handles two things in Oracle: it signals to DBWR
that dirty buffers must be written to disk, and it also writes log sequence numbers to
datafile headers and the control file. It does not, however, write dirty buffers to disk
—DBWR does that. It also doesn't write redo log information to disk, only LGWR
does that. Finally, it does not read data from disk into memory for user processes—
the server process performs this task. **(Topic 7.3)**

17. D. To prevent users from waiting if a redo log member cannot be archived

Explanation The choice identifying the reason for multiplexing redo logs as to
prevent users from waiting if a redo log member cannot be archived is probably the
best answer. You do not have enough information to tell if there is an increase in
storage space on your host machine; besides, multiplexing is also supposed to

prevent I/O bottlenecks between the ARCH and LGWR processes—which improves redo log performance, not degrades it. However, in some cases, such as when two redo log members are on the same disk, you might see some performance degradation associated with double-writes to disk. Finally, there will always be a dependency on the redo log buffer, because users write their redo entries there instead of directly to disk. **(Topic 7.1)**

18. C. LOGICAL_WRITES_PER_SESSION

Explanation Each of the following choices indicates an appropriate resource profile, except for LOGICAL_WRITES_PER_SESSION. LOGICAL_READS_PER_SESSION is the number of reads to the buffer cache that are permitted in the session before Oracle must terminate. CONNECT_TIME defines a hard timeout for connections to the database before Oracle closes the session. IDLE_TIME is another timeout that defines how long a session can be connected while doing no work. All these parameters indicate settings within a resource profile. So, because LOGICAL_WRITES_PER_SESSION is not a real resource profile setting, that choice is the correct answer. **(Topic 14.2)**

19. B. `alter system`

Explanation The `alter system switch logfile` statement is used to manually switch a log file. `alter database` is not used, nor is `alter user`, nor is `alter redo log`, which incidentally isn't even a real SQL statement. **(Topic 7.3)**

20. D. `default role`

Explanation You cannot use the `default role` clause in the `create user` statement, because no roles have been granted to the user yet. This is an interesting little fact to keep in mind about the `create user` statement that may find its way onto your OCP exam. Other than that, assigning a `temporary tablespace`, password with `identified by`, or a user profile, are all fair game. **(Topic 17.2)**

21. B. `identified by`

Explanation Of the choices given, only the `identified by` clause indicates a clause that can be issued in the `alter user` statement by the users themselves. All the rest are managed by the DBA. This is, of course, true in the absence of the user being granted the `alter any user system` privilege, but there is no indication in the question that should cause you to believe that the user has the `alter any user` privilege. **(Topic 15.2)**

22. A. `alter profile default limit COMPOSITE_LIMIT 3500;`

Explanation To perform the action indicated in the question, you would use the `alter profile default limit COMPOSITE_LIMIT 3500;` statement. RESOURCE_COST is not an appropriate `init.ora` parameter; instead, you would use RESOURCE_LIMITS. You wouldn't in fact need to make a change to a licensing parameter in the `init.ora` file at all. Finally, changing a resource limit for the profile doesn't alter its cost or its composite limit. **(Topic 14.3)**

23. D. `grant`

Explanation Giving a role to a user is the same process as giving a privilege to a user—it also is handled with the same command, `grant alter user` may be used to switch the default role later, but not until the role is actually granted. Because we are only working with one user, there is no need for a systemwide or databasewide alteration. **(Topic 16.2)**

24. B. `select`

Explanation Because undo segments are allocated for all transactional statements, all the DML statements will force the user to acquire an undo segment. However, no undo segment gets allocated when the `select` statement is issued, making that the correct answer. **(Topic 1.1)**

25. A. In the PGA

Explanation When dedicated servers are in use, session information is stored in the PGA for the session. If MTS was in place, the shared pool would have been the correct answer. Session information is never stored in the buffer cache or redo log buffer. **(Topic 1.1)**

26. A. `quota on`

Explanation The `quota on` clause in a `create user` statement will limit the amount of space the user can allocate in a tablespace with his or her own tables. It will usually not, however, impose consistent limits on the amount of data a user can add to his or her own or another user's tables `default tablespace`, `profile`, and `identified by` have nothing to do with tablespace space allocation. **(Topic 15.1)**

27. D. Much free space left for `updates` and space left free by deletes not actively filled in by Oracle

Explanation A high `pctfree` value (25 is fairly high) will leave much free space for `updates` to increase the size of each row, while a low value for `pctused` (30 is low) means that space left free by table `delete` operations will not return the block to a freelist quickly. Little free space left for updates, and space left free by deletes actively filled in by Oracle means that `pctused` is high (60 to 70) and `pctfree` is low (5 to 10). Little free space left for `updates`, and space left free by `deletes` not actively filled in by Oracle means that `pctfree` is low (5 to 10) and `pctused` is low (20 to 30). Much free space left for `updates`, and space left free by `deletes` actively filled in by Oracle means that `pctfree` is high (20 to 30) and `pctused` is high (60 to 70). **(Topic 9.3)**

28. C.   Dispatches user process access to a shared server

Explanation   DNNN, where NNN is a three-digit number (009 in this case), indicates a dispatcher process, which is a process that runs in the MTS making that choice the correct answer. DBWR writes dirty buffers to disk, making that choice incorrect, whereas CKPT writes the current redo log number to datafile headers during checkpoints and log switches, making that choice incorrect. The LGWR process writes redo log entries to disk. **(Topic 1.2)**

29. B.   In the shared pool

Explanation   When MTS is in use, session information is stored in the shared pool. Only when dedicated servers are being used will Oracle store session information in the PGA, making that choice incorrect. Session information is never stored in the buffer cache, redo log buffer, or large area. **(Topic 1.2)**

30. D.   VARCHAR2

Explanation   Views adopt the datatype of the columns from the base tables they select from, as long as there are no data conversion functions present in the view. In this case, the underlying column is a number, but there is also a TO_CHAR operation on that column, making the resulting datatype in the view a VARCHAR2. **(Topic 11.2)**

31. D.   NLS_SORT

Explanation   The NLS_SORT parameter enables you to define overriding sort order according to a language other than the national language set for the database. NLS_DATE_FORMAT is not use here, because that simply identifies the date format. NLS_RULE is an invalid national language set variable. One potential distractor in this situation is the NLS_LANG variable, which is used to define the language set the database will use. NLS_LANG consists of *language_territory.charset* and therefore it can implicitly influence the sorting, while NLS_TERRITORY helps Oracle identify the peculiarities of the geographical location the database runs in. **(Topic 18.4)**

32. C. You can use varying-length multibyte character sets as both character sets on your database.

Explanation You can *not* use varying-length multibyte character sets as both character sets on your database, so the choice stating you can shouldn't enter into consideration when choosing character set and national character set for your database. Other than that, you should consider making your character set US7ASCII or a superset of it (although the national character set can be whatever you choose), your national character set and character set should be closely related where possible, and Oracle supports only English-like languages as its character set for entering SQL and PL/SQL commands. **(Topic 18.1)**

33. A. V$NLS_PARAMETERS

Explanation The view you might use for this purpose is V$NLS_PARAMETERS. NLS_DATE_FORMAT is actually an initialization parameter, not a view, so you should be able to eliminate that one immediately as a choice. DBA_DATES is not a real view, so you should be able to eliminate that as choices as well. This leaves you with V$NLS_VALID_VALUES. You should investigate the database views supporting language specifications before taking OCP Exam 2. **(Topic 18.5)**

34. B. NLS_CURRENCY

Explanation The NLS_CURRENCY parameter could be set in your database to indicate the currency symbol is not $. NLS_SORT enables you to alter the default sort order in support of other languages. NLS_LANG is the parameter that indicates to Oracle the national language for this database, whereas NLS_DATE_FORMAT is used to indicate the date display characteristics. **(Topic 18.3)**

35. A. BACKGROUND_DUMP_DEST

Explanation You can find your ALERT file in the directory specified by the BACKGROUND_DUMP_DEST initialization parameter because the ALERT file is similar in behavior to a background process trace file that tracks—except that it tracks systemwide events, not just events occurring for one background process. USER_DUMP_DEST is used to identify the location for user trace files from user sessions. LOG_ARCHIVE_DEST is used to identify where Oracle places archived redo logs. CORE_DUMP_DEST is where Oracle places core dump files from failed processes. **(Topic 3.1)**

36. C. Oracle puts the tablespace into read-only mode after the last transaction against that tablespace commits while preventing subsequent DML until the change happens.

Explanation Only after the last transaction commits does Oracle put the tablespace into read-only mode. The tablespace cannot be put into read-only mode before a transaction against data in that tablespace commits due to the locks on mutating database objects held by the incomplete transaction. This point eliminates choice A. Oracle does not need to wait until the users all log off, however—Oracle can change tablespace status after the transaction commits, eliminating choice B. Finally, choice D is incorrect because Oracle returning an error is the behavior Oracle demonstrated in versions prior to Oracle. **(Topic 8.5)**

37. A. Using a bitmap in the space header segment

Explanation The principle behind locally managed tablespaces is that the space management is handled using a bitmap stored in the datafile header rather than by storing available space information in the data dictionary. Thus, choice B is incorrect. The locality of the database into which the information is stored is not relevant, either, so choice D is also incorrect. Finally, choice C is incorrect because Oracle does not store information integral to the operation of your database in a flat file, due to complex recovery issues inherent in doing so. **(Topic 8.2)**

38. B. Session memory for MTS configuration

Explanation The large pool, when configured, will be used by Oracle to store session memory for MTS configuration. This relieves the burden on the shared pool to store this information when MTS is in use, leaving more room for SQL parse trees. Only the shared pool may be used for storing SQL parse trees, so choice A is incorrect. Choice C is also incorrect because session memory in the dedicated server configuration is always stored in a private area seen only by that process. Finally, choice D is incorrect because the buffer cache is used for storing all block buffers, and there is no real concept of *overflow* with respect to this memory area. **(Topic 1.1)**

39. B. `alter table set unused column`

Explanation The `alter table set unused column` command marks a column as being unused in the table without actually removing any data from the column or table. The operation executes quickly because the only change actually made is to the data dictionary in the Oracle database. The `alter table drop column` command is more extensive and long-running, but also removes the actual data from the table, thus freeing up space, so choice A is incorrect. Choice C is used for changing the datatype definition of a column and is incorrect. Choice D deallocates all storage for a table, leaving only the definition intact, which is also incorrect. **(Topic 11.8)**

40. A. PGA

Explanation Data in temporary tables in Oracle is stored in the sort area, and the sort area is a part of your PGA. Because the table is temporary, there is no way for Oracle to store the data either in your buffer cache or in any tablespace other than TEMP. Thus, choices B, C, and D are all incorrect. The reason temporary table data might be stored in your TEMP tablespace is because the temporary table data might fill your sort area. In this situation, Oracle behaves as every version of Oracle behaved, and puts overflow in the temporary tablespace used for disk sorts. **(Topic 1.1)**

41. D. `recseparator`

Explanation The `recseparator` keyword in your SQL*Loader control file enables you to define a character other than "newline" that separates records. Thus, multiple rows of data can be stored on one line, or a single line of data can be found spanning multiple lines. Choice A is incorrect because the `fields separated by` clause defines the column separation delimiter, not the line delimiter. The `fields terminated by` clause defines a character to be found when SQL*Loader reaches the end of a column, making choice B incorrect as well. Finally, `trailing nullcols` identifies to SQL*Loader that, if additional columns are found in the table for which there are no records in the load file, then SQL*Loader will place a NULL value for that column. Thus, choice C is incorrect. **(Topic 1.1)**

42. A. Estimate statistics.

Explanation You can compute statistics, but not estimate statistics, on Oracle indexes when you rebuild them. Thus, choice A is correct, and choice B is incorrect. The `rebuild` clause does enable you to rebuild in another tablespace as well by simply specifying the `tablespace` clause in the `alter index rebuild` command. This feature was actually implemented in Oracle8. Thus, choice C is incorrect as well. Finally, choice D indicates that the index can be rebuilt online, whereas users are still modifying data in the table. This is a new feature in Oracle, so choice D is incorrect. **(Topic 12.3)**

43. B. LOG_ARCHIVE_MAX_PROCESSES

Explanation This question is tricky because one of the choices looks deceptively similar to the correct answer. Choice B is the correct name for the parameter used to define how many ARCH processes Oracle should run. Choice A does not identify an actual `init.ora` parameter, but looks like it *should* be right. It is important that you can distinguish the real from the imaginary on your OCP exam. Choice C is incorrect because although you can define how many archive destinations Oracle should maintain with LOG_ARCHIVE_MIN_SUCCEED_DEST, Oracle does not automatically start a specific number of ARCH processes based on the value for this parameter. Finally, choice D is incorrect because the LOG_ARCHIVE_START parameter merely tells Oracle that an ARCH process should be started at the time the instance is started, but by itself LOG_ARCHIVE_START tells Oracle to start only one ARCH process. **(Topic 7.4)**

44. D.   %ORACLE_BASE%\oradata

Explanation   Oracle significantly enhanced its support of the Oracle Flexible Architecture (OFA). Database Configuration Assistant now installs all Oracle datafiles under an oradata\<SID> directory within the software home tree in NT environments. In contrast, prior versions of Oracle would place all datafiles under the database directory, so choice C is incorrect for Oracle. Choice A is incorrect because only the admin components will be placed under the admin directory in the ORACLE_HOME tree. However, this is also an OFA-compliant way to set up the Oracle environment, so it is also important to understand. Finally, choice B is incorrect because Oracle-supplied DBA scripts are found in the rdbms\admin area. **(Topic 2.3)**

45. A.   25

Explanation   The bits in the local-management bitmap in each datafile will either represent one block or many blocks. The bit will represent many blocks only if UNIFORM SIZE is used, in which case the number of blocks represented by one bit equals the number of blocks in each extent. In this case, the block size is 4KB, while the uniform extent size is 100KB, meaning that each extent contains, and each bit represents, 25 blocks. **(Topic 8.1)**

46. C.   Based on the number of blocks in the table plus blocks in associated indexes

Explanation   When sizing the keep pool, ensure that there is enough room for the entire table plus all associated indexes. If one or the other is omitted, you may size the keep pool too small and lose blocks, resulting in I/O operations later to read either table or index data back into memory. You wouldn't base the size of the keep pool on anything from your shared pool. **(Topic 1.1)**

47. D.   NLS_DUAL_CURRENCY

Explanation   NLS_DUAL_CURRENCY is used for EU countries supporting two currencies so that dual currencies can be identified in the database. NLS_TERRITORY may identify their national currency, but not necessarily the euro, eliminating choice A. The NLS_LANG parameter is used to identify the national language, but not the currency, making choice B incorrect. NLS_COMP is used for enhanced comparison operations, not to support dual currencies, eliminating choice C. **(Topic 18.5)**

48. D.   The `insert` fails at the time it is issued, but the transaction will continue.

Explanation   A nondeferrable constraint cannot be deferred by the `alter session set constraints=deferred` statement. Therefore, the `insert` statement will fail. However, statement failure does not cause a transaction to fail. Therefore, choice D is correct. **(Topic 13.1)**

49. C.   '948695'

Explanation   A reverse key index reverses the values stored in the index for high-speed search purposes. Given the value by the question, choice C is correct because the choice presents the indexed value reversed. Choices A, B, and D are thus logically incorrect for this same reason as well. **(Topic 12.1)**

50. B.   Create an index-organized table to store the data.

Explanation   Index-organized tables take less space to store than a comparable table-plus-primary-key setup. Because the table will only be accessed via the primary key, there is no need for additional indexes. Furthermore, for storage reasons, the DBA won't want to create more indexes, eliminating choice A. Choice C is incorrect because dropping the primary key will reduce storage but has the unwanted effect of making data difficult to access. Choice D is incorrect because increasing `pctfree` makes a table require more storage to store the same number of rows. Review the discussion of index-organized tables. **(Topic 11.1)**

51. D.   Set `password_reuse_time` to 1095

Explanation   The password_reuse_time profile option represents the number of *days* that must pass before a password can be reused. Because you want to restrict reuse to a three-year period, you will set password_reuse_time to the number of days in three years, which is 1,095 (assuming no leap year in that three-year period). Choices A and B are both incorrect, because the values used represent the restriction as a number of years and months, respectively. Choices C and E are incorrect because they are meaningless values designed to distract you from the real answer. **(Topic 14.1)**

52. B.   STARSKY can no longer create tables, but HUTCH can.

Explanation   Because the `create table` privilege was revoked from STARSKY, that user will no longer be able to perform the task given by the privilege. However, unlike object privileges, system privileges are not revoked from privilege grantees when the grantor loses the privilege. Thus, HUTCH keeps the ability to create tables even when STARSKY loses it, making choice A incorrect. You do not lose the privilege in any of the actions shown in the question, which eliminates choices C and D. **(Topic 16.2)**

53. C.   The user issues the `set role` command, and then issues the DML commands.

Explanation   Because the user has been granted the nondefault role, that user must issue the `set role` command to activate the role so he or she can use the privileges associated with that role. The user cannot simply issue the commands, because the role is not a default one for the user, making choice A incorrect. However, the solution is not to make this role a default role for the user, as indicated by choice C with the `alter user` statement (using the `default role` clause). For one, the user cannot issue this command on himself or herself—he or she would require DBA intervention. For another, because the application superuser privileges are meant to be nondefault privileges, making this role a default role would defeat the purpose of password protection on the role itself. **(Topic 17.2)**

54. B.   Availability of space on disk where datafiles are added

Explanation   To increase the size of a tablespace, you must have additional disk space Oracle can use to store its datafiles. You do not need to use `autoextend` in order to increase the size of a tablespace, however, making choice C incorrect. Choice A is also incorrect because that consideration is a factor only when reducing the size of a tablespace. Finally, choice D is incorrect because block information is not stored in memory in support of increasing the size of a tablespace. **(Topic 8.3)**

55. A.   The DEVELOPER profile shows a value of 230,000 for COMPOSITE_LIMIT.

Explanation   A value of 230,000 for COMPOSITE_LIMIT is pretty high, and can most likely accommodate a few minutes' worth of queries from developers. This is the only choice that is not a potential culprit for the problem. Choice B is suspect because developers would be disconnected if the DBA manually killed their sessions. Choice C is also a problem because a low value for CPU_PER_SESSION (measured in $1/100$ seconds) means that developers would be allotted absurdly low CPU time when connected to process their queries. Finally, choice D is a problem because a connection time of ten minutes as measured by CONNECT_TIME would kick the developers off the system after a few minutes, as indicated by the question. **(Topic 14.3)**

56. A.   CREATE_CATALOG_ROLE

Explanation   Of the choices given, only CREATE_CATALOG_ROLE is a role not created automatically when the Oracle database is created. SELECT_CATALOG_ROLE gives the user access to dictionary information, making choice B incorrect. EXP_FULL_DATABASE enables the user to export every database object using the EXPORT utility, making choice C incorrect. Finally, choice D is incorrect because IMP_FULL_DATABASE enables the user to import the entire contents of an export dump file into the database. **(Topic 17.4)**

57. B.   Performance

Explanation   Even though index rebuilds can take place online in Oracle, you still have to consider the performance degradation inherent in the overhead required to rebuild the index online. This question is a challenging one because choices B, C, and D are all interrelated. Although the best performance will be experienced when the system is most idle, choice C is not the right answer because it identifies a course of action to take, not a factor to consider in determining the course of action. Choice D is also wrong, because system idleness is determined as a combination between user activity and batch processing. Finally, choice A is incorrect because in a 24×7 environment, no downtime is permitted. **(Topic 12.3)**

58. D.   The `alter tablespace coalesce` command

Explanation   Although the `alter table coalesce` command can be used to coalesce small chunks of free space into larger ones by SMON, this command does little about row chaining or migration at the table level in the Oracle database. Choice A is wrong because `analyze` populates the CHAIN_CNT column in DBA_TABLES, which tells the DBA how many rows are chained in the table of the database. Choice B is wrong because DBMS_DDL contains a procedure that analyzes objects for cost-based optimization. Choice C is also wrong because DBMS_UTILITY contains a procedure that analyzes every object in a user's schema for cost-based optimization. **(Topic 8.5)**

59. C.   Bring the tablespace online.

Explanation   Once you issue the `alter tablespace move datafile` command, you can then bring the tablespace online, provided the file appears where you told Oracle it would appear with the command from the question. Remember, alter tablespace only updates the Oracle data dictionary and control file with the new filesystem location information. Oracle does not actually move the file for you. You would take the tablespace offline before issuing the alter tablespace move datafile command, and you would also move the file first, making choices B and A incorrect, respectively. Finally, use of IMPORT as indicated in choice D is appropriate for transportable tablespaces, a subject not tested by this question. **(Topic 8.5)**

60. B.   C55278B93918BF29

Explanation   Oracle always sets a password to whatever string literal you assign using the `alter user identified by` command. Enclosing the data shown in DBA_USERS for password information in double quotes does not circumvent Oracle's security measures for not showing a password in plaintext in the data dictionary, so choice A is wrong. Also, although GIANT cannot connect until `create session` is granted to the user, this fact itself is irrelevant because the question asks about the password, not connectivity status, making choice C incorrect as well. Finally, Oracle does not lock new user accounts by default, so choice D is also wrong. **(Topic 15.2)**

Answers to Practice Exam 3

I.   A.   The listener spawns a new server process.

Explanation   When dedicated servers are in use in Oracle, the listener will spawn a new dedicated server for every user process that contacts the listener to establish service with Oracle. Because MTS is not in use, choice B is wrong because no dispatcher process will be running on the Oracle database. Oracle background processes do not communicate with server processes directly, so choices C and D are incorrect as well. **(Topic 1.2)**

2.   C.   Fetch data from disk into memory.

Explanation   The only step Oracle will execute in support of a user query from the choices given is fetching data from disk into memory. Choices A, B, and D are all incorrect because they indicate steps Oracle will execute in support of data change commands such as `insert`, `update`, and `delete`, but not in support of queries. **(Topic 1.1)**

3.   A.   Make changes to data block in memory.

Explanation   When users issue `insert` statements in Oracle, the server process always makes the changes in memory, not on disk. So, choice A is correct. Choice B is incorrect because Oracle would never parse a statement if the parse tree for an identical statement already exists in the shared pool. Choice C is incorrect because undo information is only written for `update` or `delete` statements. Finally, choice D is incorrect because redo for a transaction is never written to the datafile, it is written to the online redo log. **(Topic 1.1)**

4. C.   Use of OFA reduces support headaches by standardizing filesystem layouts for all Oracle installations.

Explanation   Choice C correctly describes a cornerstone of OFA-compliant infrastructures in that the filesystem layout of Oracle files is standardized for easy location. Choice A is incorrect because OFA distributes software, database, and administrative filesystem components into different areas so that they are easy to find and don't conflict with one another from an I/O perspective. Choice B is incorrect because enabling DBAs to arrive at their own filesystem layouts using proprietary naming conventions leads to nonstandard Oracle installations and is the antithesis of OFA. Choice D is incorrect because OFA separates database objects into different tablespaces based on I/O requirements. **(Topic 2.3)**

5. B.   `orapwd file=/u01/app/oracle/database/orapwdORCL.pwd password=oracle entries=100`

Explanation   Your call to the ORAPWD utility must include reference to all three parameters: FILE, PASSWORD, and ENTRIES. Further, your reference to the password filename you want to create must include its absolute path specification unless you want Oracle to write the password file in the current directory. Choice B alone conforms to these requirements. Choices A and C are both missing reference to the PASSWORD parameter, whereas choice D incorrectly places the password file in the current directory rather than the one specified by the question. **(Topic 2.4)**

6. A.   When the instance is started

Explanation   Oracle reads the contents of your `init.ora` file whenever the instance is started. Choices B and C are both incorrect because by the time the database is mounted and opened, the instance has already been started and the initialization parameter file has been read into memory. Finally, Oracle never reads the parameter file when the database is closed, making choice D incorrect as well. **(Topic 3.3)**

7. A.   DB_CREATE_FILE_DEST

Explanation   The Oracle-managed files feature in Oracle9*i* specifies that datafiles will be created in the directory identified by the parameter named in choice A. Choices B and C are both incorrect because those locations are used for writing redo logs and control files when OMF is in use. Finally, choice D is incorrect because these directory locations are most definitely controlled by you, the DBA, when you manually specify settings for the parameters identified in choices A, B, and C in this question. **(Topic 3.2)**

8. B.   OMF will automatically remove the underlying datafiles from the host environment.

Explanation   Choice B correctly identifies the primary feature OMF offers DBAs. Choices A and C are both incorrect because they specify functionality that is standard within Oracle when a tablespace that uses particular datafiles is dropped from the Oracle database. Finally, choices B and D are mutually exclusive, making choice D incorrect by virtue of choice B's correctness. **(Topic 3.2)**

9. B.   Two

Explanation   OMF will try to multiplex online redo logs if you use it for generating your redo log files. Multiplexing requires that at least two different locations are specified for the appropriate OMF parameters. Thus, all other choices are incorrect. **(Topic 3.2)**

10. C.   `alter system suspend`

Explanation   The `alter system suspend` command is useful for periodic acquiescing of host system I/O resources, particularly when high-speed disk mirror or synchronization mechanisms are in place on the I/O devices supporting Oracle database files. Choice D shows how to continue Oracle database operation after the `alter system suspend` command has been issued, and therefore that choice is incorrect. Choice A indicates a command you would use when you only wanted to start the Oracle instance, making that choice incorrect. Finally, choice B is incorrect because making the database read only does not cease database operations temporarily. **(Topic 3.3)**

11. A.   `shutdown abort`

Explanation   The `shutdown abort` command lets you stop your Oracle database from operating on short notice, and requires that instance recovery be performed the next time the database is started. Choice B is incorrect because the `shutdown transactional` command stops the database from operating after the current transactions are ended by the user process, which may not take place on short notice if the transactions are long-running. Choice C is incorrect because the `shutdown normal` command only stops the database from operating after the last user logs off Oracle, which may not happen on short notice. Finally, choice D is incorrect because even though the `shutdown immediate` command closes the database after rolling back current transactions, the rollback activity itself may take a long time. **(Topic 3.3)**

12. C. `orclALRT.trc`

Explanation   The contents of the trace file clearly indicate that this file is the alert log for the database. You can glean this fact from observing that the trace file contents include initialization parameter settings and startup/shutdown times for the database. Choice A is incorrect because the contents of this trace file give you no indication that an error occurred with the DBW0 process. Choice B is incorrect for the same reason, insofar as you have no indication of a failure with the LGWR process. Finally, no user process information is present in this trace file, meaning that it cannot be a user process trace file as the name of the file in choice D would indicate, making that choice incorrect as well. **(Topic 3.4)**

13. A. CONTROL_FILES

Explanation   If you do not change the setting for CONTROL_FILES in the parameter file before you create a new database, there is a chance Oracle will use the control files specified by this parameter, which correspond to another database. This could lead to problems with your other database, making choice A the correct answer. Choice B is incorrect because two databases on the same host system can have the same database block size. Choice C is incorrect because you can have two Oracle databases in the same domain when both databases are hosted on the same machine. Choice D is incorrect because the shared pool size for two databases on the same host can be the same, so long as there is enough memory for both databases' SGAs. **(Topic 3.1)**

14. C. Template

Explanation   A template is a relatively new component supported by the Oracle Database Creation Assistant. This component permits the creation of many databases from a generic specification you define. Choices A and B are incorrect because clone and copy refer to the creation of another database from the actual datafiles of an original database. Finally, choice D is incorrect because a terminal is a process or machine that enables you access to a minicomputer or mainframe. **(Topic 4.2)**

15. D. SYSTEM

Explanation   Any datafile named as part of the `datafile` clause of your `create database` command will belong to the SYSTEM tablespace. Although you can create undo tablespaces for your database with the `create database` command, choice C is incorrect because the creation of an undo tablespace is defined using the `undo tablespace` clause in the `create database` command. Choices A and B are incorrect because DATA and INDEX tablespaces cannot be created in the `create database` command. **(Topic 4.3)**

16. D. SYS

Explanation The internal user has been rendered obsolete in Oracle8i and later database releases, so because you need a privileged connection to Oracle to create the data dictionary, you need to use the SYS user as identified in choice D. Choices A and B both indicate users who do not have sufficient privileges to create the data dictionary. **(Topic 4.1)**

17. B. DBA_TABLES

Explanation The views prefixed with DBA_, USER_, or ALL_ are considered part of the Oracle data dictionary, along with a select list of other views. Choice A is incorrect because V$ views are considered dynamic performance views and as such aren't part of the data dictionary. Choice C is incorrect because SYS.AUD$ is a base table in Oracle, from which dictionary views can be derived. Finally, the EMP table is a sample table that is not associated with the data dictionary in any way. **(Topic 5.1)**

18. B. DBA_SOURCE

Explanation The output in this question is clearly a PL/SQL block, the source code for which can be found in the DBA_SOURCE dictionary view. Choice A is incorrect because DBA_ERRORS is a dictionary view you might employ as part of the PL/SQL compilation process to identify syntax errors in your PL/SQL code. Choice C is incorrect because DBA_VIEWS contains information about the views in your Oracle database, not PL/SQL code. Finally, choice D is incorrect because the source code shown contains no evidence that it is associated with a trigger. **(Topic 5.3)**

19. A. set long 9999

Explanation Because the contents of the TEXT column in DBA_VIEWS is cut off before the entire output of that column was displayed, chances are good that there is some problem in the way columns of LONG datatype are set to display in SQL*Plus. Choice A is correct because it defines a nice large value for LONG column width, as opposed to choice C, which only supports 50 characters. Choices B and D are both incorrect because they configure the width of a column called TEXT in VARCHAR2 or CHAR datatype format, which is not the case for this TEXT column, which is of LONG datatype. **(Topic 5.2)**

20. A. Verify the actual directory location of your control file.

Explanation Because you have very little information in this question, your only option is to follow the logical sequence of events starting with what little information you have. This question starts by explaining the value specified for the CONTROL_FILES parameter. Because you also know that Oracle must open your control files as part of the instance startup process, the next logical step is to determine if the control files are found where Oracle expects to find them. Choice B is incorrect because you have no information that would indicate a problem with real memory. Choices C and D are incorrect because we haven't even started the instance yet, so its too early to expect problems with datafiles or online redo logs. **(Topic 6.1)**

21. D. `/u04/oradata/db1`

Explanation When you specify the DB_CREATE_ONLINE_LOG_DEST_n parameters, Oracle places control files in each of the locations you define for those parameters. Otherwise, Oracle would have used the DB_CREATE_FILE_DEST parameter in determining where to place the control files. Thus, you know that a control file will be placed in the directories identified by choices A, B, and C, but not in the directory indicated by choice D. **(Topic 6.4)**

22. C. Updates to the contents of the control file when new tablespaces are added

Explanation Even when you don't use OMF, Oracle still updates the contents of your control file whenever a new tablespace is added to your database. This is the default functionality for supporting Oracle filesystem layout that Oracle provides. Choice A is incorrect because Oracle will expect you to determine where the control files are located using the CONTROL_FILES parameter in lieu of OMF. Choice B is incorrect because Oracle will only multiplex your control files when you specify multiple directory and file locations for the CONTROL_FILES parameter. Finally, choice D is incorrect because you, not Oracle, must specify values for CONTROL_FILES in the parameter file. **(Topic 6.4)**

23. B. Make a copy of the control file with the database shut down.

Explanation When multiplexing control files, you should make a copy of the control file when the database is shut down and move that copy to the appropriate location given by the CONTROL_FILES parameter so that Oracle will maintain the multiplexed copy. Choices A and D are incorrect because they both indicate that the database should be open during control file copying, which of course it shouldn't. Finally, choice C indicates how to create a script for recreating your control file if it should be lost, which isn't relevant to this discussion. **(Topic 6.3)**

24. D. ARC0

Explanation The archiver process will make a copy of your online redo log file in the appropriate archiving destination whenever LGWR fills the current log. Choice A is incorrect because LGWR will not make this archived copy for you. The CKPT process will also not copy an online log to its archiving destination, making choice B incorrect. Finally, the DBW0 process copies dirty buffers to datafiles, and has little if anything to do with archiving filled redo logs, making choice C incorrect as well. **(Topic 7.1)**

25. D. `ora_1_asdf1234.log`

Explanation The filename specified in choice D indicates a filename Oracle might use for creating a redo log when OMF is used. Choices A, B, and C do not follow the OMF naming convention we described in this text, and therefore could not be the correct answers to this question. **(Topic 7.5)**

26. D. You created a dictionary-managed permanent tablespace.

Explanation Although its name would indicate that temporary data might be stored in this tablespace, the `temporary` or `tempfile` keywords were not used in defining the tablespace, making it impossible for Oracle to create this tablespace as a temporary tablespace. Choices A and C are incorrect because the keywords `extent management local` were not used, meaning that this tablespace could not be a locally managed tablespace. The keywords `extent management dictionary` were used, however, meaning that this is a dictionary-managed tablespace. Choice B is incorrect however, because the tablespace is not a temporary tablespace, as you already know. **(Topic 8.2)**

27. C. `autoextend`

Explanation The `autoextend` keyword indicates a clause in which you can define whether a datafile extends automatically in support of tablespace growth. Choice A is incorrect because the `default storage` clause indicates default settings for segments and extents of objects placed into this tablespace when no `storage` clause was specified in creating that object. Choice B is incorrect because the `extent management` clause is a clause used for defining whether the tablespace free space allocation will be locally managed or dictionary managed. Finally, choice D is incorrect because the `datafile` clause is used when creating tablespaces to identify the name of a datafile to create in support of this tablespace. **(Topic 8.2)**

28. C. `uniform extent allocation`

Explanation The `uniform extent allocation` clause identifies that segments allocated in this tablespace will all be the same size, as requested by the question. Choice A is incorrect because segment and extent allocation specified by `default storage` clauses will be optional and only implemented when the object placed in that tablespace has no `storage` clause of its own. Choice B is incorrect because the `storage` clause is defined on a database object placed in the tablespace to configure how segments and extents will be allocated to that object. Choice D is incorrect because the `autoextend` clause is used for determining whether a datafile can grow beyond its original size automatically in support of tablespace growth. **(Topic 8.3)**

29. C. `drop tablespace cascade constraints`

Explanation   The `cascade constraints` clause in the `drop tablespace` command is used for ensuring that any constraints between objects inside and outside this tablespace will be severed. Choice A is incorrect because you wouldn't ordinarily drop just the datafile in the context of this question. Choice B is incorrect because simply taking the tablespace offline will not remove the contraints between objects inside and outside this tablespace. Finally, though the `including contents` clause would be included in the `drop tablespace` command whenever you wanted to drop a nonempty tablespace, this clause alone won't drop the constraints between objects inside and outside this tablespace being dropped. **(Topic 8.5)**

30. D.   The change will not take effect for existing tables.

Explanation   You can change `default storage` settings for initial extents all you want, but the change will never take effect for existing tables in Oracle. Because choice D is the correct answer, and because the other choices are mutually exclusive, choices A, B, and C are all incorrect. **(Topic 8.6)**

31. D.   All tablespaces in the database

Explanation   When OMF is enabled for your database, Oracle will handle the creation and removal of datafiles associated with every tablespace in your Oracle database. This is a handy aspect of OMF that will help you minimize the storage allocation of space on your host system. Choices A, B, and C all indicate that OMF is somehow limited to managing datafile removal for only a specific tablespace, which, of course, isn't the case. Therefore, each of those choices is incorrect. **(Topic 8.7)**

32. C.   DATA

Explanation   Of the choices given, only the DATA tablespace will not be created by the Oracle when the `create database` command given by the question is issued. Choice A is incorrect because the SYSTEM tablespace is always created by Oracle when a database is created. Choice B is incorrect because the UNDOTBS tablespace will be created by this `create database` command due to the presence of the `undo tablespace` clause. **(Topic 10.2)**

33. D.   1,500KB

Explanation   Even though you specify a storage allocation of 300KB in the `storage` clause of your `create table` statement, Oracle uses the uniform extent management configuration of 500KB set when the tablespace was created. Further, since you specified three extents with the `minextents` option in the `table storage` clause, Oracle allocates three extents of size 500KB each, for a total of 1,500KB. Thus, choice D is the correct answer, and choices A, B, and C are incorrect. **(Topic 11.6)**

34. B.   `create temporary tablespace temp01 tempfile '/u01/oradata/orcl/temp01.dbf' size 100M extent management local;`

Explanation   Choice B presents the best option for creating the temporary tablespace. Although choice C is also technically correct, the syntax in choice B follows newer conventions established by Oracle. Choices A and D are both incorrect and will result in errors if issued against an Oracle database. **(Topic 8.4)**

35. A.   `autoallocate`

Explanation   The `autoallocate` clause was left out but implied in Oracle. This is the default functionality for tablespaces in the Oracle database. Choices B, C, and D all indicate clauses that must be explicitly stated in order for Oracle to use them. **(Topic 8.2)**

36. A.   The value for the `minextents` setting.

Explanation   When more than one extent is allocated to a database table on creation, chances are the table was created with `minextents` set to a value greater than one in the `storage` clause when the object was created. Oracle would never create a database table with more than one extent by default, so choice D is incorrect. Choices B and C both indicate storage settings that have no bearing on the initial number of extents allocated to a table, so they are both incorrect as well. **(Topic 8.6)**

37. C.   `select sum(bytes) from dba_extents where segment_name = 'EMP' and owner = 'SCOTT';`

Explanation   The statement for choice C indicates a query that would give you the total space allocation for the EMP table owned by SCOTT in your Oracle database. You use the `sum( )` function because there will be more than one entry in the DBA_EXTENTS view if more than one extent is allocated to that table. Choice A is incorrect because DBA_TABLES will not give you the information you need. Choice B is incorrect because DBA_FREE_SPACE contains free space information, whereas you are looking for allocated space information. Finally, choice D is incorrect because the DBA_OBJECTS view will not give you the information you need. **(Topic 9.4)**

38. C.   The user's long-running transaction has taken so long that space for undo information has been exhausted.

Explanation   Although the ORA-01555 error will affect other users in the way listed for choice B, choice C is the correct answer because the user running the long-running transaction will actually receive the ORA-01555 error. Choices A and D are not related to the "snapshot too old" error, and therefore can be disregarded. **(Topic 10.1)**

39. C.   The database will open and all undo segments in UNDO_TBS1 will be online.

Explanation   Choice C is correct due to the SPFILE feature in Oracle, which remembers the setting made with the `alter system` command from your previous instance's execution. Choices A and B are incorrect, although this was the old functionality prior to Oracle9*i* when the ROLLBACK_SEGMENTS parameter wasn't set. Finally, choice D is incorrect as well because the database definitely will open and undo segments will be online. **(Topic 10.2)**

40. D.   Oracle will return errors and the database will not open.

Explanation   Because your `init.ora` file contained an incorrect setting, Oracle mistakenly attempted to open the UNDOTBS1 undo tablespace when in fact the name of that tablespace was UNDO_TBS1. Oracle returns errors and the database will remain mounted but will not open. Choices A, B, and C are all incorrect because the database will be unable to open. The SPFILE feature is no good here because `init.ora` overrides it with the erroneous undo tablespace name. **(Topic 10.2)**

41. C.   Set UNDO_MANAGEMENT to MANUAL.

Explanation   Your only correct option in this situation is to turn off automatic undo management. Choice B would have been the right answer if it indicated you were switching UNDO_SUPRESS_ERRORS to TRUE, but it is not the correct answer as it currently stands. Choice A indicates turning on automatic undo management, which is what caused the error in the first place. Finally, choice D is incorrect because UNDO_RETENTION has no bearing on the matter asked in the question. **(Topic 10.2)**

42. D. Standard Oracle table

Explanation Although choice C initially might seem like the right answer, notice that the question states that this table experiences frequent data change activity—the bane of a cluster table's existence. Thus, you must use standard tables, and choice D is correct. Choice A is also incorrect because nothing in the question indicates that you need the functionality offered by temporary tables. Finally, choice B is incorrect because nothing in the question indicates the need for an IOT. **(Topic 11.1)**

43. C. Redo information will be generated for the creation of this table.

Explanation Of the choices given, the only statement that can be made accurately about the table created in this question is choice C—redo will be generated because the `logging` keyword was present in the `create table` command. Choice A is incorrect because you have no information that would indicate this table is being placed in a temporary tablespace. Choice B is incorrect because the uniform extent allocation of the DATA tablespace will likely override whatever settings are made in the `storage` clause of the `create table` command given. Finally, choice D is incorrect because the `nocache` keyword in the `create table` command given ensures that blocks read into the SGA as part of full table scans will be purged by Oracle quickly. **(Topic 11.5)**

44. B. OBRYAN only

Explanation Data in a temporary table is session-private; OBRYAN therefore can remove only his own data using the `truncate` command. Thus, choices indicating other users will also have their data eliminated are incorrect. **(Topic 11.5)**

45. B. When OBRYAN `commits` the transaction

Explanation This temporary table was defined to retain records until the end of a user's transaction. Thus, when OBRYAN ends his current transaction, Oracle removes OBRYAN's data from the temporary table. All other choices indicate wrong answers because they either refer to users other than OBRYAN or to a scenario other than the end of OBRYAN's transaction. **(Topic 11.5)**

46. A. Immediately following statement execution

Explanation Once the `alter table drop column` statement is issued, Oracle removes the column from the table immediately. Choices B, C, and D are all incorrect because they indicate that the column will be removed at some later point when another command is issued, which is not the case for the `alter table drop column` command shown in the question. **(Topic 11.8)**

47. D.   Querying the DBA_UNUSED_COL_TABS view

Explanation   The DBA_UNUSED_COL_TABS view contains a listing of unused columns and tables that contain unused columns. Choice C is incorrect because it refers to the wrong dictionary view name. Choices A and B are both incorrect because they refer to methods you cannot use to find a listing of unused columns. **(Topic 11.8)**

48. A.   Less restrictive locks on underlying base tables

Explanation   Oracle reduced restrictions on the locks used for rebuilding indexes online in Oracle to permit that functionality. Choice B is incorrect because more restrictive locks would reduce the likelihood that online index rebuilds would be possible. Choice C is incorrect because standby databases are not involved in this process. Finally, choice D is incorrect because temporary tables are not involved in the process, either. **(Topic 12.3)**

49. B.   Oracle fills in the END_MONITORING column in the record corresponding to MY_IDX in the V$OBJECT_USAGE view.

Explanation   Because you terminated monitoring on this index, Oracle notes the date and time you did so in the corresponding record from V$OBJECT_USAGE. Oracle would only change the value in the USED column if someone used the index while monitoring was enabled, so choice C is incorrect. Choice A is incorrect because Oracle doesn't remove records from V$OBJECT_USAGE until the next time the instance is restarted. Finally, choice D is incorrect because the values for the record corresponding to MY_IDX in V$OBJECT_USAGE were cleared when monitoring was started. **(Topic 12.6)**

50. C.   The index will not be created unless all values in the EMPNO column are unique and not NULL.

Explanation   The only statement that is true from the choices given is choice C. Choice A is incorrect because the constraint uses a B-tree index, not a bitmap index. Choice B is incorrect because foreign keys in tables typically reference back to primary keys in other tables. Finally, choice D is incorrect because NULL values are not permitted in primary keys. **(Topic 13.1)**

51. A.   SYSTEM

Explanation   SERENA's tables will be placed in the SYSTEM tablespace unless you specify another default tablespace using the appropriate clause in the `create user` command. Choice B is incorrect because the table didn't contain reference to the DATA tablespace, nor is that tablespace the default for this user. Choice C is incorrect because the TEMP tablespace will be used for housing temporary segments but not permanent segments for this user. Finally, choice D is incorrect because the UNDOTBS tablespace will be used for housing undo segments not data segments. **(Topic 15.1)**

52. A. `create table mytab (col1 number primary key);`

Explanation Because JOSEPHINE has no space quota allotment in her default tablespace, she will not be able to issue the statement given in choice A. This restriction does not apply to space allocation in dictionary tables, however, so the statements indicated in choices B and C can both be issued by JOSEPHINE. Finally, choice D is incorrect because JOSEPHINE places that table created in the DATA tablespace, which is outside the realm of the question being asked. **(Topic 15.1)**

53. D. If SYS performs a disk sort, the temporary segments will be placed in the TEMP tablespace.

Explanation Of the statements given, only the statement for choice D is true. Choice A is incorrect because we have no information about SYS's actual password or account lock status that would indicate that no user can log in as SYS. Choice B is incorrect because if SYS creates a table without specifying the `tablespace` clause, the table will be placed in SYSTEM according to the dictionary info given. Finally, choice C is incorrect because the statement indicates the encrypted password value, not the actual value. **(Topic 8.4)**

54. B. `alter resource cost`

Explanation The command indicated in choice B is the one that must be issued in order to assign resource costs to resources in order for composite limits to work. Choice A is incorrect because the `alter system` command cannot be used for changing resource allocation costs. Choice C is incorrect for this reason as well, although you can set the value for COMPOSITE_LIMIT with the command shown in that choice. Finally, choice D is incorrect because the `alter user` command is used for assigning a profile to a user, not for explicit allocation of resource costs. **(Topic 14.3)**

55. A. IDLE_TIME

Explanation Idle time is not a resource that can be managed via composite limits. All other choices are incorrect because they indicate resource allocations that can be managed using the composite limit feature in Oracle resource profiles. **(Topic 14.3)**

56. C. Oracle uses the value for CPU_PER_SESSION from the DEFAULT profile.

Explanation   If a value for a profile resource is not set when the profile is created, Oracle uses the setting found in the DEFAULT profile. Thus, choice C is correct. Choice A is incorrect because Oracle doesn't use settings for other resources in order to set CPU_PER_SESSION. There is no SYS_PROFILE in Oracle unless you create that profile manually, and even then Oracle won't use it for anything other than resource management for users you assign that profile to. Thus, choice B is incorrect. Finally, choice D is incorrect because although Oracle might set CPU_PER_SESSION to UNLIMITED if that is what the resource setting is in the DEFAULT profile, if you've changed that setting in DEFAULT profile, Oracle will use the value you changed it to instead. **(Topic 14.2)**

57. B.   After 180 days, a user assigned this profile can reuse his or her password.

Explanation   Of the choices given, only choice B indicates a true statement that can be made about this profile. Choice A is incorrect because the PASSWORD_LOCK_TIME setting is unlimited, not three days. Choice C is incorrect because a PASSWORD_LIFE_TIME setting of 30 means 30 days, not 30 minutes. Finally, choice D is incorrect because PASSWORD_GRACE_TIME indicates how many days a user has to login to Oracle to change their password for the first time. **(Topic 14.1)**

58. B. `alter profile default limit password_grace_time 3 password_reuse_limit unlimited;`

Explanation   The question asks for the statement that will bar reuse of passwords and give the user three days to login to change his/her password for the first time, and choice B accommodates that request nicely. The PASSWORD_REUSE_LIMIT setting restricts reuse of passwords. That fact alone makes it easy to eliminate choices C and D. You know that PASSWORD_GRACE_TIME forces users to log in within a certain period of time to change their passwords for the first time or else the account gets locked. In contrast, FAILED_LOGIN_ATTEMPTS simply locks the account after the prescribed number of failed attempts to log in, eliminating choice A. **(Topic 14.1)**

59. D. `select distinct profile from dba_profiles where limit = 'UNLIMITED';`

Explanation   Each row in DBA_PROFILES indicates a resource setting for a profile, meaning that a single profile might have numerous rows in DBA_PROFILES. Thus, you would use the `distinct` keyword to limit output to only one row per profile, making choice D correct. Choice C would have been right if the distinct keyword was used. Choices A and B do not query the data in that dictionary view with the appropriate search criteria, making both choices incorrect. **(Topic 14.1)**

60. C.   Ability to back up the database

Explanation   Although the SYSDBA privilege is quite powerful, it is not omniscient, especially when it comes to object privileges. For this reason, choices A and D are incorrect. Additionally, because no information about granting administrative ability along with the privilege was indicated by the question, you can eliminate choice B as well. **(Topic 15.1)**

APPENDIX

A

Globalization Support

his appendix discusses Oracle's Globalization Support Architecture. This feature enables you to deploy Oracle in languages other than English. This topic comprises only 3 percent of the actual test material on the OCP DBA Fundamentals I exam. In Oracle8*i* and before, Oracle's Globalization Support capabilities were referred to as National Language Support (NLS) features. NLS is now a subset of Globalization Support. In this section, you will cover the following points on using NLS in Oracle:

- Choosing a database and a national character set for a database

- Specifying language-dependent behavior

- Using different types of NLS parameters

- Obtaining information about NLS settings

Oracle supports many different language-encoding schemes in order to produce a product that is usable worldwide. There are four different classes supported, including single-byte character sets (both 7-bit and 8-bit), varying-width multibyte character sets, fixed-width multibyte character sets, and Unicode character sets. You may be familiar with the single-byte character set US7ASCII, the 7-bit ASCII character set used in the United States. It uses single byte to store a character and so can represent 128 characters. Several 8-bit character sets are used throughout Europe to represent the characters found in those languages, in addition to those used in English. WE8ISO8859P1 is the Western European 8-bit International Organization for Standardization (ISO) standard character set and is widely used. Unlike US7ASCII, which uses 7 bits to represent a character, it uses 8 bits to represent a character and so can represent 256 characters instead.

Oracle uses varying- and fixed-width character sets to support languages like Japanese, Chinese, Korean, and other languages that use complex characters to represent language, and for Arabic and Hebrew, which add the complexity of being read from right to left. Unicode is a standard for encoding all characters usable in computers, including all characters in all languages, plus specialized print media, math, and computer characters. In this section, you will learn about choices in character sets for the database—how to specify NLS behavior in different scenarios, NLS parameters, NLS usage, and what influence language-dependent application behavior may have.

The database character set is defined during the database creation using the `character set` clause in the `create database` command. There are few options to change the character set after the database is created. The database character set can only be changed if the new character set is a superset of the existing character set. This is for the obvious reason that the existing character set of the database should be represented in the new character set. If this condition is met, then the character set can be changed by using the command `alter database` `character set`. If not, then a full export of the database, recreating the database with a new character set, and then a full import of the database should take care of it.

Choosing a Database and a National Character Set for a Database

Two character sets can be defined for your database: the *database character set* and the *national character set*. Both database and national character sets are defined when you create your database. The database character set is used for Oracle SQL and PL/SQL source-code storage, whereas the national character set is used to represent your table data. SQL and PL/SQL must be stored in a language containing all characters in U.S. 7-bit ASCII or EBCDIC, whichever is supported by your host machine. So, even if you speak Korean and want to store Korean in your database, you still need to know enough English to type in the SQL and PL/SQL commands.

The national character set is specified at the time of database creation using the clause `national character set`. If this is not specified, then Oracle defaults it to the database character set. Some special conditions apply to national character sets and text or large object variables. The CLOB, CHAR, and VARCHAR2 datatypes can store database character sets, and each has national character set equivalents, called NCLOB, NCHAR, and NVARCHAR2, respectively. The LONG datatype can only store character sets that are allowed to be database character sets. The client or user machines can have a different character set from the database character set. This is achieved by setting the environment variable. Make sure that the database character set is a superset of the client character set.

Varying-Width Multibyte Character Sets

In a varying-width character set, a multibyte character set is represented by one or more bytes per character. The value of the most significant bit is used to indicate if a byte represents a single byte or is part of a series of bytes representing a character.

Fixed-Width Multibyte Character Sets

Fixed-width character sets provide support similar to multibyte character sets, except that the format is a fixed number of bytes for each character.

Note also that the terms fixed length and varying length have different meanings for CHAR and VARCHAR2 datatypes than fixed width and variable width in the CHAR and NCHAR or VARCHAR2 and NVARCHAR2 context. In the first case, fixed width means that the data stored in a CHAR(3) will always be three characters long, even if you specify only one character of data. The one character will be padded with two extra spaces. VARCHAR2 columns will not be padded with extra blanks, so the same one character of data in a VARCHAR2(3) column will be only one character long. In the second case, fixed and varying width refer to the number of bytes used to store each character in the string.

The Need for National Character Sets

It is not possible to use a fixed-width multibyte character set as the database character set; it can only be used as the national character set. The data types NCHAR, NVARCHAR2, and NCLOB are provided to declare columns as variants of the basic types CHAR, VARCHAR2, and CLOB to note that they are stored using the national character set and not the database character set.

TIP
Your database and national character sets should be closely related for best results. Also, the trade-off between fixed-width and varying-width character sets is that fixed-width sets permit better performance in string operations, such as length( ) *and* substr( )*, but varying-width sets are better for managing space.*

For Review

1. Compare fixed-length and varying-length datatypes to fixed-width and varying-width multibyte character sets. What is meant by each?

2. Compare database and national character sets. What is meant and permitted by each?

Specifying Language-Dependent Behavior

There are several different areas where language-dependent behavior can be specified. Specifying these NLS parameters changes the default values that are based on the database and national character set defined. These parameters can be changed in the following ways:

- **By specifying the parameter in the database initialization file on the server** These settings have no effect on the client side, but only on the server behavior.

  ```
  NLS_TERRITORY = "CZECH REPUBLIC"
  ```

- **By specifying NLS as an environment variable on the client** This defines the behavior of the client and overrides the default values set for the session in the initialization parameter file. The following is an example of setting NLS as an environment variable in a UNIX system:

  ```
  # export NLS_SORT=FRENCH
  ```

- **At a session level by using the `alter session` command**

    ```
    alter session set NLS_DATE_LANGUAGE = FRENCH;
    ```

- **By specifying certain SQL functions**

    ```
    TO_CHAR(hiredate, 'YYYY-MM-DD', 'NLS_DATE_LANGUAGE = FRENCH'))
    ```

The NLS parameters defined in SQL functions have the highest priority, followed by parameters specified in the `alter session` command, followed by the environment variable, followed by the initialization parameter, and finally followed by the lowest priority—the database default parameters.

NLS Parameters

The following is a list of some NLS parameters and their specifications:

- **NLS_LANGUAGE** Indicates the language for error messages, the names of days and months, and the symbols for 12-hour time of day and calendar era; this parameter also defines the sort mechanism Oracle will use.

- **NLS_DATE_LANGUAGE** Changes the language for day and month names, and other language components of date information.

- **NLS_SORT** Changes the sort mechanism Oracle uses; for example, you can override the default sort order of the national character set to use the sort order of another character set.

- **NLS_TERRITORY** Indicates the numbering for day of the week, default date format, currency symbols, and decimal symbol.

- **NLS_CURRENCY** Identifies a new currency symbol.

- **NLS_ISO_CURRENCY** Identifies a new territory whose ISO currency symbol should be used.

- **NLS_DATE_FORMAT** Identifies a new date format.

- **NLS_NUMERIC_CHARACTERS** Identifies a new decimal (0.00) and group (0,000) separator.

NLS_LANG overrides default NLS settings for the user, using the following format: `language_territory.characterset`. Altering NLS parameters within the session is accomplished in two ways: either by using the `alter session set parm_name = value` command, where `parm_name` is the name of the NLS parameter and `value` is what you want to set the parameter to; or, you can use the `set_nls( )` procedure in the DBMS_SESSION package, which accepts two values: *parm_name* and *value*.

For Review

1. Identify two ways to change NLS parameters in your session.

2. Identify the parameter that changes the format of information in the DATE datatype.

Obtaining Information about Globalization Support Usage

You can get NLS information from your database in two ways: information about your data in various NLS formats and information about the general NLS setup for your database. The first set of information can be obtained through the standard SQL functions `to_char( )`, `to_number( )`, and `to_date( )`. These functions accept various NLS parameters and return information based on the NLS parameter you gave them.

In addition, several NLS functions are available that utilize the NLS_SORT parameter. The following code block shows output from a table with NLS parameters used to assist in providing meaningful formatting in a simple report. For this example, note the use of L, G, and D as the local currency, group or thousands, and decimal separator character markers in your formatting mask:

```
SQL> select year,
to_char(gnp,'L9G999G999G999D99','NLS_NUMERIC_CHARACTERS=''.,$''')
  2> as GNP
  3> from us_gnp;
     YEAR GNP
--------- --------------------------
     1997            $5,948,399,939.34
     1998            $6,043,345,223.34
     1999            $6,143,545,453.80
```

TIP
Experiment with the order of characters specified for the previous NLS_NUMERIC_CHARACTERS `initsid.ora` *parameter, and see what happens with your output. The appropriate order for specifying them is* D, G, L, *and* C *(which represents the local ISO currency symbol, such as USD for U.S. dollars).*

Dictionary Views Containing NLS Parameters

In addition to the V$PARAMETER view, you can find information about settings for your NLS parameters in Oracle by looking at several different views, which are in the following list:

- **NLS_DATABASE_PARAMETERS**   All NLS databasewide parameters are stored in this view.

- **NLS_INSTANCE_PARAMETERS**   All NLS instancewide parameters are stored in this view.

- **NLS_SESSION_PARAMETERS**   All NLS parameters for the active session are stored in this view.

- **V$NLS_PARAMETERS**   This is a superset of the previous three views.

- **V$NLS_VALID_VALUES**   This is a listing of all valid values for all parameters.

For Review

1. Identify the view that contains all NLS parameters for your instance, session, and database.

2. Identify a way you might use an NLS parameter in a SQL conversion function. In what other ways might this be a useful feature in Oracle?

Index

P

S

T

INTERNATIONAL CONTACT INFORMATION

AUSTRALIA
McGraw-Hill Book Company Australia Pty. Ltd.
TEL +61-2-9417-9899
FAX +61-2-9417-5687
http://www.mcgraw-hill.com.au
books-it_sydney@mcgraw-hill.com

CANADA
McGraw-Hill Ryerson Ltd.
TEL +905-430-5000
FAX +905-430-5020
http://www.mcgrawhill.ca

GREECE, MIDDLE EAST,
NORTHERN AFRICA
McGraw-Hill Hellas
TEL +30-1-656-0990-3-4
FAX +30-1-654-5525

MEXICO (Also serving Latin America)
McGraw-Hill Interamericana Editores S.A. de C.V.
TEL +525-117-1583
FAX +525-117-1589
http://www.mcgraw-hill.com.mx
fernando_castellanos@mcgraw-hill.com

SINGAPORE (Serving Asia)
McGraw-Hill Book Company
TEL +65-863-1580
FAX +65-862-3354
http://www.mcgraw-hill.com.sg
mghasia@mcgraw-hill.com

SOUTH AFRICA
McGraw-Hill South Africa
TEL +27-11-622-7512
FAX +27-11-622-9045
robyn_swanepoel@mcgraw-hill.com

UNITED KINGDOM & EUROPE
(Excluding Southern Europe)
McGraw-Hill Publishing Company
TEL +44-1-628-502500
FAX +44-1-628-770224
http://www.mcgraw-hill.co.uk
computing_neurope@mcgraw-hill.com

ALL OTHER INQUIRIES Contact:
Osborne/McGraw-Hill
TEL +1-510-549-6600
FAX +1-510-883-7600
http://www.osborne.com
omg_international@mcgraw-hill.com

Knowledge is power. To which we say,

crank up the power.

Are you ready for a power surge?

Accelerate your career—become an **Oracle Certified Professional** (OCP). With Oracle's cutting-edge *Instructor-Led Training*, *Technology-Based Training*, and this *guide*, you can prepare for certification faster than ever. Set your own trajectory by logging your personal training plan with us. Go to **http://education.oracle.com/tpb**, where we'll help you pick a training path, select your courses, and track your progress. We'll even send you an email when your courses are offered in your area. If you don't have access to the Web, call us at 1-800-441-3541 (Outside the U.S. call +1-310-335-2403). **Power learning has never been easier.**

©2000 Oracle Corporation. All rights reserved. Oracle is a registered trademark of Oracle Corporation.

Get Your FREE Subscription to *Oracle Magazine*

Oracle Magazine is essential gear for today's information technology professionals. Stay informed and increase your productivity with every issue of *Oracle Magazine*. Inside each **FREE,** bimonthly issue you'll get:

- Up-to-date information on Oracle Database Server, Oracle Applications, Internet Computing, and tools
- Third-party news and announcements
- Technical articles on Oracle products and operating environments
- Development and administration tips
- Real-world customer stories

Three easy ways to subscribe:

1. Web **Visit our Web site at www.oracle.com/oramag/. You'll find a subscription form there, plus much more!** ·

2. Fax Complete the questionnaire on the back of this card and fax the questionnaire side only to **+1.847.647.9735.**

3. Mail Complete the questionnaire on the back of this card and mail it to P.O. Box 1263, Skokie, IL 60076-8263.

If there are other Oracle users at your location who would like to receive their own subscription to *Oracle Magazine*, please photocopy this form and pass it along.

☐ **YES! Please send me a FREE subscription to *Oracle Magazine*.** ☐ **NO**

To receive a free bimonthly subscription to *Oracle Magazine*, you must fill out the entire card, sign it, and date it (incomplete cards cannot be processed or acknowledged). You can also fax your application to **+1.847.647.9735. Or subscribe at our Web site at www.oracle.com/oramag**

SIGNATURE (REQUIRED)	X	DATE	

NAME		TITLE	
COMPANY		TELEPHONE	
ADDRESS		FAX NUMBER	
CITY		STATE	POSTAL CODE/ZIP CODE
COUNTRY		E-MAIL ADDRESS	

☐ From time to time, Oracle Publishing allows our partners exclusive access to our e-mail addresses for special promotions and announcements. To be included in this program, please check this box.

You must answer all eight questions below

1 What is the primary business activity of your firm at this location? *(check only one)*
- ☐ 03 Communications
- ☐ 04 Consulting, Training
- ☐ 06 Data Processing
- ☐ 07 Education
- ☐ 08 Engineering
- ☐ 09 Financial Services
- ☐ 10 Government—Federal, Local, State, Other
- ☐ 11 Government—Military
- ☐ 12 Health Care
- ☐ 13 Manufacturing—Aerospace, Defense
- ☐ 14 Manufacturing—Computer Hardware
- ☐ 15 Manufacturing—Noncomputer Products
- ☐ 17 Research & Development
- ☐ 19 Retailing, Wholesaling, Distribution
- ☐ 20 Software Development
- ☐ 21 Systems Integration, VAR, VAD, OEM
- ☐ 22 Transportation
- ☐ 23 Utilities (Electric, Gas, Sanitation)
- ☐ 98 Other Business and Services
  _____

2 Which of the following best describes your job function? *(check only one)*

CORPORATE MANAGEMENT/STAFF
- ☐ 01 Executive Management (President, Chair, CEO, CFO, Owner, Partner, Principal)
- ☐ 02 Finance/Administrative Management (VP/Director/ Manager/Controller, Purchasing, Administration)
- ☐ 03 Sales/Marketing Management (VP/Director/Manager)
- ☐ 04 Computer Systems/Operations Management (CIO/VP/Director/ Manager MIS, Operations)

IS/IT STAFF
- ☐ 07 Systems Development/ Programming Management
- ☐ 08 Systems Development/ Programming Staff
- ☐ 09 Consulting
- ☐ 10 DBA/Systems Administrator
- ☐ 11 Education/Training
- ☐ 14 Technical Support Director/ Manager
- ☐ 16 Other Technical Management/Staff
- ☐ 98 Other _____

3 What is your current primary operating platform? *(check all that apply)*
- ☐ 01 DEC UNIX
- ☐ 02 DEC VAX VMS
- ☐ 03 Java
- ☐ 04 HP UNIX
- ☐ 05 IBM AIX
- ☐ 06 IBM UNIX
- ☐ 07 Macintosh
- ☐ 09 MS-DOS
- ☐ 10 MVS
- ☐ 11 NetWare
- ☐ 12 Network Computing
- ☐ 13 OpenVMS
- ☐ 14 SCO UNIX
- ☐ 24 Sequent DYNIX/ptx
- ☐ 15 Sun Solaris/SunOS
- ☐ 16 SVR4
- ☐ 18 UnixWare
- ☐ 20 Windows
- ☐ 21 Windows NT
- ☐ 23 Other UNIX _____
- ☐ 98 Other _____
- 99 ☐ **None of the above**

4 Do you evaluate, specify, recommend, or authorize the purchase of any of the following? *(check all that apply)*
- ☐ 01 Hardware
- ☐ 02 Software
- ☐ 03 Application Development Tools
- ☐ 04 Database Products
- ☐ 05 Internet or Intranet Products
- 99 ☐ **None of the above**

5 In your job, do you use or plan to purchase any of the following products or services? *(check all that apply)*

SOFTWARE
- ☐ 01 Business Graphics
- ☐ 02 CAD/CAE/CAM
- ☐ 03 CASE
- ☐ 05 Communications
- ☐ 06 Database Management
- ☐ 07 File Management
- ☐ 08 Finance
- ☐ 09 Java
- ☐ 10 Materials Resource Planning
- ☐ 11 Multimedia Authoring
- ☐ 12 Networking
- ☐ 13 Office Automation
- ☐ 14 Order Entry/Inventory Control
- ☐ 15 Programming
- ☐ 16 Project Management

- ☐ 17 Scientific and Engineering
- ☐ 18 Spreadsheets
- ☐ 19 Systems Management
- ☐ 20 Workflow

HARDWARE
- ☐ 21 Macintosh
- ☐ 22 Mainframe
- ☐ 23 Massively Parallel Processing
- ☐ 24 Minicomputer
- ☐ 25 PC
- ☐ 26 Network Computer
- ☐ 28 Symmetric Multiprocessing
- ☐ 29 Workstation

PERIPHERALS
- ☐ 30 Bridges/Routers/Hubs/Gateways
- ☐ 31 CD-ROM Drives
- ☐ 32 Disk Drives/Subsystems
- ☐ 33 Modems
- ☐ 34 Tape Drives/Subsystems
- ☐ 35 Video Boards/Multimedia

SERVICES
- ☐ 37 Consulting
- ☐ 38 Education/Training
- ☐ 39 Maintenance
- ☐ 40 Online Database Services
- ☐ 41 Support
- ☐ 36 Technology-Based Training
- ☐ 98 Other
- 99 ☐ **None of the above**

6 What Oracle products are in use at your site? *(check all that apply)*

SERVER/SOFTWARE
- ☐ 01 Oracle8
- ☐ 30 Oracle8*i*
- ☐ 31 Oracle8*i* Lite
- ☐ 02 Oracle7
- ☐ 03 Oracle Application Server
- ☐ 04 Oracle Data Mart Suites
- ☐ 05 Oracle Internet Commerce Server
- ☐ 32 Oracle *inter*Media
- ☐ 33 Oracle JServer
- ☐ 07 Oracle Lite
- ☐ 08 Oracle Payment Server
- ☐ 11 Oracle Video Server

TOOLS
- ☐ 13 Oracle Designer
- ☐ 14 Oracle Developer
- ☐ 54 Oracle Discoverer
- ☐ 53 Oracle Express
- ☐ 51 Oracle JDeveloper
- ☐ 52 Oracle Reports
- ☐ 50 Oracle WebDB
- ☐ 55 Oracle Workflow

ORACLE APPLICATIONS
- ☐ 17 Oracle Automotive

- ☐ 35 Oracle Business Intelligence System
- ☐ 19 Oracle Consumer Packaged Goods
- ☐ 39 Oracle E-Commerce
- ☐ 18 Oracle Energy
- ☐ 20 Oracle Financials
- ☐ 28 Oracle Front Office
- ☐ 21 Oracle Human Resources
- ☐ 37 Oracle Internet Procurement
- ☐ 22 Oracle Manufacturing
- ☐ 40 Oracle Process Manufacturing
- ☐ 23 Oracle Projects
- ☐ 34 Oracle Retail
- ☐ 29 Oracle Self-Service Web Applications
- ☐ 38 Oracle Strategic Enterprise Management
- ☐ 25 Oracle Supply Chain Management
- ☐ 36 Oracle Tutor
- ☐ 41 Oracle Travel Management

ORACLE SERVICES
- ☐ 61 Oracle Consulting
- ☐ 62 Oracle Education
- ☐ 60 Oracle Support
- ☐ 98 Other _____
- 99 ☐ **None of the above**

7 What other database products are in use at your site? *(check all that apply)*
- ☐ 01 Access
- ☐ 02 Baan
- ☐ 03 dbase
- ☐ 04 Gupta
- ☐ 05 IBM DB2
- ☐ 06 Informix
- ☐ 07 Ingres
- ☐ 08 Microsoft Access
- ☐ 09 Microsoft SQL Server
- ☐ 10 PeopleSoft
- ☐ 11 Progress
- ☐ 12 SAP
- ☐ 13 Sybase
- ☐ 14 VSAM
- ☐ 98 Other _____
- 99 ☐ **None of the above**

8 During the next 12 months, how much do you anticipate your organization will spend on computer hardware, software, peripherals, and services for your location? *(check only one)*
- ☐ 01 Less than $10,000
- ☐ 02 $10,000 to $49,999
- ☐ 03 $50,000 to $99,999
- ☐ 04 $100,000 to $499,999
- ☐ 05 $500,000 to $999,999
- ☐ 06 $1,000,000 and over

If there are other Oracle users at your location who would like to receive a free subscription to *Oracle Magazine*, please photocopy this form and pass it along, or contact Customer Service at +1.847.647.9630

Form 5   OPRESS

About the BeachFrontQuizzer™ CD-ROM

BeachFrontQuizzer provides interactive certification exams to help you prepare for certification. With the enclosed CD, you can test your knowledge of the topics covered in this book with more than 175 multiple choice questions.

Installation

To install BeachFrontQuizzer:

1. **Insert the CD-ROM in your CD-ROM drive.**

2. **Follow the Setup steps in the displayed Installation Wizard. (When the Setup is finished, you may immediately begin using BeachFrontQuizzer.)**

3. **To begin using BeachFrontQuizzer, enter the 12-digit license key number of the exam you want to take:**

   OCP Oracle9*i* Database Fundamentals I Exam   411660497323

Study Sessions

BeachFrontQuizzer tests your knowledge as you learn about new subjects through interactive quiz sessions. Study Session Questions are selected from a single database for each session, dependent on the subcategory selected and the number of times each question has been previously answered correctly. In this way, questions you have answered correctly are not repeated until you have answered all the new questions. Questions that you have missed previously will reappear in later sessions and keep coming back to haunt you until you get the question correct. In addition, you can track your progress by displaying the number of questions you have answered with the Historical Analysis option. You can reset the progress tracking by clicking on the Clear History button. Each time a question is presented the answers are randomized so that you will not memorize a pattern or letter that goes with the question. You will start to memorize the correct answer that goes with the question instead.

Practice Exams

For advanced users, BeachFrontQuizzer also provides Simulated and Adaptive certification exams. Questions are chosen at random from the database. The Simulated Exam presents a specific number of questions directly related to the real exam. After you finish the exam, BeachFrontQuizzer displays your score and the passing score required for the test. You may display the exam results of this specific exam from this menu. You may review each question and display the correct answer.

NOTE
For further details of the feature functionality of this BeachFrontQuizzer software, consult the online instructions by choosing Contents from the BeachFrontQuizzer Help menu.

Technical Support

If you experience technical difficulties, please call (888) 992-3131. Outside the United States call (281) 992-3131. Or, you may e-mail **bfquiz@swbell.net**.

ORACLE SOFTWARE LICENSE AGREEMENT

YOU SHOULD CAREFULLY READ THE FOLLOWING TERMS AND CONDITIONS BEFORE BREAKING THE SEAL ON THE DISC ENVELOPE. AMONG OTHER THINGS, THIS AGREEMENT LICENSES THE ENCLOSED SOFTWARE TO YOU AND CONTAINS WARRANTY AND LIABILITY DISCLAIMERS. BY USING THE DISC AND/OR INSTALLING THE SOFTWARE, YOU ARE ACCEPTING AND AGREEING TO THE TERMS AND CONDITIONS OF THIS AGREEMENT. IF YOU DO NOT AGREE TO THE TERMS OF THIS AGREEMENT, DO NOT BREAK THE SEAL OR USE THE DISC. YOU SHOULD PROMPTLY RETURN THE PACKAGE UNOPENED.

LICENSE: ORACLE CORPORATION ("ORACLE") GRANTS END USER ("YOU" OR "YOUR") A NON-EXCLUSIVE, NON-TRANSFERABLE DEVELOPMENT ONLY LIMITED USE LICENSE TO USE THE ENCLOSED SOFTWARE AND DOCUMENTATION ("SOFTWARE") SUBJECT TO THE TERMS AND CONDITIONS, INCLUDING USE RESTRICTIONS, SPECIFIED BELOW.

You shall have the right to use the Software (a) only in object code form, (b) for development purposes only in the indicated operating environment for a single developer (one person) on a single computer, (c) solely with the publication with which the Software is included, and (d) solely for Your personal use and as a single user.

You are prohibited from and shall not (a) transfer, sell, sublicense, assign or otherwise convey the Software, (b) timeshare, rent or market the Software, (c) use the Software for or as part of a service bureau, and/or (d) distribute the Software in whole or in part. Any attempt to transfer, sell, sublicense, assign or otherwise convey any of the rights, duties or obligations hereunder is void. You are prohibited from and shall not use the Software for internal data processing operations, processing data of a third party or for any commercial or production use. If You desire to use the Software for any use other than the development use allowed under this Agreement, You must contact Oracle, or an authorized Oracle reseller, to obtain the appropriate licenses. You are prohibited from and shall not cause or permit the reverse engineering, disassembly, decompilation, modification or creation of derivative works based on the Software. You are prohibited from and shall not copy or duplicate the Software except as follows: You may make one copy of the Software in machine readable form solely for back-up purposes. No other copies shall be made without Oracle's prior written consent. You are prohibited from and shall not: (a) remove any product identification, copyright notices, or other notices or proprietary restrictions from the Software, or (b) run any benchmark tests with or of the Software. This Agreement does not authorize You to use any Oracle name, trademark or logo.

COPYRIGHT/OWNERSHIP OF SOFTWARE: The Software is the confidential and proprietary product of Oracle and is protected by copyright and other intellectual property laws. You acquire only the right to use the Software and do not acquire any rights, express or implied, in the Software or media containing the Software other than those specified in this Agreement. Oracle, or its licensor, shall at all times, including but not limited to after termination of this Agreement, retain all rights, title, interest, including intellectual property rights, in the Software and media.

WARRANTY DISCLAIMER: THE SOFTWARE IS PROVIDED "AS IS" AND ORACLE SPECIFICALLY DISCLAIMS ALL WARRANTIES OF ANY KIND, EITHER EXPRESS OR IMPLIED, INCLUDING, BUT NOT LIMITED TO, THE IMPLIED WARRANTIES OF MERCHANTABILITY, SATISFACTORY QUALITY AND FITNESS FOR A PARTICULAR PURPOSE. ORACLE DOES NOT WARRANT, GUARANTEE OR MAKE ANY REPRESENTATIONS REGARDING THE USE, OR THE RESULTS OF THE USE, OF THE SOFTWARE IN TERMS OF CORRECTNESS, ACCURACY, RELIABILITY, CURRENTNESS OR OTHERWISE, AND DOES NOT WARRANT THAT THE OPERATION OF THE SOFTWARE WILL BE UNINTERRUPTED OR ERROR

FREE. ORACLE EXPRESSLY DISCLAIMS ALL WARRANTIES NOT STATED HEREIN, NO ORAL OR WRITTEN INFORMATION OR ADVICE GIVEN BY ORACLE OR OTHERS SHALL CREATE A WARRANTY OR IN ANY WAY INCREASE THE SCOPE OF THIS LICENSE, AND YOU MAY NOT RELY ON ANY SUCH INFORMATION OR ADVICE.

LIMITATION OF LIABILITY: IN NO EVENT SHALL ORACLE OR ITS LICENSORS BE LIABLE FOR ANY DIRECT, INDIRECT, INCIDENTAL, SPECIAL OR CONSEQUENTIAL DAMAGES, OR DAMAGES FOR LOSS OF PROFITS, REVENUE, DATA OR DATA USE, INCURRED BY YOU OR ANY THIRD PARTY, WHETHER IN AN ACTION IN CONTRACT OR TORT, EVEN IF ORACLE AND/OR ITS LICENSORS HAVE BEEN ADVISED OF THE POSSIBILITY OF SUCH DAMAGES. SOME JURISDICTIONS DO NOT ALLOW THE EXCLUSION OF IMPLIED WARRANTIES OR LIMITATION OR EXCLUSION OF LIABILITY FOR INCIDENTAL OR CONSEQUENTIAL DAMAGES SO THE ABOVE EXCLUSIONS AND LIMITATION MAY NOT APPLY TO YOU.

TERMINATION: You may terminate this license at any time by discontinuing use of and destroying the Software together with any copies in any form. This license will also terminate if You fail to comply with any term or condition of this Agreement. Upon termination of the license, You agree to discontinue use of and destroy the Software together with any copies in any form. The Warranty Disclaimer, Limitation of Liability, and Export Administration sections of this Agreement shall survive termination of this Agreement.

NO TECHNICAL SUPPORT: Oracle is not obligated to provide and this Agreement does not entitle You to any updates or upgrades to, or any technical support or phone support for, the Software.

EXPORT ADMINISTRATION: You acknowledge that the Software, including technical data, is subject to United States export control laws, including the United States Export Administration Act and its associated regulations, and may be subject to export or import regulations in other countries. You agree to comply fully with all laws and regulations of the United States and other countries ("Export Laws") to assure that neither the Software, nor any direct products thereof, are (a) exported, directly or indirectly, in violation of Export Laws, either to countries or nationals that are subject to United States export restrictions or to any end user who has been prohibited from participating in the Unites States export transactions by any federal agency of the United States government; or (b) intended to be used for any purposes prohibited by the Export Laws, including, without limitation, nuclear, chemical or biological weapons proliferation. You acknowledge that the Software may include technical data subject to export and re-export restrictions imposed by United States law.

RESTRICTED RIGHTS: The Software is provided with Restricted Rights. Use, duplication or disclosure of the Software by the United State government is subject to the restrictions set forth in the Rights in Technical Data and Computer Software Clauses in DFARS 252.227-7013(c)(1)(ii) and FAR 52.227-19(c)(2) as applicable. Manufacturer is Oracle Corporation, 500 Oracle Parkway, Redwood City, CA 94065.

MISCELLANEOUS: This Agreement and all related actions thereto shall be governed by California law. Oracle may audit Your use of the Software. If any provision of this Agreement is held to be invalid or unenforceable, the remaining provisions of this Agreement will remain in full force.

YOU ACKNOWLEDGE THAT YOU HAVE READ THIS AGREEMENT, UNDERSTAND IT, AND AGREE TO BE BOUND BY ITS TERMS AND CONDITIONS. YOU FURTHER AGREE THAT IT IS THE COMPLETE AND EXCLUSIVE STATEMENT OF THE AGREEMENT BETWEEN ORACLE AND YOU.

Oracle is a registered trademark of Oracle Corporation.